Integrating Learning Through Story

The Narrative Curriculum

Carol Lauritzen, Ph.D.
Eastern Oregon State College

Michael Jaeger, Ed.D.
Eastern Oregon State College

D0074074

Delmar Publishers
I(T)P® An International Thomson Publishing Company

Albany • Bonn • Boston • Cincinnati • Detroit • London • Madrid • Melbourne
Mexico City • New York • Pacific Grove • Paris • San Francisco • Singapore
Tokyo • Toronto • Washington

NOTICE TO THE READER

Cover Illustration: Pete Palumbo
Cover Design: Brucie Rosch

Delmar Staff

Publisher:	William Brottmiller
Acquisition Editor:	Jay Whitney
Associate Editor:	Erin O'Connor Traylor
Project Editor:	Marah Bellegarde
Production Coordinator:	James Zayicek
Art and Design Coordinator:	Carol Keohane
Editorial Assistant:	Glenna Stanfield

COPYRIGHT © 1997
By Delmar Publishers
a division of International Thomson Publishing Inc.

The ITP logo is a trademark under license

Printed in the United States of America

For more information contact:

Delmar Publishers
3 Columbia Circle
Box 15015
Albany, New York 12203-5015

International Thomson Editores
Campos Eliseos 385, Piso 7
Col Polanco
11560 Mexico D F Mexico

International Thomson Publishing Europe
Berkshire House 168-173
High Holborn
London WC1V 7AA
England

International Thomson Publishing GmbH
Königswinterer Strasse 418
53227 Bonn
Germany

Thomas Nelson Australia
102 Dodds Street
South Melbourne, 3205
Victoria, Australia

International Thomson Publishing Asia
221 Henderson Road
#05-10 Henderson Building
Singapore 0315

Nelson Canada
1120 Birchmont Road
Scarborough, Ontario
Canada M1K 5G4

International Thomson Publishing—Japan
Hirakawacho Kyowa Building, 3F
2-2-1 Hirakawacho
Chiyoda-ku, Tokyo 102
Japan

1 2 3 4 5 6 7 8 9 10 XXX 02 01 00 99 98 97 96

Library of Congress Cataloging-in-Publication Data

Lauritzen, Carol.
    Integrating learning through story: the narrative curriculum /
Carol Lauritzen, Michael Jaeger.
        p.   cm.
    Includes bibliographical references and index.
    ISBN 0-8273-7418-6
    1. Curriculum planning.   2. Narration (Rhetoric)
3. Interdisciplinary approach in education.   4. Interaction analysis in education.
    5. Constructivism (Education)   I. Jaeger, Michael
(Michael J.)   II. Title.
LB2806. 15.L38   1997
375'.001—dc20

96-4765
CIP

Contents

DEDICATION

We are grateful to the many teachers and children who have so willingly invited us into their classrooms. The students and teachers of Ackerman Laboratory School on the Eastern Oregon State College campus deserve our special appreciation. Their classrooms provided a wonderful setting for much of the initial research on the narrative curriculum. Ackerman's 61 year tradition in teacher education ends in 1996. We will miss the daily presence of the children and our colleagues who exemplify a caring community of learners.

We are also grateful to our students, colleagues, and friends who read all or parts of the manuscript and offered helpful suggestions and encouragement. We thank them and all the others who have added richness to our story.

We dedicate this book to Michael's sons, Aaron and Eli, and to Carol's sons, Nathan and Zachary, who have been our most important teachers.

Acknowledgments

Our appreciation is extended to the reviewers enlisted through Delmar Publishers for their constructive criticism and helpful suggestions. They include:

Joanne Bernstein, Ed.D.
Brooklyn College
Brooklyn, NY

Kent Freeland, Ph.D.
Morehead State University
Morehead, KY

Theresa Sullivan-Steward, Ph.D.
Sangamon State University
Springfield, IL

Richard Swerdlin, Ed.D.
University of South Texas
Denton, TX

Joan Thompson, Ph.D.
Catholic University of America
Washington, DC

Deborah Tulloch, Ed.D.
College of Saint Elizabeth
Morristown, NJ

Audrey Wright, Ed.D.
Central Missouri State University
Warrensburg, MO

Introduction:
Telling Our Story

"The universe is made up of stories, not atoms."
— Muriel Rukeyser

We would like to tell one of those stories that make up the universe—
the story about how this book came to be written. By sharing our
story, we hope to give you some insight into the nature of the book and
how you might read it.

In our first few years at Eastern Oregon State College, each of us
(Michael Jaeger and Carol Lauritzen) carried out our own educational
research interests. Michael designed and compiled approaches to the
teaching of concept/process science and Carol investigated literature-
based learning. Our interest in the integration of science and literature
began with discussions about ways to correlate children's books with sci-
ence-concept units. These discussions led to our first collaborative workshop for teachers in our region.

We planned the workshop curriculum around the science concept of
interaction. The purpose was to demonstrate that important concepts are
integral to many different environments and that organizing units of
instruction around these concepts would correlate several subject areas.
In the workshop, teachers did experiments that illustrated mechanical,
chemical, and environmental interactions and read children's literature
that emphasized human interactions. Manipulations with gears, pulleys,
and levers were paired with *The Question Box* (Williams, 1965), a story
about an elaborately geared clock that protected a village by tolling a
warning of any invading force. Both the literature and science experiences
illuminated the concept of interaction.

In our discussion on the long drive home, we, at first, acknowledged
our innovations and successes but we soon began to realize that our
attempt to merge disciplines was superficial. We had pieced together
activities because they had one commonality: Gears, pulleys, and levers
interact (science). People and machines interact (literature). As we strug-
gled over how we might restructure the merging of the two disciplines,
Carol ventured, "Why not start with *The Question Box* ? That way, the
need to work with gears and pulleys could come out of the story."

That conversation sparked our journey toward the narrative curriculum. We realized that we needed to revise our thinking about curriculum. We threw away our workshop plans and started anew. We revisited the work we had done previously. Carol had already found positive effects with story in mathematical learning (Lauritzen, 1991; Lauritzen, 1992). Michael had designed science curriculum based on historical accounts (Jaeger, 1991). We recognized that story was important to both of us and played a key role in our way of knowing and learning.

We read research from each other's discipline areas and tried to negotiate the language barriers between science and language arts. Michael believed that science should be a generative process by which students construct meaning from experience. Carol believed that students develop into readers and writers by being immersed in a context of real language use. For her, meaning is a transaction between a text and a language user. Ensuing translations and discussions made it apparent to us that we shared a common learning theory (constructivism—explained in detail in chapter 3) and the view that learning should take place in a meaningful environment. We sought a curriculum that was based on these shared beliefs. Finding no existing curricula that fulfilled our requirements, we started to examine possibilities. The collaborative work that followed is reflected in the pronoun "we" used throughout this book.

Because we started our research from two separate disciplinary perspectives, we began to explore what other educators had done in integrated curriculum. Much of the literature we found called for integration as the primary rationale for curriculum organization. Examples of thematic, topic, or process models for integration were common. We noticed that most curriculum units that employed one of these organizational strategies were designed by first making an *a priori* decision that there should be some mathematics, science, language arts, social studies, fine arts, and so forth in the unit. Each unit was an attempt to relate the disciplines to a common topic in order to demonstrate the meaningfulness of the parts.

We examined numerous units that were, in reality, just reorganizations of content. The "integration" resulted from shifting ideas from various subject areas into units that were related in a way selected by the curriculum planner. We began to question the merits of this design. To explore this type of curriculum organization, we created our own unit based on the topic of "Octopus." What we found was, on one hand, humorous:

- Octopus math—do base eight, practice multiplication tables by eights
- Octopus science—examine the biology of octopi
- Octopus social studies—map the regions of the world where giant octopi are found
- Octopus language arts—read *20,000 Leagues Under the Sea*
- Octopus physical education—walk like an octopus

▌ Octopus art—cut out a construction paper octopus and make crepe paper legs

▌ Octopus health—sample different octopus foods and find their nutritional value

On the other hand, we were disappointed because this kind of unit seemed to us to be synthetic, arbitrary, and really no better than the traditional organization by separate subject areas. In some ways, it seemed less beneficial for learning because it forced the disciplines to fit into less-than-optimum contexts. For example, mathematics is most likely learned better without an "octopus entanglement" and art is not art when it is relegated to "crafts" or cast as the handmaiden of other content areas. In addition, it seemed to us that topical, thematic, and process integration did not create ideal environments in which to practice the tenets of constructive learning. Since neither children nor adults would naturally decide to learn multiples of eight as an adjunct of learning about octopi, we had to "crowbar" the activity into the setting. Because the teacher chooses the topics and the linking activities, units easily distill to teacher-directed instruction in which only the teacher can see the connections. Curriculum is right back where we started—teacher-directed, teacher-controlled, teacher-transmitted.

How could we engage our learners in authentic ways that would lead to authentic explorations? We wanted no "crowbarring" in our curriculum. As we wrestled with the pitfalls of using traditional curriculum organizers while attempting to honor a constructivist perspective and to forward the broad goals of schooling, stories kept returning to our discussions as an integrative force. Perhaps we could use children's literature as a way to organize the curriculum. We knew quite a bit about literature-based studies, so we began to explore the prospects of merging constructivism, goal-based learning, and story as a curriculum model.

What happened next was a bit of serendipity. Carol pulled a group of picture books off the shelf that she thought might have potential. Naturally, she started at the beginning of the shelves which included authors with names from A to E! Together we read through the books and chose the one that had the most appeal for us. This wonderful book, *Very Last First Time* (Andrews, 1985), became the prototype story for our model. By studying this piece of children's literature, we learned that a rich, compelling story with a universal theme was ideal for containing and organizing the curriculum. Study and field research allowed us to see how readers interacted with this and other stories and how, if given the opportunity, developed inquiries and resolutions from the text. Stories led to questions we would normally encounter in social studies, science, language arts, health, mathematics, art, technology, music, and other areas. As teachers we did not have to invent connections—they were already there! Our instructional role was to support and facilitate learners so they could find the connections and possibilities for themselves. We discovered that their learning occurred beyond discipline boundaries. It was transdisciplinary.

We worked directly with elementary school children and with teachers in our region to test curriculum developed from a story-based, constructivist perspective. Our original focus on science and language arts shifted to concerns about curriculum, learning theory, and goal-based instruction. We conducted workshops and participated in study groups to gather insights from teachers about how they utilize goals, how they believe that children learn, and how they construct curriculum. Experienced elementary and secondary school teachers worked with us for several years to transform the ideas into a cohesive design. Facilitated by a constructivist instructional strategy, our cohorts generated new implementation strategies, applications, and modifications to the overall model. Implementation of the curriculum design in local schools and assessment of these experiences indicated positive results with both elementary and secondary school students. The years of experience teaching and collaborating with current teachers not only gave us important critical insights about the practical considerations of the model, but also gave us the personal stories that make theory meaningful.

The result of these years of work, thought, and study is a belief system, supported by theory and field research, that transcends the design of our original workshop by a quantum leap:

- We believe that a map for curriculum can be found in story because story is the most meaningful context for making sense of a chaotic world. Making meaning of chaotic events is what education is all about. Therefore, in this book we present a curriculum which utilizes narrative as its framework.
- We believe that students must construct meaning rather than memorize information. Therefore, in this book we present learning from a constructivist perspective.
- We believe that curriculum suited to prepare students for the 21st century should have as its foundation a set of broad goals for learning—namely, helping students to think critically, creatively, and reflectively when making decisions and solving problems.

The last piece of the puzzle fit into place as we tried to help new teachers acquire the ability to plan and implement learning using the model. If novice teachers could be successful with a goal-based, constructivist, and story-organized curriculum then we believed that we definitely had something worthwhile. Along with development of the model, we created an undergraduate teacher education block based on our work (Lauritzen & Jaeger, 1994).

Each term elementary school teacher candidates have an opportunity to learn in the same way we had been suggesting for children. We start their six-week experience with a good story. We have read compelling stories such as *The Bone Wars* (Lasky, 1988) and *The Bamboo Flute* (Disher,

1993). We have played the role of pioneers on the Oregon Trail and handicapped students negotiating an unfriendly campus. We have taken field trips to places such as a local, dilapidated hot springs resort to see what we could learn. Students developed personal and small group inquiries from these experiences and then communicated their findings to their fellow students and teachers. We have been amazed at the scope and depth of learning that took place. We have learned about the swagmen of Australia, Native American culture, geologic faults, post-traumatic stress disorder, musical instrument design, the technology of wheelchairs, the preservation of dinosaur bones, and volumes and volumes more. Feedback from these students has revealed positive attitudes about their own learning using this model.

The real test, however, was to determine whether student teachers could transfer the kind of curriculum that they had experienced as learners to their own teaching. At first they found this a difficult task. They were so enthusiastic about the information they had learned that they wanted to transfer all they knew to their own students. With mentoring, however, these teachers did create constructive, goal-based, story-framed curriculum.

We have learned a great deal from these students about how to communicate our curriculum model. We learned that it was impossible to transmit the meaning of the model by simple verbal explanation. Our students constructed their own meaning from their experiences. We learned that it was impossible to provide a single experience and expect long-term understanding. Students reported that it was usually the third time through the model that they really grasped how it worked.

What we have learned from trying to help our teacher education students understand this kind of learning and teaching is that it would be ineffective to just write what we know and hope to transmit that understanding to the reader. We must practice what we preach by providing rich contexts with which our readers may interact. We must provide a dialogue to help them construct their own meanings. Readers may have years of exceptional experience in the classroom, advanced degrees, and considerable knowledge to bring with them as they open the pages of this book. As constructivists, we acknowledge this academic and experiential prior knowledge and ask that you activate it as you engage in the experiences in this book.

We recognize that readers have already created a set of beliefs in logical and meaningful ways. We acknowledge that no book or isolated experience is likely to erase concepts of teaching, learning, and curriculum held by the reader. We acknowledge that we cannot simply tell teachers how to construct curriculum. Therefore, we try to provide a text that allows readers to utilize their prior knowledge, interact with new ideas, and construct new meaning about a curriculum which is authentic and powerful and also fulfills the broad goals of education. We have found that this is no easy task. We spent a great deal of time thinking about the nature of the book. How would we structure the contents, ideas, and experiences so that they might be interactive with the reader? How could we facilitate a constructive perspective in the learners as they interact with the text? What would we do to allow for the value of social learning?

After much discussion and debate, we decided to relate as personally as we can what we have offered our own students. The chapters that present foundations of the curriculum design each unfold with an experience. As much as possible we want the reader to interact with the experience, responding to its possibilities and perspectives. We will relate how others have responded to these experiences, but we honor the fact that the reader will have unique and important insights. We will help the reader think about possible meanings and make generalizations. At the conclusion of each chapter we will ask the reader to linger with questions and reflections. We would encourage all readers to consider their own lingering questions in addition to ours. In chapters when it seems appropriate to consider ideas outside the scope of this book, we offer suggestions of companion readings that may stimulate further thought. The reader may find that this book differs from their expectations of what a text is supposed to be since it includes numerous stories, anecdotes, and quotes, and the chapters are not of uniform length and style.

In chapter 1, we invite the reader to follow us and a group of children within the context of the book, *Very Last First Time*. You will see how the children interact with the context to generate inquiries. You will witness their explorations and celebrate their resolutions. Chapter 1 is intended to give an overview of the nature of narrative curriculum so that you can see the big picture before examining the parts. At the conclusion of the chapter we relate its events to the content of the other chapters. Therefore, we recommend that you read chapter 1 first. After that you can make your own decisions about what should come next for you.

Through the process of new experience, personal and shared vision, and collected insights, new understandings can be generated. We hope that the reader of this book constructs meaning about learning, about contexts for that learning, and about the role of teachers in facilitating that process. Our hope is that this book will support your thinking about what children experience as they learn and about what you can do to assist them in that learning. As a result, we anticipate the addition of your story of learning to the universe.

CHAPTER 1

A "Very Last First Time"

This is a book about curriculum—how we think about it, how we plan it, and how we make it come alive with our students. The experiences that follow in this chapter and in the balance of the book are detailed, real-life examples of one paradigm of curriculum design. This design, which we have entitled "narrative curriculum," endeavors to embody the critical elements of educational reform. This first chapter will provide an overview of the curriculum in order to provide a picture of the "whole" before we examine the parts.

To provide this whole picture, we (the authors, Carol Lauritzen and Michael Jaeger) will recount an entire cycle of curriculum developed with and for a group of elementary school students in the fall of 1994. The one-week unit was based on the story, *Very Last First Time* (Andrews, 1985).

To open the unit, Carol and Michael welcomed the group of 8- to 12-year-old students to a cozy spot on the carpet so that they could interact with the picture book Carol brought to share with them. Their comments follow:

Vanessa:	It's a story.
Holly:	It's named *Very Last First Time.*
Carol:	What do you notice about the cover of the book?
Steve:	He's digging a hole.
Kristen:	Eskimos!
Debra:	He's in the north.
Travis:	It looks like a desert with some snow there.
Steve:	It looks like he's ice fishing.
Carol:	This story is written by Jan Andrews. She lives in Ottawa, Canada. The illustrations are by Ian Wallace. I hope you'll talk about the book and share what you are thinking.

Carol began reading the story:

Eva Padlyat lived in a village on Ungava Bay in Northern Canada. She was Inuit. And ever since she could remember she had walked with her mother on the bottom of the sea. It was something the people of her village did in winter when they wanted mussels to eat. Today, something very special was going to happen. Today, for the very first time in her life Eva would walk on the bottom of the sea alone. (Andrews, 1985, unpaged)

Karl:	She's like… not gonna like it, maybe.
Doug:	It's gonna be cold.
Jennifer:	It is a very strange custom. People don't need to walk on the bottom of the sea, especially in the winter.
John:	She doesn't want to do it. It is the first time and she might not know where to go.
Douglas:	And I don't think she should go. She might drown. If you go to the bottom it's really dark down there.
Jennifer:	It would be the last time she does it!
Travis:	Her first and last time.

As Carol continued with the story she encouraged the students to interact with the text and pictures. The students posed many questions and made many comments and observations during the next twenty minutes. For example:

John:	I think there are no trees because it is too cold and it's above the tree line.
Doug:	The village looks really isolated.
Jennifer:	It looks old but it's not because there are modern things too.

Mike:	What if the tide comes back?
Steve:	What if they can't find the hole?
Jake:	Why don't they have a flashlight?
Sara:	What are those rocks? It looks like rock totem poles.
Elizabeth:	Why don't they have a lamp?
Jennifer:	Maybe it is a custom.
Kristen:	It looks like a cave.
Elizabeth:	Are the shadows real?
Jacob:	I don't see how she can get to the bottom of the ocean.
Carol:	How deep is it under there?
Sarah:	How can you light a candle under water?
Jake:	What if the tide comes in and washes her out?
Sarah:	Where did those pictures on the ice come from? Maybe some people went down there and carved them.

During the reading of the book, Michael had been recording the students' questions. When the interactive read-aloud was complete, Michael focused the students' attention on the list he had made. He asked, "What would you like to know more about?" The students added other ideas to their list. In all, they compiled over three dozen questions about what they had seen or heard in the book.

Michael then circled one of the questions and said, "One of the things you wanted to know was 'Where do Eva and her mother live? What is it like there?'" Students responded with speculations and suggestions about where the story took place. Michael then asked, "How could we find out about this place?" The students brainstormed means of pursuing their inquiry about the geographic area that the story depicted. They offered many possible resources: encyclopedias, books about Eskimos and Inuits, a letter to the author, atlases, *National Geographic*, a telephone call to someone in the region, and the story itself.

A student named Karl reread to the whole group the section of *Very Last First Time* that gave the place name: Ungava Bay, Northern Canada. With this information and an invitation to find out, children used all of the available resources to explore the question: "Where was this place and what did it look like?" Students examined maps and atlases and globes. They found Ungava Bay on the 60th parallel, about the same latitude as St. Petersburg, Stockholm, and Anchorage. Travis found the tree line on a *National Geographic* map and deduced that since the setting was tundra, the story must have occurred on the upper regions of Ungava Bay, north of the tree line. Vanessa made a linguistic discovery about the words "Inuit," "Inuuk," and "Inuk" which she recorded in her journal (fig. 1.1). Doug and John found a map that showed where each subgroup of the Inuit was located. Elizabeth and Sara paged through many resource texts and showed

others a picture of an Inuit village that resembled the illustrations in the book. Several students watched all or part of a documentary video about the Netsilik Eskimo group.

The first day of the unit concluded with all students recording their findings in their learning logs so that they could recall what they and others had discovered. Kristen found and noted the explanation for the rock piles we had observed in the book illustrations (fig 1.2). Elizabeth's entry

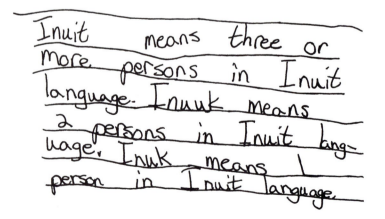

FIGURE 1.1 Vanessa's journal entry about vocabulary

reflects her strong interest in the video and the information she gained from it (fig. 1.3).

After the first day of working together, a comprehensive list of the students' questions had been compiled and organized as shown in figure 1.4. On the following day, Carol focused the students on these questions as a way of directing their explorations.

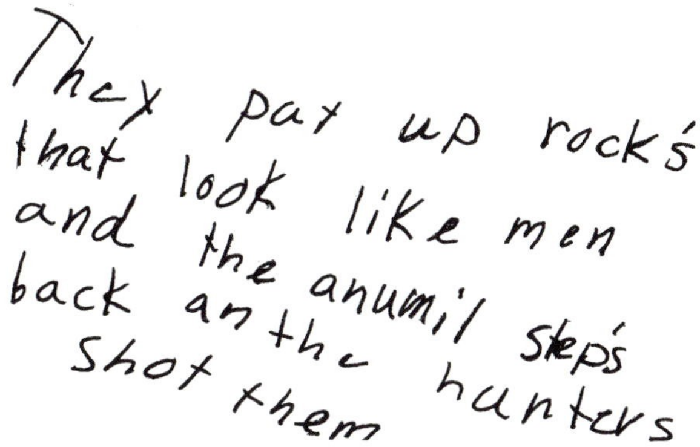

They pat up rocks
that look like men
and the anumil steps
back an the hunters
shot them

FIGURE 1.2 Kristen's journal entry about rock sculptures

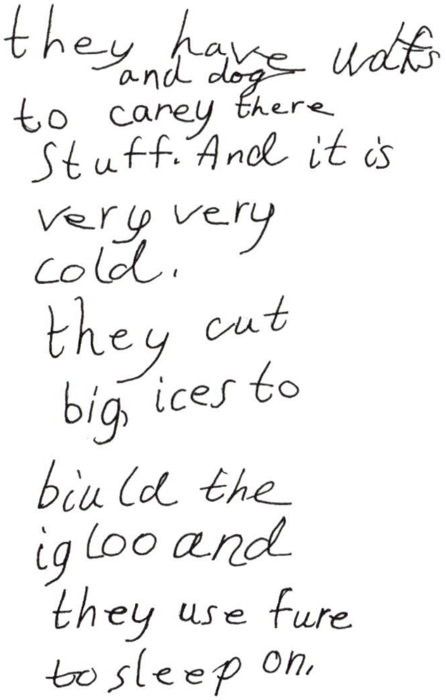

they have udts
and dog
to carey there
stuff. And it is
very very
cold.
they cut
big ices to

biuld the
igloo and
they use fure
to sleep on.

FIGURE 1.3 Elizabeth's journal entry about Eskimo video

FIGURE 1.4 Organized listing of student inquiries generated by *Very Last First Time*

What are the customs of the Inuit?
- Is it a custom to go under the ice?
- Will she do it again?
- Do the pictures in the book show a true picture of Eva's culture?
- Why would they do this in winter and not summer?
- What else do these people do?

What is it like under ice? (What could Eva really see?)
- Was the author realistic with the pictures?
- What were the images in the rocks or ice?
- Was that Eva's imagination?
- What were the snow/rock men in the pictures?

How does the ice freeze?
- Is it salt water that freezes?
- How could the water freeze with the waves crashing?
- Why was the ice yellow colored?
- What was the thickness of the ice?

How much time did she have under the ice?
- How did she light the candles?
- How much time would she have using a candle?
- When would the tides return?

How do living things survive under the ice?
- What are mussels and why would they eat them?
- What are other examples of tide pool life there?
- How do tide pool animals live under the ice without water?

How do people in this area get food, electricity, and other materials for living?
- Where would they buy groceries?
- Where did the electricity come from?
- Why snowmobiles and snowshoes at the same time?
- Why didn't she use a flashlight?

What would it be like to be under the ice?
- How light was it?
- What would it smell like?
- What would the depth of the ocean be?
- What would it sound like?

She asked students how they might pursue each of these sets of questions. They responded by brainstorming sources of informative print materials to study, experiments or experiences that might give insights, and contacts to make. When the students had exhausted their wealth of information, Carol and Michael introduced other possibilities that were not part of the children's prior knowledge. All these ideas were recorded on a large chart, which included a column for recording possible end products. Again the children provided all the ideas they had and the teachers introduced additional ideas. Finally, the students helped design a scoring guide by which their work would be assessed. This scoring guide included assessment of both process and products.

Students were introduced to the materials and resources that we had collected to support their inquiries: an extensive set of textbooks, journals, and other print media, a videotape of an Inuit family, a telephone contact of the mayor of a town in the Ungava district, materials that could be assembled into a model demonstrating the action of ice forming on the bay, seashore books, sets of preserved life from coastal areas, candles, tide tables, measurement devices, and calculators. (See resource list at the end of the chapter.) All of these materials were assembled according to the questions posed and study areas were established so that students could group themselves according to their interests.

Each subsequent day of the unit began with the students and teachers meeting together in circle. The students made a commitment to the explorations they would be completing that day and what they intended to accomplish. On each workshop day, each group reported the status of their studies and agreed to complete a particular aspect of their work.

Within the workshop cycle, the children explored a number of interesting avenues.

Elizabeth and Kristen were attracted to the video and viewed it in its entirety. While watching, Elizabeth became intrigued with the idea of making an igloo. She began cutting out squares of paper with tabs to glue together. As Carol observed her becoming frustrated with this construction technique, she prompted Elizabeth to consider other possibilities rather than abandoning her exploration. Together they gathered sugar cubes, Styrofoam, and biodegradable packing bubbles. Carol demonstrated how

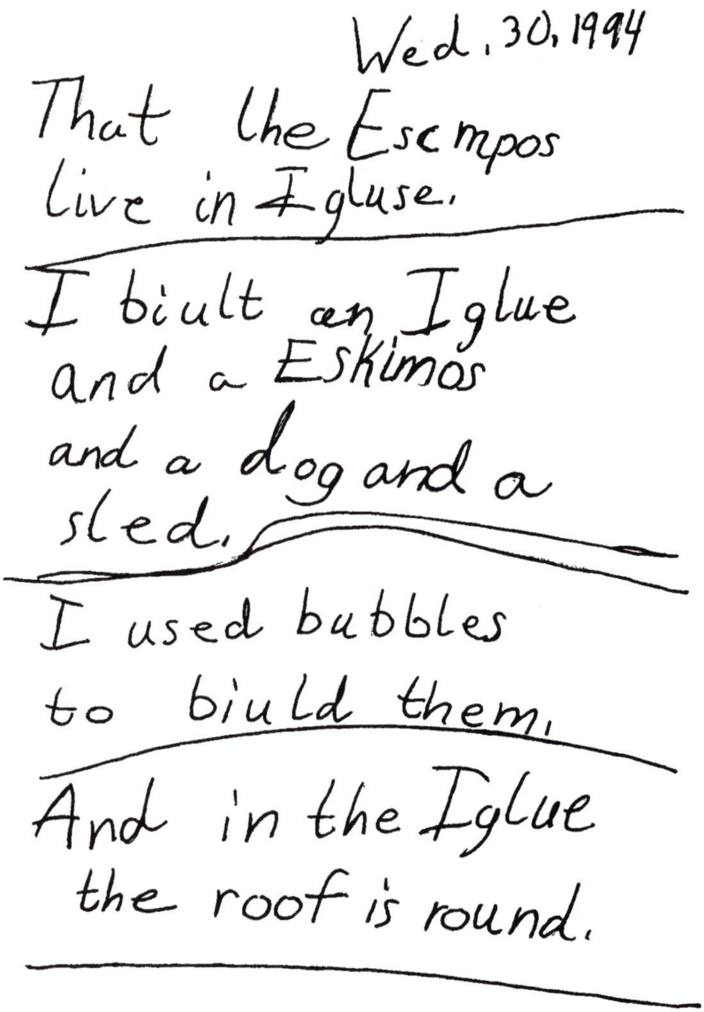

Wed, 30, 1994

That the Escmpos
live in Igluse.

I biult an Iglue
and a Eskimos
and a dog and a
sled.

I used bubbles
to biuld them.

And in the Iglue
the roof is round.

FIGURE 1.5 Elizabeth's journal entry about making igloos

I BLt A Iglo To
Day

FIGURE 1.6 Jake's journal entry

the bubbles would stick together with a bit of moisture and Elizabeth was a builder. In a somewhat breathless way she recorded her workshop project (fig. 1.5). Steve and Jake became interested watching Elizabeth and invented their own methods of "ice" construction. Using glue guns, sugar cubes, foam blocks, and packing bubbles, these two boys created "ice" homes. Jake wrote proudly of his product (fig. 1.6).

Kristen followed a different direction as a result of watching the video. She was excited to find the same family featured in a *National Geographic* article. Of particular interest to her was their method of fishing and the fishing spear. Using a large stick she created a model of the tool and compared it to those she had read about in the magazine. She recorded her construction process in her journal. (fig. 1.7). In the spirit of social learning, Steven was also affected by Kristen's project. Although he had not engaged in spear-making, he had watched Kristen and listened to

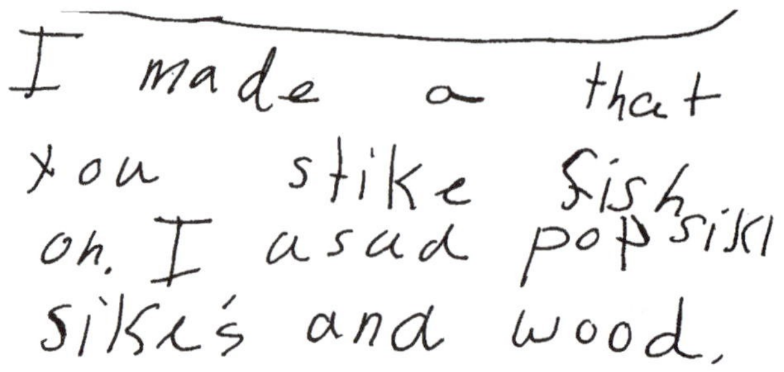

I made a that
you stike fish
oh. I asad pop sikl
sikes and wood.

FIGURE 1.7 Kristen's journal entry about fish spears

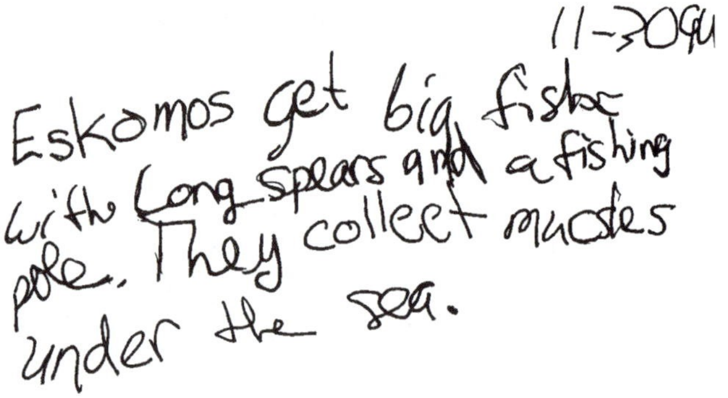

11-30-94

Eskomos get big fishr
with long spears and a fishing
pole. They colleet muodes
under the sea.

FIGURE 1.8 Steven's journal entry

her explain her work. He reported in his journal what he had learned through her experience (fig. 1.8).

Holly, Anne, and Debra became interested in Eva's potential peril under the ice and wanted to know how long she might have had before the tide came in. Since Eva's candle had burned out, these three began experimenting with candles to see how long they could burn. First they marked off an inch on the candle, burned the candle to the mark, timed how long it took to burn, and multiplied this time by the total length of the candle. During a later workshop, Michael demonstrated how they might use a balance scale to weigh the candle, burn, and reweigh. They eagerly tried this method of calculating burning time. They also enjoyed tipping the candle to let the melted wax flow away and discovering how to make the candle produce dark smoke. Carol questioned them about the relationship of these explorations to Eva's experience in the book. They decided that tipping the candle would alter the results since a tipped candle would burn more quickly than Eva's stationary ones. Their journals are a delightful blend of drawing and writing and demonstrate how individuals engaged in the same event make personal meaning of it (figs. 1.9–1.11).

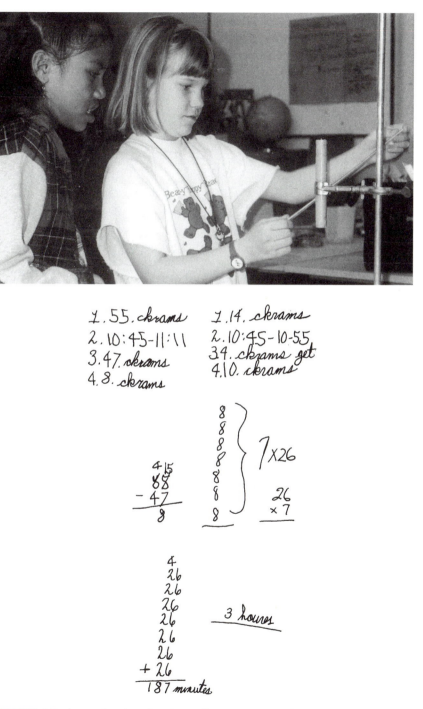

1. 55. ckrams   1. 14. ckrams
2. 10:45-11:11   2. 10:45-10-55
3. 47. ckrams   3.4. ckrams get
4. 8. ckrams   4.10. ckrams

                   8
                   8
                   8
                   8   7 X 26
                   8
       4 15   8
        8 5   26
      - 47   8 × 7
        8

         4
        26
        26
        26
        26   3 houres
        26
        26
      + 26
      187 minutes.

FIGURE 1.9 Journal entry about candle measurement

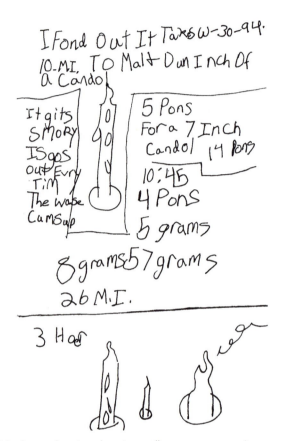

FIGURE 1.10 Journal entry about candle measurement

Two groups of students were intrigued with how ice could form on the ocean. They initially believed that ice could not form since Ungava Bay was salt water and also because the water was in motion from waves and tides. They were willing to put their ideas to the test through experimentation. They began an inquiry into making a model of the bay, with wave action and ice. Using batteries and a motor, they devised a system that could keep waves slapping against the edges of their container. Jennifer, Daniel, and John decided to include the salt water aspect of the problem. They wanted to know how much salt to add to simulate sea water. Carol suggested some possible avenues for determining the correct proportions but the group decided (in their words) to be "unscientific" and just guess. They also added a sand base, rocks, and other debris to their ocean container to simulate a beach and shore. By wiring a speed control between the batteries and the motor of their wave making machine, they experimented with the force of the waves on the shoreline.

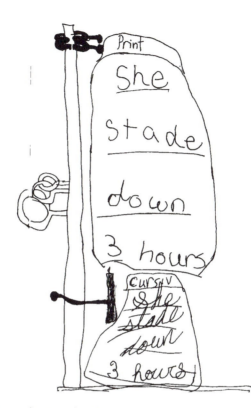

Print

She
stade
down
3 hours

cursiv
She
stade
down
3 hours

FIGURE 1.11 Journal entry about candle measurement

Jennifer's journal gives a sketchy recording of the progress of their experimentation (fig. 1.12). She seemed to record just enough to remind herself of what had happened but found the doing more compelling than writing about it. Initially, their exploration had been a copy of the wave machine made by another group of students but by springboarding from that group and capitalizing on their invention, this second group was able to move their model closer to an actual ocean setting. The first group, however, made their own discoveries. They realized that their experiment would be spoiled if the battery was depleted while the model was in the freezer. (Sometimes television commercials do have a positive effect.) They wanted to know how to prevent this possibility. Michael demonstrated how to wire batteries together in parallel and they made a power pack to keep their wave machine going all night.

Doug and Vanessa wanted to know more about the mussels themselves and the tide pool environment. They used a shell collection and

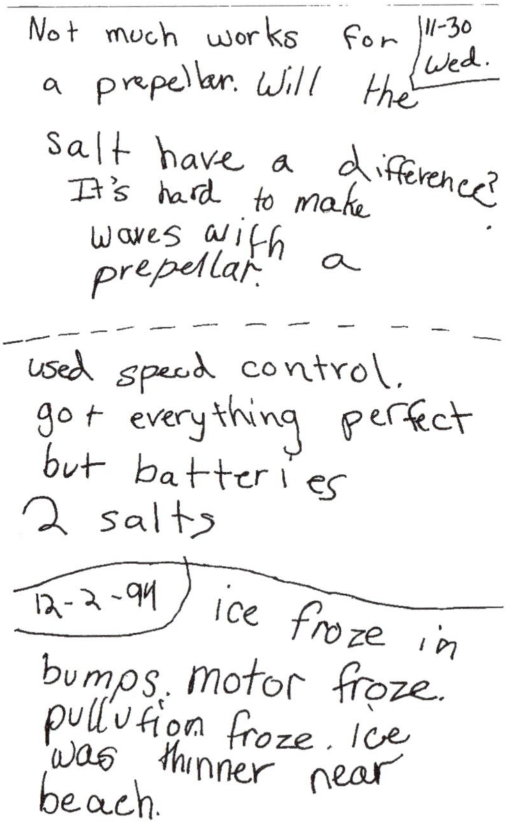
11-30 Wed.
Not much works for a prepellar. Will the salt have a difference? It's hard to make waves with a prepellar.

used speed control. got everything perfect but batteries 2 salts

12-2-94 ice froze in bumps. motor froze. pullution froze. Ice was thinner near beach.

FIGURE 1.12 Jennifer's journal entry

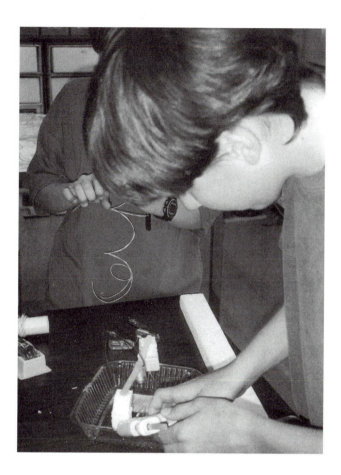

print material to gain information. Vanessa records what she learned in the form of a question and answer (fig. 1.13).

At the end of each workshop time, students and teachers again gathered in the circle area. They shared their explorations of the day by reading or paraphrasing from their journals or speaking spontaneously about what they knew or had learned or were still puzzling about. Students contributed ideas about how they might continue their studies and suggestions were offered between groups about how problems might be solved.

As we brought our explorations from *Very Last First Time* to a close, we asked the students to prepare a final presentation about their findings. Each group gave a short and informal oral demonstration of what they had discovered and how that discovery helped answer a question that the story had initiated.

The ocean model explorers found that salt water would indeed freeze and that waves froze too! The surface of the ice became a series of small

> What are mussels and
> Why do people eat them?
> The mussel is a member
> of the clam family. It
> is a black and blue shell
> with mussel meat inside.
> People eat the meat
> inside the shell.

FIGURE 1.13 Vanessa's journal entry about mussels

hills—just as depicted in the book. As they tilted their model of the ocean to simulate the tide moving, they saw pockets of air develop just where Eva would have walked.

The candle and tide explorers found that there was a difference among various types of candles and how long they might burn. They inferred that Eva must have had a candle of approximately 1″ in diameter and 9″ long because of its appearance in the book. If this were so, they calculated, then the candles could have lasted about three hours. They also compared the two methods they had used to determine burning time for the candles and reported that the weighing method predicted more burning time than the length method.

The individuals that studied culture found many interesting things. Kristen found that the rock totems, as she called them, were really rock piles that were assembled by the Inuit to herd caribou in desired directions. Elizabeth reported that the magazine article and the video that she had watched featured the same family. She succeeded in her igloo construction and added a dog, sled, and child to accompany her dwelling. Doug and Vanessa learned and informed the group about the reasons for eating mussels.

As teachers, we shared our personal inquiries with the children. Carol reported her interests in determining what this area must look like and showed slides that she had borrowed from a local geography professor who had traveled in the Arctic. The students remarked on how the villages looked similar to the one shown in the book and how isolated and cold things looked. Carol also showed the class some drawings typical of Inuit art. She remarked that the drawings looked very similar to the visions that the artist had painted in the book. Some students then speculated that the images in the book illustrations might represent the artist's, or perhaps Eva's, imagination or a portrayal of a spirit world.

Michael shared his interest in the mussels themselves. He told the children how the mussels have a glue that causes their byssal fibers to adhere to the rocks and how the sticky substance is now being examined by chemists seeking to develop a new technology for gluing under water. He provided the students with live mussels to examine and explore. Using diagrams of the external anatomy, students tried to identify parts of their mussels. Then Carol invited the students to place the mussels in a cooker. The mussels were steamed for a few minutes to open the shells. Students had an opportunity to examine the internal anatomy and to identify any parts that they might recognize with the help of an anatomy diagram. Michael demonstrated how to eat the mussel and (even amidst the shrieks of "Gross!") many took a taste test. Journal entries showed the strong impressions the mussels left on the students (figs. 1.14–1.16).

A final return to the story allowed students to think about why Eva would have walked alone on the bottom of the sea to collect mussels to eat and what the phrase "very last first time" now meant to them. Many of the children, especially the younger ones, thought the phrase meant that she would not go back under the ice again.

Elizabeth related it to her own experience of building igloos: "Well, it was my first time building one of those things and it's going to be the last time. I think it's your first time and then it's your—it's your very first time and it's your last time." Sara stated with assurance, "It's the first time she did it, but she didn't want to do it anymore so it's her last time." Some of the students thought she might go again but not alone. "I thought it meant that it was her first time alone, but it was also her last time. With somebody she might go again" (Debra). Some of the more advanced students

12-2-94

found all parts.
found out that mussells
smell like the sea

hinge dorsal surface
umbo
beak
posterior

mussles are GROSS!

FIGURE 1.14 Journal entry about mussels

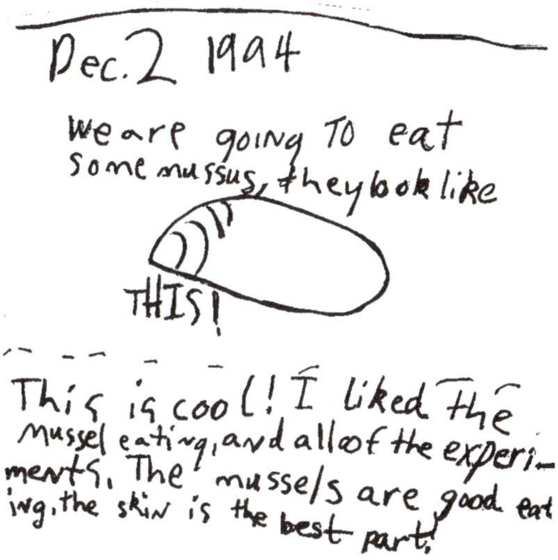

Dec. 2 1994

We are going to eat
some mussus, they look like

THIS!

This is cool! I liked the
mussel eating, and all of the experiments. The mussels are good eating. the skin is the best part!

FIGURE 1.15 Journal entry about mussels

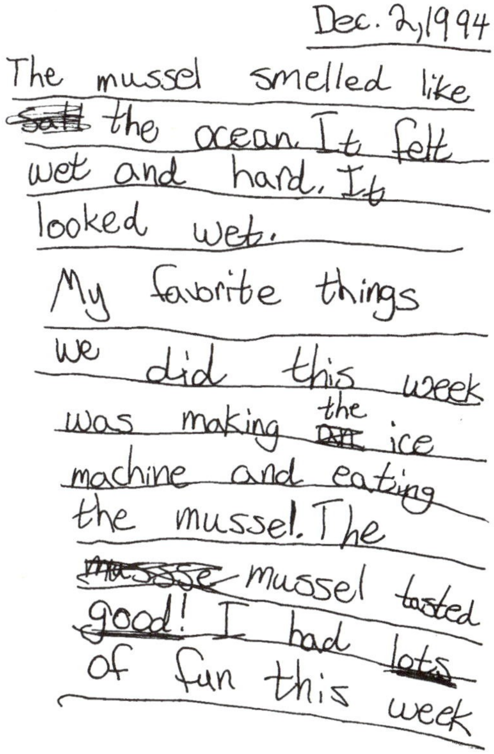

Dec. 2, 1994

The mussel smelled like
~~salt~~ the ocean. It felt
wet and hard. It
looked wet.

My favorite things
we did this week
was making the ~~ice~~ ice
machine and eating
the mussel. The
~~mussse~~ mussel ~~tasted~~
~~good!~~ I had ~~lots~~
of fun this week

FIGURE 1.16 Journal entry about mussels

had different explanations. "It meant it was the very first time she went under the ice alone and she couldn't do it again. She can't go under the ice alone for her first time again" (Kristen). "It means that she can only go down under the ice by herself for the first time. She can only go down there the first time once" (Holly). "That she'll never have to do it the first time again. She'll be more experienced the next time. And then it won't be her first time anymore and she'll have more experience" (Jennifer). "Because if it was going to be her first and her last time it would probably say 'my very first and last time.' But I think it probably meant because you can't have the first time for the same thing twice" (Mike). After hearing these explanations from the other students, the puzzled look on Vanessa's face turned to one of satisfaction as she exclaimed, "Oh, now I get it!"

✾ Reflections

The curriculum experience that we have related in this opening chapter is real. As teacher/researchers, we audio- and videotaped the instructional sessions, documented student work, and interviewed the students who were involved. We made notes and reflected upon our experiences. We asked our colleagues to observe and offer feedback. Our purpose was to collect all the information necessary to capture a complete learning cycle that would then serve as a prototype from which to launch the balance of our discussion concerning the theory and practice of curriculum organization. We believe this example (and similar ones described throughout this book) provides a vision for how learning and teaching must evolve from their present structures to a radical new paradigm. We will endeavor to be comprehensive as we propose a model for curriculum design in the following chapters. We hope to provide new ideas for how to create contexts for learning, how we believe children learn best, how goals should direct our efforts, how teachers must become transformed into facilitators of learning, and how classrooms must change to accommodate these ideas.

To examine these perspectives in brief, let us return to the *Very Last First Time* experience. The discussion of this exemplar will introduce the major concepts that we believe are central to the narrative curriculum and point to the chapters in the text where they will be discussed in more detail.

Starting with a Story

To begin, we see that Carol's interactive read-aloud initiated our curriculum unit. In the thirty minutes or so of shared listening, questioning, and hypothesizing, students were captured by the drama and intriguing nature of the story as well as the emotional appeal of its messages. A young girl's passage under the ice, in a place halfway around the world, was a story that our students could both relate to and wonder about. Their musings were framed into inquiries: "Who are these people? Why do they gather mussels under the ice? Why is it significant that she goes alone? What was it like under the ocean? How could ice be on top of the sea like that?" These authentic student inquiries demonstrated that the students were interested in what the story offered them. They were hooked and wanted to know more. Kristen demonstrated this when she said, "We tried to figure out what the "very last first time" meant and we did lots of experiments about freezing ice and how long Eva was under the ice." The questions that were generated from this picture book proved that story had the power to motivate learners to ask questions and actively seek to answer them.

The decision to base the curriculum on a story was significant and essential. *Very Last First Time* provided the context that led children to study Inuit culture, arctic geography and climate, the nature of ice and tides, how candles burn, mathematical problem solving, model building, and the biology and nutrition of mussels. In finding out about these things students practiced the foundational processes of learning, communicating, quantifying, and using appropriate technologies. When needed, students acquired new information and skills through teacher facilitation. The story had presented wonderful possibilities and the explorations that followed helped us understand the story better as well. (Figure 1.17 diagrams the

FIGURE 1.17 The narrative curriculum: Students experiencing the curriculum as a story

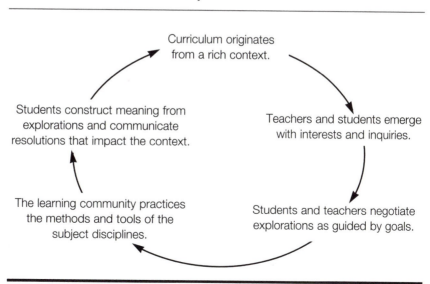

Curriculum originates from a rich context.

Teachers and students emerge with interests and inquiries.

Students and teachers negotiate explorations as guided by goals.

The learning community practices the methods and tools of the subject disciplines.

Students construct meaning from explorations and communicate resolutions that impact the context.

recursive pattern of the curriculum.) Doug's comments show the new understanding he gained:

> Salt water can freeze though. Even though the salt usually could stop it from freezing it does freeze. We were thinking that maybe the salt water probably wouldn't let it freeze because it was salt, but it did. So it kind of answered one of my questions. Can salt water freeze? Because there was ice on the top of the salt water and I wanted to know how could it freeze. I learned that mussels have vitamins, proteins, and minerals. I remember what the mussels tasted like. It tasted pretty good. I figured out that they tasted good so she [Eva] would like them probably.

The power of story to support curriculum has both anecdotal and theoretical rationale. Jennifer's words reinforce our belief:

> In regular school you just do an experiment. This was based on something. I like it better because when you just do regular school and you do an experiment then you may learn something from it and when you do it based on the book then you learn about it and you learn more about the book.

In chapter 2 we explore the critical aspects of story and advocate narrative as an ideal structure in which authentic, student-generated learning can take place. The chapter will generalize story as context and will establish a counterpoint to traditional curriculum that is structured by topic or chronology. Many more examples of stories and their applications are given in chapter 7. In that chapter we provide a structure and a process for selecting stories that can provide a rich context for the narrative curriculum.

Constructing Meaning

The *Very Last First Time* unit illustrated how we organized opportunities for student learning. The curriculum is negotiated between teacher and student, and the learning is constructed in a meaningful way by the student. For example, students who were curious as to how ice formed in arctic bays had some ideas about how they might find out. They suggested that they might read a book or ask an expert. As teachers we supplied additional suggestions and ideas that students did not have in their prior experiences. With these choices, students made decisions about what they wished to explore and how they believed they might resolve their inquiries. Through the interaction of their prior knowledge and the new information provided by the teacher, the learners developed many ways of exploring, interpreting, and representing their findings.

As teachers we tried to share the learning experience. We scrambled for materials, supplied support, rerouted dead ends, and rejoiced in small discoveries. Students created new ideas about how the ice was formed, how the Inuit lived, why the people probably ate mussels, and how long Eva had to walk around under the ice. The children had invented (constructed) new meanings from the experiences lived and evidences gathered. They built on previous knowledge to make new knowledge from something they had read, heard, seen, or made with their own hands.

Interviews with the students more than a week after the experience give insight into the meanings they constructed.

> *Karl.* We learned how the ice keeps the waves moving and stuff and only the top freezes and the bottom can go out with the tide and stuff. We didn't quite understand how the people walked under the ice, and so that helped us understand that a lot. We learned a lot of stuff about the candles that they probably used and that it's a tradition.

> *Holly.* I learned about the Inuits and they walked on the bottom of the ocean and it's in Canada. I liked lighting the candles and seeing how long it took for them to burn down to the end. It told us how long she was down there before her candles burned out.

Sara.   I learned what mussels were and how they stick to the rocks and stuff. They didn't look very appetizing. She probably eats them a lot more than me. In the winter they don't have very much food probably.

Jennifer.   You have to hook a lot of batteries together to get it to work a while to see how water could freeze with waves crashing and moving. It freezes in really weird positions. It doesn't matter what color the wires are as long as you have two wires. If your battery gets wet then you're not going to be electrocuted, but it won't work as well and neither will your motor. What comes out of the wall is usually direct and the battery has like a covering on it. Like you wouldn't take out a wall socket and move it someplace else, but you can take out a battery. You have to hook them up so that all the plus sides face the same way and all the minus sides face the same way. That she'll never have to do it the first time again, she'll be more experienced the next time. Well, she'll know next time that she probably shouldn't go… that she should keep better track of the time. And that it won't be her first time anymore and she'll have more experience.

Vanessa.   I learned that mussels are a member of the clam family. I learned that mussels taste pretty good and that waves freeze when the temperature is cold enough. I also learned that Inuk spelled with one "u" means one person and Inuut spelled with two "u's" is two people and Inuit is three people.

John.   I learned that the Eskimos do walk under the ice and the tide can go out and the ice will stay there. I also learned how the mussels actually look on the inside of the shells. I thought it was pretty disgusting looking.

Steve.   We studied about the Eskimos, the Inuits, and how they walked under the ice in the ocean. [Mussels have] this special kind of glue that will stick under water. That mussels open if you put them in boiling water. And that they don't look too great when they're opened. Yeah, it tasted pretty good. Because when you warm them up they're like hot and they like keep you warm. And they're easy to get to eat.

This constructive approach to teaching and learning is the second tenet of our vision. Karl expresses the rationale from a child's point of view:

I liked more freedom. Instead of just the teacher telling you what to do, you had freedom to choose what you wanted to study about. If you don't have the choice, then you're kind of forced into it. Then you don't really like it because you want to use your own ideas. Everything pretty much helped me understand why they went under the ice, how they went under the ice, about their culture.

Karl's comments point to a wonderful bonus that this learning paradigm offers. Each learner, regardless of gender, ethnicity, regional orientation,

developmental need, or prior knowledge has the opportunity to act within the narrative curriculum and make personal sense of the universal themes embodied in story. Because learners can grow from their own prior knowledge to new understandings appropriate to their own needs, the constructive approach offers an advantage over curricula designed by specific objective standards. In our class, some students made growth in understanding of how other cultural systems work, some gained insights about first-time experiences and rites of initiation, and others developed skills in interpreting natural-world phenomena. Students involved in the same story, but in other classrooms, may grow in different ways and may construct alternative explanations. We believe that the constructive approach offers the broadest opportunity to honor the learner regardless of background and to provide the appropriate scaffolding to support personal educational growth.

In chapter 3 we immerse ourselves in this new way of thinking about learning, in order to challenge traditional models of instruction that assume the purpose of teachers and curriculum is to transmit a compendium of information and skills to students. In chapter 8 we consider the developmentally appropriate roles of students in curriculum planning.

Goal-Based Curriculum

Even though we acknowledge that this kind of teaching and learning is a departure from the status quo, it rests firmly on the foundation of traditional goals for schooling. As we plan, as we create possibilities for learners, and as we assess, we follow the beacon of goals—the broad reasons why teachers and students engage in the process of schooling. In our *Very Last First Time* scenario, the children were listening, talking, writing, reading, experimenting, making, using tools, and interpreting results. These engagements are no accidents of the curriculum or conveniences that were added to fill the instructional time we had with students. Rather, we had clear, defined goals for this unit which were articulated at each step of our planning and teaching. We wanted students to develop skills in writing and recording observations, so we offered a journal especially designed for the unit and made specific recommendations, and sometimes requirements, that students write. We wanted students to read to find information and so we provided a multitude of resources that we speculated would help them find out about their work. We wanted students to express themselves orally, so we provided a forum for students to share what they knew and how they had found out and coached them in making effective presentations. We wanted students to use their hands, experiment, test hypotheses, and propose theories, so we provided them with opportunities to explore and helped them design those explorations.

In chapter 4 we present the idea that broad goals are the real power behind the curriculum. We survey the variety of foundational and life-skills goals that have been proposed for 21st-century learners and discuss why the narrative curriculum is well suited for addressing the needs of goal-based reform. We also show how assessments reflect the processes and products of explorations and culminating events and how assessments inform instruction.

Planning

As we prepared this unit, we thought extensively and intensively about what we would do, about what students might do, and about what we hoped they might accomplish. We chose *Very Last First Time* after much consideration about the match between the level of sophistication of the story and the developmental level of our students, about the possible inquiry that might be generated from the story, about what questions the students might have and what explorations they would pursue, and about how we would create a learning environment that would both encourage students to explore areas of interest and foster their progress toward important learning goals.

Creating a meaningful curriculum that employs the narrative context, the constructive approach to learning, and a foundation of goals requires a synthesis of purpose and logistics. We suggest a planning model that blends these purposes evenly and arises from our beliefs about students and learning. (Figure 1.18 provides a summary of these beliefs.) In chapter 5 we

---

FIGURE 1.18 Beliefs about curriculum

- We believe that curriculum should emerge from natural organizers such as literature, human history, and contemporary issues.
- We believe that learning is best facilitated in an environment that encourages students to construct their own meaning from experience.
- We believe that the purpose of curriculum is to organize the efforts to forward the broad goals of schooling and that these goals must shape and give rationale for all that occurs in the name of education.
- We believe that students should have a formative voice in curriculum planning and implementation.
- We believe that teachers should provide learners with resources, tools, concepts, and skills that will help them successfully investigate their world.
- We believe that learning should occur in an environment that both expects and celebrates a community of learners.
- We believe that curriculum should be designed to embrace diversity of all kinds and should use the richness of each learner's prior knowledge and experience to the maximum benefit of the community of learners.

---

discuss the ways in which we conceptualize this nexus of curriculum theory. And, although we believe in the value of a good theory, chapter 6 moves the theory into a planning model that has worked well with teachers and students as they think about and implement curriculum planning.

More Questions

There are many more issues that were not illustrated in the scenario: How did we pick the narrative? How did we decide to arrange the learners into groups? Why did we choose to have students do some things under teacher direction and allow them to do other things on their own? How did we decide what kind of explorations to offer to the students or when to direct their interest to avenues that we thought more informative? What else were we thinking as we generated this unit of curriculum? The following chapters are dedicated to addressing these and other issues about the narrative curriculum. Chapter 9 provides logistical considerations for teachers seeking solutions to natty, in-the-midst-of-action problems. Finally, chapter 10 provides stories of teachers in different settings who have tried the narrative curriculum and who relate what they have learned in the process.

We hope that as you interact with the stories, scenarios, theory, and applications in each chapter your thinking about learning will be stimulated in a challenging way. By the time you finish the book we hope you will be planning curriculum with the model. Like Eva, you will be venturing into new territory that can be frightening, but with the guidance and support you will receive from us and others and the belief in the resources you have within yourself, you can take the risk of trying something new. We hope that our story leads into your story, a story of your own "very last first time" with learning and teaching.

◈ RESOURCE LIST

General—Inuit

Bockstoce, J. (1983, July). Arctic odyssey. *National Geographic, 164 (1)*, 100.

Carpenter, E. (1959). *Eskimo*. Toronto: University of Toronto Press.

Chadwick, D. H. (1979, December). So empty, yet so full. *National Geographic, 156 (6)*, 737.

Educational Resources. (1967). *At the autumn river camp*. (The Netsilik Eskimo series.) Watertown, MA: Author.

Fullard, H. (1979). *The atlas of Canada and the world*. Raintree, WI: George Philip.

Honigmann, J. J., & Honigmann, I. (1965). *Eskimo townsmen*. Ottawa: University of Ottawa Canadian Research Centre for Anthropology.

Jenness, D. (1967). *The people of the twilight*. Chicago: University of Chicago Press.

Judge, J. (1983, February). Peoples of the arctic. *National Geographic, 163 (2)*, 144.

Matthews, S. W. (1987, January). Ice on the world. *National Geographic, 171 (1)*, 79.

Momatiuk, Y., & Eastcott, J. (1977, November). The Inuit of Umingmaktok: Still Eskimo, still free. *National Geographic, 152 (5)*, 624.

Mowat, F. (1952). *People of the deer*. Boston: Little, Brown.

Nelson, R. K. (1969). *Hunters of the northern ice*. Chicago: University of Chicago Press.

Newman, P. C. (1987, August). Canada's fur-trading empire. *National Geographic, 172 (2)*, 192.

Poncins, G. D. (1941). *Kabloona*. New York: Reynal & Hitchcock.

Reynolds, B. (1984, June). Eskimo hunters of the Bering Sea. *National Geographic, 165 (6)*, 814.

Rousseliere, G. M. (1971, February). I live with the Eskimos. *National Geographic, 139 (2)*, 188. [Same family as in the video]

Stefansson, V. (1926). *My life with the Eskimo*. New York: Macmillan.

Teal, J. J. (1970, June). Domesticating the wild and woolly musk ox. *National Geographic, 137 (6)*, 862.

Wahl, E. (1961). This land: *A geography of Canada*. Toronto: Oxford University Press.

Zahl, P. A. (1972, March). Portrait of a fierce and fragile land. *National Geographic, 141 (3)*, 303.

Children's Literature—Inuit

Andrews, J. (1985). *Very last first time*. New York: Atheneum.

Bleeker, S. (1959). *The Eskimo, arctic hunters and trappers*. New York: Morrow.

Bringle, M. (1973). *Eskimos*. New York: Franklin Watts.

Ekoomiak, N. (1988). *Arctic memories*. New York: Henry Holt.

Glubok, S. (1964). *The art of the Eskimo*. New York: Harper & Row.

Harrington, L. (1973). *The polar regions*. Nashville, TN: Thomas Nelson.

Iglauer, E. (1966). *The new people, the Eskimo's journey into our time*. New York: Doubleday.

Jenness, A. (1970). *Dwellers of the tundra, life in an Alaskan Eskimo village*. Toronto: Crowell-Collier.

Joosse, B. M. (1991). *Mama, do you love me?*. San Francisco: Chronicle Books.

Kendall, R. (1992). *Eskimo boy: Life in an Inupiaq Eskimo village*. New York: Scholastic.

Kusugak, M. A. (1992). *Hide and sneak*. Toronto: Annick.

Pitseolak, P. (1977). *Peter Pitseolak's escape from death*. New York: Delacorte.

Reynolds, J. (1993). *Frozen land: Vanishing cultures*. San Diego: Harcourt Brace.

Children's Literature—Tide Pool Information

Amos, W. H. (1984). *Exploring the seashore*. Washington, DC: National Geographic Society.

Bendick, J. (1976). *Exploring an ocean tide pool*. Chicago: Garrard.

Hogeboom, A. (1951). *Sea animals and how to draw them*. New York: Vanguard.

Malnig, A. (1985). *Where the waves break: Life at the edge of the sea*. Minneapolis: Carolrhoda.

Swenson, A. A. (1979). *The world within the tidal pool*. New York: David McKay.

CHAPTER 2

Story: A Felicitous Context for Learning

Activating Prior Knowledge

What does *story* mean to you? What is your definition of the term? How might your definition compare to that of other educators, linguists, or philosophers?

Are there any stories that you find helpful in describing who you are and what you hold dear?

Has story ever played a role in your learning or in engaging students in learning?

Chapter Highlights

We introduce the concept of story as a theoretical construct, a container for the experiences of humankind, by providing a vignette of one powerful story and its effects on learners.

We advocate story as a means of bringing meaning to, and for organizing, ideas and information.

"Father said, 'We can take very little with us.'" The instructions allowed each voyager to take only one personal item and one book on their escape from the dying blue Earth. Pattie took a dark green book with gold tooling. It had flowery end pages and a creamy silk ribbon to mark the place. Its pages were quite empty. Her siblings, Joe and Sarah, and all the others ridiculed Pattie about her choice because it was the games and books that filled the long silences of space travel to their new world. After many months of anticipation, the travelers embarked upon the planet. It was a land of lakes and craggy glittery rocks—a beautiful silent land of symmetrical snow-topped mountains shining silver and gray. Pattie, the youngest, was given the privilege of naming the new world. She christened it "Shine." As the space pioneers explored Shine, they quickly discovered the crystalline nature of every aspect of the planet. The grass and plants cut their feet and the plants and trees seemed to be made of glass and were unlike those on Earth. Father invented a way to use the trees by melting and splitting the wood to form a hut. The children discovered candy-like tree sap, green jellyfish-like creatures in the lake, and the curious Boulder Valley of the moth people. Life on Shine was unsure because the source of food was uncertain. The settlers had tried to raise their rabbits by feeding them the plants of Shine, but the crystalline nature of the tissue killed every animal. Nothing would grow in the vegetable patches. It seemed that they would surely die of starvation if their primary crop—wheat—failed. Father was instrumental in planting the crop. Using the book on intermediate technology that had been his selection to bring to the new world, Father had determined to become a contriver of machines and now had a vital role in the fledgling society. At first the wheat grew green and tall. There was great hope in the community that they might yet be saved from starvation. When the wheat started to mature, however, the grains had become crystalline just like everything else on Shine. Not desiring to end in a fate similar to the rabbits, the people of Shine were prepared to take their pills of last resort. Pattie and Sarah, however, decided to try. They ground a stolen handful of wheat, added water, made a dough, rolled out a thin pancake, cooked it over the fire, and ate it. Father was alarmed when he discovered their folly and was prepared to see both children meet the same fate as their rabbits. Instead, the children awoke the next morning feeling quite well and the community was saved. As the group prepared for the winter, they had a need to record the division of the shares of food. Father sent Joe to get Pattie's blank book despite her protests. When he opened it he discovered it was filled with large, round, shaky writing which everyone begged him to read. Father began in a surprised voice: "Father said, 'We can take very little with us.'" (Paton Walsh, 1982, *The Green Book*, summarized)

◈ Responses to *The Green Book*

A summary does not do justice to this wonderful story but it serves to high-light its setting, characters, action, and dilemmas. You will want to read *The Green Book* in its entirety to enjoy the author's craft and to appreciate the role that story has in this book. As you reflect on the story, what interests you? What would you like to know more about? What might you do to satisfy those interests or questions?

We have offered this text to several groups of learners. All ages, 8-year-olds to adults, respond in unique and interesting ways. Fifth graders were interested in why the earth was dying, why it was going blue. They wanted to know when the book was supposed to have taken place, about rocket travel, and about the length of the journey. They were interested in jellyfish ("Will a jellyfish really burn like that?") and eating the glasslike particles ("Could you eat anything that is crystalline and still live?"). Our adult learners were equally fascinated by possibilities in the book:

Where are they going?
Why were they allowed to take so little?
What was the disaster?
Why did so many bring Robinson Crusoe and no one thought to bring Shakespeare?
What happened to Mother?
What were their ages?
What was the population of Earth?
Why no wind?
No clouds yet rain? How?
Why did it get dark so quickly?
What will the "pill" do?
What is a rivulet? Treacle?
How could crystalline plant life exist?
What kind of life cycle did the moth people have?
What was the function of the guide?
How are people's roles in society determined? What has value?

Dozens more questions and puzzles were generated during the reading and discussion of the book. After the questions, actions often followed. Children and adults alike have pursued their questions by thinking, discussing, researching, and experimenting. Explorations made possible by this story include:

▌ drawings based on interpretations of text descriptions of land forms and scenery of Shine

- discussions about the kinds of books and/or personal items one might take on a journey such as this
- identifying stories worth keeping and telling them to one another
- observation of meal worms as possible parallels to the moth people in the story
- experimentation with dance as a way of communicating information and feeling

Members of one of our adult classes were particularly interested in the area of "intermediate technology," the role of contriver, and the kinds of contrivances that might be made from materials available to the Shine pioneers. They collected all sorts of discarded items and began planning and experimenting to make articles useful to an emerging society. An amazing array of contrivances were made and demonstrated: jellyfish-collecting nets made from plastic berry containers, water purification apparatus and hydroponic gardens from sheets of plastic and wooden supports, simple

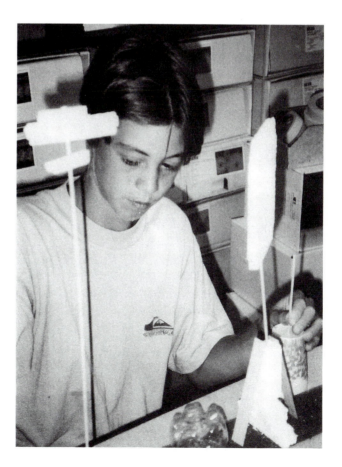

looms made of cardboard and string for weaving moth wings into cloth, as well as games, weapons, tools, and ornaments. They also presented brief and entertaining "commercials" to convince other members of the group that their contrivance was valuable to the community. The process, as well as the products, involved in these constructions provided evidence that students had planned original work based upon a significant aspect of the story, had developed an action plan for making the contrivance, used materials and tools properly, and had demonstrated and communicated convincingly about its applications and utilities.

The Green Book grabbed the interest of our learners. They wanted to know more about the people of Shine, about Pattie, about Sarah and Joe. They wanted to know how the planet worked. They wanted to know what would happen next. The interests of the learners were motivated by the story and the story was made richer in the process. As the setting, the motivations of the characters, and the scientific and logistic credibility of the story were pondered, the story grew in meaning. The students were better able to understand the motivations of the characters and to make sense of life as it might have been lived in a new place. They were led back into the story to consider its message and how it spoke to them in their present lives. The story had entertained, but had also done something more. The story had captured the imagination of the readers and activated them to consider possibility. The story provided a compelling context for learning.

🕸 What Is Story?

Our knowledge of story begins in the preschool years. Very young children can both understand and tell well-formed stories (Baker & Stein, 1981; Applebee, 1978). We use the word *story* frequently in statements such as "she told a story" or "I read a good story in that book" but most of us have considerable difficulty when asked to define it. The work of a number of linguists has determined that stories have a stable pattern which allows for specific types of information and logical relationships. Temple and Gillet (1989) summarize this work:

> …Stories are about characters whose actions are sequentially organized and causally related. Characters have roles and the roles are motivated. Who people are, what they do, why they do it, and what difference it makes—these things are explained by stories. Stories are, thus, explanatory devices that help us make sense of the random and inexplicable happenings of everyday life. People aren't characters until stories make them so. Events aren't grouped in logical chains until a storyteller groups and imposes logic on them.

In this book, we designate as stories only those texts that are fully articulated. They include all requirements of story: setting, characters, action directed toward goals, causation, and significance. There is much of literature that is not story, just as there are many stories that are not works of literature. It is also important to remember that story does not necessarily refer to fiction. Stories can be factual, as in the telling of an event that has happened in your personal life. History, too, can be communicated as story. On the other hand, stories may be products of an author's or storyteller's imagination. Regardless of the origin of the story, it is a partial recounting of everything that takes place. The story maker chooses the portion that will give shape and meaning to the events. So even the stories that seem realistic are never actual reality (Rosen, 1986).

Many writers, as well as dictionaries, use *narrative* as a synonym for *story*, although narrative also refers to "a kind of life story, larger and more sweeping than the short stories that compose it. Narrative is the study of how humans make meaning of experience by endlessly telling and retelling stories about themselves" (Connelly & Clandinin, 1988, p. 24). We will follow the common practice of using these terms interchangeably except that we give narrative a particular meaning in the phrase *narrative curriculum*. Here, narrative refers to a story as a structure that organizes ideas and events of curriculum into a storylike form in order to given them meaning.

◈ Why Story?

Then, why story? What makes *The Green Book*, or for that matter, any good and fully articulated story so special? Why does story give us meaningful strings to pull? Why does story provide a compelling context for learning?

To Remember

Narrative is a fundamental human activity: "it is simply there like life itself... international, transhistorical, transcultural" (Barthes, 1977, p. 79). Humans are storytelling organisms who individually and socially lead storied lives. Stories are fundamental structures of the human experience dating back to preliterate cultures, and are still retained as a primary mode of modern communication. Storytelling and the storyteller are fixtures of both the past and the present.

The function of the storyteller in preliterate cultures was to perpetuate the culture and community memory of a people. Patriarchal stories of the Old Testament, for example, were orally transmitted for centuries before scribes put quill to scroll. The stories, parables, and allegories of the Hebrews and the stories of other ancient cultures contained the elements of belief systems, historical records, and common culture. Stories provided the vehicle for communication of law, religion, ethics, and values. As containers of information, stories provided early cultures with efficient ways of remembering complex concepts and systems.

In a metacognitive way, story provides a structure for remembering. For example, aboriginal peoples of Australia know nothing of maps. Instead they tell stories rich with place names and their positions. The story provides a verbal map of the relationship of each place to other places. To know the story meant that you had a means of finding your way over the land. To not know the stories is quite literally to be lost (Avi, 1992). Story is an important metacognitive organizer for information—a pattern which the brain can easily recognize and can then layer specifics upon. Research shows that information that is not structured narratively suffers loss in memory (Mandler, 1984). Children and adults benefit from the organizing framework of story.

To Parallel Life

Each of our lives is a story, a living narrative of our existence. Physician and poet William Carlos Williams talks about the lives of his patients by saying, "Their story, yours, mine—it's what we all carry with us on this trip we take, and we owe it to each other to respect our stories and learn from them" (quoted in Coles 1989, p. 30). When we relate how we spent our summer vacation, how the fishing was, where we stayed, and the people we met, we do it as story. In this way stories are easy for learners to understand because they are based on a simple, understandable structure. Stories have real and believable characters that solve real problems, a pattern analogous to life. Because of this parallel, "narrative structure allows children to identify with a character being propelled through a conflict that reaches a resolution" (Lauritzen, 1991). A visceral bonding occurs between ourselves and the characters. As the characters in the story are confronted with circumstances, trials, and epiphanies, we share in their emotions: we triumph in success, cry in grief, feel joy in accomplishment and fear in anticipation. We take ownership of their story as our story. Through stories, learners can experience other lives vicariously and develop an awareness and understanding of their own lives in the process.

> One integrates life as story because one has stories in the back of the mind as containers for organizing events into meaningful experiences. The stories are means of finding oneself in events that might not otherwise make psychological sense at all. (Hillman, 1979, p. 43)

To Make Meaning

Stories provide learners a means for making meaning. They allow us to tell about things that we know either tacitly or consciously, to help us rediscover or reinvent our reality and thereby understand it more deeply and meaningfully. Bruner (1990), in *Acts of Meaning*, argues that narrative thinking brings the child into the arena of human culture. He says that it is narratives that give pattern and continuity to human experience and therefore stories are powerful instruments of learning. "I have wanted to make it clear," he says, "that our capacity to rend experience in terms of narrative is not child's play, but an instrument for making meaning that dominates much of life in culture" (p. 97). Rosen (1986, p. 230) suggests:

> Narrative has an importance much deeper and broader than the purely literary values we customarily give to it and …it has a preeminence among the discourse options open to us [because]… it is a primary and irreducible form of human comprehension and it is the central instance or function of human mind.

Story gives us a framework for imposing order on what would otherwise be random events. Story selects and organizes chaotic events, enabling us to discern how diverse elements come together into meaningful experiences. Story allows the learner to link isolated facts into connections that make sense, something that Calkins (1991, p. 185) says is critical for humans:

> For all of us, the life we're given amounts to "We had Coke, and then we had a hot dog." The rest depends on what we make of it. Being human means we can remember and tell stories and pretend and write and hope and share, and in this way we add growth rings of meaning to our lives. Being human means that in addition to going through the motions of our lives, we need to turn back and celebrate our lives. We need to paint and write and make believe and tell stories and represent and reminisce. We need to develop the eyes to see. What human beings fear most is not growing old, but growing old without things adding up.

Narratives are a way of making sense of reality and of the events that continually fill our lives (Erasmus, 1989). Fully articulated stories are based upon central themes, universal truths, and/or moral outcomes. These conceptual organizers arrange the patterns of a text (oral or written) in such a way to help the receivers of the text construct the big ideas contained in and between its lines. A story has the power to convey concepts in powerful and meaningful ways. As Egan (1979, p. 120) states:

> Stories are the most effective tools for making their content meaningful. They are also effective ways of introducing the concepts of otherness by

building into their structure notions of causality, logical relationships, the movement of time. The potential of fictional stories for clarifying the concepts of almost any curriculum area should not be underestimated or ignored.

Explaining who we are and how we function through narrative is evident in the words of a Native American medicine man:

> Too many of you don't know the stories... You can't know certain things without them. I've done the chants for many years now... The chants get results. I can't explain it to you. But the most important thing is that you have to know the stories, the legends, in order for the words and the rhythms to make sense, in order for you to know your language and your culture. (Brown, 1991, p. 89)

The stories and legends are the conceptual and spiritual organizers for the chants and healing rituals. Stories provide learners with organizational structure. Algorithms, processes, and streams of facts are like chants without a context—they simply do not work without the story to make meaning.

> We tell ourselves stories in order to live. We live... by the imposition of a narrative line upon disparate images, by the "ideas" with which we have learned to freeze the shifting phantasmagoria which is our actual experience. (Didion, 1979, p. 11)

To Learn in a Meaningful Context

Each new reform initiative in education in the past decade has broached the words "meaningful context" in some manner or another. This clarion call is the antithesis of decades of instruction in which the curriculum has been split into bite-sized chunks that are easy to swallow but provide little nourishment: workbooks of spelling words and reading skills, math problems, science nomenclature, names, dates, people, places, events, facts, or as we like to call it, "stuff." The "stuff" curriculum fails to motivate teacher or learner because it lacks connectedness between the parts.

The National Council of Teachers of Mathematics' Standards (NCTM, 1989), for example, is clear in its call to rearrange the piecemeal curricula (Frye, 1989). It emphasizes a vision of:

- A curriculum for all that includes a broad range of content, a variety of contexts, and deliberate connections
- The learning of mathematics as an active, constructive process
- Instruction based on real problems

Math futurists see learning less as a set of arithmetic processes and procedures and more as an ability to approach real world problems through authentic experiences—less drill and practice of algorithmic routes to solve a multitude of similarly stated problems and more experimentation, observation, manipulation, and interpretation of experience by use of mathematical tools.

Other disciplines are similarly involved in the debate about curriculum organization. For social studies educators, the legacy of John Dewey's ideas about organizing learning around classroom projects and social action still persist:

> History becomes especially accessible and interesting to children when approached through stories, myths, legends, and biographies that capture children's imaginations and immerse them in times and cultures of the recent and long-ago past. Teachers will find in history many resources to foster these ends: lively, compelling stories and biographies that catch children up in the real problems, issues, and dilemmas encountered by people at various times in history, and that disclose the variety of perspectives, feelings, motivations, and responses of different peoples involved in the situation. (National Center for History in the Schools, 1995, unpaged)

Recommendations from these educators suggest that students will be more apt to understand the human condition and the significance of events if they become personally linked with the events and characters of the past and present. These personal historical stories create logical containers for knowing. If we learn about the Civil War from the textbook's compendium of facts we are less likely to develop a sense of the drama of human conflict than if we focus the curriculum on a more localized and intimate historical story. *Pink and Say* (Polacco, 1994), a children's book that traces the friendship of two boys fighting for the North, is an example of such a context. This is a story whose theme addresses the human condition in the brutality of war and the transcendental kinship of all humans. In this context we first understand the whole picture and can then seek to place the detail of names, dates, times, and actions as they help us interpret the story.

> Historical narrative imposes order on events, implies that the events it treats have a beginning and an end, and that causation can be assigned... The conflict at the heart of historical fiction forces awareness that this set of events could be constructed differently, even while it enlists the reader's identification with the protagonist's cause. (Levstik, 1989, p. 116)

A narrative context invites inquiry and leads to in-depth study so that learners can begin to understand how knowledge in a domain is used (Pappas, Kiefer, & Levstik, 1995, p. 169).

For language arts educators, the importance of context is well established in the practices of literacy learning. Whole language curricula and literature-based study provide structures for organizing knowledge and learning skills. Probably more than any other discipline, language arts educators have recognized the need to arrange learning opportunities into logical structures characteristic of human experience. The participants in the 1987 English Coalition Conference envisioned school as a place where learners could use language to understand themselves and others, to make sense of their world, and to reflect on their own lives. They called for an end to fragmentation of curriculum (Jensen, 1989). Templeton (1995, p. 17) summarizes the discipline's attention to the issue of context: "The ways in which readers engage in and respond to any literacy activity depends fundamentally on the contexts in which the activity occurs."

Aesthetic educators have also recognized the power of more holistic contexts for learning. Montana's Framework for Aesthetic Literacy (Hahn, 1994, p. 8) stipulates "aesthetic encounters" as the context for learning. "The aesthetic encounters take place in the studios, museums, theaters, libraries, concert halls, classrooms, streets, and parks of the community." The encounters are "thick, rich environments" that are "culturally significant and worth our attention." In the recommended middle school curriculum, a powwow serves as one encounter (context) for learning. Students attend a powwow, hear an elder talk about the culture, and read about Native American history. This rich context provides the medium for further questions and research. Elements of dance, music, dress, artistic interpretation, cultural context, art objects, artistic processes, history, and religion are explored within the curriculum.

Some disciplines are just on the verge of accepting new ways of organizing their knowledge. Although the sciences have been traditionally bound to scope and sequences of content as organizational patterns, several trends do portend a reorganization of the curriculum around " important issues in the community and world;… a particular student's interest;… a particular investigation" (National Research Council, 1994, pp. vi–7). Though still tangential to the mainstream of how science curriculum is generally regarded by educators, Martin and Miller's (1988, p. 259) commentary is indicative of newer thought:

> The very nature of such [science] texts is unscientific. Static, linear, and nonparticipatory, they stand in stark contrast to the dynamic, cyclic, and directly involving mode of science that is so inviting to young children. These texts offer children no stories, no connections between forms and forces, between observers and observed. Without this profound connectivity which is the lifeblood of science, the body of scientific knowledge can be reduced to a corpse. Through the storytelling mode, scientific knowledge can be kept alive for children.

Broader perspectives of the total school curriculum offer the most challenges to fragmented, noncontextual curriculum design. The need for meaningful context has been one of the major justifications in the recent trend toward integrated curriculum. The movement toward curriculum integration has propelled a search for solutions that transcend the traditional subject-area approaches to learning. Finding links between mathematics, science, language arts, social sciences, and aesthetic pursuits has become important in educational restructuring. Context becomes an essential element in linking different disciplines in meaningful and authentic ways.

A holistic view of curriculum is shared by many who see real-world, people-centered issues as the natural way in which humans organize their learning and knowing. Beane (1991) urges that the curriculum be based on the common interests and needs of the students and that its content be drawn from the intersection of adolescents' concerns and world issues. The 1995 Association for Supervision and Curriculum Development (ASCD) Yearbook (Beane, 1995) is a plea for coherent curriculum which includes several proposals for contexts that would lead to coherence. Wiggins (1995, p. 116) concludes:

> Thus, we can say that the ultimate coherence of curriculums depends on students having repeated opportunities to directly experience not just adult work but the context of that work: the challenges, messes, and dilemmas at the heart of a profession knowledge in use.

Iran-Nejad, McKeachie, and Berliner (1990, p. 511) state:

> research indicates that the more meaningful, the more deeply or elaboratively processed, the more situated in context, and the more rooted in cultural, background, metacognitive, and personal knowledge an event is, the more readily it is understood, learned, and remembered.

Story has great potential to meet the criteria that these authors stipulate for understanding, learning, and remembering events. Wells (1986, p. 194) champions this potential in his rationale for story as a meaningful context for curriculum.

> Constructing stories in the mind—or storying, as it has been called—is one of the most fundamental means of meaning making; as such it is an activity that pervades all aspects of learning. . . Through the exchange of stories, teachers and students can share their understandings of a topic and bring their mental models of the world into closer alignment. In this sense, stories, and storying are relevant in all areas of the curriculum.

Because story reflects the real world, the conflicts, dilemmas, puzzles, mysteries, and dramas depicted are authentic. One of our students,

Garrick, said it well: "With narrative we take a piece of life and learn from it and that's what we do every day."

To Accommodate Individual Differences

Story has a unique charm in that it has the power to capture the entire spectrum of learners. A good story is a good story for all ages. For example, we have read the picture book *Galimoto* (Williams, 1990, explored in detail in chapter 3) to young children, middle grade students, and adults. Each age group reacted to the text with interest. Young children were interested in the central character of the book, an inquisitive African boy. They wanted to know more about what the boy was doing and why he was interested in collecting certain materials. Middle grade students wanted to consider where the story took place, why the main character was using a shoe box, although everyone looked barefoot, and what life was like in this village. Adult learners were no less intrigued by the book. Some were interested in the gender roles depicted by the book. Others wanted to know about the social relationships of the characters. *Galimoto* invited all learners to interact with the story at their levels of ability and interest.

Humans construct meaning as they process a text, either oral or written. The transactional view of reading as proposed by Rosenblatt (1938/1976, p. 25) asserts that "the literary work exists in the live circuit set up between reader and text..." Because of this, the text is created anew by each person who interacts with it, yielding multiple interpretations among readers or within the same reader over time. Numerous reports of literature study (Gilles, 1990; Eeds & Peterson, 1991; Leal, 1993) show that students of varying backgrounds and abilities differ in their interpretations and the meanings they create from text. Because stories are approachable from any background, they resonate across cultures and ages. *Owl Moon* (Yolen, 1987) holds 5-year-old Yup'ik children in Alaska spellbound (Marylee Bates, personal communication, February 20, 1993) as well as children in Arizona (Barone, Eeds, & Mason, 1995). Children and their parents in Tacoma took delight in the book (Egawa, 1990), as did adult students of children's literature. Hickman (1992) reports the responses of children at various age levels to the same book. Although there were differences in the nature and sophistication of the responses, Hickman found that "all of us—and I include myself among those who responded—constructed meaning in consideration of the whole as more than the sum of its parts" (p. 191). All of those who interacted with the text, from kindergarten students to adult professors, found significant ways to connect with the story.

Since story can be approached from a variety of intellectual and developmental levels, everyone has the opportunity to find a measure of delight.

Story invites learners, whatever their social, academic, or developmental station, to stretch their minds, and to inquire and explore the possibilities.

To Join a Community

Story provides a sense of community with its common points of reference. Below are listed some phrases that are related to stories we know. See how many of them trigger a story for you.

"Sour grapes"
"La llorona"
"The people of Chelm"
"Loaves and fishes"
"To be or not to be"
"Deng Ge and the candlewick fairy"
"Call me Ishmael"
"The night Max wore his wolf suit and made mischief..."
"Playing the dozens"
"Listen, my children, and you shall hear..."

With each story that we share, we feel a closer relationship with each other. If we know the same stories, we share much more than just the information contained in the pages of a book.

> Although storying may have its roots in the biologically given human pre- disposition to construct mental stories in order to make sense of percep- tual information, it very quickly becomes the means whereby we enter into a shared world, which is continually broadened and enriched by the exchange of stories with others. (Wells, 1986, p. 196)

The community instills its truth through shared story and seeks under- standing through examination and reexamination of the anthology of expe- rience. Barton and Booth (1990, p. 174) state this elegantly:

> But most of all, we sing the praises of story—that most simple and com- plex creation of all the arts, resonating from caves and echoing from the moons of distant planets. We are all part of the story tapestries of our tribes, our threads woven into yours, each tale embroidered with the strands of others, for all time.

The use of story to bind community is powerful, in a practical sense. Michael recounts an experience with science educators in which story played a pivotal role in shaping community from a sense of chaos:

> There were almost fifty science educators from four states struggling to draft a common statement of goals on which all could agree. There were

long discourses, bulleted lists, explanatory prose, miscommunication, and heated debate. We were not of common purpose and were headed for four separate visions. I remembered a story that seemed to relate the key ingredients of the goals we were so desperately trying to communicate and asked the group if I could share it. In a few short moments of telling the story *Come Back, Salmon* (Cone, 1992), the individual isolation melted and the community jelled. Somehow the story of young children repairing a polluted stream, returning salmon fry to the spawning beds, and then awaiting the return of the fish from the sea was common experience whereby all could agree upon the goals of science education. Story had done what the collective intellect and hours of rhetoric could not—it formed a community with shared experience and common understanding.

Karla, one of our students, explained how story builds a sense of community: "Stories offer counsel, comfort, and connection to the lives of others."

Story brings each of its remarkable strengths to all—from the ancients huddled around a fire in a forest hut to present-day people seated at computers in high-tech offices. Story has not lost its power over the ages, but rather has found renewed vigor (Denman, 1991). Children today need story as much or more than at any other time. They are experiencing an increasingly chaotic world characterized by a glut of information bombarding them from all sorts of media, a decreasing sense of personal safety, and an undercurrent of despair. Children in the best of circumstances have lives that are fragmented with crowded schedules of school, sports, lessons, organizations, and family obligations. Less fortunate children affected by broken families, drugs, violence, homelessness, and hunger face a life filled with daily difficulties. We have an obligation to give children not only a nurturing environment but also the words and the language forms to combat these difficulties. Story can provide developing children with a means to validate their feelings, promote insights, and nourish hope (Barton & Booth, 1990). Stories offer all children an opportunity to find sense in chaos, to link their experience with others, and to be a part of a community—in sum, to share in the power of story. Because of story, "our personal existence, however trivial it may seem, takes on a cloak of significance" (Denman, 1991, p. 4).

◈ *The Green Book* Revisited

Reexamine *The Green Book* summarization at the beginning of the chapter for a moment. Consider why it lures us to want to know more about the characters, setting, and action. What is it about this book that appeals to us? Why was this story able to communicate important ideas, relationships, and universal truth?

When we examine the responses of our learners to this text, we see the power of story reflected. The story of *The Green Book* helps us remember; it parallels life; it fosters meaning-making; it provides a meaningful context; it accommodates individual differences; it invites us into a community.

By reconstructing the story of *The Green Book*, learners remember the essential elements of the story and are immediately able to recall the pieces of information, events, concepts, and experiences contained there. The story allows our learners to not only remember the essence of the story itself, but more importantly allows them to discover why we read that particular book. They remember that *The Green Book* helped us to identify why story is so powerful. Pattie's choice of the blank book to take on the journey at first seemed foolish, yet at the conclusion of the book we understand otherwise. We remember that the keeping of a community's story, the recording of human events and relationships, and the preservation of culture is the essence of *The Green Book*.

The Green Book allows our learners to make meaning through discussion of important conceptual issues. Through Pattie's decision, through the actions and reflections of Father, through the moral dilemmas presented in the conflicts of the colony, we shared and re-created the dilemmas for ourselves. By paralleling life's nadirs and zeniths, the story facilitated our understanding of how the world works.

We learned in a meaningful context. Imagine 20 students scurrying about building contrivances made of sticks, foil, and plastic tape. Their zeal and motivation was created from the context of survival. The story provided that tension and urgency. There was a meaningful context that linked the actions and interests of our learners to something that had purpose and reason.

Each learner approached *The Green Book* from individual perspectives. Some of our younger children were very interested in areas that adults simply skipped over. Some questions adults pursued were eschewed by others. The rainbow context of the story invited a multiplicity of responses and inquiries.

Finally, *The Green Book* helped our learners to form a community. After the shared experience of reading the book, we heard many conversations about possibilities and exploration of meanings. Now, learners can recall experience through the common language of the story. They themselves make story out of their experience. Students still recall their construction of contrivances, their growing of wheat seeds, the writing in their own blank books. In adding to their own story, they reflect and bring meaning to their experience. Dewey (1938) tells us that the purpose of education is to bring meaning to experience. And Wells (1986, p. 196) reminds us of the process. "Making sense of an experience is to a very great extent being able to construct a plausible story about it." Story helps to fulfill the purposes of education.

Lingering Questions

Many individuals have difficulty conceptualizing story as a way of communicating the meaning of human experiences rather than just a fictional tale. How can we continue to develop our understanding of the concept of story?

We have indicated that organizing curriculum by a scope and sequence of facts and concepts—discrete facts learned within discrete subjects—should be questioned. We view narrative structure as a compelling alternative. Is a change from the traditional divisions of schooling needed? Does story offer a good alternative or are other alternatives more viable?

Companion Readings

Since we have only summarized *The Green Book* (Paton Walsh, 1982), we highly recommend that you read this story in its entirety. We suggest *Stories in the Classroom: Storytelling, Reading Aloud and Roleplaying with Children.* (Barton & Booth, 1990) for a perspective on the importance of story, the role of story in making meaning and a compendium of application possibilities. If you would like to read an in-depth treatise on narrative as a cultural way of thinking and knowing, Bruner's *Acts of Meaning* (1990) provides important background.

CHAPTER 3

Constructivism: A Theory of Learning

Activating Prior Knowledge

How and where do children learn what they know? What do children already know before they come to school? Is this knowledge important?

If we want to help children acquire new concepts or ideas, what instructional environments and teaching practices are most successful in bringing about long-lasting change in what they know and believe?

Chapter Highlights

The scenario that opens this chapter features a constructivist lesson based on a children's book. In an analysis of this lesson we compare constructivist and transmission teaching.

Constructivism is defined and its seven tenets are then introduced with vignettes, illustrations, and curricular implications.

Constructivism is differentiated from discovery.

Students bustle about as they await the start of class. A group clusters around Michael, the teacher, as he arranges some materials. They are eager to discover what new inquiry is in store for them. Michael signals the class of 8- and 9-year-olds that it is time to begin and holds up a shoe box. "What do you think might be inside my special household storage box?" Students wonder why he calls it a "special household storage box" since it looks like an ordinary shoe box to them. They offer many suggestions about the possible contents. Michael lifts the lid and begins to show the students the things that he has collected over the past few weeks—rubber bands, popsicle sticks, plastic bags, cardboard tubes. "What do you think of all these things I have saved?" Students are asked to record in their journals ideas about the materials in the box. They write: "I would throw them away. They're useless." "My mom uses the plastic bags for trash. The other stuff, I don't know." "You could shoot the rubber bands at somebody."

Michael now asks the class to sit in a circle around him as he brings out a picture book titled *Galimoto* (Williams, 1990). "What do you think this book is about?" he asks as he shows the cover of the book. Students speculate about the title *Galimoto* and wonder about what it means. They talk about the boy on the cover and suggest that the setting might be in Africa or perhaps the Caribbean. They are curious about what the boy is doing with the wires.

Next the students and the teacher read the book interactively.

> Kondi opened an old shoe box and looked inside. These were his things. They belonged to him. Inside the box there was a ball made of many old plastic bags, tightly wrapped with string. There was a knife Kondi had made from a piece of tin can and a dancing man he had made from dried cornstalks. In Kondi's box there were also some scraps of wire. He had been saving the wires for something special. Now he took them and the knife from his box. 'I shall make a galimoto,' Kondi told his brother, Ufulu. (Williams, 1990, unpaged)

As the story unfolds, Kondi finds, trades, begs, and borrows wires for his galimoto.

While he reads the story and shows the pictures to the class, Michael invites the children to respond by asking questions such as, "What do you think Kondi is going to do next? Why do you think that? Do you see anything in this picture that you have a question about? Is there anything you would like to know more about?" Students ask their own questions about what a galimoto might be, about where this place might be, about why there are shoe boxes and no one seems to wear shoes, and about what kind of chant the women were singing as they worked. They wonder and guess about the action of the story and the characters and their way of life. As the story closes, students discover that Kondi's galimoto is a wire model of a truck. Other children in the village had constructed their own galimotos. Cars, trucks, boats, motorcycles—all were galimotos.

Michael returns to the shoe box of materials. "I guess I can throw these things away now!" The class responds with resounding disapproval. "We could use some of that stuff," recommends one student. "Let's make something," another suggests. The class eagerly decides to experiment with the materials to see if they might create something. One member of each cooperative group selects popsicle sticks, plastic bags, rubber bands, and cardboard rolls from the shoe box. Michael asks the groups what they can do if they do not have enough supplies. "We can be like Kondi and trade with others to get what we need," a student suggests. A busy hum of activity fills the room as students experiment with the materials, trade with others for needed items, sketch their creations, and take notes in their journals. Students share their creations: cars, paddle boats, parachutes, bag trees, a catapult-shooting game, merry-go-rounds, and a host of other inventions and models.

As the students demonstrate their crafts, Michael asks them to think about the materials in the shoe box once again. He asks them to write about what uses they have found for household trash. "Look back to your first writing in your journal. Do you think differently now about popsicle sticks and plastic bags?" They report: "Junk isn't what it seems." "I didn't think these things had any value, but with a little imagination I can make a toy." "Things we throw away might be recycled into something useful." "Other cultures like Kondi's make better use of their environment and resources. We ought to do the same." The class discussion continues about how materials can be reused and what they could invent collectively if they saved more of these things.

⬥ How We Construct Meaning

The introductory scenario offers us a backdrop for a discussion of learning. We will consider a fundamental question: "How do we learn best?" Perhaps because it appears too theoretical and nebulous, curriculum designers often skip over this most fundamental question. Yet, we believe that to base curriculum on an idea of how humans learn is not only appropriate, but critical. To skip to planning curriculum without some agreement about how we learn is akin to selecting an automobile without regard to the energy system it employs. You might be very impressed by the style, appointments, and comfort of the car only to realize that it runs on an exotic fuel or perhaps does not even have an engine! A theory of learning is essential to curriculum development because it fuels our thinking in making curriculum choices.

The lesson sequence just presented is based upon important tenets about how people learn best. Fosnot (1989, p. 19–20) enumerates:

1. Knowledge consists of past constructions.
2. Constructions come about through assimilation and accommodation.
3. Learning is an organic process of invention, rather than a mechanical process of accumulation.
4. Meaningful learning occurs through reflection and resolution of cognitive conflict and thus serves to negate earlier, incomplete levels of understanding.

By choosing these tenets to describe learning, we have aligned ourselves with a constructivist perspective. Constructivists view thinking and learning differently from other learning theorists.

> The learner is actively constructing knowledge rather than passively taking in information. Learners come to the educational setting with many different experiences, ideas, and approaches to learning. Learners do not *acquire* knowledge that is transmitted to them; rather, they *construct* knowledge through their intellectual activity and make it their own. (Chaille & Britain, 1991, p. 11)

Take a moment to return to the *Galimoto* lesson to analyze how it employed the constructivist perspective of learning. In it, we honored what learners knew about common objects and what might be done with them. We encouraged students to make meaning of the experiences and to personalize their findings. We provided an experience with the potential to create cognitive dissonance in the learner. As planners of this lesson we had adopted a paradigm about how people learn before we crafted our curriculum. Each decision that we made about how to arrange activities, how to facilitate learning, and how to structure assessment was fueled by constructivist tenets about learning.

◈ Constructivism Contrasted with Transmission

The constructivist perspective is a departure from what educators have commonly practiced. To bring that difference to light, examine how we might have structured some of the same content and activities based on what might be called a transmission model of learning as opposed to a constructive one. Figure 3.1 outlines a transmission lesson plan and figure 3.2 shows the kind of results that might be expected. In contrast, figure 3.3

FIGURE 3.1 *Galimoto:* Transmission lesson

TLWDAT: (The Learner Will Demonstrate the Ability to:)

1. listen interpretively
2. list materials that are normally thrown away but which may have utility
3. make an accurate model

ANTICIPATORY SET:
Read *Galimoto* aloud to the class

LESSON:
Give Objective of Lesson: "Today we are going to be like Kondi. He made a toy from scraps of wire—using materials that would have been thrown away. You too will make a toy from wire (pipe cleaners) that I have brought for you."

Give Model: "Here is one that I have made as a model. See how I have bent the wires to make a wheel?"

Check for Understanding: "Now children, what will we be doing today?" (Students respond.)

Guided Practice: Give students time to build their galimoto. Teacher monitors as individuals shape cars, trucks, helicopters, wagons from pipe cleaners.

ASSESSMENT:
Examine student models to determine how closely they match the models in the book.

Written Quiz:

1. What are some uses of discarded materials?
2. What is a galimoto?
3. How did Kondi get materials for his galimoto?

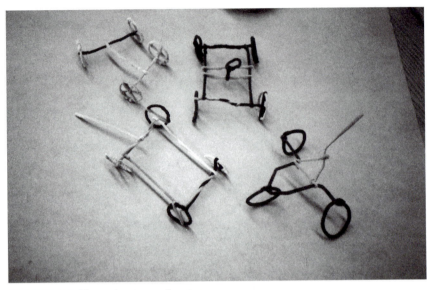

FIGURE 3.2 Pipe-cleaner galimotos

FIGURE 3.3 *Galimoto:* Constructivist plan

GOALS:
Appreciating the links between science, technology, and society
Communicating new ideas

LESSON:

- Activation of prior knowledge through questioning students about the nature of materials and their possible uses—show items in a shoe box
- Have students record their responses
- Interactive reading of *Galimoto*
- Allow for exchange of reactions and questions
- Reexamine text and pictures as needed
- Student exploration with materials from the shoe box to "be like Kondi"—to transfer the story theme to their own lives
- Students present their creations to the rest of the class
- Students discuss what they have learned
- Students write a reflection in journals

ASSESSMENT:
Watch and listen to students as they work. Evaluate student communications of their creations. Compare beginning and ending journal entries to determine any changes in views.

FIGURE 3.4 Constructivist vs. transmission model

Transmission Model	Constructivist Perspective
■ Closed-ended instruction	■ Open-ended instruction
■ Teacher-directed learning	■ Student-directed learning
■ Ignores prior knowledge	■ Utilizes prior knowledge
■ Transmits knowledge	■ Generates knowledge
■ Externally motivated	■ Intrinsically motivated
■ Isolates skill instruction	■ Capitalizes on context

delineates how the lesson was actually taught. These results were the various student constructions reported in the previous section. A constructivist lesson design assumes a different philosophical, psychological, and epistemological basis. In figure 3.4 we have listed some major contrasts between the objectivist (transmission) and constructivist perspectives. The transmission model assumes that the learner is the recipient and benefactor of the teacher's or the textbook writer's experience and knowledge. The lesson and its supportive strategies are methods to transmit that knowledge to the learner. Metaphorically, the learner is a sponge or receptacle which we fill up with the collected wisdom of the common culture.

Because the transmission model starts with the premise that the learner will be taught a certain piece of information or skill, prior knowledge is ignored and unimportant. Assessment must measure whether the objective has been met. Learning outside the defined objective is considered irrelevant. Since the objectives are set by the teacher or dictated by the district and state, motivation for learning is external. Students make galimotos because they are directed to do so and are evaluated based on their skill to copy the model. The teacher does all the thinking. The students are commanded to work rather than invited to make meaning from an experience. Instruction is controlled and confined.

⬙ Tenets of a Constructivist Perspective

In contrast, instruction designed from a constructivist perspective is open-ended. To hone our understanding of this view of human learning, let's explore the basic principles of constructivism. We have synthesized and summarized the research (Callison, 1991) by listing characteristics of constructive learning:

- Learners come to school with a wealth of prior knowledge. Learning is an interaction between the learner's use of prior knowledge and school experiences.
- What learners know is constructed meaning which did not exist before the learner created it.
- Learners make meaning about the world by logically linking pieces of knowledge, communications, and experiences.
- These belief systems are often incomplete explanations or misconceptions.
- Belief systems are held until they are modified or replaced by a more satisfactory explanation.
- Direct instruction is unlikely to change belief systems.
- Learning takes place when confrontation with new experience creates dissonance.
- Learning is facilitated by social interaction.
- Learning takes place best in a meaningful context.

Each of the principles represents a significant idea about learning. In the following sections, we offer an illustrative vignette, discuss each principle, and offer some implications for curriculum development.

Learners come to school with a wealth of prior knowledge. Learning is an interaction between the learner's use of prior knowledge and school experiences.

Adult learners, including elementary teachers, are asked about electricity. "What kinds of things can shock you?" Learners report such things as household current, lightning, car batteries, and the batteries used in toys, flashlights, and other common items. Given a 1.5 volt "D" cell battery, individuals are asked to touch each side of the battery with one hand. Many approach the task with trepidation for fear that they may be shocked but most of the learners observe that they feel nothing. When wires are added to the ends of the cell, many of those who saw no hazard in holding a battery now are cautious. Several have reported that they check the charge of a battery by holding it to their tongues to feel the spark. Experience with various forms of electricity and, in some cases, fear of electrical shock either facilitates or interferes in the adult's observation and use of batteries.

Prior knowledge is "the sum of a person's previous learning and development; ...experiences which precede a learning situation, story, etc." (Harris & Hodges, 1981, p. 29). It is the accumulation of information, ideas, and schemata which is generated by all the experiences we have, both in and out of school. All learners arrive at school with a wealth of information and experience. Constructivist theory demands that we be aware of students' prior knowledge, their conceptions and their suppositions, for it is in the interaction of this prior knowledge and current experiences that learning takes place. Thus, knowing what children know is a most important beginning for teaching and learning (Ausubel, 1968). Prior knowledge is important in constructing new ideas and frameworks and forms the bridge or barrier to further conceptual change (Pines & West, 1986). Learners accommodate new concepts by generating links to the existing knowledge (Driver & Bell, 1986). By assessing prior knowledge and organizing new experiences that complement and challenge the student, effective learning is achieved (Finley, 1985). This tenet is amply supported by research studies in reading which demonstrate that individuals understand what they read in relationship to what they already know. These findings are summarized in figure 3.5.

The implications of this knowledge are both a boon and a challenge. The boon is that if we recognize that learners are already adept at many things and already know a wealth of information, then we can tap into those strengths and use them as resources in the classroom. A teacher we know who adopts this philosophy proudly says that she has 28 experts in her class—all children have particular abilities, expertise, or special knowledge.

The challenge is in thinking about how the curriculum can accommodate this prior knowledge. If curriculum is a carefully delineated scope and sequence that dictates specifics, then, for some children, repetition is a wearisome reality. Colonial history of the United States is

FIGURE 3.5 The effect of prior knowledge on reading comprehension

Anderson et al., 1977	Two groups of college students, one consisting of majors in music and the other majors in physical education, were asked to read an ambiguous passage about "Rocky on the mat."	The music majors interpreted it as a jailbreak and the physical education majors thought it was a description of a wrestling match.
Steffensen, Joag-Dev, & Anderson, 1979	Students from the United States and India read letters about an Indian wedding and an American wedding.	Readers remembered more of the culturally matched passage and elaborated on it more appropriately than on the passage from the other culture. They produced more distortions of the culturally mismatched passage.
Reynolds et al., 1982	Black and white students read a passage about two boys "playing the dozens."	The white students who were from an agricultural area generally recalled the event as a fight. The black students more often recognized that the boys were just joking and having fun.
Lipson, 1983	Students in private Jewish and Catholic schools all read a neutral passage as well as passages specific to the two religious groups.	High-achieving students had learned to suppress their background knowledge and assume the interpretive frame of the instructional material.
Bloome & Green, 1985	Students were asked to respond to a reading passage by answering multiple choice questions from a reading workbook and then questioned about the process they had used to choose their answers.	Students were much more likely to comprehend text when they had culturally appropriate prior knowledge.

taught in elementary, middle, and high school because we anticipate that students will not retain the information. But what if they do? We recall one high school junior in a U.S. history class who declared as the pilgrims landed on Plymouth Rock for at least the third time in his educational career, "I'm not coming back to this class until we get to the twentieth century." If the curriculum is arranged in such a way that we repeat and rehash the same content, then we dismiss our learners' prior experiences. For other children, failure to recognize their prior knowledge means that they are expected to learn something for which they have no background. This happens, for example, when mainstream textbooks are used with children who are not part of the majority culture. One kindergarten teacher in a native school in Alaska was heard to exclaim with exasperation, "Do you realize how much of this textbook is based on understanding farms!" Her young students had never seen anyone tend a garden, much less have a concept for farms. In either the repetition or omission case, the learner is not well served. Curriculum must always allow learners to build upon their prior knowledge and grow from it.

What the learners know is constructed meaning which did not exist before the learner created it.

Children's language yields many examples of constructions that are original. Nathan was 2 when he went on his first wilderness canoe trip. His favorite word at the time was "juice." On encountering river rapids, he promptly named them "whee-juice," a meaning constructed by him that was an apt description of his experience. When 4-year-old Zachary was poked by a needle, he said, "It sparkles me!" To him, dollar bills were "straight money" and he excitedly called from the shower one day to invite his mother to "look at all the soap droppings!" At age 5, he liked riding his bike on "soft" roads, meaning smooth, and when he ran out of clean socks, he said his drawer was "blank." And during a snow day when he was 6, he announced, "School was crossed out." Children make similar inventions in their writing. Phillip, a kindergartner, draws a picture of a car and labels it "labrgne" and 7-year-old Debbie writes "I wish for high-hill-shoes but my mother things I'm to young but who kers" (Temple, Nathan, Temple, & Burris, 1993, p. 134). Both in speech and in writing children are creating meanings and inventing structures that are unique and which do not exist prior to the child's creating them.

We know that children construct knowledge because they possess so many ideas that adults do not teach them (DeVries & Kohlberg, 1989). This is true of adults as well—they have many ideas which no one has taught or told them. A primary tenet of constructivist theory is that knowledge is the result of individual constructions of reality. "Meaning is not conveyed but evoked" (Wheatley, 1991, p. 11). "Learning involves organizing self experiences in a way that makes sense" (Driver & Bell, 1986, p. 453). ..."through the continual creation of rules and hypotheses to explain what is observed" (Brooks, 1990, p. 68). Each individual invents the truth. Wells (1986, p. 89) advises teachers to "recognize that their perspective cannot be transmitted directly, but must be constructed by children for themselves, through a process of building on what they already know and gradually elaborating the framework within which they know it."

Learners make meaning about their world by logically linking pieces of knowledge, communications, and experiences.

As part of a book response activity, adults had to predict how long different kinds of candles might burn. There were birthday cake candles, votive candles and short multipurpose ones. To our surprise, one adult learner was convinced that one kind of candle, because it was in a metal cup, would never burn out. The learner linked his prior knowledge and observations to form what was to him a logical explanation of the candle. From his point of reference, wax did not burn but simply melted and dripped off candles. A metal container contains the dripping and therefore the candle would never burn out.

All of us make sense of our world through individual and often, non-conventional, or non-science, ways. Children make sense of their world by employing causal explanations and generalizations to impose some order on experiences (Hewson, 1986). These "alternative frameworks" (Driver & Easley, 1978) are ways in which learners make sense of the natural phenomena around them. Alternative frameworks are often counter to conventions of science. It is common, for example, for people to think that the reason it is warm in the summer is because the sun is closest to the earth during that season, that one can be shocked from a common "D" cell battery, or that we see more in a mirror if we stand back. Researchers have cataloged a plethora of misconceptions in the sciences (Shymansky &

Kyle, 1988). In one classic example, Nussbaum (1979) collected children's ideas about how the earth was situated as a cosmic body (fig. 3.6). In their rich descriptions of earth as disc, semi-sphere, and flat plane, it is clear that these inventions are attempts to make sense of various pieces of knowledge and observations. Pines and West (1986) ask that we not be alarmed at these misconceptions, but rather that we marvel at the children's creative abilities to make sense of the world.

Although the area of naive conceptions has been most studied in the sciences, studies of other disciplines also reveal the human proclivity for making sense out of experiences. Gardner (1991) describes stereotypes, simplistic interpretations, and little tolerance for the abstract, the irregular or the experimental as evidence for misconceptions in social sciences, humanities, and the arts.

The implications of this understanding are important for curriculum and instruction. Brooks and Brooks (1993) state that a guiding principle of constructivism is to adapt curriculum to address students' suppositions. If we know that learners come to school with rich prior knowledge and pre-conceived notions about how the world works, then it is important that we

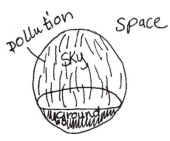

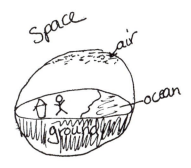

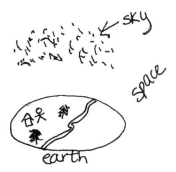

FIGURE 3.6 Students' ideas of the earth-space relationships

make an attempt to detect these belief systems. Learners' constructions of their own systems—that the earth is warm in the summer because it is closer to the earth, that all Native Americans own horses and live in tepees, or that all music should be harmonious and have a regular beat—should provide educators with meaningful starting places for curriculum. It is at the counterintuitive junctures of our world that we can most critically and beneficially spend our time and resources.

 Belief systems are often incomplete explanations or misconceptions. Belief systems are held until they are modified or replaced by a more satisfactory explanation.

Carol's mother lives in north central Nebraska, very near a fossil find. Although she had lived there for her whole life, she never had seen the site. One summer, Carol's family returned to Nebraska and arranged an expedition to see the fossil digs. Walking up to a road cut in the sand hills of Nebraska, Carol's mother viewed a bright white layer of sea shells. "You know, I have been told all my life that this area was once an inland sea, but I never truly believed it until this moment."

Alternative frameworks are not replaced easily. Learners will find ways to adjust their old ideas before assimilating new ones. Children and adults hold their belief systems until they are directly confronted by some new phenomena. Learners are often unwilling to give up their personal frameworks even in the face of observable phenomena that are in conflict with their explanation (Feher & Rice, 1988). Studies in reading have shown that readers will let their background knowledge override the text if the two are in conflict (Lipson, 1982; Reynolds, Taylor, Steffenson, Shirey, & Anderson, 1982; Smith, Readence, & Alvermann, 1984). Teachers also demonstrate this trait.

> One of the most common observations made in the literature about teach-ers' belief systems concerns the remarkable persistence of beliefs. Once formed, beliefs resist change, even when change is expected. . . . Research tells us that underlying belief systems are so strong that they resist change even when practical circumstances would seem to dictate change. (Wyatt & Pickle, 1993)

This resistance to change is a significant aspect in understanding learn-ing. If learners are in fact reluctant to leave self-constructed explanations of the world, then how can those frameworks be challenged and replaced with more conventional constructs? The answer to this question rests in first acknowledging that conceptual change is gradual, arduous, and often threatening. To learn means, in Piagetian terms, to accommodate new con-structs into older structures. To affect conceptual change, learners need an environment of new experiences and communications that confront their conceptions. Posner, Strilke, Hewson, & Gertzog (1982) assert that people will resist change unless they are confronted with something different and become dissatisfied with the former. Learning is characterized by a process of interaction between the student's mind and the new experience. Such a learning environment enables students to modify their existing cognitive structures (Kyle & Shymansky, 1989). Finley (1985) found that direct expe-rience with the phenomena in the form of hands-on experimentation was an effective way of confronting naive conceptions.

We must recognize that learners can easily comply with "correct" answers while no underlying change in understanding or belief has taken place. The quick route to successful performance seldom leads to compe-tence, insightfulness, or expertise (Blais, 1988). For example, research with primary-level children (Kamii, Lewis, & Jones, 1991) shows that the teaching of rules or algorithms is counterproductive in developing an understanding of the meaning of place value. In work with children near Birmingham, Alabama, teachers discovered that if children were encouraged to produce their own algorithms in solving problems that they were more likely to understand the function and meaning of place value in operations such as addition and subtraction. By invention of their own methods of adding the ten's and one's place values, children gained an understanding of the representations of the symbols. Teachers found that students gave more correct answers for mathematics problems by using invented algorithms than using an imposed set of rules. Learners who constructed their own meaning about how mathematics problems could be solved became successful. Their conceptions were molded by their own observations and experiences. For students given a step-by-step method of symbol manipulation, however, no greater understanding of mathematics was gained and fewer problems were solved correctly.

We must overcome our tendency to provide the learners with explanations of our expert knowledge. "Giving students the ideas impairs the robustness of what students learn, their depth and breadth of understanding, and their self-confidence" (Simon, quoted in O'Neil, 1992, p. 4).

Direct instruction is unlikely to change personal belief systems.

For a moment, think about getting ready for work in the morning. You brush your teeth and look in the bathroom mirror above the sink. After you check your face for leftover toothpaste, you decide that you would like to see the rest of your body. What should you do to see more of yourself? We have asked this question of child and adult learners alike and generally receive the response, "Back up and you can see more of yourself."

We next ask that groups of learners to take mirrors and experiment to corroborate their assumptions. When asked to report findings, some say they can indeed see more of themselves by getting farther from the mirror, an observation consistent with their initial assumptions. Some groups report that there is little or no change in what can be seen. These divergent findings cause some learners to dispute observations different from their own.

Finally, we mount a large mirror on the wall and ask several volunteers to make observations in front of the group. Most learners, when they are confronted by this controlled circumstance, make the observation that there is no change in the amount of the body that they can see as they move farther from the mirror. However, there are some that will maintain their initial position even though what they see offers no corroboration. One student that we had asked to do this experiment repeatedly reported that she saw more as she moved back. After others continued to report differently, her face wore a surprised look as she realized that she did not want to believe what she saw!

It takes more than a transmission model to change the conceptual structures that people invent for themselves. Michael was unable to convince anyone about the mirrors. No amount of "telling" adequately reforms anyone's beliefs. In order to change, learners must actively hypothesize, check, and change their ideas (Driver & Bell, 1986).

> The more likely it is that students have misconceptions, and the more important deep understanding of a concept is, the more educators must minimize the amount of direct telling to students and maximize pupils' direct construction."(O'Neil, 1992).

Growth in knowledge and thinking occurs gradually, with each new adjustment laying groundwork for further adjustments. Learners require a "coherent, internally stable set of explanatory structures that account for the individual's experience and that resolve as many apparent anomalies as possible" (Hewson, 1986, p. 161). Problem-centered curricula, in which students engage in meaning making, provide an environment for conceptual change (Wheatley, 1991). Such a learning environment enables students to modify their existing cognitive structures.

Of course, we recognize that there are some kinds of information (as distinct from knowledge) that can be transmitted from authority to recipient. Facts, dates, and place names are pieces of information that can be easily transmitted from teacher, text, or media to learners. Caine and Caine (1991) refer to this kind of attainment of information as route learning. We can learn the route to our destination by remembering to walk three blocks north, turn right, walk two blocks east and stop at the yellow house. We have only step-by-step instructions on how to proceed. Learning routes is necessary when the information is a kind of knowledge that cannot be constructed. Our discussion about human learning focuses upon conceptual, or map, knowledge. This kind of knowledge is broader than route learning because it provides the learner with the schema of the problem instead of an algorithm for solution. By having a concept of a town and the skills of using a compass, a map, and an address, learners armed with a broader understanding can invent their own routes. This kind of learning involves learners in understanding the whole as opposed to just the parts.

To illustrate the difference between map and route learning, consider the example of baking bread. For Michael, bread baking is a series of steps he takes—a route. First measure ingredients, mix materials as directed, knead dough a certain length of time, allow time to rise, knead again, and so forth. To Michael, the list of directions are mindless mandates that control behavior. He does not know the reasons for what he is doing. Sometimes the bread turns out just fine and other times it fails. When it fails he has no understanding of which variable was at fault. For him the route was something that he followed dutifully. If there had been a mistake or misprint in the recipe, he would have happily complied. Carol, on the other hand, doesn't need a recipe. She has a concept of "bread"—a map. Carol scoops flour out of the bin without measuring, substitutes some ripe banana for sugar, adds extra milk powder for the calcium, and adjusts the amount of shortening, seeking a tasty, low-fat loaf. She kneads the bread until it feels right—knowing how the gluten forms and the yeast works. She can easily detect an anomaly in a new recipe because she knows how the materials interact to make the dough.

The differences we find between these two ways of knowing are the differences between being a cog on an assembly line versus being a craftsperson. As a route learner we do one piece of the learning, tighten one nut on the giant machinery of the curriculum—we learn one fact, practice one skill. As a craftsperson, however, we know the whole system. We know the problem that our machine solves, the plans to make the product, the utility of the pieces, and the expected performance of the product. As a map learner we see the end point of our labors and understand how all activities contribute to the whole.

Broad concepts, language learning, problem solving, invention, and storytelling all demand map learning. It is this sort of learning that cannot be simply transmitted from one person to another by telling. As John Dewey (quoted in Blais, 1988, p. 6) reminds us:

> No thought, no idea, can possibly be conveyed as an idea from one person to another. When it is told, it is to the one to whom it is told, another fact, not an idea . . . Only by wrestling with the conditions of the problem first hand, seeking and finding his own way out, does he think.

When a learner has formed an idea, a concept or schema, bits of information that fit with that schema can then be easily transmitted to them.

 Learning takes place when confrontation with new experience yields dissonance.

Elementary school students had just returned from a field trip during which they had taken temperature readings in various parts of a lake they had visited. When they compared their findings students were puzzled by the radically different data they had collected. As the group sat on the classroom floor examining their numbers and handling their thermometers, one student, after a pause in the conversation, inquired: "How does a thermometer work anyhow?" His question generated a variety of responses from the others. One student speculated that external pressure pushed against the glass tube which made the red level rise. Another thought the material in the bottom of the tube was a solid and heat made it melt and flow up the tube. Even though, according to their teacher, these students had previously had lessons on Fahrenheit and centigrade and read the thermometer each day, none of the students had a correct explanation of what was happening. One boy volunteered that he had a book at home that showed how to make a thermometer and he would build one. The next day the boy brought his apparatus to class and demonstrated how the liquid went up into the straw when it was immersed in boiling water and how the level dropped when the liquid was cooled. He explained that everything expands in heat and shrinks in cold—even roads. As the children watched the liquid move up and down the straw, their ideas became more closely aligned with a more mature concept of the workings of a thermometer. Children created a new concept of the thermometer only as a function of their natural confrontation with concrete events.

As Resnick's (1985) research demonstrated: "…effective instruction must aim to place learners in situations where the constructions that they naturally make… are maximally likely to be correct and efficient" (pp. 28–29). If we wish to help the learner construct new meaning, we must resist the notion that we can simply pour the new knowledge atop the old.

Pines and West (1986) suggest that learners will consider changing personal belief systems when confronted by an event that directly challenges or corroborates their prior experience. For example, most students believe that a force is required to move an object continuously through space because of their experiences in a friction-laden world. This deep belief will persist unless learners are immersed in an experience that creates a cognitive dissonance. If they are allowed to manipulate pucks on a frictionless surface or allowed to experiment with computer simulations that eliminate the forces of friction, the new way that they observe objects to move challenges the old beliefs.

Stereotyping is another example of a belief system resistance to change. Gardner (1991) describes the human proclivity to overgeneralize and to create personal meanings that class, or stereotype, people's actions. Events such as the ascent of a political party, the advent of a revolution, or the downfall of a character in a tragedy are open to alternative explanations. A particular analysis, no matter how complex, is not necessarily the correct one. Creating opportunities for learners to experience alternative explanations and to voice exceptions is essential if stereotypes or simplistic explanations are to be changed.

The process of creating intervening experiences for learners is the task of the curriculum and the teacher. If we adhere to the caution that we cannot simply stamp in correctness, then our task as teachers is to create curricular "events." Curriculum and instruction must provide events and foster exploration. If the teacher in our vignette had simply inserted yet another lesson that told students about thermometers, it might have been an effective way of transmitting information, but would it have been effective in changing beliefs about how thermometers work? Lectures by the teacher about the shortsightedness of stereotypes may convey information, but will they change convictions? Curriculum must anticipate the formation of important concepts and provide confrontative events. Therefore, the curriculum should employ a method for broaching the most essential human questions and beliefs and must be organized in such a way that the learners will adopt these as their own important issues.

One perception about constructivism might be that we want learners to create their own private universes. Not so. "Teachers must guide students toward current, best understandings. 'There isn't just one truth, but there isn't no truth either'" (Resnick quoted in O'Neil, 1992, p. 5). What we want to do in school is to create circumstances, events, and experiences so that learners will come to construct meaning that contributes to informed understanding of how the world works.

Learning is facilitated by social interaction.

A group of third graders have decided to focus their book discussion on the topic of grandparents. Following the conclusion of their discussion group, the children made the following reflections.

> Ben continued, "This group has changed my way of thinking. I used to go to my Grandma's house and not think anything about it. Now I go and I see her as a special person. I value her more. She seems so caring and funny. I notice more when I go to her house. She has become more interesting. It is like starting over and getting to know a new friend."
>
> Luke hesitated, "I was really afraid to go over to my grandparents'. I knew I had changed and I was afraid they would be the same. I was wrong. I noticed how much they loved life. I started listening to them more. I wanted to learn from them. I don't really think they changed, but I changed and now I look at them differently."
>
> Carl nodded his head in agreement and said, "I always felt my grandparents were special. I wasn't necessarily changed in my thinking about them but I changed a lot in my thinking about school. This group made me think. I can't wait to read other books and discuss their meanings." (Kauffman & Yoder, 1990, p. 144)

These three children's reflections demonstrate the power that their group discussion had to change both their beliefs and actions. Each student recognized the impact of the books they had read, their peers, and their grandparents. They give testimony to the importance that social interaction has on the shaping of meaning.

Observations of peers, shared insights, and collaborative constructions are powerful tools in the process of conceptual change. Learners are
receptive to the leading of other learners and will often modify or adopt a
new construct invented as a collective effort more readily than if offered
as a distant truth.

> If a particular prediction we have made turns out to be corroborated by
> what another person does, this adds a second level of viability to our
> schema that in turn strengthens the experiential reality we have con-
> structed." (Yager, 1991, p. 54).

> Piaget attributed great importance to social interaction. To him such
> exchanges were indispensable, both for children's elaboration of logical
> thought and for adults' construction of sciences. (Kamii, 1989, p. 32).

Kamii (1985) reports several studies that demonstrate the importance
of social interaction for the construction of mathematical knowledge. On
the basis of these studies, she reaches the conclusion that:

> Insofar as peers and adults constitute the child's social environment and thus
> the objects of his social interaction, they influence his construction of math-
> ematical knowledge in very important ways. They fuel the child's mental
> activity by such indirect means as saying something that casts a doubt in his
> mind about the adequacy of an idea. They also do things that become for him
> an impetus for making a new relationship. (Kamii, 1985, p. 31)

Gergen (1982, p. 270) sums up the importance of social interaction:
"Knowledge is not something people possess in their heads, but rather
something people do together." The community of learners is a context for
providing and reflecting on experience and for developing new explanations of the world. In a constructivist classroom one would expect, therefore, to see groups of students conversing with each other and with their
teachers and struggling together with problems.

Learning takes place best in a meaningful context.

A group of our preservice teachers asked us to conference with them
before they were to teach a unit on Native Americans. As we listened to
their lesson ideas we recognized that they were organized in an objectivist,
or transmission, mode.

> First we are going to show the children pictures and examples of the kinds of
> dwellings that Indians lived in. We are going to give them pictures of hogans,
> wigwams, tepees, and then have the students assemble models of each.

We asked the teachers to describe the parts of the lesson and they dutifully identified the anticipatory set, the objective, the lesson, practice, and assessment. We asked them to consider how the children were learning in this mode. Was it a constructive opportunity or was it a version of the transmission model? After considerable brainstorming and discussion, the students redesigned the lesson:

> We decided that we will show the students pictures of the habitats in which the Indians lived. We will have pictures of deserts, forests, and grasslands. We will ask students to brainstorm things that they thought the Indians might have been able to gather from these environments to build shelters. We hope to challenge students to think about how they might make a shelter from the items suggested and then supply them with materials for experimenting. After they have made a shelter we will ask them to comment about how they put it together and what features it has.

Several days later we watched children debate with one another about the possible design of their shelters. They experimented with the materials and built and rebuilt their structures. They reported to the rest of the class about what they had created. The spokesperson for the desert environment group explained their shelter:

This one would be for the chief and it would hold all of his family. It's made out of clay, sticks, and rocks. We can get the rocks from where they fall down off the cliffs. There are flaps for doorways. We made these flaps so you can open and close them so when it's colder out you can close it and when it's hotter out you can open it. The hole in the top lets out smoke and can be closed off if it rains. Ladders go up to the top and they climb up that way and they are safe up there when it floods sometimes.

One boy in the prairie group talked about their shelter and its construction:

We took the sod and make a square but we made this much room for a little door. We did this about four or five times until we did it the way we wanted it. Then we made a hole for the fire exhaust to go up. Then we put the buffalo hide on top and put sticks through it to help it stand up and keep the rain from getting in.

A girl in that group added:

We did this like five times like he said. All the other times we just put the straw and hay all over it and didn't bundle it up or anything and then we thought this area would have a lot of tornadoes and so if we bushelled [sic] it and bundled it together, it would be better.

These explanations reveal that, in solving this problem, students constructed meaning about the nature of shelters and their relationship to environments and human needs.

The learners were highly motivated to solve the problem and construct their own interpretations of how humans interact with nature. We attribute this successful learning, in part, to the compelling nature of the context itself. Students were engaged because they were part of the context. They were members of a community needing to build a shelter from the materials of their environment. "Evidence is accumulating that participating in a learning community sustains interest in learning, permits higher order integration of ideas, and fosters the internalization of social processes of constructing meaning" (Guthrie, Bennett, & McGough, 1994). The context aroused the students' interest, curiosity, and desire to perfect the project. Since intrinsic motivators such as involvement, curiosity, and a sense of competence are so much more powerful in lifelong learning than external motivations such as compliance, educators should aim to build contexts that create intrinsic motivation (Guthrie, 1995).

If our student teachers had taught their transmission lesson, then children would have been able to label various types of dwellings and build model copies of them, but they would not have received the benefits of a compelling context. No doubt they would have dutifully complied to the teachers' wishes, but their motivation would have been external and their attitude would have been neutral or even negative. Context is also critical because it helps learners make connections. In our example, learners related the natural environment to the types of shelters that people construct and how they work together to build them. In the transmission lesson, there are no connections to be made. If learners are to make conceptual connections about their world, how can this be accomplished if their educational experiences are unrelated dollops of information? Meaningful, whole contexts that offer students rich possibilities and challenges are critical for learning.

A Differentiation Between Constructivism and Discovery

The differences between transmission and constructivist approaches are illustrated in the previous vignette. In a transmission lesson, the endpoint is predetermined. The tepee would either look like the picture or it would not. The learning would have been closed. The constructivist lesson, on the other hand, was marked by a question mark, not by a period.

The distinction between discovery and constructivism is not quite so clear. Although some suggest that constructivist learning theory is discovery, we disagree. In a discovery lesson the teacher sets up the experience and circumstances such that when the first domino falls, all the rest fall in a predictable pattern. Discovery lessons are designed so that learners can arrive at only one possibility (if they follow directions correctly). The teacher expects that all of the students will arrive at the predicted endpoint at the conclusion of the lesson.

The constructivist point of view is broader in scope than discovery. Learners invent their own realities instead of discovering the teacher's reality. We might say that Columbus discovered America, but Jefferson invented a republic. America was already a continent when Columbus discovered it. He found what was already there. Jefferson invented a concept. He created a vision that had never been seen before. The teacher directing a constructivist lesson would expect that learners make meaning about experiences. They will invent visions which may never have been seen before.

Summary of Constructivist Tenets

Both child and adult have experienced the natural world on a daily basis and have observed common events and special phenomena through the senses.

Mirrors reflect; candles drip; sparks jump from electrical equipment; Nebraska plains look very dry and unlike the sea. These experiences are arranged in ways which are meaningful to the learner and which satisfy or explain the way things are. It seems logical that we should see more as we move back from a mirror. Since there is no ash, then it makes sense that the wax is not consumed. Batteries are approached with fear of shock. Nebraska is a long way from the ocean. Once those explanations are embedded, learners are reluctant to let go. Humans have a propensity to defend and protect their perspectives. Even when confronted with conflicting or challenging observations, learners often hold tenaciously to their beliefs.

No amount of "telling" facilitates conceptual change. Even after expert testimony to the contrary, the individual still believes that candles that do not drip are never consumed, that batteries can shock, that one can see more if the mirror is further away. Carol's mother, even though she was taught about the geologic history of her home region, still remained skeptical. The social aspect of the learning cannot be underestimated in each of these instances. For example, Carol's mother might not even have had the experience if it had not been for the family choosing to walk those road cuts and to collectively view them. Anne goes home after the mirror experiment and asks her roommate what she sees in the bathroom mirror! What was needed in each of these learning situations was an opportunity for the learner to have new experiences, to incorporate the new with the old in order to create a new structure, and to interact with others in a social setting. The constructive perspective allows for open-endedness: The natural curiosities of the learners lead to experimentation and observation, which in turn lead to new questions for exploration. Knowing becomes a generative process of building meaning through new experiences.

As a theoretical ground for learning, constructivism impacts on both teaching and curriculum. The role of the teacher becomes that of analyzing and drawing upon the learner's current state of knowing, providing an environment and context for learning, coaching, guiding, and facilitating. The goals of curriculum are not a set of disparate behavioral objectives, but rather a broader learner empowerment. Instead of simply imparting a body of information, the teacher helps children enrich and understand their personal, lived-through experience. Knowledge becomes not something that sits on a shelf but the dynamic interaction of people. Teachers grounded in a constructivist view have a distinct attitude toward their students—a respect and understanding of their students' knowledge and ability to learn (Jaeger & Lauritzen, 1992).

✎ Application of the Constructivist Model to the Classroom

How can teachers apply the theoretical base developed in the *Galimoto* scenario and the discussion of a constructivist view of learning? In the next section, we describe the beginning of a third grade science lesson which you are invited to continue. Considering the ideas of prior knowledge, logical constructions of meaning, resistance to change, social influence, and contextual variables, what would you do as a teacher to facilitate learning here?

Tom, the student teacher Carol was observing, held up a paper ruined by a watery, ringed stain. The third graders responded with a lot of sympathy and attempts to comfort him when they saw it was the piece that he had been writing and sharing with the class for several weeks. Then Tom, with a genuinely frustrated but inquiring tone, asked the class to help him figure out how his paper had been ruined, where the stains had come from, and how they could prevent this from happening to someone else's writing. The students offered a lot of ideas and explanations. Water spilled out of a glass; it came from a can of soda that was wet; the ink got hot; the paper was moist. Tom responded by telling them he knew an experiment they could do that might demonstrate where the water came from. In a few minutes, the children were clustered in groups around large cans containing ice water. There was quite a bit of noise as the children started voicing their observations that the can was getting "foggy." Then some of the children said that water was running down the outside of the can. The paper towels that were under the cans started to get wet. At this point, Tom, thinking that children would arrive at the correct explanation, asked them to identify the source of the water. He and I were both surprised when the majority of the students asserted that the water had oozed through the can, that the metal had somehow leaked the water to the outside.

What would you, as the teacher, do at this point?

Teacher Behaviors in a Constructivist Setting

Although we might suggest several alternatives to Tom as he taught that lesson, consider what happened next and compare your ideas about how to proceed with his:

Tom started to repair the students' misconception by telling them the principles of condensation, but when he started this explanation, he detected a change in the students' behavior. They stopped paying attention and started playing with the ice water. So, he changed tactics. He asked the students if the same thing would happen if the water was warm. James answered that it wouldn't because warm water would move up. Only cold moves down. "How could we test that idea?" Tom asked.

"We could put a paper towel over the can and after a while see if it got wet," the child proposed. Tom arranged for James to set up the experiment in a corner of a room. A bit later, all the children observed a dry towel except James, who, firmly based in his belief, thought the towel felt moist. Still, the students had not changed their minds about the source of the water so Tom asked them to think about other times and places they had seen water on things. They related ideas about milk cartons, cold Cokes from the vending machine, dew on the grass in the morning, and foggy glass in the bathroom after a shower. Tom guided discussion further by asking about the nature of containers used for storing liquids. Students agreed about the impermeable nature and safety of canning jars. Tom encouraged the students to find out if water droplets would form on the surface of a tightly capped jar containing ice water. Students were soon engaged in this experiment using jars. All the groups reported that water had formed on the outside of the jars. This was strong enough evidence for most of the children to begin to consider other sources for the water. To help them, Tom wiped the chalkboard with a wet towel. The children watched as the wet disappeared before their eyes. "Where did the water go?" Students suggested that it was absorbed by the blackboard, that it disappeared, evaporated, changed, and that it went out the door and up in the sky to become part of a cloud. Amazingly, not one of them related the water on the outside of the jar to the water lost from the chalkboard. Unfortunately, at this time, the children had to go to lunch. Yet, they left with a glow from the excitement of investigation. After surveying the classroom littered with science paraphernalia, Tom sat down for a follow-up discussion of his lesson. He began making plans to help the children continue their explorations.

What constructivist tenets did you find Tom putting into practice? He acknowledged that his learners came to school with an array of prior knowledge. They had seen foggy glass, sweating bottles, canning jars, and dew on the grass. They had made logical explanations of the phenomena. Knowing that the children were not going to be easily moved from their ideas about the moisture, Tom provided new experiences that would confront their conceptions and provide a measure of dissonance. Fostered in a context conducive to socially constructed meaning, new observations led students to make new constructions about how the world works. Tom allowed his students to invent an answer that satisfied the observations. Tom's instruction illustrates that a teacher's beliefs about how children learn have important implications for how the teacher acts.

🕮 Some Objections to Constructivism

At this point, you may be thinking of some of the objections to this view of learning and teaching. These objections include the shift from teacher-centered to student-centered curriculum, the lack of texts and materials that accommodate this style of learning, the length of time required to construct meaning as compared to simply telling and memorizing information, and the enormous change that would be required in the behavior of teacher and learner.

This perspective of learning may be alarming to some because it shifts the emphasis from teacher to learner. How can those who retain the accumulated wisdom of the ages (teachers) relinquish their right to transmit that information to those who do not have it? This view is shared by those who have a vision of a common cultural literacy. Knowledge of the names, dates, places, and relationships is valued by a significant portion of the population. The tenets of constructivism are dissonant to those who believe that the purpose of K–12 education is to inculcate learners with the essentials of western culture. Other critics fear that we are wasting time having students reinvent the wheel. We would reply that although we do not need more wheels, we do need more inventors. And, in the process of inventing, students will learn the skills needed for that invention and many others.

Some view constructivism as a laissez-faire approach to education in which teachers create fun activities in which children can do anything and learn or not learn as they wish. This is a romantic notion far from the actual tenets of constructivism. As Blais (1988, p. 3) forcefully states:

> "Constructivism is not a wimpy, say-nothing, your-ideas-are-fine theory. It does not say that knowledge is something that the learner *ought* to construct for and by himself. Rather, it says knowledge is something that the learner *must* construct for and by himself. There is no alternative. Discovery, reinvention, or active reconstruction is necessary." (emphasis added)

Whether we wish to acknowledge it or not, learners do create their own meanings. Rosenblatt (1938/1976, p. 51) reminds us:

> Nevertheless, the student's primary experience of the [literary] work will have had meaning for him in these personal terms and no others. No matter how imperfect or mistaken, this will constitute the present meaning of the work for him rather than anything he docilely repeats about it.

Teachers with a constructivist perspective realize that "all people ever have is their own understanding: you can tell them all sorts of things, but you can't make them believe it unless they also construct it for themselves" (Duckworth, quoted in O'Neil, 1992, p. 4). Sometimes these meanings are idiosyncratic. The teacher must have the vision for what the learner will become and the ability to provide the appropriate experiences for the learner to reach this vision.

We realize how hard it is to change to constructivist, theory-based teaching. Most of us have not had any classroom experience with constructivist learning. Our teachers were, most likely, objectivists who transmitted information. Teachers need "analoge experiences"—opportunities to engage in the type of learning they would be implementing with their students. They also need reflection and discussion in order to make the link between their own experiences and their classrooms (Riley, Morocco, Gordon, & Howard, 1993). The constraints of meeting district and state guidelines, of covering material, and of toeing the line of standardized testing also make it difficult to change to a constructivist approach. However, the reasons for changing to a constructivist approach are compelling when the benefits to the students are considered. As Brooks (1990, p. 70–71) states:

> Constructivism doesn't say, as critics claim, that you can't teach people anything; it guides us in finding out how to teach them... Our task, then, is to understand and nurture the learning and development of our students. We must not do for them what they can, and must, do for themselves.

Lingering Questions

Transmission teaching remains a powerful and pervasive force in U.S. schools. If we adopt a constructivist approach will we jettison behavioral objectives? Is there a role for transmission teaching in 21st-century schools?

For teachers reared on the transmission model and the direct instruction design for lesson plans, there is much to learn in order to teach with a constructivist perspective. How will the classroom be transformed and how will teachers learn to function differently in a constructivist setting?

Companion Readings

Galimoto is a fine piece of children's literature that should be read to appreciate our opening scenario. *The Search of Understanding: The Case for Constructivist Classrooms* (Brooks & Brooks, 1993) provides a good overall perspective on the implications of constructivist teaching. *The Young Child As Scientist* (Chaille & Britain, 1991) is one book which gives specific examples of constructivist teaching.

CHAPTER 4

The Goals of Schooling

Activating Prior Knowledge

What is your vision of students graduating from public school? What would be the major concepts you want them to have learned?

Goals 2000, SCANS, state and national content standards, and outcomes-based education represent whole systems of ideas and directions for what schools should be doing. Are you aware of other goal systems?

Chapter Highlights

We first ask our readers to involve themselves in a story about how immigrants established a community in the upper Midwest. This story evokes the central question of schooling: "What is worth knowing?"

To illustrate the sources of goals, we present examples from national, state, and local levels as well as those from various disciplines.

We then examine what goal-based curriculum looks like and provide an exemplar that demonstrates the logical relationships between stated goals, student explorations, and assessment.

Inge is seated at a table preparing potatoes for the evening meal. The snow swirls and howls outside. "I wonder when Olaf will be coming from the mine." She pauses and looks out the window as she soliloquizes about life in northern Minnesota. She and Olaf had moved to northern Minnesota last spring to find work in the lumber mill, but since Frank Hibbing had accidentally found rich iron ore, Olaf had become a miner instead. It was a hard life, Minnesota. Long winters, hot summers. Late freezes to spoil the fruit and early freezes to spoil the vegetables. Bears, mosquitoes, isolation.

Still, this life was better than the possibilities of her homeland. Opportunities for Inge had been bleak since all the good farmland was owned by the wealthy and her family's farm was too small to divide among all the children. She was destined to a life of washing, baking, and cleaning for others until she received a letter from Olaf in America. Through their families, Inge was suggested to Olaf as a wife. Olaf had managed to save enough money to buy her passage to the United States. The letter communicated the details of the arrangements and a proposal to Inge. It had seemed the only choice for her to make.

With a blast of cold air the cabin door opened and then slammed shut. Olaf shivered as he huddled over the wood stove. "A cold one, doncha know." Olaf's teeth chattered as Inge poured him a cup of hot coffee to warm his frozen hands. "Mr. Hibbing says we've hit a new core of the stuff that's richer than all the rest. Looks like we'll have work for years to come." Olaf sat down at the table massaging his hands on the cup. He gave Inge a cheery grin, ice crystals still clinging to his red beard.

"Does that mean that Frank will be hiring more folks to help at the mine?" Inge asked hopefully. Winters in northern Minnesota could drag on for years, it seemed, without the benefit of human company.

"You betcha," Olaf said as he cocked his head. He exuberantly explained what Hibbing had said. "There's going to be carpenters, wagon masters, loaders, blacksmiths, engineers, and common laborers coming in here."

"Where is Mr. Hibbing going to put all these people? Where will they live?" Inge asked. Most of the previous folks had been laborers who worked seasonally in the mill and were content to live in makeshift tents.

"Mr. Hibbing is going to set aside some of his land for a town," Olaf replied. "He has agreed to provide building materials for houses and he wants us to organize a meeting of the new workers when they get here this spring to plan the town!"

We began our graduate-level curriculum class one evening playing the dramatic roles of the story. (Resources from which we created this story are listed at the end of the chapter.) Staying in the characters of Inge and Olaf, we invited the class members to join us at a town meeting to decide the future plans of Hibbing, Minnesota. "Friends, neighbors," we said, "you are newcomers here but we want you to help us decide what we need for a good town. By the way, what did you say your name was?" We asked them, in role, to think about what occupations, businesses, and services we needed for a real community. Each person contributed possibilities. An English teacher suggested that we needed a library. A vocational education teacher suggested a smithy. Others wanted banks, restaurants, stores, and farms. One music teacher even suggested a dance hall (and other morally questionable establishments).

As these participants in our drama made suggestions about "our" town, it became "their" town because they began to don the personae of the characters they had selected as contributors to the town. As a group, we planned the town on a large paper grid illustrated in figure 4.1. There was considerable discussion about the scale that we were going to use as we mapped the town. "What will each grid represent?" "Let's have each square equal a city block." "We won't have enough space on this paper. How about making each square a mile?" Conversation about scale and possibilities for placement of parks, streets, business districts, and homes consumed a significant amount of class time.

Later we asked the group to brainstorm the materials that might have been available to the Minnesota pioneers of the 1880s. Logs and lumber, rock, cement, sheet iron, marble, clay, and brick were listed. We then offered the group these kinds of materials in their metaphorical forms: popsicle

FIGURE 4.1 Plat map of Hibbing, Minnesota

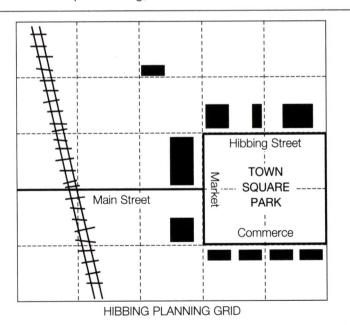

HIBBING PLANNING GRID

sticks (planks), straight pretzels (logs), pie tins (sheet iron), modeling clay, plaster of paris (cement), and Styrofoam (marble, rock, and brick). For the next hour, the students built their structures to the scale of a tiny cut-out of Frank Hibbing, the mine owner: log cabins, marble banks, clapboard churches, tin restaurants. We learned to sand our pretzels to notch the ends like a log cabin and to chink the gaps with a flour-and-water paste. We learned to saw the Styrofoam into blocks that could be joined with plaster of paris. We learned how to lay planks of popsicle sticks into walls and walkways. The town sprang up from our imaginations.

We felt the participants had a good sense of the time and place but we wanted them to develop a sense of ownership of the town as real people would. As we concluded our initial experience with the development of Hibbing, we asked our class to develop their chosen characters and to share their character in such a way that other town members would come to know them also.

When the class next met, members shared diary entries, music, dramatic presentations, and letters. Each presentation was an invention of the persona they had become as a citizen of Hibbing. They had researched the era and had probed into the region and times and had assembled a rich autobiography from the resources they gathered. Figure 4.2 shows one individual's findings written as a letter to her parents.

Our experience as citizens of Hibbing could have concluded at this point but as we finished hearing the Hibbing residents create their identities with our model of the town as a backdrop, a stranger strode into the room. It was none other than Frank Hibbing, the owner of the mine and lands that the townspeople had settled. (Actually he was a colleague we had cajoled into playing the role.) "I'm afraid I've got some good news and some bad news, folks!" Frank explained that his assayers had just confirmed that a new lode of high-quality iron ore had been discovered that would bring

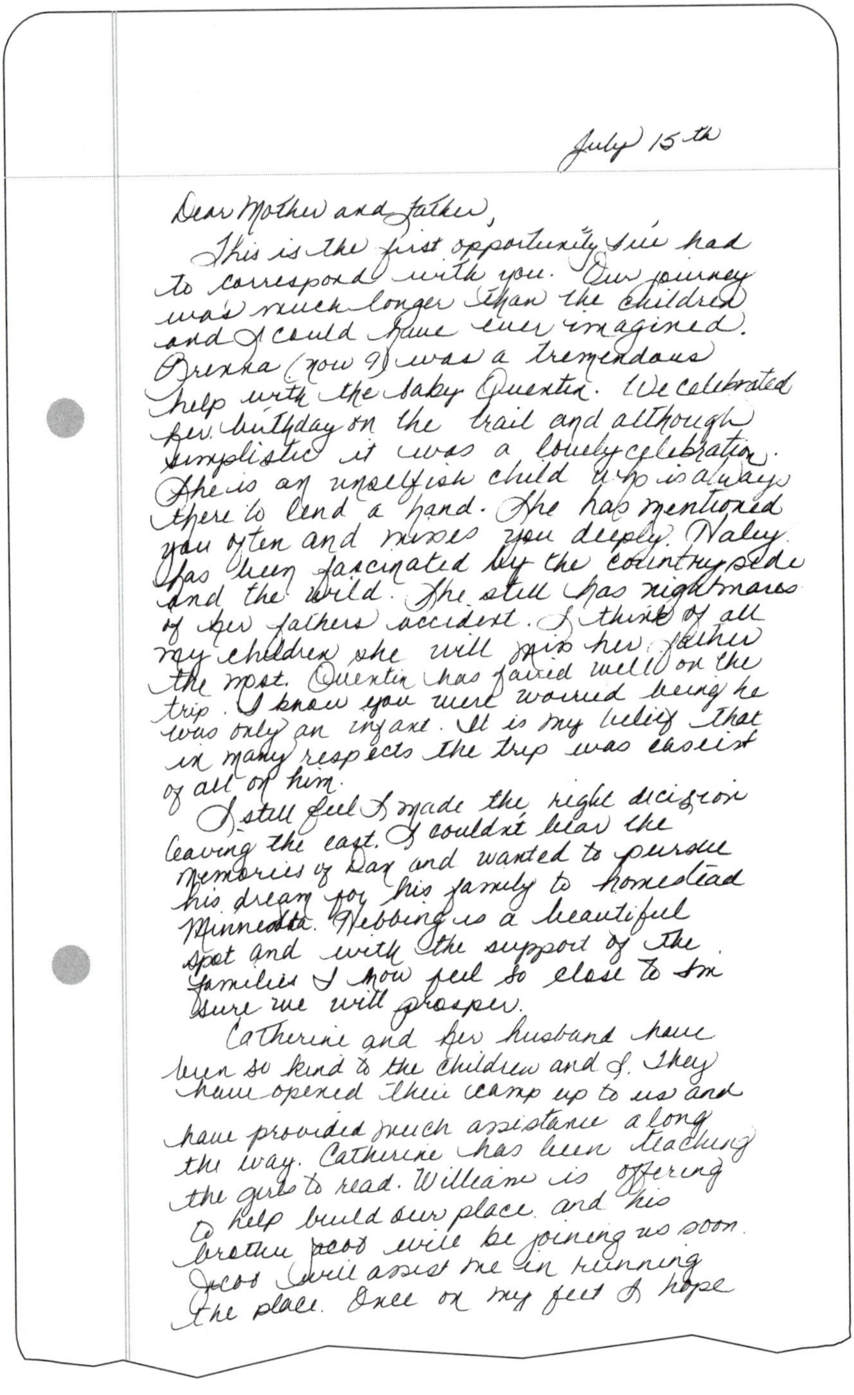

July 15th

Dear Mother and Father,

This is the first opportunity I've had to correspond with you. Our journey was much longer than the children and I could have ever imagined. Brenna (now 9) was a tremendous help with the baby Quenten. We celebrated her birthday on the trail and although simplistic it was a lovely celebration. She is an unselfish child who is always there to lend a hand. She has mentioned you often and misses you deeply. Haley has been fascinated by the countryside and the wild. She still has nightmares of her father's accident. I think of all my children she will miss her father the most. Quenten has fared well on the trip. I know you were worried being he was only an infant. It is my belief that in many respects the trip was easiest of all on him.

I still feel I made the right decision leaving the east. I couldn't bear the memories of Dan and wanted to pursue his dream for his family to homestead Minnesota. Hebbing is a beautiful spot and with the support of the families I now feel so close to. I'm sure we will prosper.

Catherine and her husband have been so kind to the children and I. They have opened their camp up to us and have provided much assistance along the way. Catherine has been teaching the girls to read. William is offering to help build our place and his brother Jacob will be joining us soon. Jacob will assist me in running the place. Once on my feet I hope

FIGURE 4.2 A letter from Hibbing

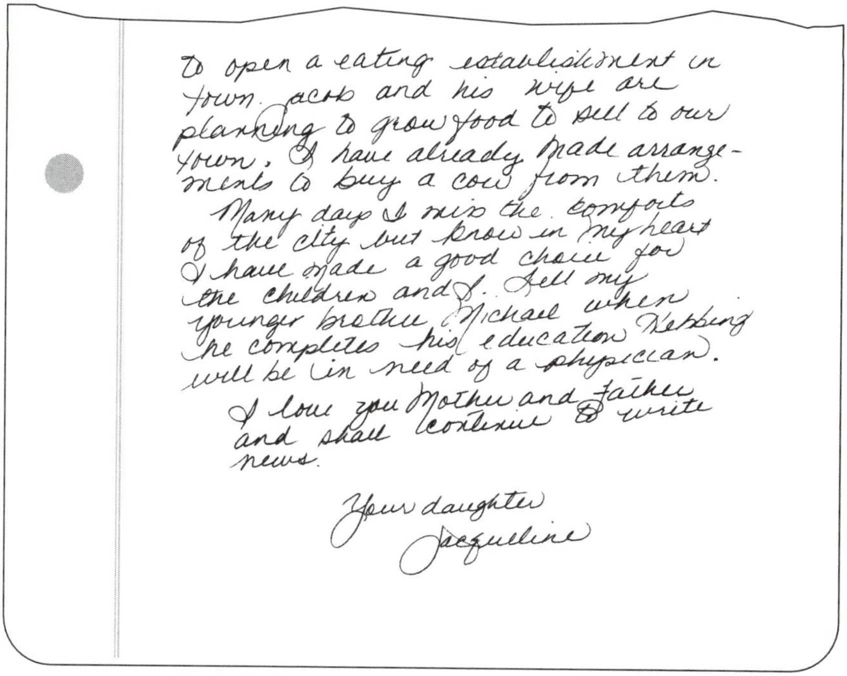
To open a eating establishment in town. Jacob and his wife are planning to grow food to sell to our town. I have already made arrangements to buy a cow from them.

Many days I miss the comforts of the city but know in my heart I have made a good choice for the children and I. Tell my younger brother Michael when he completes his education Hibbing will be in need of a physician.

I love you Mother and Father and shall continue to write news.

Your daughter
Jacqueline

FIGURE 4.2 A letter from Hibbing (continued)

more revenues to Hibbing. The only difficulty was that this new ore was located directly under the town that had just been completed!

Our class erupted with indignation at the prospect of disrupting the town. "No, we won't move our town! We've worked hard to plan and build it." Several students insisted, "Dig some other place!" And the citizens of Hibbing began working together to solve this new problem.

Reflections on "The Town That Moved": What Should Be Learned at School?

We have described "The Town That Moved" as a point of reference for exploring a fundamental question about curriculum: What should we learn at school? What prior knowledge did our learners need to participate in the story? What new knowledge did they acquire? What skills did they either practice or need to learn as they became active participants in the ongoing drama of the town? What instructional goals directed this piece of curriculum? What knowledge, skills, and goals do you connect with:

▮ the introductory dramatization and town meeting?
▮ the mapping and building of the town model?
▮ the character research and sharing?
▮ the problem of moving the town?

When we asked these same questions of our students who participated in "The Town That Moved" experience, they supplied us with an impressive list:

▮ an ability to listen interpretively
▮ an ability to communicate with oral and written language
▮ an ability to use reference materials and resources to find out about the geography, history, and setting of the region and time
▮ an understanding of the town as a system
▮ an ability to measure and calculate scale of buildings
▮ an ability to interact in a collaborative and cooperative way
▮ an ability to use hand tools and materials to make a product
▮ an ability to think creatively

The class had selected broad categories of behaviors, skills, and conceptual understandings as important outcomes. They recognized that certain prerequisite skills were important in order to plan the town:

▮ the ability to measure
▮ the ability to use maps and symbols
▮ the ability to use scale to relate real to representational
▮ the ability to plan collaboratively
▮ the ability to communicate plans to others

The class speculated that without these basic tools of learning, our town would not have been very well designed. Some parts of the community might have been missing; buildings of all sorts of proportions might have been erected; architecture unrelated to possible materials or era would have been planned; and the area that we had set aside might not have accommodated our plans. We might even have disagreed about the purpose of the project and no town would have been made!

The class turned the question back to us: "What was your purpose in having us do this story?" We did indeed have specific goals in mind when we planned this experience for the class. We wanted our learners to achieve several broad goals:

▮ to work cooperatively and collaboratively
▮ to apply personal learning and discipline perspectives to a specific project
▮ to communicate learning through a variety of media

- to utilize and develop personal language arts skills
- to become transdisciplinary problem-solvers
- to utilize a wide array of resource materials, including primary and secondary sources

Before we had selected "The Town That Moved" story and activities, we had decided on these goals to direct us. But how did we arrive at these particular goals? The simple answer is that we just knew them. Although there is truth in this statement, we will be a bit more analytical about the source of goals.

◈ Goals: Where Do They Come From?

First, we need to clarify what we mean by goals. Many writers have used a variety of terms almost synonymously: purpose, aim, goal, objective, outcome, standard. Those who try to distinguish between the terms sometimes create hierarchies of use in which one of the terms, such as *purpose*, labels overall general statements and a term such as *objective* designates a specific skill or piece of information. In this chapter, we are dealing with the general expectations of schooling and we have chosen to use the term *goal* to label these broad statements describing the purpose of education. A goal is generally stated in terms of what the student will know or be able to do, however, goals are sometimes stated in terms of what schooling should accomplish.

Each group that holds a stake in schooling identifies the goals it deems important. National, state, local, and disciplinary goals all designate what some group believes should be happening in classrooms. From what do these stake holders derive their ideas? The philosophical and social foundations of American schooling are the historical pieces that shape current belief. We will not engage in reviewing these except to consider the broader concerns and sources that transcend the current national debate.

Every generation of American society seems to spawn its own problems. And, in every generation, school is called upon to solve society's ills. As a new nation emerged and manifested its destiny westward, moral corruption loomed as one of society's most significant enemies. During the last part of the 19th century, the moral issue of primary concern was health. Alcohol and tobacco abuse was considered a national scandal. Schools were assigned the task of fixing the problem. The goals of schools are stated in textbooks of the era:

> If wrong habits are formed in childhood, the power to correct them in maturer years is often wanting; and even if efforts in that direction prove successful, still the evil remains. (Brown, 1872)

> The above series [Steele's Science] was originally prepared (as their general titles indicate) to supply the demand created by the laws for temperance instruction in public schools in the United States. (Steele, 1891)

> It is believed that the study of the human body, together with a knowledge of the effects of alcohol upon it, will do much to make the coming generation wise, temperate, and moral. (Stowell, 1893)

The goals of schooling implied by these statements directed textbooks, curriculum, and instruction for decades.

Similarly, every subsequent national crisis has triggered the development of new goals for schools. Goodlad (1979, p. 45) summarizes the origins of goals by identifying the major social, political, and economic influences in United States education:

> Viewed historically, goal statements reflect both some concern for the times and for social purposes designed to remedy a condition or to produce a more desired one. Over time, shifts have occurred. The shift in the U.S. over more than three centuries has been from discipline honed by the classics and religion to civic, religious, and vocational responsibility; to worthy membership in home, community, state, and nation; to concern for justice and respect for others; to appreciation for democratic values; to respect for self and development of individual talents.

Wars, natural resources management and conservation issues, competition for domination of space, environmental concerns, and recently, realities of Asian and European economic successes have each, in turn, contributed to national rhetoric about the expectations of schooling. One might argue, at the approach of a new century, that the priorities for schooling have shifted once again because of a concern for lack of economic vigor and flawed international status or because of the concern for the well-being of children in negative social conditions. Still, in an analysis of goals articulated in recent decades, core commonalities exist. Goodlad lists twelve discrete goals for schooling derived from an analysis of over 100 existing goal statements. (See figure 4.3.) As Goodlad said:

> There is no need to begin from scratch... on the assumption that we have no goals for schooling. Rather, we should be addressing ourselves to such questions as the meaning and significance of such goals, their implications for educational practice, and whether or not we intend to carry out what these goals seem to imply. (p. 46)

The source of goals is both institutional and personal, pragmatic and philosophical. As we will see in the following examples, goals are debated, created, compiled, and written by many individuals and diverse groups who identify, and rally support for, what they believe schooling should accomplish.

FIGURE 4.3 Goals for schooling in the United States (Goodlad, 1979)

---

1. Mastery of basic skills or fundamental processes
2. Career education/vocational education
3. Intellectual development
4. Enculturation
5. Interpersonal relationships
6. Autonomy
7. Citizenship
8. Creativity and aesthetic perception
9. Self-concept
10. Emotional and physical well-being
11. Moral and ethical character
12. Self-realization

National Goals

Current national-level goals are formed by committees of scholars, legislators, educators, or business people. Probably the most well-known current work is the National Education Goals 2000 effort. These goals are stated as the fundamental expectations of what schools should achieve. Figure 4.4 is a summary of this sweeping recommendation that ranges across the aesthetic, technical, and economic goals of education. How these goals translate into operational definitions and implied practices are uncertain except that specific assessments will be employed to track their progress. Mathematics, reading, science, and foreign languages are to be monitored with standardized examinations (National Education Goals Panel, 1992). These assessments generally measure the acquisition of content.

An example of national benchmarks for schools that focuses on goals for student achievement can be found in the SCANS report (U.S. Department of Labor, 1991). It describes a three-part foundation of basic skills and attributes all learners should have as a result of schooling. (See figure 4.5 for a summary of SCANS recommendations.) Because of "the globalization of commerce and industry and explosive growth of technology on the job" the terms for young people's entry into the world of work have changed (U.S. Department of Labor, 1991). These national goals aim to provide the nation with a skilled population of workers and so are somewhat in contrast to the Goals 2000 listing. Presumably, if one gets a job, is successful, and contributes to the economy, then the SCANS goals would be met. On the other hand, receiving a high Scholastic Aptitude Test (SAT) score might adequately demonstrate the end point suggested by the Goals 2000 report. We mention these two different approaches to illuminate the

---

FIGURE 4.4 The National Education Goals (The National Education Goals
Panel, 1992)

By the year 2000…

All children in America will start school ready to learn.

The high school graduation rate will increase to at least 90 percent.

All students will leave grades 4, 8, and 12 having demonstrated competency
over challenging subject matter including English, mathematics, science, foreign
languages, civics and government, economics, arts, history, and geography,
and every school in America will ensure that all students learn to use their minds
well, so they may be prepared for responsible citizenship, further learning, and
productive employment in our Nation's modern economy.

The Nation's teaching force will have access to programs for the continued
improvement of their professional skills and the opportunity to acquire the
knowledge and skills needed to instruct and prepare all American students for
the next century.

United States students will be first in the world in mathematics and science
achievement.

Every adult American will be literate and will possess the knowledge and skills
necessary to compete in a global economy and exercise the rights and responsibilities of citizenship.

Every school in the United States will be free of drugs, violence, and the unau-
thorized presence of firearms and alcohol and will offer a disciplined environment conducive to learning.

Every school will promote partnerships that will increase parental involvement and
participation in promoting the social, emotional, and academic growth of children.

---

curricular implications of adopting one or both forms. Schooling that follows from adoption of a goal structure that honors "knowing" should differ from one based on a goal structure of "doing."

State Mandates

Although national benchmark goals can set the general dimensions of the
purpose and nature of schooling, states are often more specific in their
mandates about the what and how. Although Oregon, for example, has
subscribed to many of the national standards, the state goals are tailored
to students within the state. Considering issues such as a declining forest

FIGURE 4.5 SCANS Report: Necessary skills (U. S. Department of Labor, 1991)

Basic Skills:
  A. Reading
  B. Listening
  C. Arithmetic/Mathematics
  D. Speaking
  E. Writing

Thinking Skills:
  A. Creative Thinking
  B. Decision Making
  C. Problem Solving
  D. Seeing things in the mind's eye
  E. Knowing how to learn
  F. Reasoning
  G. Ability to use tools

Personal Qualities:
  A. Responsibility
  B. Self-esteem
  C. Sociability
  D. Self-management
  E. Integrity/Honesty

products industry, a Pacific-rim economy, urban sprawl, social decay, and environmental difficulties, Oregon has created a set of goals that reflect the perceived needs of society. The Certificate of Initial Mastery outcomes listed in figure 4.6 characterize the shift in goals from students as receivers of information to students able to use information to solve 21st-century problems (Oregon Department of Education, 1993). Ohio has developed similar broad definitions. An example of this state's physical education and health goals are seen in figure 4.7.

States are also specific about the nature of goals for each discipline. Michigan, for example, has developed very complex and far-reaching goals for K–12 instruction in languages, mathematics, arts, life management, technology, careers, health, and physical education. The "Core Curriculum Standards" document includes benchmarks for elementary, middle, and high school levels and cross-referencing among the standards for the various disciplines. Figure 4.8 summarizes part of Michigan's goal structure for mathematics. Montana provides an exemplar in the aesthetic and language arts that delineates a goals structure for visual, literary, and performing arts (fig. 4.9).

FIGURE 4.6 Oregon Certificate of Initial Mastery (CIM) foundational goals (Oregon Department of Education, 1993)

Think critically, creatively, and reflectively making decisions and solving problems

Direct his or her own learning, including planning and carrying out complex projects

Communicate through reading, writing, speaking, and listening and through integrated use of visual forms such as symbols and graphic images

Use current technology, including computers, to process information and produce high-quality products

Recognize, process, and communicate quantitative relationships

Participate as a member of a team, including providing leadership for achieving goals and working well with others from diverse backgrounds

FIGURE 4.7 Ohio State Health and Physical Education Goals (Ohio State Board of Education, 1995)

HEALTH AND PHYSICAL EDUCATION
- Evaluate the harmful effects of drugs of abuse, alcoholic beverages, and tobacco
- Demonstrate the ability to protect oneself from injury or disease
- Demonstrate ability to engage in exercise, movement, and individual and team sports
- Maintain personal levels of physical fitness and design a program for lifetime fitness
- Assess personal fitness status which includes cardiovascular endurance, muscular strength and endurance, flexibility, body composition, and nutrition
- Participate in community recreational options

Discipline-Centered Goals

National and state goals are often influenced by each discipline's concern about standards for its own subject areas. Led by the National Council of Teachers of Mathematics (1989) with its *Curriculum and Evaluation Standards for School Mathematics*, many professional organizations and coalitions have begun the process of establishing standards within specific disciplines. These organizations are attempting to provide leadership in the improvement of teaching and learning in their respective areas and to establish standards against which local and

---

FIGURE 4.8 State of Michigan, Content Standards for Mathematics
(Michigan Department of Education, 1994)

Patterns, Relationships, and Functions: Content Standard 1: Students recognize similarities and generalize patterns, use patterns to create models and make predictions, describe the nature of patterns and relationships, and construct representations of mathematical relationships (patterns).

Elementary	Middle School	High School
Recognize, describe, and extend numerical and geometric patterns.	Describe, analyze, and generalize patterns arising in a variety of contexts and express them in general terms.	Analyze and generalize mathematical patterns including sequences, series, and recursive patterns.
Represent and record patterns and relationships in a variety of ways including tables, charts, and pictures.	Represent and record patterns in a variety of ways including tables, charts, and graphs, and translate between various representations.	Analyze, interpret, and translate among multiple representations of patterns including tables, charts, graphs, matrices, and vectors.
Use patterns to describe real-world phenomena.	Use patterns and their generalizations to make and justify inferences and predictions.	Study and employ mathematical models of patterns to make inferences, predictions, and decisions.
Explore various types of patterns (repeating, growing, shrinking).	Explore and describe patterns for linear expressions and other near-linear patterns such as step and constant functions.	Explore patterns (graphic, numeric, etc.) characteristic of families of functions; explore structural patterns within systems of objects, operations, or relations.
Apply their experiences with patterns to help solve problems and explore new content.	Use patterns and generalizations to solve problems and explore new content.	Use patterns and reasoning to solve problems and explore new content.

---

state agencies can measure their own curriculum guides. The NCTM Standards, for example, are definitive statements about what is valued in mathematics education.

FIGURE 4.9 Montana Content Standards for Aesthetic Literacy: Learning in Visual, Literary, and Performing Arts (Hahn, 1994)

Students will LEARN to Perceive and Analyze

They should have an informed acquaintance with exemplary works of visual, literary, and performing arts from a variety of cultures and historical periods. They should be able to develop and present basic analyses of works of art from structural, historical, and cultural perspectives, and from combinations of those perspectives. This includes the ability to understand and evaluate work in the various arts disciplines.

Students will LEARN to Communicate

They should be able to communicate at a basic level in dance, music, theater, and the visual arts. They should be able to communicate proficiently in the language arts and in at least one art form.

Students will LEARN to Connect Cultures and Other Content Areas

They should be able to relate various types of arts knowledge and skills within and across the arts and other disciplines.

Students will LEARN to Interact and Reflect

They should develop attributes of self-discipline, cooperation, responsibility, and reflectiveness in the performance, production, and processes of the arts.

They describe the criteria for the curriculum of a quality mathematics program, the instructional conditions necessary for mathematics to be learned, and the methods of evaluating students' progress and curricular programs. Each curriculum standard... includes the content to be learned, *the expected student outcomes*, a discussion of the content and examples that illustrate the particular focus. (Frye, 1989, emphasis added)

Reports from disciplinary groups often provide both general rationale and specific content guidelines in the form of goal statements or outcomes for learning. Although all science educators do not agree to their formulation, the National Science Education Standards (National Committee on Science Education Standards and Assessment, 1994) includes 200 pages of detail about processes and concepts that all students should understand. Figure 4.10 gives an example of only one of the content strands from these guidelines that emphasize conceptual understandings. As an interesting comparison, the National Science Teachers Association has created its own guidelines (shown in figure 4.11) that are more oriented toward content by topic (National Science Teachers Association, 1993).

History and geography have well-developed goals formulated by academicians and social science educators. Figure 4.12 presents an overview of standards in historical thinking (National Center for History in the Schools, 1995) and figure 4.13 enumerates the national geography standards (National Council for the Social Studies, 1994). These listings of goals attempt to represent what historians and geographers envision as the ideal end point of learning.

FIGURE 4.10 Excerpts from National Science Education Content Standards (National Committee on Science Education Standards and Assessment, 1994)

Motions and Forces

The motion of an object can be described by its position, direction of motion, and speed. This motion can be reported and can be represented on a graph.

An object that is not being subjected to a force will continue to move at a constant speed and in a straight line.

If more than one force acts on an object, then the forces can reinforce or cancel one another, depending on their direction and magnitude. Unbalanced changes in speed and/or direction of an object's motion.

FIGURE 4.11 Important Facts Common to All Natural Sciences (National Science Teachers Association, 1993)

Grades 6–8

    Definition of an inch in centimeters
    The speed of light in a vacuum
    Value of absolute zero on a Celsius scale
    The density of liquid water
    Boiling point of water
    Freezing point of water
    Speed of sound in air
    Speed of sound in water
    Definitions of day, hour, and year
    Names of common acids and bases
    Names of common elements that are insulators
    Names of common elements that are conductors

FIGURE 4.12 Excerpts from National Standards for History (National
Center for History in the Schools, 1995)

---

1. Historical thinking skills that enable children to:

    ▌ differentiate past, present, and future time
    ▌ raise questions: seek and evaluate evidence
    ▌ compare and analyze historical stories, illustrations, and records from the
       past
    ▌ interpret the historical record
    ▌ construct historical narratives of their own

2. Historical understandings that define what students should know about the his-
    tory of families, their communities, states, nation, and world. These under-
    standings are drawn from the record of human aspirations, strivings, accom-
    plishments, and failures in at least five spheres of human activity: the social,
    political, scientific/technological, economic, and cultural (the philosophical/reli-
    gious/aesthetic), as appropriate for children.

Local Goal Development

Schools very often create their own set of goals with or without the
advantage of national, state, or discipline-based influence. Michael can
remember when his school district developed goals for all learners by
collecting hundreds of statements describing learner outcomes.
Teachers, parents, administrators, and students compiled goals for
schooling and labeled them with colored sticky dots to prioritize them.
The items that had the most red dots were claimed as the district's pri-
ority goals.

Examples of local attempts to prioritize goals are varied. Some are
broad collections of statements and are more characteristic of national
goals. Hartsfield Elementary School in Tallahassee, Florida, compiled this
sort of statement (fig. 4.14). Professionals within individual schools in a
district are then able to interpret these goals and to create curriculum they
believe will best accomplish the expected outcomes. Other districts, such
as Kent (WA) School District, provide grade-by-grade structures for each
discipline that specify not only broad goals but also detail the routes for
achieving those goals (fig. 4.15).

Even individual school communities decide upon goal structures for
their students. Oregon's program, "Onward To Excellence" helped individual schools set the goal priorities they believed were most valid for their
own schools. Through a goal-setting process, the school community

---

FIGURE 4.13 National Geography Standards (National Council for the
Social Studies, 1994)

The goal of Geography for Life is to produce a geographically informed person who
sees meaning in the arrangement of things in space and applies a spatial perspective to life situations. The geographically informed person knows and understands:

The World in Spatial Terms
1. how to use maps and other tools and technologies
2. how to use mental maps to organize information about people, places, and
   environments in a spatial context
3. how to analyze the spatial organization of people, places, and environments

Places and Regions
4. the physical and human characteristics of places
5. that people create regions to interpret the world's complexity
6. how culture and experience influence people's perception of places and
   regions

Physical Systems
7. the physical processes that shape the patterns of Earth's surface
8. the characteristics and spatial distribution of ecosystems

Human Systems
9. the characteristics, distribution, and migration of human populations
10. the characteristics, distribution, and complexity of cultural mosaics
11. the patterns and networks of economic interdependence
12. the processes, patterns, and functions of human settlement
13. how forces of cooperation and conflict among people shape division and con-
    trol of Earth's surface

Environment and Society
14. how human actions modify the physical environment
15. how physical systems affect human systems
16. the changes in use, distribution, and importance of resources

The Uses of Geography
17. how to apply geography to interpret the past
18. how to apply geography to interpret the present and plan for the future

---

assembled a set of personalized goals for the school. Some schools selected academic achievement in areas such as reading or mathematics. Others
picked behavioral traits such as students as citizens or students as leaders.
Here at Eastern Oregon State College, the laboratory school developed
goals through a collaborative process involving staff and parents. Figure
4.16 lists the goals of Ackerman Laboratory School.

FIGURE 4.14 Local school district goal statement: Hartsfield Elementary,
Tallahassee, Florida (Hartsfield Elementary School, 1995)

Belief Statements

- High expectations lead to high achievements.
- Education is the collaborative responsibility of students, staff, parents, and the community.
- Learning is enhanced in a positive, nurturing, and disciplined environment where students respect themselves, others, and the educational process.
- Each student will be a self-sufficient, lifelong learner with a sense of purpose, responsibility, and appreciation for cultural diversity.
- Each student will master basic skills and apply critical and creative thinking to solve problems and seek solutions.
- Each student is respected for his/her uniqueness and is taught accordingly.
- Each student will demonstrate personal integrity through morally motivated behavior.
- The Hartsfield school community is committed to the shared purpose of applying technology to our learning.

It is clear that goals derive from a variety of sources. Most teachers recognize these multiple contributions to setting the purpose of education, as we do. Our collective total of over 40 years in the classroom has given us considerable experience with different curricula, local school needs, parental concerns, district directives, discipline-based standards, state mandates, national benchmarks, and research-based guidelines for schooling. From all these experiences we have constructed an internal set of goals that we consider important. And, in addition, because we teach in a social context, we seek agreement between the goals we have constructed and their external sources.

◈ Why Goals?

We have established that our scenario of "The Town That Moved" was based upon a set of goals. We have also established that the goals we have for students are ultimately a compilation of what we believe is best for our local students as influenced by national, state, district, and discipline-based concerns for schooling. We have yet to establish why goals are vital prerequisites for curriculum planning.

Let us describe a new lesson sequence for you—one that fails to employ goals in the curriculum-planning process. As you read figure 4.17, work backward to see if you can identify what the purpose of this unit was. What

---

FIGURE 4.15 Kent School District fourth grade learner objectives in language arts (Kent School District, 1995)

Students in language arts will...
1. read independently and interpret a variety of literary forms including Native American legends, realistic fiction, poetry, and reference materials, and summarize through activities such as artistic presentations and oral and written communication.
2. speak effectively to practice appropriate social communication and correct usage in daily interactions, and practice formal and informal speaking through oral critiques, speeches, and role playing.
3. write effectively to compose clear sentences, paragraphs, stories, and/or informational reports.
4. demonstrate the ability to use active listening skills to collect information gained from speakers or from listening to a variety of cross-cultural literature.
5. respond to a variety of oral and written cross-cultural literary forms, and express ideas clearly through means which include media, visual arts, and performance.

Concepts
1. Understanding symbols, patterns, and structures can promote effective communication.
2. The tools of universal communication can promote creative thinking and understanding.
3. Individuals can powerfully respond to ideas and attitudes through appropriate communication.
4. Understanding individuals in universal contexts can lead to better understanding of self.
5. Creative experiences can develop awareness and confidence in communication.

---

goals did you infer from this instruction? The first thing we noticed when examining this curriculum was that the only way we could efficiently and accurately describe the unit was to list events. It is a gallimaufry of activities. Although loosely webbed from the story *Blueberries for Sal* (McCloskey, 1948), the curriculum focuses less on the story and more on the topic of bears (fig. 4.18). The glue that holds this piece of curriculum together is not adhesive and is so sparsely applied that the curriculum really does not hold together at all. The goal of the unit appears to be to learn about *Blueberries for Sal* or bears, but why should that be a goal? What is the rationale for this sort of instruction? As Kohlberg and Meyer (1972, p. 449) state:

> The most important issue confronting educators and educational theorists is the choice of ends for the educational process. Without clear and rational educational goals, it becomes impossible to decide which educational

---

FIGURE 4.16 Ackerman Laboratory School broad goals (Eastern Oregon
State College, 1990)

Aesthetic and Artistic Development
    to appreciate the arts
    to think, learn, and communicate through the arts

Emotional and Social Development
    to develop a positive, realistic self-concept
    to develop independence
    to set appropriate goals and feel satisfaction in accomplishment and effort
    to cope with change
    to develop friendships
    to learn from others
    to enjoy living and learning

Intellectual Development
    to sustain and extend natural curiosity
    to develop thinking through meaningful learning experience
    to use language to facilitate thinking and learning
    to become an independent, lifelong learner

Physical Development and Well-Being
    to learn and practice safety measures
    to take care of and respect their bodies
    to develop an awareness of good nutrition
    to develop a wide variety of motor skills while maintaining physical fitness
    to develop an appreciation and enjoyment of human movement
    to learn social skills in physical activity setting

Social Responsibility
    to value and respect individual contributions
    to value, respect, and appreciate cultural identity and heritage
    to accept and demonstrate empathy
    to become a responsible member of society
    to respect and care for environment
    to adapt to a changing world

---

programs achieve objectives of general import and which teach incidental
facts and attitudes of dubious worth.

The kind of integration and confusion of goals in a *Blueberries for Sal*-type
curriculum seems unlikely to be the most effective way to help students grow
in meaningful ways. "The best way to characterize these units of instruction is
as a collection of activities that are more likely to fragment than to integrate
students' understanding" (Lipson, Valencia, Wixson, & Peters, 1993, p. 260).

The teacher who developed the *Blueberries for Sal* unit is representative of those who have not developed a true sense of linkage between the goals of learning and what learners actually do on a day-to-day basis. One consequence is that some teachers come to view goals as a pejorative or a nuisance. These teachers plan activities that appeal to them and that they think will appeal to students and then go back and index their plans to the mandated goals because it is required. Other teachers may be so caught up in the "what-do-I-do-Monday" anxiety that they fail to focus on how what happens on Monday is related to the goals toward which we are heading. A third group dismisses the importance of goals through an overgeneralized

---

FIGURE 4.17 *Blueberries for Sal* activity list

Day 1: Read *Blueberries for Sal* (McCloskey, 1976) aloud
Have the students reread the story silently and write vocabulary words that are new to them
Have the students make a story map for *Blueberries for Sal*
Read poems about bears
Sing "The Bear Went Over the Mountain"
Start a KWL (What I Know, What do I Want to Learn, What I Learned) for bears

Day 2: Reread *Blueberries for Sal*
Point out punctuation marks
Do a cloze procedure (reading comprehension) on a page of text
Continue working on the bear KWL
Read other bear books
Read *Corduroy* (Freeman, 1968)

Day 3: Do a readers' theater of *Blueberries for Sal*
Chart sentences from story
Draw pictures to match script
Read *Winnie the Pooh* (Milne, 1926)
Recite poems and songs about bears

Day 4: Serve blueberry muffins
Talk about blueberries and picking
Read about panda bears
Read *Little Bear* (Minarik, 1957)
Recite poems and songs about bears

Day 5: Finish KWL chart—what we learned about bears
Read about polar bears
Write paragraphs about bears
Read *The Biggest Bear* (Ward, 1953)

(The unit continues for five additional days in the same vein.)

FIGURE 4.18 *Blueberries for Sal* unit

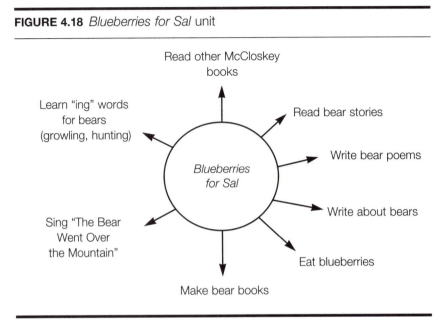

sense of coverage, such that they simply say, "I'm sure I covered that goal. It's in there somewhere!" They delude themselves unless the goals are specifically operationalized by discussing them with students, providing feedback to students related to the identified goals, and tracking student progress toward expert exhibition of goal attainment.

Goals: When Should They Be Considered?

The curriculum webbed from *Blueberries for Sal* would have had much clearer direction if the planner of the activities had first selected goals appropriate to the students in the classroom. It is important to first establish goals and then to plan the experiences to achieve those goals. As a contrast to *Blueberries for Sal,* let us examine a piece of curriculum that establishes goals in the early stages of curriculum planning and then continues to acknowledge these goals as beacons for guiding daily instruction.

Goal-Based Unit: The Dust Bowl

Three teachers, Debbie Field, Angie Kautz, and Robyn Miller, collaborated to form a unit around the events of the Dust Bowl migration of the 1930s. Three basic goals guided their curriculum unit: To understand the human

experience, to promote the utility of human collaboration and cooperation, and to practice mathematical relationships and applications. Their
decision to employ these goals within this unit was an interactive process
that required considerable brainstorming of possible ideas and testing to
see if students would be engaged in authentic explorations that would
advance the purpose of the stated goals.

They settled on the concept of engaging students in a simulation or
reenactment of immigrants traveling to California from Oklahoma along
Route 66. Students were arranged in family groups and given identities,
based on actual migrants, that they would assume for their journey. The
requirements were to keep a journal of where they were, how many miles
they traveled, how much gasoline they used, what expenditures they needed to make for food or lodging, and how they felt about the journey. Each
day their guides (teachers) would present the family group with an event
card that simulated real dilemmas on the trail: a flat tire, a bee sting, dirty
clothes. The family groups would wrestle with solving the problems and
engage in sharing various chores associated with the problems' solutions.

The main goal of the unit came from a state framework and is general.
"To understand the human experience" is a goal that speaks to larger questions about who we are as humankind and what kinds of experiences characterize our history. Through the simulation of the Dust Bowl migration,
the teachers enlisted many tactics to provide students with firsthand experiences. When students first started the journey they met in a dark room
where the floor was covered with a thin coat of dirt. As they sat in the dust
a fan swirled the air with grit. (Students were given painters' masks to protect them from inhaling any particulate matter). Segments of the film version of Steinbeck's *Grapes of Wrath* were shown and a readers' theater
describing conditions in Texas, Colorado, and Oklahoma in the 1930s was
presented. During the daily journeys the students fixed a flat tire, washed
clothes in a tub with a scrub board, ate beans out of a can, weeded a way-
side for wages, kept financial records, and made simple toys and musical
instruments out of discarded junk. This allowed students to experience
some of what it might have been like to be a migrant. The girl who experienced the trek as Nelda Bancroft wrote as she began the journey:

> I [am] happy that we will be able to go to California and have a life with-
> out all the dust and wind. We will be able to grow crops and have jobs that
> can pay us well. I don't want to leave all my stuff here and I know I will
> never be able to go back and get it.

A diary entry partway through the trip shows the feelings of the boy in
the character of Leo Bancroft: "I am happy but worried because I might die
but I have confedens [sic]." And at the end of the migration, the voice of
Rosalene Bancroft (fig. 4.19) is a loud exclamation of emotion. These diary

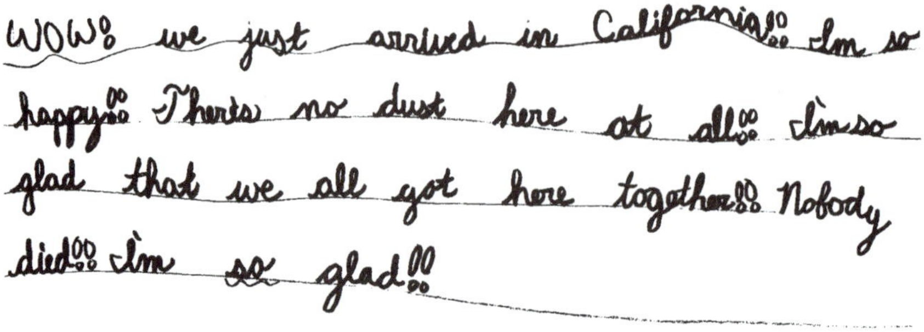

WOW! we just arrived in California! I'm so happy! There's no dust here at all! I'm so glad that we all got here together! Nobody died! I'm so glad!!

FIGURE 4.19 Journal entry of Rosalene Bancroft

entries, which are just samples of the student recollections, journals, and enthusiasm for this experience, make it clear that they have a greater understanding of what being an "Okie" was really like.

To track collaboration and cooperation, another goal for the unit, the check sheet shown in figure 4.20 was designed to monitor student progress. Class periods were designed in such a way that students had to interact and solve problems as a team. The teacher had ample opportunities to observe students in this endeavor and to give formative feedback, helping students grow in areas such as consensus building, respecting divergent views, and listening effectively.

The mathematical goal required both formative, daily attention and a summative assessment. As students recorded their family's decisions about how much money was spent and how many miles they traveled, some students had difficulty in keeping the numerals in the appropriate columns and in processing the totals. Both teacher and student worked

FIGURE 4.20 Checklist for cooperation and collaboration

Checklist: Cooperate and Collaborate

___ the student effectively defines problems, issues, and tasks within the group

___ the student performs various roles within the group

___ the student establishes and participates in open and clear communication

___ the student engages all team members

___ the student works towards consensus

___ the student respects divergent points of view

___ the student listens to views of others

each day on this task and found that it required considerable energy to use mathematics as a tool for daily living. To track the students' cumulative progress, teachers created a scoring guide (fig. 4.21) to assess each student's final analysis of the family's expenses. An example of what students generated is seen in Vanessa's journal (fig. 4.22). When the scoring guide was applied to this student work, progress toward the goal could be recorded.

For these teachers, goals provided the starting place for their planning and a way to make decisions about what explorations they would encourage in the classroom. Although they acknowledged that there were many other things in operation in the unit such as map reading, writing and speaking skills, and hand skills, they made a concerted effort to select just a few goals to be the overall purpose and compass points of their efforts. These goals were related to one another as well. In order to understand the human experience of the Dust Bowl, students needed to understand that part of the survival of these migrants was due to their ability to cooperate and collaborate. Another part of that human experience was to understand

---

FIGURE 4.21 Scoring Guide: Quantification

Scoring Guide: Quantification

___ Demonstrated *proficiency* in the quantifying process
    ___ student is able to interpret a problem situation, which includes selecting information to solve specific problems
    ___ student is able to develop and apply appropriate problem-solving strategies
    ___ student effectively solves the problem and is able to verify the solutions
    ___ student can effectively communicate results

___ Demonstrated *progress* in the quantifying process
    ___ student exhibits marginal ability to interpret a problem situation, which includes selecting information to solve specific problems
    ___ student has difficulty developing and applying appropriate problem-solving strategies
    ___ student has difficulty solving the problem and is able to verify the solutions
    ___ student exhibits marginal ability to communicate results

___ Demonstrated *emerging* skills in the quantifying process
    ___ student is unable to interpret a problem situation, which includes selecting information to solve specific problems
    ___ student is unable to develop and apply appropriate problem-solving strategies
    ___ student is unable to solve the problem and is unable to verify the solutions
    ___ student is unable to communicate results

VANESSA	GAS	COST OF GAS	FOOD	WATER	$ EARNED
WEEK 1 DISTANCE: 400	20 gallons	.12 x 20= 2.40 $2.40	.70¢	.15x4= 60¢	$1.00
WEEK 2 DISTANCE: 450	23	$2.76	.70	.45	Ø
WEEK 3 DISTANCE:	17	$2.04	$.90	$.45	$.75
Total	6 0	$7.10	$2.30	$1.50	$1.75

FIGURE 4.22 Vanessa's record of the trip to California

the need for, and lack of, money that these migrants had. The progress toward the goals was made even easier due to their interelatedness. Because of this focus and clarity of purpose, students and teachers were able to see progress in each of the identified goal areas.

So why is this so important? Couldn't we do this Dust Bowl unit without the statement of goals and the emphasis on formative tracking of progress toward those goals? Yes, but we would run the risk of either being so totally unfocused that we lose the point of why we were doing the unit in the first place or we might default to the common denominator of instruction—the transmission of facts and information. Let us elaborate a bit on each point. Goals are a way of keeping us honest, loyal to the purposes of why we are in the classroom. They help us steer our efforts and check to see if we are on course. If teachers had not identified mathematical applications as a goal for their Dust Bowl unit, would they have created the need for students to track the financial matters of their family with such acuity? Teachers acknowledged that the daily finance and travel log was difficult for many students and, because it was, they recognized that it was just what students needed to do! Sometimes we avoid the hard things because we like to see students being successful. If we choose this route too often, when will students ever be challenged to increase their learning?

Establishment of goals led to a curriculum that helped students move toward more mature understandings.

Goals also give teachers permission to engage in curriculum and instruction that they otherwise would be reluctant to do. For example, as a classroom teacher, Michael always felt students should engage in projects, create innovative solutions to issues, use materials and tools, and work in small groups. Still, during the weeks of noisy creation in his classroom, he was concerned that these experiences were not really the science or mathematics he was expected to teach. He had been given a textbook that supposedly contained the only valid goals for instruction and he felt the tension between it and the alternative he practiced in his classroom. He did not have the benefit of stated goals to authorize what he was doing. If goals are clearly articulated and honored, then teachers are given the permission to do those things they once pursued from intuition. On the other hand, teachers who are engaged in innovative curriculum can justify their choices by pointing out to their challengers that they are forwarding the mandated goals. One social studies teacher said it best when apprised of the newer reform agenda goals, "Deep down I always thought that this was the way I should teach, but now I have the permission to teach this way." This teacher, like many others, has discovered the power and elegance that goal-based teaching offers.

Summary

Before any curriculum planning can take place, teachers must have a clear sense of two things: how children learn and what is important for them to learn. We addressed how children learn in chapters 2 and 3, and this chapter examined what different groups believe is important for children to learn. We do not venture to tell you which set of goals you should adopt, we only advocate that you have a clear goal structure in place. Normally teachers receive support in creating a goal structure from their state departments of education and their local districts, but even if this input is not available, all teachers should be vested with a definitive and forceful vision of what is important for children to learn as a result of schooling. Then, as you plan curriculum, you can select the focus of each unit from that vision.

Goals should buoy the curriculum and give it purpose and direction. We see goals as balloons that support and provide energy for the curriculum. Without well-articulated goals for schooling, we are like Alice in Wonderland (Carroll, 1918):

"Cheshire Puss," she began rather timidly…"Would you tell me please which way I ought to go from here?"

"That depends a good deal on where you want to get to," said the cat.

"I don't care where," said Alice.

"Then it doesn't matter which way you go," said the cat.

Lingering Questions

A dilemma that we feel in articulating goals is that they often seem at counter purposes. How can we encourage students to be self-directed, creative, and independent, and at the same time have content goals that require specific acquisition of knowledge?

You will notice that we have not specified which goals you should select, only that all teachers and all school systems should have clearly identified goals. What goals do you believe should be the guiding force of 21st-century curriculum?

One cannot talk about goals without assessment soon entering the discussion. How is assessment related to the selection of goals?

Companion Readings

The 1995 yearbook of the Association for Supervision and Curriculum Development, *Toward a Coherent Curriculum* (Beane, 1995), offers many viewpoints on the role of goals in creating coherent curriculum, stimulates thought about which goals should be selected, and offers ideas about the alignment of goals and assessment.

Chapters 2 and 3 of *A Place Called School* (Goodlad, 1984) discuss an interesting study of the source of goals.

Resource list for "The Town That Moved"

Finsland, Mary Jane. (1983). *The town that moved*. Minneapolis: Carolrhoda.
Hibbing Chamber of Commerce. Pamphlets and brochures.
Hibbing Daily Tribune, Centennial Edition. July 22, 1993.
Mestek, Patricia. (1992). Personal communication.

CHAPTER 5

Narrative Curriculum: A Connection of the Three Foundations

Activating Prior Knowledge

How would you explain to other professionals or to parents the foundations on which curriculum should be designed?

Chapter Highlights

Employing the three major aspects presented in the previous chapters, this chapter proposes a curriculum model that uses narrative as the context for learning, goals to buoy learning, and constructivism as the theory for learning.

What framework unites the three foundations that we have presented in the first chapters? What arrangement of the curriculum starts with broad goals, searches for a meaningful context, and values constructive learning? In keeping with our strategy of providing experiences to our reader prior to suggesting possible solutions, we offer here another scenario to introduce the model of curriculum that integrates our stated foundations. For those of you eager to explore the model itself, go ahead to the section titled "The Model Explained" and then return to the scenario to see the model in action.

The scenario features two experienced teachers brainstorming a unit of instruction. We have asked them to be deliberate in communicating the thought processes they use as they plan instruction. As they retrace their steps in planning this piece of curriculum, participate with them in their brainstorming while they invent a learning experience for their middle school students.

◈ A Scenario of Curriculum Construction

Sophie: Let's spend some time brainstorming the unit we were talking about doing next term with our middle school kids. I was thinking we could review what we need to accomplish and design some general directions for curriculum. Did you have any thoughts about what general directions we need to take with this unit?

Lou: An important area in which my students need practice is in the art of resolving conflict. Kids seem to be so prone to argument instead of exchanging ideas. When they have conflicting viewpoints they resort to fighting.

Sophie: So you want them to defend a viewpoint without arguing?

Lou: Having an open mind, realizing that maybe somebody else's ideas could shape theirs, is an important aspect of communication that they need to work on.

Sophie: OK, that's a goal. Don't we also want them to defend their viewpoint from a knowledgeable position? We don't want them to just state their opinion. We want them to support it with research or data that they have collected.

Lou: The other thing that I have noticed with this age group is that they really romanticize certain things like war and violence. I'd like to create an opportunity for them to examine this.

Sophie: I know what you mean. They hear stuff in the news about Bosnia or Iraq or some other conflict and their solution is always "nuke 'em!" They solve problems on a very low level of moral development. What we need to do is give them a chance to lift themselves to a higher moral plane of decision making.

Another goal that I think fits here is one that is in our social studies curriculum. We need to have students understand the patterns of why people engage in conflict and how conflict has been resolved in the past.

Lou: We might be able to use a world civilization background—conflicts in history and man's long record of inadequate conflict resolution.

Sophie: I wonder if I could fit some of our science goals here. I was thinking about our state framework of Science Common Curriculum Goals that requires us to think about science, technology, and society.

Lou: Wouldn't that fit with the first two goals? One of the aspects of science-technology-society (STS) could include exploring the relationship of weapons of war and science and their impact on society. It sounds like the social studies goals and science goals are very similar. Communicating position without conflict will fit right in.

Sophie: Then, language arts serves as the means for communicating their findings about technology, war, or the historical context that led to conflict.

Lou: Are there other things we want to have our kids work on that might complement the goals we have chosen?

Sophie: Well, we probably don't want to choose too many goals, we might forget why we are teaching the unit! I do think that the new mathematics standards ask us to pay particular attention to how to solve problems through authentic and real experiences. We need to allow students to apply their mathematical knowledge to any problems they might encounter in this unit.

Lou: This might be best accomplished in a social setting where peers can collaborate to form solutions.

Sophie: The other goal that I would really like to see accomplished with my students is having them feel comfortable with the use of tools, materials, and processes of technology. They need to have an ability to use their hands to experiment and craft—and I am not talking about just scissors, paste, and tape. I would like to see students use some tools and materials that are unfamiliar to them.

Lou: So, what do we have so far? Expressing conflicting points of view without arguing, using research to support a position, solving authentic problems, addressing issues of science-technology-society, collaborative problem solving, and practicing hand skills.

Sophie: That's a lot. We may not be able to address all of these goals in the unit we plan, but they will give us a focus in the rest of our planning.

Lou: Do you have a context in mind that might facilitate these goals?

Sophie: I have been thinking of a context that might work very well here. It is an historical account from the campaigns of Alexander the Great. Here is the synopsis that I have been working with:

In 322 B.C., Alexander the Great marched his armies along the coast of the eastern Mediterranean summarily subjugating everyone in his path. The only substantial fortress keeping him from the bounty in Egypt was the city of Tyre situated on the coast of what we now call Lebanon. The newer part of the city of Tyre was on an island and the older part of the city was on the mainland.

Although most cities resigned quickly to Alexander's demands for allegiance and subjugation, Tyre resisted. The city and its people had a long history of economic success and naval prowess. The city had been besieged before and had not willingly succumbed to a conquering army in over 1,000 years. Alexander demanded entrance to the city, but the Tyrians rejected his requests. The long siege began.

Without a navy, Alexander was faced with the longest, most difficult, and most costly challenge of his military career. He was faced with the imposing fortress of Tyre:

▌ An island separated by one-half mile of sea as deep as 20 feet near the shore
▌ A 150-foot wall of stone and gypsum mortar protecting the shore side of the island
▌ The wall defended by thousands of well-equipped soldiers
▌ A formidable navy harbored on the lee (protected) side of the island with ships called triremes (oared boats without sails)
▌ Catapults and other devices capable of firing rocks and flaming missiles at anyone close to the island (some with a capability of tossing 50-pound rocks up to 400 yards)
▌ A fresh water supply on the island
▌ Access to trade from the sea
▌ Strong winds and rough seas in the separating channel (Williams, 1907)

Alexander was faced with an important decision. Should he skip the city and allow his back to be left vulnerable from the sea or should he siege the city at a high cost and delay his eventual showdown with Darius, the Persian king at his flank? We know what he thought about the problem because the Greek historian Arrian quotes Alexander in a speech to his officers:

> Friends and allies, I see that an expedition to Egypt will not be safe for us, so long as the Persians retain the sovereignty of the sea; nor is it a safe course, both for other reasons, and especially looking at the state of matters in Greece, for us to pursue Darius, leaving in our rear the city of Tyre itself in doubtful allegiance, and Egypt and Cyprus in occupation of the Persians. ...But, if Tyre were captured, the whole of Phoenicia would be in our possession, and the fleet of Phoenicians, which is the most numerous and best in the Persian navy, would in all probability come over to us. (Godolphin, 1942)

Alexander had a dream that night that confirmed his desire to take Tyre. He saw the god Heracles taking him by the hand and leading him into the city. Heracles was a god that employed labor in accomplishing his tasks, so Alexander interpreted the dream to mean that the siege would be long and arduous. He would take the city by force. Alexander had access to the old city of Tyre on the mainland, its 50,000 inhabitants, the forested mountains of Lebanon, and his army of more than 30,000.

Sophie: I was thinking that this story has good potential for student inquiry.

Lou: In most history books Alexander is presented as a hero... an august figure. The way you tell this story he seems more like a real person. And the Tyrians seem very human as well.

Sophie: I think the reason this story appeals to me, and to others who have heard it, is that it makes the personalities real and believable.

Lou: The story is compelling and has lots of possibilities. The characters are rich, the setting has lots of puzzles and questions that might be asked, the action is certainly captivating, but most of all the story has a universal theme. Point and counterpoint, the very idea we want the students to engage, resolution of conflict, technology and society. It is all there.

Sophie: The context seems to work well with the science-technology-society (STS) and conflict resolution goals. I can see where the students could research either side of the conflict and develop a rationale for their actions. What about the other goals? Will the story support hand skills or problem solving?

Lou: The students could decide to construct examples of the siege towers or fortifications. Hand skills are certainly a possibility here. Problem solving in mathematics seems integral to trying to calculate the engineering problems of the siege: how the catapults operate, what volume of rock would be needed to build a causeway to the island, or specifications for building the fortifications.

It also appears that this story has plenty of opportunity for our students to make meaning about modern-day conflicts through their experiences with historical characters. Let's try it.

Sophie: How will we organize the unit so that we don't simply give all the information to the students? We want them to construct their own meaning, don't we?

Lou: Yes, we both believe in a generative model of learning. We could present the story from both a Greek and a Tyrian voice. That might set the stage for the class to ask questions about the conflict. The class could divide up so that one group and one teacher are Tyrians and the others are Greeks. From their respective viewpoints they would have to resolve the conflict.

Sophie: So we give them the initial circumstance, collect their ideas, and then make suggestions about what they might do?

Lou: I think we need to be careful that it is their idea of what they want to explore. We need to ask guiding questions and we can give them challenges, but it is important that they choose how they will solve the questions they wish to examine.

Sophie: I can envision the class becoming engaged in role playing the two cultures, researching the setting and background of each, building the fortifications or models associated with the siege, and collaborating with their peers to make a final product.

Lou: I think it has good potential. Let's brainstorm a list of questions that kids might think of. That way we can gather resources and materials that might be needed ahead of time.

Sophie: Okay, but let's do it later. After all this hard work, I'm ready for a nap!

◈ The Model Under Construction

We asked you to interact with our two teachers brainstorming their curriculum. Take a few moments now to think about the process in which you and they engaged.

- Was there a pattern from which the unit was planned?
- How were goals addressed?
- Where did learning theory apply?
- How was the context selected?
- How were the students' interests and needs considered?
- How were explorations selected?

We asked one of our curriculum classes to design a graphic organizer based on the same experiences and information that we have thus far presented in this book. We gave them tape, scissors, and the symbols and labels in figure 5.1. You might like to try this exercise too! We expected that everyone would arrive at the same general arrangement of parts. What we found, however, was that each individual crafted a different visual picture of what made sense to them about how the curriculum was designed. Our learners had constructed their own meaning, not discovered ours!

We realized that many of their ideas were an improvement on our original model and we went about modifying our own graphic organizer as we learned from our students. What an incredible experience—both for teachers

FIGURE 5.1 Graphic organizer pieces

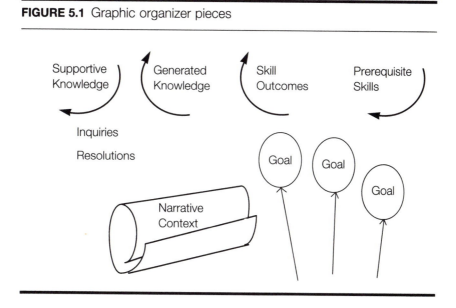

to learn from students and for students to recognize themselves as teachers. In the process we had collectively constructed new knowledge and had generated new meaning for our work. As we continued to reflect about our students' contributions and as we prepared to write this chapter, we created the current depiction of the model as shown in figure 5.2. Each part of this diagram represents an important tenet that acts simultaneously with the other tenets to create the curriculum. The balloons are goals that provide support or purpose for the curriculum. The scroll represents a story that provides a natural containment for the context of the curriculum. The interactive arrows of prior knowledge and new knowledge represent the interactive, constructive nature of the learning process. In this one figure we illustrate all the principles important to curriculum design.

You may have constructed a different model from the symbols in figure 5.1. That is to be anticipated and embraced. Since we recognize that all individuals construct their own meaning about the experiences they encounter, each visualization of a concept has the potential for uniqueness. At present, our model satisfies us and helps us communicate our thinking graphically. We offer it more as an aid to focus our attention on how we construct curriculum, rather than to market a particular graphic organizer. Your visual portrayal may have more appeal than ours. In fact, if you feel that your representation better communicates the concept, send it to us. We will learn from you!

FIGURE 5.2 The narrative curriculum model

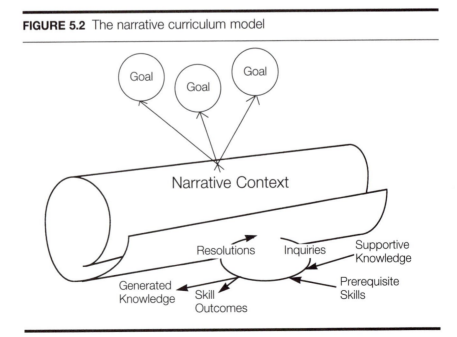

◈ The Model Explained

Goals

The scenario we presented is obviously a condensed and edited version of how actual curriculum planning would occur. In a normal process, there would be numerous short brainstorming sessions, avenues pursued that lead to dead ends, and interferences of all kinds. However, even with all the realities and constraints of school life, we believe teachers can be reflective about what makes curricular sense and can collaborate to create meaningful learning opportunities for students. As we return to our curriculum brainstorming scenario, note that our teachers were first interested in the goals for their learners. They addressed the needs of the learners and tried to fit the mandates of school, district, state, and nation with internal rationale for what middle grade youngsters ought to master. As we have discussed before, we see the goals as buoying the curriculum—balloons elevating and giving direction to the curriculum. The goals must be agreed upon before any other activity can take place.

The teachers selected a number of goals that seemed to articulate themselves naturally. The historical context, science-technology-society (STS), communication and research, hand skills, and problem solving mesh well as mutually supportive goals. As the teachers planned this unit, one stated goal led logically to others. Different disciplines often write surprisingly similar goals, which when illuminated in the light of broad goal attainment, merge into commonality.

From examining goals from a variety of sources, we have found that there are some broad goals that are honored by many disciplines. Every discipline expects the learner to be a good communicator, for example. The National Science Teachers Association, the National Council of Teachers of Mathematics, and the National Council of Teachers of English all specifically address the goal of communication in their description of standards. Mathematicians describe the goal of communication as a student's ability to convey ideas about mathematics, to deal with it in social contexts, to make connections, and to explain their thinking as they learn and become involved in mathematics (NCTM, 1989). Language arts professionals are in the process of creating standards that emphasize using the language arts to communicate with power and excellence for a variety of purposes (NCTE and International Reading Association, 1996). Scientists' version of the communication goal is stated as "the ability to communicate ideas and share information with fidelity and clarity" (American Association for the Advancement of Science, 1990, p. 192). Although stated in various forms, the basic ideas are comparable. The recognition that disciplines share mutual aims provides an obvious starting point to help streamline our efforts to forward the goals.

In our opening scenario, several goals that are mutually shared by at least two disciplines are apparent. Since students will be dealing with issues of war and technology in the siege of Tyre, debating the merits of others' ideas, and developing commentary on the relationships between technology and war, goals articulated by both the sciences and the social sciences can be addressed. For example, in social science we could apply the standard put forth by the National Center for History in the Schools (1995):

Standard 5. Historical Issues—Analysis and Decision Making
A. Identify issues and problems in the past.
B. Compare the interests and values of the various people involved.
C. Suggest alternative choices for addressing the problem.
D. Evaluate alternative courses of action.
E. Prepare a position or course of action on an issue.
F. Evaluate the consequences of a decision.

In science, we could apply the science-technology-society goals put forth by the Oregon Department of Education (1988, pp. 42–43):

Goal 6.0 Describe how society influences science and technology.
A. Describe how society's support influences science and technology.
B. Recognize that society controls science and technology through the allocation of resources.
C. Recognize how individual wants and needs are positively and negatively influenced by technology.
D. Assess the worth of a given course of action or policy after considering possible impacts on individual, society, and the earth's environment.
E. Analyze authoritative data to determine what optional positions are possible on a specific issue.

The degree of overlap between these two lists is significant. By clustering these goals, we can create a learning experience that will satisfy both standards. Knowledge of these goals and alignment of similarly stated language is an important step in determining which goals to employ.

The weaving of synergistic goals requires collaboration and critical thinking. In addition, teachers must know the goals they are expected to address to satisfy the myriad of responsibilities for their students' learning. We would argue against a formulaic goal selection strategy e.g., one language arts goal, one science goal, one social studies goal, and one arts goal. A forced integration of goals is like trying to put the stepsisters' feet in Cinderella's glass slipper. Instead, teachers need to assemble likely goals that mesh in a complementary manner.

The model first and foremost depicts goals as providing and supporting the purposes of the curriculum. We have shown only three balloons to lift this specific piece of curriculum. We might have shown more or less, but the symbolism seems important in the small number of balloons. A modicum of goals is important because it puts a reasonable demand on the teacher's ability to plan and assess. If we choose too many balloons we may create a unit of curriculum that tries to do too much. When teachers are able to plan with goals that are closely related, as did the teachers in our scenario, more goals can be addressed. Problem solving in the historical context, communicating points of view, and understanding science-technology-society (STS) can be viewed as aspects of the same goal: problem solving. If, on the other hand, we had selected four diverse goals, such as to cope with change, to learn and practice safety measures, to learn through the arts, and to understand the scientific concept of system, the lack of overlap would create fragmentation. In planning lessons and in facilitating learning, teachers can realistically heed only a small number of directives. To ask appropriate questions and to lead learners in specific ways requires focus. A preponderance of unrelated goals causes confusion and muddles our assessment of our learners.

Context

Once the teachers in our scenario had agreed upon the goals, they next searched for a meaningful context for instruction. Teachers' conscious awareness of the desired goals allows them to examine a story for its potential to access these goals. Then, the recurring question becomes, "Can we reach our goals through this context?"

The Alexander narrative illustrates several important features of a successful context: it is a story with a compelling theme, it has potential for exploration, and it makes a good match with the desired goals. We have chosen the scroll to represent the story, or narrative, that provides the context for learning. The scroll is unfurled and upon its leaves are the setting, characters, and action of a story. Although we will discuss how we select narrative contexts in chapter 7, it is important to state here that the selection of this context was no accident. Many other possibilities were explored concurrently with the Alexander scenario. Only after reflection and brainstorming was this context judged worthy of being a vehicle for the unit.

One of the parameters that frames our context selection is the developmental needs and interests of our students. Middle school students are, in Egan's terms, romantic in their interactions with story (Egan, 1990). The idea of adventure, heroes, drama, action, and intrigue are natural points of resonance for students from 8 to 15 years old. We could be fairly certain that the milieu of the siege of Tyre would attract learners who view the world in a romantic fashion.

Many other kinds of subtle interactions give teachers insight about which contexts will be effective and which will not. As the teachers approached this unit they believed that their students would react favorably to the idea of experimenting with materials to solve the siege of Tyre problem. Because they knew the students' prior knowledge, preoccupations, interests in reading, popular culture, and habits of mind, they could predict with some accuracy their reactions. This intuitive awareness of appropriate context comes from a close relationship between students and teachers and depends upon a sensitivity for and faith in the learners.

All students may not find the siege of Tyre compelling. They may have a different orientation to what they find interesting and motivating. The reminder to teachers is that we must go beyond our own view of the context to look at it through our students' eyes. Will they be interested? Will they be connected to a deeper meaning, or theme? Will they find something that they want to pursue? Will they be challenged?

The criteria at work in selecting the context deals not only with the quality of the story and the storytelling, but also with the interests of the learners. As the possibilities in the Alexander story were explored, the teachers tried to match the possibilities in the story with the philosophy of a student-centered approach. When teachers examine a context, they recognize the potential for success when they sense: "Ah, kids are going to connect to this and want to learn about it." The teachers in our scenario examined the story, identified the point-counterpoint which led to the development of siege weapons and fortifications, and recognized the appeal for their middle level students. These considerations help ensure that students will be more active and willingly engaged in learning.

Learning Theory

Another concern is the nature of the students' learning. It isn't enough that we select lofty goals and a context for learning, we must also carefully choreograph learning experiences. Since the teachers in this scenario have adopted a constructivist theory of how conceptual learning is facilitated, the strategies employed to implement the curriculum are critical.

We have depicted the interaction of context with the learner as a recursive loop. As the teacher or student reads or participates in the story, questions, puzzles, wonderments, ideas, assertions, and feelings are generated. We have labeled these responses as "inquiries" in the model. As students listen to the Alexander story, for example, they ask questions related to the characters, setting, action, and meaning of the narrative. Until learners ask their own questions about things of importance to them, there will never be any genuine ownership of learning (Freire, 1973). In the Alexander story, the following types of questions emerge:

How could they have made a catapult to throw rocks accurately?
What would a trireme look like?
How did they make siege towers?

What does this area look like today?
What was the story of Heracles?
In what other sieges did Alexander engage?
Who were the Tyrians and what was their history?
Why was Alexander so intent on conquering the world?

The resolution of the first question alone ("How could they have made a catapult to throw rocks accurately?") requires initial research, experimentation, collaboration, and communication. Learners may read about archaeological evidence of catapults, use similar materials to make their own models, work together to share ideas for planning the most effective tools, and demonstrate their findings to others.

Inputs to the learning cycle include the use of prior knowledge and previously acquired skills. Students bring to the story their own background of ideas about catapults, perhaps from movies, videos, books, or having had experience with slingshots or the like in a scout project. The prior knowledge of how rubber bands work, what catapults may or may not have looked like, and other life experiences contributes greatly to how the question is addressed and the tactics that are employed. Skills, too, are to be acknowledged. Skills contribute to a learner's ability to address the question and the level at which information is retrieved and processed. For example, learners who are able to do library research or electronic information retrieval will resolve catapult-related questions and problems differently from those who are unable to use these skills.

The curriculum model allows students to approach the text from their individual levels of learning. Growth for students begins with their current levels of knowledge and skill attainment. Acquisition of new knowledge and skills results from the interaction of their current levels and their exploration of the narrative. When learners investigate catapults, for example, they generate new meaning about simple machines, technology, and sources for materials. Just as information is learned and concepts are generated from explorations, skills are enhanced. For example, as learners build catapults and test their ability to toss rocks at targets, mathematical skills in estimating, graphing, and measuring success rates can be developed. Teachers discover that when they teach a new skill based on its immediate utility for solving a problem, students acquire it readily.

The model depicts arrows pointing toward the scroll and emanating from the scroll in order to visually represent a constructivist approach to learning. We utilize prior knowledge, offer challenging experiences, and facilitate acquisition of new knowledge and skills in a social setting. The arrows represent the recursive, cyclic nature of learning. The outcome of the learning and the resolution of the question contribute to the understanding of the story. This point will be discussed in more detail in chapter 6.

Model Summary

The graphic organizer illustrates our allegiance to goals, our assertion that narrative provides a meaningful context, and our belief in meaning making as a primary way of knowing. It provides us not only with a method of communicating the pedagogical tenets that inform our decisions, but also with a reference point to which we may refer to ensure that our work is indeed consistent with our theories.

We now invite you to return to chapter 1 and see if the model we have presented is active in the opening scenario. Analyze the curriculum by scanning the unit based on *Very Last First Time* and reflecting on the questions in figure 5.3.

◈ Transdisciplinary Learning: A Natural Consequence of Narrative Curriculum

The reader may be impatient with us at this point on at least one particular point: the integrated curriculum. Although we have introduced this book as addressing the integrated curriculum, we recognize that we have said very little on that topic so far. We have delayed the discussion until now because we believe that all curricular decisions should be based on

FIGURE 5.3 Questions for testing the curriculum model

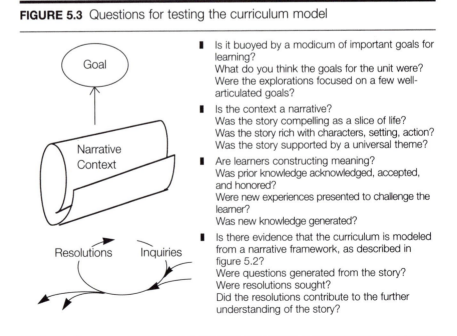

- ▪ Is it buoyed by a modicum of important goals for learning?
  What do you think the goals for the unit were?
  Were the explorations focused on a few well-articulated goals?

- ▪ Is the context a narrative?
  Was the story compelling as a slice of life?
  Was the story rich with characters, setting, action?
  Was the story supported by a universal theme?

- ▪ Are learners constructing meaning?
  Was prior knowledge acknowledged, accepted, and honored?
  Were new experiences presented to challenge the learner?
  Was new knowledge generated?

- ▪ Is there evidence that the curriculum is modeled from a narrative framework, as described in figure 5.2?
  Were questions generated from the story?
  Were resolutions sought?
  Did the resolutions contribute to the further understanding of the story?

how children learn and the goals that designate what is to be learned. From these, a curriculum design can be proposed. Much of current literature makes an integrated approach a primary rationale for curriculum organization. Thematic, topic, or process models are cited as designs for integration. Units are planned to include some mathematics, some science, some language arts, some social studies, and so forth in a unit of instruction; this results in existing curriculum being regrouped into new packaging. The motive behind this regrouping is to bring diverse subject-area activities together, in order to give each part meaning.

We disagree with this strategy. We have designed curriculum that first evolved from broad goals and ideas of schooling, from the way we believe students learn best, and from meaningful contexts for that learning. We have made no demands that the curriculum be multidisciplinary, yet the curriculum design we advocate results in authentic learning that is *trans*-disciplinary by nature. The authentic nature of the context and the inquiries of students identify the disciplines needed to serve the learning. The narrative curriculum framework is a way to achieve integration without the use of a shoehorn or a crowbar to force all the disciplines in beforehand.

Transdisciplinary is an unfamiliar word to most. We have appropriated it from Drake (1991) to call attention to the view we take toward integration and the role of the disciplines in the curriculum. Transdisciplinary means both "across" and "beyond" the disciplines. Just as we must cross geographical boundaries to reach a destination, we cross disciplinary boundaries when we engage in inquiry and exploration. In our example of the siege of Tyre we wanted to understand how Alexander the Great went about defeating the Tyrians. To understand all we could about the story required us to read the historical narrative supplied by Herodotus, to interpret the Greek mythology that may have motivated Alexander to action, to study and experiment with primitive technologies available to the ancient Greeks, to craft models that represented the setting, and to debate ideas and possibilities with our peers. Our pursuit of resolutions to our inquiries led us across many disciplinary boundaries. In fact, it led us beyond disciplinary restrictions altogether. We didn't stop at any boundary because we were stepping into a new discipline. Rather, we ranged over a wide area to investigate our area of personal passion, using the road maps of the disciplines to help structure our exploration.

Let us separate what we mean by "disciplines" from that of "subjects" since in much of our educational tradition the two terms have been used interchangeably. For example, some would say that studying history is engaging in the discipline of history. However, studying history does not make one a historian. Neither does learning the content of science make one a scientist. There is an important difference between the discipline and the subject matter often studied in school. Disciplinary thinking requires that we engage in inquiry, exploration, and demonstrations of our learning according to the methods that each discipline has developed. To engage in a discipline we need to know its tools, processes, style of discourse, and organization. The way practitioners in each discipline ask questions, set about their work, collect information, and communicate their findings has a distinct flavor. Authors are frequently asked to describe their writing processes and while their accounts show individual differences, the commonalities reveal the discipline of writing. Historians engage in their work using a methodology called historiography. We could learn a lot about the subject of history without ever acting as a historian. When we ask students to acquire information about people, places, and events of the past, they are learning the subject of history. If students have opportunities to ask questions, to pore over diaries and eyewitness accounts, and to formulate their own ideas about the meaning of events, then we have begun to expose them to how historians practice their discipline.

The transdisciplinary nature of the narrative curriculum adopts the definition of "discipline" as a way of gaining knowledge and perspective about the world. As we engage a context and seek to learn more about things that interest us, the authentic disciplinary method can be activated. If we want to know about what kind of catapults were used to hail missiles on the Tyrian fleet, we could read about it, or we could activate the scientific method and engage in experimentation. This ability to adopt different perspectives adds power to learning.

We believe the narrative framework to be a natural way of integrating learning without inventing inauthentic linkages. When the three foundations of curriculum—narrative context, goals, and constructivism—are united, integration is a natural and welcome consequence.

Lingering Questions

Are there other tenets we should consider important enough to include in a curriculum model?

If the model is used and a resultant unit is not transdisciplinary (that is, the study remains within the confines of a single discipline), is it still a worthy unit? Do all units have to be integrated?

CHAPTER 6

Narrative Curriculum: The Planning Template

Activating Prior Knowledge

How do you plan curriculum? How do you think other teachers develop units? What are the key concerns that should enter into curriculum design?

Chapter Highlights

In this chapter a planning template helps move us from the theoretical into the practical. It demonstrates how goals, narratives, and disciplinary heuristics interact in the process of developing curriculum.

FIGURE 6.1 Stories in chapters 1 through 5

Chapter 1:   The picture book provides the context for curricu-
Very Last First Time   lum in a mid-level elementary classroom.

Chapter 2:   The chapter book introduces the concept of the
The Green Book   power of story as a container for curriculum.

Chapter 3:   The picture book provides both a pattern of con-
Galimoto   tructivist learning and a context to stimulate learn-
                                        ers' construction of meaning.

Chapter 4:   The collaborative story making challenges us to
"The Town That Moved"   think about what is worth knowing.

Chapter 5:   The historical vignette offers planners a chance to
"The Siege of Tyre"   manipulate the theoretical tenets of curriculum
                                        making.

In the first five chapters of this book you have had the opportunity to interact with a series of stories. Their purposes are summarized in figure 6.1.
Very Last First Time engaged us as transdisciplinary learners and portrayed the narrative curriculum. *The Green Book* illustrated the power of
story and provided us with a rationale for using narrative as the context for
learning. *Galimoto* exemplified the process of constructing meaning from
experience. As we identified with the 19th-century characters in "The
Town That Moved," we began to create a vision for 21st-century citizens
and the rationale for schooling. "The Siege of Tyre" provided us with an
opportunity to theorize about the nature of curriculum while considering
the variables of story, constructivist learning, and goals. As we thought
about how these pieces fit together, we created a theoretical framework.

◈ The Planning Template

To move from the theoretical to the practical is often a precipitous leap.
Where shall we proceed from this point? We have found that a planning
template helps us create narrative curriculum. The template (fig. 6.2)
reminds us of the principles of the narrative curriculum while capturing
the theoretical organization of curriculum in a one-page visual format.
    Across the top of the template is a keyword listing of the goals that we
have chosen to guide curriculum planning. You may wish to substitute your
own list of goals. The arrows indicate that goals interact with all of the
other aspects of the template. Across the bottom are reminders of when to

FIGURE 6.2 Narrative curriculum planning template

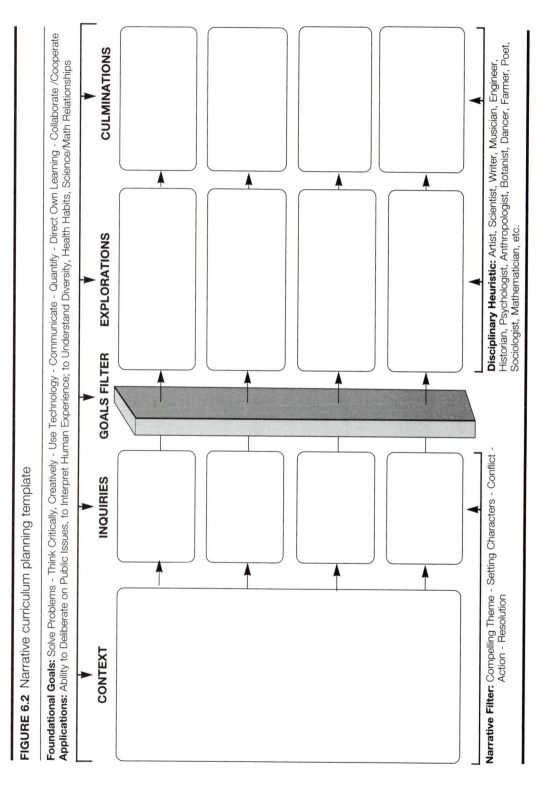

Foundational Goals: Solve Problems - Think Critically, Creatively - Use Technology - Communicate - Quantify - Direct Own Learning - Collaborate /Cooperate **Applications:** Ability to Deliberate on Public Issues, to Interpret Human Experience; to Understand Diversity, Health Habits, Science/Math Relationships

CONTEXT   INQUIRIES   GOALS FILTER   EXPLORATIONS   CULMINATIONS

Narrative Filter: Compelling Theme - Setting Characters - Conflict - Action - Resolution

Disciplinary Heuristic: Artist, Scientist, Writer, Musician, Engineer, Historian, Psychologist, Anthropologist, Botanist, Dancer, Farmer, Poet, Sociologist, Mathematician, etc.

consider the role of narrative and of the disciplines. The rest of the template moves from left to right to show a planning sequence. We will follow that sequence as we write this chapter. Ideally, there would be arrows after "Culminations" that would bring us back to the "Context." Unfortunately it is hard to represent a three-dimensional process on two dimensions.

To discuss the template, we needed names for the parts. We found that choosing terms was often difficult. Many words that appealed to us based on their dictionary definitions have developed connotations or connections that we feared might lead readers to the wrong associations. As we examine the template, we will also explain our choice of terms.

Since planning is a process, we have attempted to write this chapter in such a way that you may engage in the process of planning. After each part of the template is explained, we offer a planning invitation to you. As with any other invitation, you are free to R.S.V.P. negatively or affirmatively!

◈ Context

Context is "the overall situation in which an event occurs" (Davies, 1975, p. 157). Applied to school, context is the overall situation in which learning occurs. It is the environment that surrounds the learner and the learning. Etymologically, *context* derives from the Latin root meaning "to weave together." In terms of education, then, the context weaves together all learning. For most school experiences, context has not been an important consideration. Teachers in a transmission mode propel their students from topic to topic like a freight train through an encyclopedia. Students acquire bits of content baggage as they are moved from ancient Egypt to multiplying mixed fractions, from parts of speech to one-celled organisms. The trip is an endless string of unrelated bits of information organized by arbitrary limits of time, place, process, or skill. There is nothing provided to help students link these disparate items. To convince students that these topics have meaning and connection with the real world, each lesson is buttressed with an external rationale and motivation for learning.

Although historical inertia of past practices and an overwhelming volume of textbooks follow this encyclopedic organization of curriculum, authentic human experience presents a conflicting view. The world presents us with problems, issues, and challenges that carry with them an eclectic mix of concepts, information, and skills. If, for example, you plan to remodel your kitchen, what will you need to learn and know? The curriculum would arise from the skills and knowledge required to do the job. Blueprints and design require us to learn about scale, measurement, and building codes. Laying flooring demands that we will learn how to cut, glue, and grout tiles. The remodeling project defines the kind and amount of learning that takes place. We advocate an antithesis to the topic-driven organization so prevalent in schools. We believe that schooling is a significant portion of the life of children and that curriculum should be like life. Or, as Harste (1994) puts it, "We see curriculum as a metaphor for the lives we wish to live and the people we wish to be." Therefore, the basis of curriculum should be a meaningful context, with students acting in meaningful ways within that context.

For us, choosing an authentic context interacts with selecting the goals that focus a unit. The curriculum emanates from and is limited by the interactions that emerge. In the template, the context is depicted by a rounded box, a shape which signifies that the context is a container for the curriculum. It provides the security of natural boundaries for study. Because authentic contexts take place in real settings, involve characters, pose questions, and seek resolutions, they have all of the characteristics of a fully-articulated story. To remodel a kitchen we have a problem, we act, and there is resolution. This beginning, middle, and end nature of the narrative context forms a natural containment and keeps our study within the boundaries of the story.

When we select a narrative, we look at it as a context, not as a stimulus. Narrative cannot simply be an anticipatory set that engages us at the start and then we go on with instruction as usual. It is not a springboard to launch the learning, but rather a map that supports us in making sense of what we are doing. The narrative serves as a reference point and a lifeline that prevents us from drifting and getting lost. To keep reflecting from experience to story and from story to experience builds meaning (fig. 6.3).

FIGURE 6.3 Recursive learning

Learner constructs new meaning

Learner brings experience to story

It is the cycle of the learners interacting with the narrative that builds concepts and constructs new meaning. The learners emerge from this cycle with more meaning about the story and themselves (Rosenblatt, 1938/1976).

As we have noted in previous chapters, story provides the motivation, organization, and meaning making of the narrative-framed curriculum and it is therefore critical that we choose a story that attracts the learner and has potential for fostering inquiry. To demonstrate how the interactive process of context selection works, let us return to *Very Last First Time*. How did we decide to use this book? What were our procedures? What tests did we employ to determine if this context would meet our needs?

First and foremost, we were drawn to the story itself. The story of Eva alone under the ice captured both our emotions and our intellects. We believed it would appeal to our students both because of its strangeness and its universal appeal. The students' curiosity would be aroused by the wonder of what to them were unusual events in an equally unusual place. However, we believed they would also recognize the universal message that applied to them. "Part of what draws children to *Very Last First Time* is not simply the going under the ice but the fact that this is a story of initiation, a story that says if you are careful when you are going into danger, you will find too you have brought with you the things you need" (Jan Andrews, personal communication, July 19, 1995). In preliminary interactive readings with people of all ages we found that the story effectively claimed the reader's or listener's attention. We knew we had a good story that generated much interest and many inquiries. *Very Last First Time* makes us want to know more. We are interested in Eva because she is a believable character with whom we empathize. Her problems become ours; when she hears the tide roar and her candle snuffs out, we worry about what will happen next. Contexts that we select for the narrative curriculum must have this compelling human drama that draws us to want to know more about the places, characters, actions, and resolutions of the story. The selection of narratives will be explored more fully in chapter 7.

Knowing that the story had the power to attract and stimulate, we next looked for its curricular potential. Examining the text from a disciplinary perspective, we searched for possibilities to branch from the text to curriculum. Was there potential here for forwarding important concepts and processes of various disciplines? Summarizing the main aspects of the story, we highlighted the sections of potential interest to teacher and students. As you look at the story summary in figure 6.4, see if you agree with what we found compelling. The highlighted sections provided an authentic reason to explore maps, earth-sun-moon systems, tides, littoral zones,

FIGURE 6.4 Examining *Very Last First Time* as a narrative context

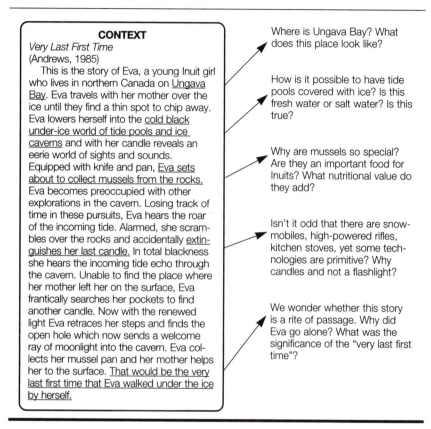

nutrition, technology, and Inuit culture. This story was a context rich in potential for inquiry and exploration. And, in the process of working through the inquiries and explorations, students would learn content that is often included in the traditional curriculum of the elementary school.

The Narrative Filter

How do we decide if the curricular adjuncts are valid? There were many other possibilities in the text suggested by words and pictures. Couldn't we also use these as links to many more topics? How do we separate the critical, core areas from tangential ones? To answer this question we use the story map. The story map tests to make sure the context has all the key elements of a fully articulated story and it keeps the curriculum planner linked to the major thrust of the story. A large body of research has demonstrated that stories can be parsed into essential components, which can then be displayed using a graphic organizer called a story map (Mandler & Johnson, 1977; Stein & Glenn, 1979; Fitzgerald & Spiegel, 1983). The map helps us decide if the story is indeed a fully articulated story, and it helps identify the issues that are related to the text directly and those that are tangential or circumstantial. The story map we prepared for *Very Last First Time*, shown in figure 6.5, helped us identify its key elements. As we planned possible inquiries and explorations, we referred to the map to determine if our ideas were directly associated with the story or were only loosely attached and therefore out of bounds. We would feel justified in finding out about Ungava Bay and the region, but would not engage in a study of Canada as a result of the story. We would find out about mussels and related sea creatures, but not launch into a study of the ocean. The story map helps corral our possible interests and keeps them central to the story itself.

There are significant reasons for keeping the strings of inquiry close to the core of the story. When we take a globe and demonstrate the length of day near the Arctic circle, when we learn more about Inuit culture, when we taste mussels for ourselves, we learn more about Eva and her environment. Our new knowledge has contributed to the story in a reflective way.

FIGURE 6.5 Story map of *Very Last First Time*

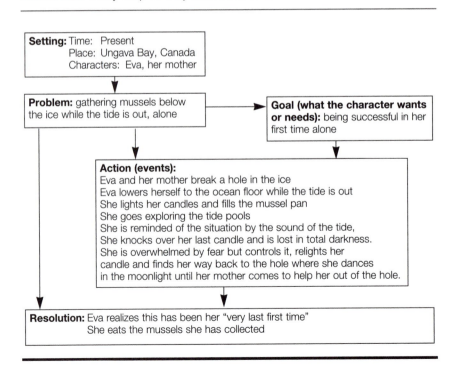

Setting: Time: Present
Place: Ungava Bay, Canada
Characters: Eva, her mother

Problem: gathering mussels below the ice while the tide is out, alone

Goal (what the character wants or needs): being successful in her first time alone

Action (events):
Eva and her mother break a hole in the ice
Eva lowers herself to the ocean floor while the tide is out
She lights her candles and fills the mussel pan
She goes exploring the tide pools
She is reminded of the situation by the sound of the tide,
She knocks over her last candle and is lost in total darkness.
She is overwhelmed by fear but controls it, relights her
candle and finds her way back to the hole where she dances
in the moonlight until her mother comes to help her out of the hole.

Resolution: Eva realizes this has been her "very last first time"
She eats the mussels she has collected

If we stretched our learning into a study of Canada, we *might* develop deeper understanding of the story and of our relationship to it, but probably not. The story map reminds us of the inquiries that are integral to the essence of the story, those that will encourage the recursive nature of learning.

The story map is part of the narrative filter, a screen for contexts. The filter requires us to look both at the elements of a fully articulated story (the purpose of story mapping) and at the essential aspect of story: its underlying themes. Since we are clarifying terms in this chapter, we need to explain what we mean by *theme*. We use it in the literary sense of indicating the underlying idea of a story. It is the message the author wishes to convey about life and it is the meaning the reader preserves long after the details of the story are forgotten. Some guidelines adapted from Perrine (1983) help us understand theme.

▌ Theme must be expressible as a statement with a subject and a predicate.

▌ Theme must be stated as a generalization about life.

▌ Theme is the central and unifying concept of a story.

▌ One should avoid any statement that reduces the theme to a familiar saying or trite expression.

We agree with Perrine (1983) and Lukens (1990) that themes need to be stated as sentences. Lukens explains:

> Why not say, "The theme of *Charlotte's Web* is friendship"? Notice what happens if we do state the theme this simply. Friendship is too broad a term: "Friendship is fraudulent," or "Friendship is a useless luxury," or "Friendship is all giving and no receiving." Any of these statements concerns friendship and might reasonably be explored and proven in literature, but none is the truth of E. B. White's story. When we force ourselves to make a specific statement based upon the facts of the story, we define the theme more carefully. (p. 90)

Themes are too complex and abstract to be expressed by a single word or short phrase.

Theme has been used quite differently by other writers, especially those discussing integrated curriculum. Sometimes theme is used to refer to topics such as bears, apples, dinosaurs, or insects. Many authors caution against these sorts of topics and advocate themes that are more conceptual, with meaningful relationships embedded in them (Edelsky, Altwerger, & Flores, 1991; Routman, 1991; Stevens, 1993; Manning, Manning, & Long, 1994). However, even these authors are still using theme as a label of the organizer of the curriculum. Thus, ideas diverse as "laughing out loud" and "oceanography" and "appreciating cultural differences" are listed as themes. While we like what these authors say about children and learning, we differ from them in our use of the term *theme*. For us, theme is a statement of meaning rather than a curriculum organizer.

The narrative filter reminds us of the importance of theme. It also helps us eliminate superficially attractive contexts from authentic narratives. Using topics such as penguins, flight, and Texas, or concepts such as community, cycle, and system as contexts fails to capitalize on the inherent benefits of story. Topics and concepts are fields of information without the rhythm of story and they have no inherent theme, no essential kernel of meaning. There is no opportunity to enrich one's personal story if there are no stories with which to interact. Story, by definition, is a structure that provides meaning and a way of knowing. The narrative filter forces us to examine our chosen context to ensure that all the benefits of narrative are intact for the learner.

An Invitation to Use the Template: *Selecting a Context*

Before you begin your own narrative curriculum planning, we thought it might be helpful if we elucidate our process of examining each variable. While we do not literally make a chart and fill in the boxes with "yes" and "no" as we have shown in figure 6.6, we used this graphic form to make our thinking apparent to you. The example for this "think-aloud," *The Green Book*, generated an extensive list of inquiries. Note how we have tested each possible inquiry with a set of criteria.

We first asked the question, "Does this book contain a fully articulated story?" Can we find all of the key elements? Does it have a significant underlying theme? As we outlined the setting, characters, and other elements on the story map we found that it indeed was a fully articulated story (fig 6.7). We also found that the book's themes welcomed many opportunities for connections: Humankind's proclivity to pioneer, the role of stories and written records in human culture, the role of technology in society, and the interaction of cultures.

We next generated a lengthy list of possible student inquiries by carefully rereading the text. We then tested each possible inquiry with the second question, "Are the potential inquiries and explorations authentic to the context?" Several of the inquiries failed that test immediately. We found some questions like "Can we eat ground glass?" tangential to the main issues the book raises. On the other hand, several inquiries were key to our further understanding of the story. Questions related to the characters and their motivations, to the nature of the planet and its natural system, to the organisms they encountered, and to the problems of the settlers matched the essential elements of story.

The third question asks whether the context will match the interests of our students. Because we knew that our students were interested in fantasy

FIGURE 6.6 Screening possible inquiries

Brainstormed list of inquiries from *The Green Book*	Are the potential inquiries and explorations authentic to the context?	Is this a compelling context and inquiry that will interest your students?	Are there opportunities to access the disciplines?
What would you take on a voyage?	Yes	Yes	Yes
What book would you take?	Yes	Yes	Yes
What would you do with a blank book?	Yes	Yes	Yes
What happened to the earth?	No	Yes	Yes
What would make it change color, to become colder?	No	No	No
What causes heat on a planet?	No	Yes	Yes
How did they navigate?	No	No	Yes
How do magnetic fields work?	No	No	Yes
Gravity in space?	No	No	Yes
Why don't things fall in space?	No	No	Yes
What was the length of journey and the time spent?	Yes	No	Yes
How fast did they go?	No	No	Yes
What does this landscape look like?	Yes	Yes	Yes
How do you know the water and air is good?	Yes	No	Yes
What causes weather?	No	No	Yes
Why is there no weather?	No	No	Yes
Why no riffles where water meets lake?	No	No	No
How long are the days?	No	No	Yes
What kind of calendar would work?	No	No	Yes
Why immediate and complete darkness?	No	No	Yes
What would the crystals look like?	Yes	Yes	Yes
Why can't you crosscut trees?	No	Yes	No
What about the biology of the moth people?	Yes	Yes	Yes
What were the jellyfish like?	No	Yes	No
Why is wheat so important?	Yes	No	No
What's a seed drill?	No	Yes	No
What is intermediate technology?	Yes	Yes	Yes
What are Candy Trees? Like maple trees?	Yes	Yes	Yes
What was the life cycle of the moth people?	Yes	Yes	Yes
What was their dance? A mating ritual?	No	Yes	Yes
How did they plant, care for, harvest the wheat?	Yes	No	Yes
What was the "pill" they talked about?	No	Yes	No
Why did the people like the idea of recording the story of their colonization?	Yes	Yes	Yes

FIGURE 6.7 Story map of *The Green Book*

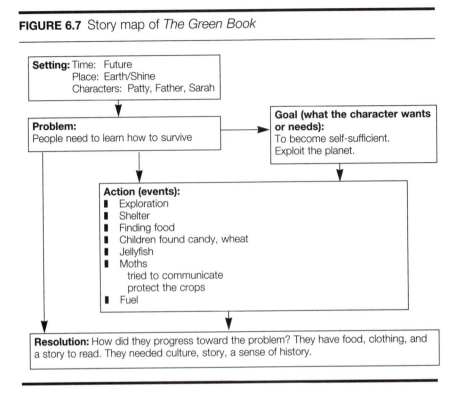

and adventure it was a good bet that they would like this book. Prior experience with students of various ages also helped confirm the potential this book had to stimulate readers of any age.

Finally, we considered the question, "Will there be opportunities to access the disciplines?" Can we think like artists, astronomers, explorers, and so forth as we begin to delve into the inquiries? As we examined the list, there were a few questions that we could not readily identify as supporting a disciplinary way of knowing. These were dropped in deference to others that showed a clear invitation to think in a particular disciplinary manner. We knew that puzzles about the moth people, for example, would lead us to an opportunity for students to engage in observational processes practiced by scientists. Interpreting what the planet looked like exercises both an aesthetic eye and an interpretive reader's eye. Screening the inquiry possibilities with the criteria questions assured us that the remaining inquiries were valid and would lead to valuable explorations. This sifting of possibilities allowed us to proceed with the planning process with confidence that we were remaining true to our principles of curriculum design.

FIGURE 6.8 Criteria for context

Criteria for Context

1. Is it narrative in structure?
   > Can we find the key elements of story?
   > Does it have a significant underlying theme(s)?

2. Are the potential inquiries and explorations authentic to the context?

3. Is it a compelling context that matches your students' interests?
   Can you generate interest for this story among your students?

4. Are there opportunities to access the disciplines?

We now invite you to select a context for yourself. We have provided a short story in Appendix A that may have potential as a narrative context. As you read "The Pine Tree Shillings," use the questions in figure 6.8 to help guide your thinking.

To record your thinking, fill in the sections of the story map (a blank one is included in Appendix A). Then, summarize the story in the context space on a blank template (also in Appendix A). Underline those key areas that you believe to have potential for exploration. Brainstorm some of the disciplinary perspectives that could be brought to the context. In addition, consider the match between the context and your students. For example, we brought the pine tree shilling story to one group of fifth graders who had some background knowledge of colonial America and who had been reading some of Hawthorne's "Wonder Tales." They immediately took to the story, as did a group of graduate-level students in a mathematics education class. Students with other backgrounds might not.

Other contexts may come to mind or other pieces of literature may be considered as a narrative context. Experiment with several sources and filter these sources with the questions we have suggested. You may also wish to examine contexts that may not pass the narrative filter test. For example, many instructional units are based on topics such as rivers, bears, the Civil War, penguins, flight, and so forth. Try one of these examples or one of your choice and determine whether it meets the criteria of a meaningful context.

❖ Inquiries

With the context firmly established, the next portion of the template assists with planning inquiries and explorations (fig. 6.9). This process involves at least three conscious actions: deciding which inquiries and explorations will be encouraged, shaping explorations according to a disciplinary heuristic, and planning explorations that are consistent with selected goals. Educators have used the term *inquiry* to represent a range

FIGURE 6.9 Planning inquiries and explorations

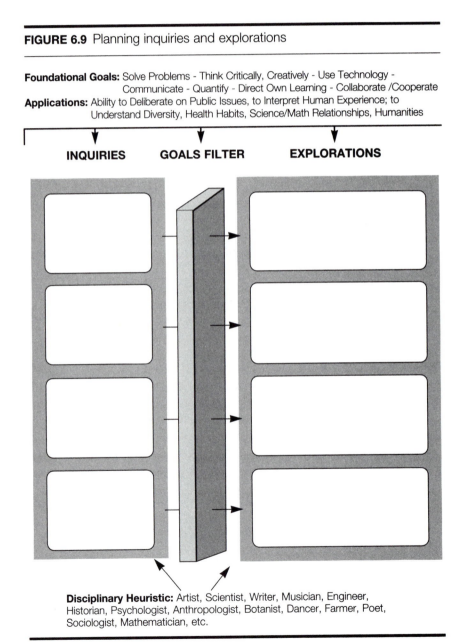

Foundational Goals: Solve Problems - Think Critically, Creatively - Use Technology - Communicate - Quantify - Direct Own Learning - Collaborate /Cooperate
Applications: Ability to Deliberate on Public Issues, to Interpret Human Experience; to Understand Diversity, Health Habits, Science/Math Relationships, Humanities

INQUIRIES   GOALS FILTER   EXPLORATIONS

Disciplinary Heuristic: Artist, Scientist, Writer, Musician, Engineer, Historian, Psychologist, Anthropologist, Botanist, Dancer, Farmer, Poet, Sociologist, Mathematician, etc.

of meaning, from the act of stating a question to defining a theory of learning. We use *inquiry* to mean a search for truth, information, or knowledge. This definition leads to a broad and permissive path that invites learners to explore the world in all possible ways.

How are inquiries evoked from the context? Does the teacher plan all inquiries ahead of time? Do students generate all the questions and then pursue what they find compelling? Or is there a mix of both these perspectives?

Students' Roles in Inquiries

A context is chosen based on the inquiries the teacher believes it will generate. But we must also examine the text from the students' perspectives. What will students be interested in? What will their questions be? Experienced teachers are usually good at picking out those things that students will find interesting or puzzling. With continued experience we become increasingly accurate in predicting which questions students will pose. We sketch into the template the questions that students are likely to ask and the ones that we find compelling.

Initially, then, the inquiries reflect ideas that we believe are critical and those that we believe children will suggest. However, we must always leave space for the inquiries students generate that we did not anticipate. These must always be considered valid and valuable. Our planning at this point does NOT create a list of what must be done but rather generates a plan of what is possible so that we can be prepared for the possibilities. Students' input is always the deciding factor in what inquiries are actually pursued. How teachers solicit inquiries and subsequently arrange inquiries for consideration will be discussed in chapters 8 and 9.

Disciplinary Perspectives on Inquiries

A second consideration that shapes our inquiries focuses on the nature of how the different disciplines approach problems. How would an astronomer, an author, an anthropologist, an oceanographer, and a sociologist, to name a few, approach the context of *Very Last First Time?* What inquiries would these professionals pursue? We find it helpful to have students pose questions from these perspectives because it broadens the scope and depth of inquiry. The disciplinary heuristic is the filter that we use to describe this process. What questions would practitioners in these disciplines ask? What would they be interested in? For a scientist, *Very Last First Time* has some tantalizing puzzles that beg inquiry: What tidal or freshwater system created these ice caverns? Are there special types of sea creatures living here? Is this frozen salt water or fresh water? Is it possible to see the moon directly overhead at that latitude? For an anthropologist, other things may stand out: Is Eva's story a rite of passage? What specific group of Inuits is represented? What is the evidence that this village has adopted Anglo-European traditions? Each discipline offers a separate vantage point, a way of knowing embedded in the process and patterns practiced by its patrons. In this respect the heuristic encompasses not only content of the subject or the facts of information, but also the nature of how the disciplinary expert thinks.

If both students and teachers address inquiries in this manner, many more questions are raised and many more opportunities arise for achieving goals. We ask students to "think like a _____" and to ask questions or to tell what they would want to know from that perspective. For example, when we provided mussels for students to explore, we asked that they put themselves into the roles of biologist, nutritionist, and musician. Students generated different lists of inquiries from each heading based on their prior knowledge and perceptions of what would be important to each professional. As a biologist they suggested that we could look inside to see the parts of a mussel, that we look in a book to find out more about how the creature lives, that we perform some kind of experiment to see how it moves and reacts to touch. Students thought that a nutritionist might want to know about the food value of the mussel. How many calories? How could we cook it? Did it have any important vitamins and minerals? From a musician's perspective the inquiries centered on making instruments from the shells and the lyrics of songs we might create to describe the mussel and mussel collecting and eating.

This process requires, of course, that students and teachers have some understanding of disciplinary heuristics and that they are able to consciously control means of inquiry. The role of the teacher is critical. By prompting examination though a particular disciplinary lens and by modeling that perspective by thinking aloud, the teacher can open up new ways of knowing and extend the realm of possibilities for exploration. The teacher must be able to articulate disciplinary questions in order to model the thought processes of the core disciplines. Teachers must realize the distinction between the content of a discipline and its worldview. This may seem insurmountable for those who have learned history, science, math, art, and language as contents to memorize. Learning the disciplines as ways of knowing is worth the effort because they are powerful tools for inquiry and exploration.

An Invitation to the Planner: *Generating Inquiries*

You may wish to continue your planning template by creating inquiries from the context. Remember that these should emerge from the main aspects of the context and should be related to theme, setting, characters,

conflict, action, or resolution of the story. Inquiries may be stated as questions or simply as things you would want to know more about.

For now, list all the inquiries that seem to fit. You may need to add to (or delete) the spaces provided for this purpose since there is no magic number of inquiries resident in "The Pine Tree Shillings" or any other narrative context. After you have generated inquiries from the narrative, test them with the criteria found in figure 6.10.

After the context is presented to the students, the inquiries should be adjusted by selecting those with the greatest potential for satisfying all of the aforementioned issues. Ideally, a few carefully chosen inquiries that interest both teacher and students will remain. These inquiries must contribute to a way of knowing about the world and students' personal

---

FIGURE 6.10 Criteria for inquiries

Criteria for Inquiries

1. Is the inquiry directly related to an essential element of the text?

2. Does the inquiry lead to a resolution that will help the learner understand more about the context? Does the inquiry support the recursive nature of learning?

3. Does the inquiry honor the heuristic of a discipline?

4. Have you allowed for inquiries from the students?

---

experiences within it; they must help students practice a disciplinary perspective; and their exploration must move students toward the achievement of selected goals.

This process usually takes several passes of looking at the context, posing questions, testing possibilities, and predicting the most effective avenues of exploration. With practice, a curriculum planner can complete this process in fewer, more intuitive steps.

The Goals Filter

We now have a rich context and a group of selected inquiries. We have found it critical at this point to remind ourselves of goals. As we asserted emphatically in chapter 4, goals must buoy the curriculum and provide a rationale for learning. Goals must be part of the curriculum planner's schema so that they act simultaneously with the selection of the context. However, we want inquiries to be open to all possibilities that both the students and teachers generate. As in brainstorming, all ideas are first accepted, and only then evaluated. Thus, the goals need to be reconsidered at this time. Although written text forces us to discuss the parts of the template sequentially, we have tried to portray with our graphic organizer that in our thinking, goals operate concurrently with the selection of the context and they filter the inquiries before explorations are designed.

A curriculum planner must explore many different possibilities while maintaining a solid grasp on the set of goals for which the planner is responsible. For example, we found several opportunities for authentic inquiry in *Very Last First Time*. In the example shown in figure 6.11, we have indicated the goal of understanding diversity as a critical element in directing the students' work and thought. Sifting all of the inquiries through the filter, we found only a few that could serve the goal. Questions that enhanced our learning of other cultures, such as "Does the Inuit culture celebrate rites of passage?" and "What are the images on the walls of the ice caves?" address the goal. Other inquiries such as "Where do they get their supplies?" and "How do animals in the tide pools live under the ice?" may better serve other goals. If students can explore and use resources to pursue their inquiries then we have honored the goal of self-directed learning and problem solving. If students use language to collect data, invent meaning, and report findings, then we have honored the broad goal of communication. If students are encouraged to examine the differences and similarities in Eva's culture and story to their own culture and story, then we are shaping an understanding of diversity. The potential of the story to generate these opportunities for learning are weighed with the internal understanding teachers have

---

FIGURE 6.11 The goals filter in action

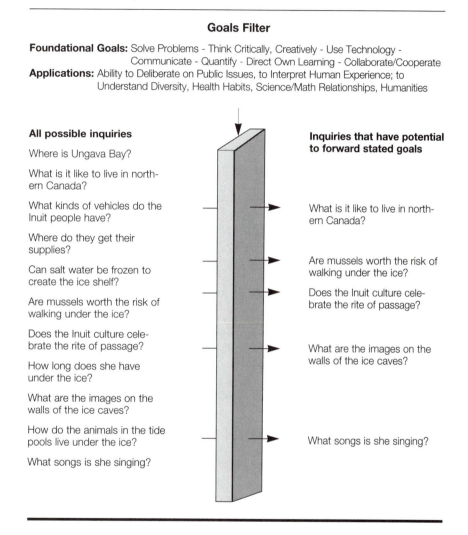

Goals Filter

Foundational Goals: Solve Problems - Think Critically, Creatively - Use Technology - Communicate - Quantify - Direct Own Learning - Collaborate/Cooperate
Applications: Ability to Deliberate on Public Issues, to Interpret Human Experience; to Understand Diversity, Health Habits, Science/Math Relationships, Humanities

All possible inquiries

Where is Ungava Bay?

What is it like to live in northern Canada?

What kinds of vehicles do the Inuit people have?

Where do they get their supplies?

Can salt water be frozen to create the ice shelf?

Are mussels worth the risk of walking under the ice?

Does the Inuit culture celebrate the rite of passage?

How long does she have under the ice?

What are the images on the walls of the ice caves?

How do the animals in the tide pools live under the ice?

What songs is she singing?

Inquiries that have potential to forward stated goals

What is it like to live in northern Canada?

Are mussels worth the risk of walking under the ice?

Does the Inuit culture celebrate the rite of passage?

What are the images on the walls of the ice caves?

What songs is she singing?

---

about the purposes for schooling. In this way, the use of goals filters the inquiries and subsequent explorations, thereby focusing our energies more efficiently. We must always have a purpose for what we do.

We must resist the temptation to be charmed by a story and simply nod at the goals while planning activities. We can collect a variety of activities related to *Very Last First Time* and then tick off the goals that might be related as a post-facto rationale for the curriculum we have invented. Putting it another way, we decide what we are going to do, then justify it by naming goals that may incidentally be served. This is an unacceptable practice since it leads easily to a "curriculum-as-activities" approach. Furthermore, it indicates that the curriculum planner does not have ownership of goals or does not recognize the important role of goals in education.

We must also guard against forcing contexts to serve goals that are ill-suited. We could have chosen quantification as a probable goal for the context of *Very Last First Time*. Quantification means that students are able to recognize when and how to apply mathematical relationships. Some of our explorations from *Very Last First Time* did require the use of numbers and mathematical manipulation so we may be tempted to cite quantification as a goal for the unit. But, to do so would not necessarily forward that goal. If quantification were the goal we had to address, then we would need to find a story that does present a focus on, or authentic context for, quantification. The goal filter prevents the curriculum planner from attributing a goal to a context without careful consideration. Using the planning template in this way requires that teachers understand and own the goals so that they can choose contexts that naturally produce inquiries in the designated goal arena.

Concerns About Content

It is usually at about this point that teachers begin to wrestle with the question of content. We can anticipate some of your worries: How will I be able to cover the information that we are required to teach? How will I fit all the necessary information into this kind of a curriculum? How will content be articulated between grade levels?

We respond to these questions by asking a question: What information is important, critical, or vital to the schooling of a child? (By information here we mean typical textbook content, such as the three classes of simple machines, the seven types of sentences, the major battles of the Civil War and their dates, the functions of vitamins, the operational definitions of mathematics such as numerator and dividend, and the rules for badminton.) Your reception of the narrative curriculum depends on your answer to that question. If your answer agrees with Hirsch's (1987) notion that acquiring a common core of information is an absolute requirement for students, then the narrative curriculum becomes problematic.

As an example, let us suppose that we must teach the three types of machines in third-grade science. If every child must be able to give the operational definition of a plane, pulley, and lever, and list an example of each, then there are faster and more efficient ways of transmitting that information. (See chapter 3, transmission model of teaching.) Transmitting information negates child-centered curriculum and relegates the function of planning to simply having our own way. Although it would be valid, hypothetically, to develop a narrative curriculum that came from a story about a pharaoh, and then anticipate that students would be interested in pyramid building and ultimately the simple machines the Egyptians employed, that curriculum would still be unlikely to lead to the required objective. Although students may use pulleys, planes, and levers if they make pyramid models, must they learn operational definitions to be successful? The operational definitions, classifications, and hierarchical layers were created to organize the content curriculum. This kind of information is of little value when we pursue real problems and apply information in living our lives.

The decision about the value of specific content is critical. After all, the content curriculum is our heritage. In our own educational histories we all dutifully marched through courses and textbooks acquiring what textbook authors and publishers believed to be important, if not essential, information. We all learned facts, names, dates, lists, and symbols, but was all this "stuff" critical for living intelligent, moral, and happy lives? Darling-Hammond (1994, p. 490) raises another important reason for reconsidering a curriculum driven by content.

> While it is possible to reach a knowledge-based consensus among members of the teaching profession about how children learn well and what the implications of that are for practice, questions of precisely what pieces of content children should learn, how, and when are in some sense irresolvable. Knowledge is exploding at an ever more rapid rate, and decisions about particular ways of construing that knowledge are always to some extent arbitrary... Given that there is too much to be known, we will never derive a national answer that reveals the Truth about exactly which facts students should know or which subtopics they should study at particular moments in their lives.

Noddings (1995a) argues against the dogma of content by questioning whether we should force all students to study a narrowly prescribed curriculum devoid of content they might truly care about, while ignoring the wider range of human capacities. It is difficult to wrest ourselves free from the content that we have traditionally called curriculum, but we must open ourselves to new ways of thinking. In doing so, we do not advocate a no-content approach. Rather, content should be a natural outgrowth of meaningful contexts in which students acquire and apply knowledge.

Our experience has shown us that children engaged in narrative curriculum do learn a great deal of content. If we choose contexts carefully, inquiries and explorations will generate both traditional curriculum content and new information previously unvisited by school textbook writers. The examples we have presented in this book demonstrate the rich content that emanates from a meaningful context. Facts about the Arctic Circle, Canada, Inuits, mussels, byssal fibers, tides, Northern Lights, tide pools, batteries, motors, circuits, rheostats, igloos, Eskimos, latitude, longitude, Oslo,

Ungava Bay, sled dogs, and ice fishing were just a few of the pieces of information that sprang up from the exploration of *Very Last First Time*. Students learned things that are normally taught in several different grade levels of traditional science, social studies, and language arts. They learned other things that are found nowhere in the traditional curriculum. They learned these things because the curriculum had been shifted from an arbitrary organization of content to a logical one based upon a specific context.

Ultimately, as teachers, we must decide if we have the freedom and risk-taking ability to make this shift and depart from the scope and sequence spiral. One way to begin is to devote a portion of the total school time to narrative curriculum. Not comfortable with leaving the traditional curriculum totally, teachers and schools might choose an alternative curriculum model during part of the day or part of the year. Fort Pitt Elementary School, for example, decided to depart from the traditional curriculum one week out of each month (Hartman, DeCicco & Griffin, 1994). Other plans of compromise can be negotiated.

We recognize that due to the issue of content coverage, some curriculum planners may find the narrative curriculum to be too risky. Indeed, if we are unable or unwilling to reexamine the role of content in the curriculum then the narrative curriculum has little chance of succeeding. Because we believe that foundational goals are by far the most important rationale for schooling, we do not limit our children's learning to the hegemony of a perceived common culture of content. For those who consider particular pieces of information as necessities, the narrative curriculum may not be the most appropriate model.

An Invitation to the Planner: *Selecting Goals*

As in the previous invitation section, let us talk through how we operationalize the process of selecting the focus goals of a unit. Figure 6.12 illustrates how we analyze the context and inquiries from *The Green Book* according to criteria about goals.

FIGURE 6.12 Criteria for goals

Criteria for Goals

1. Does the context have potential in facilitating the goals of schooling?

2. Are the goals that are assigned to the context clearly related to possible inquiries and explorations that emerge?

3. Are the assigned goals central to the intended instruction or are they attributed after the activities have been chosen?

To objectively examine the context and inquiries, we ask, "Do they have potential to facilitate the goals of schooling?" Which of our established set of goals interact with the context and inquiries to meet the needs of learners? An important thing to remember here, as we described in chapter 4, is that we have already established a set of goals for our students. At this point, our task is to select from that set of goals those which will receive attention in conjunction with the context. From *The Green Book* context, we determined that many of the inquiries would lead students to engage in personal research. Experimentation, model building, and artistic interpretation are logical explorations related to these inquiries. The goal of self-directed learning seems an ideal match. Further, as we look at the hand skills students will use in manipulating materials and tools we know that we can target appropriate uses of technology as a second goal. Finally, we have an ongoing need to activate the goal of effective communication. There appears to be ample opportunity for students to read, find information, write, share orally, create visuals, and consider the role of literacy and literature in society and personal life.

Finally, we asked the question: "Are the assigned goals central to the intended instruction or are they attributed after the activities have been chosen?" The three goals that we chose are ones that make sense to us as we think now about the inquiries and as we think ahead to possible explorations. We might have chosen to focus on other goals, but we did not because they were not integral to the context. We did not select the goal of "appreciating diversity" because no diversity issues were apparent. If we had selected this goal, we would have had to require students to engage in activities such as considering the gender roles and class systems suggested in the narrative. These issues are tangential to the main action and theme of the story—focusing on them would create a situation we are trying to avoid.

The process of looking for contexts, brainstorming inquiries, and thinking about possible explorations is highly interactive with our established goals. We made a decision about which goals could be best served as we thought about the possibilities the context might offer. Once we made our decision and identified the focus goals, we used them as continual compass points to direct our work. Ever after, in the planning, in facilitating explorations, in helping students come to resolutions, and in assessing learning, goals were our constant guides.

You may now wish to return to the template that you have started and use the goals filter. You should select goals that fit your current professional situation. You may wish to replace the goals we have listed at the top of the template with those that are particular to the school, district, or state in which you teach or will teach. If you are not currently working from a foundation of goals, it may be helpful to you to post an appropriate set of goals in some conspicuous place so that you will begin to internalize them.

🔶 Explorations

From the inquiries generated by students and teacher we move to planning explorations. Explorations are investigations, adventures in discovery. *Explore*, according to *Webster's Ninth New Collegiate Dictionary* (Mish, 1989), has three meanings. To explore is to investigate, study, analyze, and become familiar with by testing or experimenting. To explore also means to travel over new territory for adventure or discovery. Lastly, to explore means to examine minutely. The Latin root reminds us that to explore is to search out. All these meanings combine to form our concept of exploration. Exploration implies that learners are actively doing something. To achieve their purpose, they travel where they need or want to go even though neither they, nor their teacher, are always sure of what they will find. We avoid the use of the word *activity* because it connotes a form of action limited by rules and sets of directions to achieve a known result.

Explorations that arise from simple questions, such as "Where is Ungava Bay?" are fairly straightforward opportunities to discover. As teachers, we call on students' prior knowledge of atlases, maps, globes, or other media sources as a strategy for finding out. The students' simple exploration can be to find Ungava Bay on a map or in an atlas. If these tools are unknown to the students, teachers will have to plan lessons to teach them the necessary skills. However, even these seemingly simple inquiries can turn out to be complex. The "Where is Ungava Bay?" question led to discussions of tundra and tree lines, length of a day during various seasons, and climate at various latitudes.

Complex inquiries require even more complex explorations. To find out whether salt water will freeze, students need to experiment with fresh and salt water to explore freezing points. We may need to consult weather maps, tide charts, or even experts knowledgeable about the region. The exploration may be a process of trying to find out rather than a resolution that yields a specific answer.

The critical elements of planning explorations are rooted in previous dialogue about goals and disciplinary heuristics. Explorations must forward goals and must honor the way of knowing that a discipline demands. Let us elaborate once again with an example which is summarized in figure 6.13. In *Very Last First Time* a great deal of tension is created when Eva is isolated in darkness under the ice. We fear for her safety and wonder if the tide will overcome her. We want to know how long she has to find her way out. Thus, we felt that a valid inquiry to pursue was the passage of time. This is reinforced by the response of nearly all readers of this story who ask the same compelling question, "How long has she been under the ice?" One way of determining the passage of time was the burning of her candles. Another way of determining time is by investigating how long the tide stays out.

FIGURE 6.13 Screening possible explorations

Brainstormed list of explorations from *The Green Book* inquiries	Does the exploration empower students to determine a resolution to the question?	Does the exploration afford the students an opportunity to acquire or refine process skills?	Does the exploration forward the goals that we have assigned to the instructional unit?	Does the exploration offer students a direct linkage to the question posed?	Is this exploration something a disciplinary expert is likely to engage in?
Inquiry 1: What would you take on a voyage? Possible exploration: Students could brainstorm lists of materials and their rationales as a "lifeboat" exercise.	Yes	Yes	No	Yes	No
Inquiry 2: What book would you take? Possible exploration: Students could survey various people in the community to determine their book choices.	Yes	Yes	Yes	Yes	Yes
Inquiry 3: What would you do with a blank book? Possible exploration: Students could create their own blank book and use it to record their own findings and recollections of learning.	Yes	Yes	Yes	Yes	Yes
Inquiry 4: What does this landscape look like? Possible exploration: Students could create visual or three-dimensional images of the planet's features from the description provided in the story.	Yes	Yes	Yes	Yes	Yes
Inquiry 5: What would the crystals look like? Possible exploration: Students could create crystal gardens from various chemical sources and examine structure with a hand lens.	Yes	Yes	No	No	Yes
Inquiry 6: What is intermediate technology? Possible exploration: Students could identify a need in the community and create an intermediate technology solution.	Yes	Yes	Yes	Yes	Yes
Inquiry 7: What was the life cycle of the moth people? Possible exploration: Students could examine the life cycle of the meal worm or wax moth and compare the stages of growth.	Yes	Yes	Yes	Yes	Yes

Planning an exploration that helps resolve this matter must be interactive with the selected goals. If we had set critical thinking as one of the primary goals for this unit, then we would try to match the exploration to that end. In this example, we would give students a variety of candles, have them devise a measuring system for length or mass, and then plan an experiment to test the longevity of different candles. In another exploration, they learn about the movement of the tide through the use of tide charts, simulation of tidal movement on the earth, and visual representations of tidal movement. Then they compare the results of the two explorations to determine how much time might have passed. We have honored our critical thinking goal by directing the exploration in a particular manner.

We might have selected another goal—understanding the human experience. Then the exploration would be different. We might ask students to simulate Eva's experience under the ice by sitting in a darkened room, playing an audio tape to simulate the tide, and lighting a single candle. We might ask students to study the shapes Eva sees on the rocks and walls under the water and to draw the images they would see there. As students reflect on the simulation, they may relate to Eva's encounter and become more aware of the human experiences of others.

In each of these cases we might also ask, "Is this the approach or the nature of the exploration that a disciplinary expert would take?" If critical thinking had been our goal for students as they explore candles and tides, then what disciplines provide a suitable methodology? Scientists would approach the inquiry with the perspective and acquired skill of their discipline: how to form a hypothesis, how to plan a controlled experiment, how to collect and analyze data, and how to generalize upon the results are some of the heuristics that would operate here. If we had opted to have the goal of "understanding the human experience" operational in this inquiry, then a different heuristic would be active. A sociologist, artist, or psychologist would bring a different set of perspectives, skills, and interests: How to characterize and chronicle human observations, how to communicate impressions and emotions, how to generalize about traditions, culture, and their meaning. We must be aware that goals and disciplines interact as we craft explorations and that certain natural affinities do develop. We forward a goal by selecting the disciplinary heuristic that seems best suited for that purpose. Consider exploring how much time Eva had under the ice from an artistic perspective. Would that discipline contribute the most to resolving the question? Likewise, would an empirical, experimental approach by a scientist be appropriate for communication of the emotional impact of the experience?

The goal filter and the referral to the disciplinary heuristic keep us aware of the purposes of our explorations and provide the planner with consistent feedback about the appropriateness of activities. As we have suggested in the previous sections, goals must be actively engaged before we begin to decide what our explorations will be. We may decide to dissect, identify, and study mussels as a way of learning more about Eva's quarry. However, if we had not identified a goal that gives purpose to this exploration beforehand, then it probably fails to effectively move students toward anything purposeful. To learn about mussels may be a fun diversion for an hour or two, but unless we can become better observers, journal writers, problem solvers, or dietitians, we should not revere the activity as particularly valuable in itself.

Planning the explorations further requires consideration of the third tenet of constructivist curriculum—the way learners build meaning. Because we believe that learners need to create meaning from experience, we should take a constructive approach to designing explorations. Within explorations, students should have opportunities to activate prior knowledge, share new experiences with others, and make meaning from those experiences. Materials, activities, and resources should give learners tools and strategies rather than prescribed routes to follow. For our exploration of sun-planet systems, solar radiation, and seasons in arctic areas, we chose to provide students with the tools to demonstrate how the rays of the sun heat the earth's surface. Since the challenge was to explain why Ungava Bay would be cold, students used globes, lamps, and thermometers to demonstrate their ideas. We could have created a lesson that would have transmitted the knowledge to students in a direct fashion using a simple demonstration, a reading assignment in a textbook, a film, or a lecture. But, because we believe that conceptual understanding arises from the learner's construction of meaning, the exploration was designed to allow students to generate their own ideas. A social setting in which exploratory and collaborative talk (Peterson, 1992; Wells & Chang-Wells, 1992; Pierce & Gilles, 1993) were encouraged facilitated active learning.

Gathering resources and materials is time-intensive work, not restricted to the narrative curriculum planning process, but certainly a necessity for it. In our work with *Very Last First Time*, for example, we had to plan well in advance to have materials available when the unit began: maps, globes, databases, print resources, lamps, thermometers, wax paper, meter sticks, charcoal, drawing paper, water, containers, access to refrigeration, trays, mussels, a knife, a hot plate, napkins… and much more! We also had to be willing to scramble for additional resources according to student-generated inquiries. This kind of teaching and learning requires that we do our best to assemble an environment for learning that allows students to explore.

An Invitation to the Planner: *Considering Explorations*

As you work with the nearly complete "The Pine Tree Shillings" planning template, think about the inquiries that you have posed. What explorations would be possible? As you craft ideas for student explorations, test what you have planned for students to do by answering the questions

---

FIGURE 6.14 Criteria for explorations

Criteria for Explorations

1. Does the exploration empower students to determine a resolution to the question?

2. Does the exploration offer students a direct linkage to the question posed? In other words, if we proceed with the planned exploration, will it likely provide insights about the question and feedback to the narrative?

3. Does the exploration forward the goals that we have assigned to the instructional unit? For example, if you have assigned a goal of "Collaborative and Cooperative Learning" in the template, is the exploration likely to forward that goal in a direct way?

4. Does the exploration afford the students an opportunity to acquire new process skills or refine previously learned ones?

5. Is this exploration something a disciplinary expert is likely to engage in?

---

in figure 6.14. Notice that the emphasis here is on how students could find out, *not* how the teacher could inform.

The space on the template allows for only a brief title or description of the exploration. The materials, supplies, and more elaborate plans for instruction need to be written outside the template. One method that expands this process is to write the short exploration summary on the template and then to index the detailed plans with a number or letter. Chapter 10 includes several examples of this style of planning.

Culminations

As we reach the end of a story, the resolutions to the problems and challenges presented are finally realized. The cycle embodied by a fully articulated story anticipates the cycle of our curriculum planning. Just as we have created an opportunity for the learner to pursue the resolution of their own inquiries, we must provide an opportunity to celebrate the culminations of those explorations. We conclude the planning process by considering the possible culminations that students will offer as they conclude their work.

Culmination means to reach the highest, climatic, decisive point. Learners involved in active exploration reach destinations that are truly high and decisive points of resolution. The products of our explorations are culminations. Whatever we discover, however we communicate that insight, and any tangible products from our quest, all contribute to culminations.

Culminations provide opportunities for learners to publicly share the products of their explorations.

There are few vivid and compelling recollections of school that can compare to the celebrations of learning. We recall animated children reciting tales they invented to describe how local natural places came to be named. We recall students adamantly advocating the models they had created to solve the problem of lack of playground facilities. We recall five young women performing a readers' theater they had written about pioneer life on the Oregon Trail. We recall a challenged learner weary from pounding copper sheets into model coins make a profound realization about the value of work and reward. We recall these culminations of learning as journeys completed—as true celebrations of accomplishments. These are the things we, as teachers and as learners, cherish about the learning process.

Culminating events can be one of the most powerful aspects of the narrative curriculum. As we have noted before, explorations should be designed to help students answer their own inquiries. The results of explorations, or culminations of learning, are by their nature recursive. Whatever we find out informs us about the inquiry and returns us to the context from which we began. This connectedness gives a reason for engaging in our explorations and meaning to our findings. Students have little difficulty in placing a value on what they know. Phrases like "this helped me understand more about…" or, "now I understand why…" abound in the oral and written reflections of students.

Because culminations are shared within the community of learners, they inform us and link us with others engaged in related quests. Interesting things happen when learners share their findings in culminating events. First, we notice that learners are keenly interested in each others' work. Because all learning is contained by the original context, the culminations of learning are all linked. We have noticed that students are more likely to respond to others' findings interactively. For example, children who created model gliders from balsa wood kits were keenly interested in another group's attempt to create paper gliders from a computer-generated planning program. They compared their products and dialogued about how they had done their work. This authentic attentiveness to others' findings contributes to each student's acquisition of new knowledge.

Culminations are also an incredible opportunity to demonstrate learning to external audiences. When learners are given an opportunity to share their findings with parents, professionals, and others outside the classroom, learning becomes externally validated. One vivid example comes to mind. One of our classes had chosen to explore some ways of enhancing community recreation opportunities. Their inquiry led them to explore possibilities for improving the local playground. They created models that depicted what they would like to see installed on the playground—mazes, swinging ropes, forts. Initially students engaged in this exploration more in a sense of play and hypothetical practice rather than any real-world action. When the school principal and a member of the city council became interested in their work, a new sense of zeal enveloped the students. Suddenly the anticipation of an authentic audience elevated their investment in the project. By the time they were ready to share what they had created in their work, they were students with vision. Clearly, if the external audience had not been part of the culminating event, students would have sensed less "realness" in their learning experience.

We can create many opportunities for culminating events. Students can prepare presentations, poster sessions, dramatic representations, multimedia productions, debates, and aesthetic interpretations. For mature learners it is appropriate to be open-ended about these opportunities. We might simply negotiate with students the amount of time they have to communicate their findings and let them decide how to do it. For less sophisticated learners, teachers may provide patterns and modalities for communication of findings. This may be especially appropriate if specific goals for communication have been identified. We may, for example, require that students create some visual image related to their work if we had identified that portion of the communications goal as critical. We may require students to report data in tables, graphs, or statistics if our goal had been quantification. Culminations allow for multiple ways of knowing and are limited only by the creative imaginations of the students and teacher. What is important is that there be a public celebration of the culminations so that all can enjoy and benefit from the products of learning.

◈ Assessment

This leads us to a discussion about assessment. Because culmination sounds final, you might infer that assessment must be close at hand. Although we have shown culminations at the end of the template, thereby implying a summative and evaluatory function, we believe learning is indicated both by ongoing processes and by end products. Although it is appropriate to think about culminations as representative of what we have learned, the avenues by which we reach the culmination are just as important.

Assessments of both process and product are directly related to the goals we seek to achieve. Products are natural consequences of learning that are summative in nature: test results, summaries of findings, results of experiments, oral reports, tangible models, dramatic renditions, and so forth. By examining the product, we can determine the skills that were employed in its formation. If an oral presentation is effective, we know that the learner has mastered the concept, organized information, translated actions into words successfully, and achieved a degree of oral competence. If a graphic representation and cogent summary of data results from experimentation, we can infer that learners have conducted a successful experiment, quantified data accurately, applied appropriate technologies, and communicated effectively.

Products can tell us much about the abilities and accomplishments of the learner, but the processes the learner has used to reach the product are equally revealing. Consider the goal of cooperation and collaboration. Could we examine a product and infer that students had worked together in effective and mature ways? Probably not. To track progress in this area we would need to keep anecdotal records, check sheets, or scoring guides as students interacted in groups.

Some goals may require both product and process assessments to monitor student progress. Problem solving requires this approach. Evidence that a process of problem solving was utilized is critical in assessing students' abilities, because they may not reach a solution for a particular problem. Students may engage in appropriate problem-solving methods, may learn much from the process, and yet not produce a significant product. A failed report, experiment, or project may not give us enough information about the methods employed in its pursuit. Therefore, assessment requires dynamic observation and record keeping of the paths that learners take in solving problems, as well as of the solutions themselves.

An Invitation to the Planner: *Providing for Culminations and Assessments*

The culminations aspect of the planning template requires us to think carefully about our expectations for the nature of the students' work. This aspect provides the answer to the question: "What will students demonstrate as a product or process of their learning?" Products and processes must be directly related to goals. If we had assigned a goal of problem solving for the unit, and the inquiry and exploration facilitate this goal, then the assessments must be directly related to measurement of progress toward that goal. You may wish to outline appropriate culminating events for each exploration. As you do this, consider the criteria in figure 6.15.

◈ Summary

The value of the template is that it allows us to think about instruction as a whole and that curriculum planning is plotted on a map that is easy to conceptualize. Planning represents possibilities for implementing curriculum

---

FIGURE 6.15 Criteria for culminations and assessments

Criteria for Culminations

- ▌ Will the culmination provide students an opportunity to share the products of learning in an authentic social setting that is reflective of the stated inquiry?

- ▌ Is the consequence of a student's learning directly related to the stated goal and can it help us determine if students are making progress toward that goal?

Criteria for Appropriate Assessments

- ▌ How will processes and products of learning be assessed? That is, will the ongoing process of the exploration itself be the consequence of learning or will the product of exploration be significant?

- ▌ What will we look for and how will we recognize it when we see it?

---

and should remain flexible as new information is learned about the needs and interests of students.

The examples provided in Appendix B show how we sketched the plans for *Very Last First Time, Galimoto, The Green Book,* "The Town That Moved," and "The Siege of Tyre." We hope that you find the template an effective way of thinking about the multitude of variables that act upon the narrative curriculum. It should help you, as a curriculum planner, to visualize curriculum that is goal based, authentically from an appropriate context, and honors a student-centered approach to learning.

Lingering Questions

How can we design curriculum considering all the factors concurrently rather than sequentially? How do we get all the important aspects to work interactively?

Is a narrative curriculum similar to the transaction that takes place between a reader and a text (Rosenblatt, 1938/1976)?

Companion Readings

The chapter by Jon Cook in *Negotiating the Curriculum* (Boomer, Lester, Onore, & Cook, 1992) offers complementary insights into curriculum planning.

CHAPTER 7

Narrative Curriculum: Selecting the Narrative

Activating Prior Knowledge

Reactivate your definition of *story*. Is it congruous with the operational definition that we elaborated in chapter 2?

Chapter Highlights

Using the broad definition of *story* as a narrative structure (setting, characters, plot, and supporting theme), we explore the sources of suitable stories to use as contexts for the narrative curriculum. The essential elements of fully articulated stories can be found in literary, historical, collaborative, and issue/problem-centered narratives. This chapter highlights several examples of each source of story and offers the reader an invitation to begin the search for others.

The biggest question for me is where do we find the stories? Many of us are topic based teachers with no knowledge of what is available. Who is able to simply spend time searching? Where do we get the time to dig up or write stories based on what we want to teach? Are there collections of books or packets available for us to purchase? (middle school social studies teacher)

I'm interested in this approach for integrated curriculum. I hope to use it sometime in the next school year. I may have to try *The Green Book* first since I had trouble finding a good piece of literature to integrate. Maybe when I have more time to relax and read I'll find something I'd like to use. Since I have a team with three other members, maybe we'll come up with something together. (sixth grade science teacher)

The comments of these two teachers may reflect your hesitation about the practicality of the narrative curriculum. Teachers who find the theory and philosophy of the narrative curriculum appealing usually ask, "Where do I find the wonderful narratives that will form the basis for the curriculum?" There is no compendium of narrative contexts compiled for instructional use, no existing anthology of children's literature collected for narrative curriculum. We will share with you some narratives that we have found to be successful. But most of all, we want to encourage you to learn to choose the narratives that will serve your goals and your students. In this chapter we offer a process for selecting narrative contexts and some guidelines for examining a narrative to determine its curricular potential. When you have acquired the ability to select narratives, you will be able to determine which narratives interact best with your curricular needs. The narrative resources throughout the book and in Appendix C are not voluminous, but they are a good starting point and there are many additional places to search. We invite you to share with us narratives you discover so that, collaboratively, we can assemble a more extensive list.

Distinguishing Alternative Roles of Narratives

Most of you have probably used stories and other forms of literature in your classroom. In fact, there are many publications presenting literature-based ideas for instruction. We find several roles proposed for the use of stories. We present them all to you even though they are not all consistent with the perspective of the narrative-framed curriculum.

Story As Anticipatory Set

Many teachers are skilled at providing lessons with a captivating lead, or anticipatory set. The purpose of this lesson device is to draw attention, focus interest, and provide motivation for learning. An anticipatory set is a stimulus or spark that ignites an objectivist lesson. After we have used the story it is jettisoned and we proceed with the main thrust of the lesson. Story can be used, and used quite effectively, in this way. (See chapter 3, figure 3.1, *Galimoto* Transmission Lesson.) A story can begin a lesson by attracting the audience to its information or ideas. For example, a short excerpt from *Dragonwings* (Yep, 1975) that describes the 1906 San Francisco earthquake might be read to a class to build interest in earthquakes. Then the class would proceed with its earthquake study without ever returning to the story. Another example of the use of a story as an anticipatory set is to read the section of *Sadako* (Coerr, 1993) in which she folds a paper crane and then move into a craft lesson on paper-folding. As a set, the story is not honored for its theme or as a piece of literature. And, the story, once used, has completed its mission and has no further part of the lesson. This application of story may accomplish its purpose of instilling interest or focusing attention, but differs significantly from the role we propose.

Story As Application

Early in our efforts to relate science and language arts, we used stories as a means to provide students alternative experiences with difficult science concepts. For instance, we developed instructional units that focused on broad concepts such as cycles, systems, and interactions. We located stories that contained these concepts and used them as ways to illustrate science ideas through a literary medium. For example, we did an experiment with two interactive chemicals and then related this to the interaction of characters in the stories *Rosie and Michael* (Viorst, 1974) and *Mine's the Best* (Bonsall, 1973). Carefully selected stories might connect to several subjects at a conceptual level. Using stories in this way as application is also a valid and powerful tool in curriculum, but not in a narrative-framed sense. Since the story forms a parallel route of understanding it can be considered of equal value to the experimental procedure. It performs a complementary function in the curriculum. This use of story enhances learning, but the story is being used as a servant to other subject areas.

Story As Closure

Using story as a way to check for understanding or for summarizing learning is related to the idea of story as application. Asking children to write a story about what they have learned or to listen to a story about what they have been learning is an application exercise in story disguise. This may be a useful tool but it is not using narrative as a context for learning.

Story As Resource

Stories are also valuable as resources. We read information-rich stories to provide insight and information about a particular topic. Here, story performs a function of providing additional insight or support for the topic that is the actual focus of the curriculum. A unit on the rain forest may include both story and informational books such as *Rain Forest* (Cowcher, 1988), *One Day in the Tropical Rain Forest* (George, 1990), and *Rain Forest Secrets* (Dorros, 1990), that students will read to develop a picture of life in the tropics. Story performs a needed function in this respect because it is an effective way to transmit some kinds of information. However, it is simply providing an ancillary source rather than framing the curriculum.

Story As Curriculum Framework

While we realize the value of the previous roles of story, our purpose is to develop the idea of story as a curriculum framework. In this role, the story is constantly in place during the entire course of the curricular unit. As the students ask questions and engage in exploration, their personal stories are being developed at the same time that their understanding of the narrative context is enhanced. The framing story supports the recursive nature of learning that we advocated in chapter 6.

❖ Sources of Narratives

The first criterion for selecting a context is the presence of all the elements that compose a fully articulated story: setting, characters, action, conflict, resolution, and a compelling theme. In chapter 2 we discussed the need for a fully articulated story, one in which the characters are involved in a conflict and reach a resolution. The narrative filter in the template is a reminder of this necessity (fig. 7.1).

There are many genres that fulfill the requirements of the narrative filter. We have used several examples in previous chapters to demonstrate a variety of possibilities. Literary sources we have used include picture books such as *Very Last First Time* and *Galimoto* and chapter books such as *The Green Book*. "The Town That Moved" is an example of a collaborative story and "The Siege of Tyre" and "The Pine Tree Shillings" are examples of historical narratives. A fourth type of narrative which will be introduced in this chapter is the issue- or problem-centered narrative.

FIGURE 7.1 The narrative filter

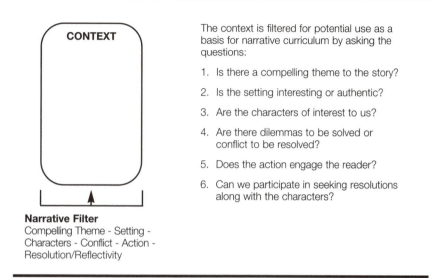

CONTEXT

Narrative Filter
Compelling Theme - Setting -
Characters - Conflict - Action -
Resolution/Reflectivity

The context is filtered for potential use as a basis for narrative curriculum by asking the questions:

1. Is there a compelling theme to the story?

2. Is the setting interesting or authentic?

3. Are the characters of interest to us?

4. Are there dilemmas to be solved or conflict to be resolved?

5. Does the action engage the reader?

6. Can we participate in seeking resolutions along with the characters?

Literary Narratives

Children's literature is a logical place to begin our search for narratives. Libraries and bookstores are lined with books that contain wonderful stories. Children's books have been written and illustrated with the intent of entertaining, captivating, instilling wonder, and provoking the thoughts of young people. We know that a fine piece of literature will, at the very least, provide an enriching interaction with a work of art. However, to be considered as a narrative context, literary sources like children's picture or chapter books must stand the test of the narrative filter as well as provide the curricular adjunct that will forward our goals. Consider the literary examples in figure 7.2. Each story we have chosen fulfills the requirements of rich setting, compelling characters, engaging plot, and universal theme. Let us take a closer look at each of these considerations.

Setting.   A rich setting invites our interest. From northern Canada to Africa, from our past to our future, rich settings indicate possibilities for inquiry. The illustrations in *The Day of Ahmed's Secret* (Heide & Gilliland, 1990) make us wonder. How do people live in modern Cairo? What are the foods shown in the market? Why are there so many different styles of clothing? As we pore through the descriptive pages of *The Bone Wars* (Lasky, 1988) we wonder what "Indian" territory looked like and where the places are in relation to

FIGURE 7.2 Literary examples of narrative contexts

Literary Source	Setting	Characters	Plot	Theme
Very Last First Time (Andrews, 1985)	Arctic Circle	Inuit girl, mother	Girl walks on bottom of sea to gather food	Meeting the challenges of new things in life
Galimoto (Williams, 1990)	Malawi, Africa	African boy, townspeople	Boy collects wires to make a toy	Enjoying our world tran- scends materialism
The Day of Ahmed's Secret (Heide & Gilliland, 1990)	Cairo, Egypt	Ahmed, father, townspeople	Boy works to earn opportu- nity to become literate	Personal iden- tity and worth is often related to ability and responsibility
The Bone Wars (Lasky, 1988)	1850s west- ern U.S.	scientists, their sons, Native Americans	Two sons of bone hunters become friends amidst fathers' profes- sional rivalry	Scientific discovery and truth must not be motivated by ego
Dragonwings (Yep, 1975)	1903–6 San Francisco	Tang Chinese men, elderly Anglo woman	Chinese family pursues dream in new world despite prejudice	People are individuals, not stereotypes
The Green Book (Paton Walsh, 1982)	Future space	father, children, moth people	Family travels from a dying earth to an un- known planet	Among the most important human needs is a sense of personal worth

modern cities and states. We wonder about the the distances covered on horseback and the appearance of the badlands. We examine setting in liter- ary narratives because it provides a gateway for learning about places and cultures outside our local experiences. A setting different from that of our own life experience is not an absolute requirement, but unfamiliar settings often generate more inquiry. Any rich setting will generate inquiries from geo- graphical, cultural, and historical perspectives.

Characters. In each of the examples cited, young people play significant roles in the stories. Eva (the Inuit girl), Ahmed (the Egyptian boy), Patty (the future pioneer girl), and Moon Shadow (the Chinese boy) are personalities that allow us to learn about ourselves. In these characters, we sometimes see a reflection and sometimes "try on" a desirable attribute. A compelling character can serve as a mirror for self-examination, a peer with whom we can compare, or a hero to emulate. Believable characters make it possible to ask ourselves in the midst of a narrative, "What would I do in that situation?" or to exclaim "Don't do that!" Inquiries and explorations that extend the character are valid investigations into the human experience.

Plot. For any literary narrative to be effective, it must have tension. What will happen to Eva on the bottom of the sea? What will Kondi make with his wires? What is Ahmed's secret? As each story progresses, we participate vicariously in the actions because they either contribute to or impede resolution of the conflict. As curriculum planners, we are interested in these tensions because they allow learners to become emotionally and intellectually involved in the narrative.

Theme. Literary sources are also desirable because they contain themes that illustrate what it means to be human. Theme is an underlying idea that unifies all the other elements of a piece of literature and it is the insight that shines through to illuminate the text. According to Lukens (1990, p. 88), "This truth goes beyond the story and comments on human beings. This discovery holds the story together so that long after details of the plot are forgotten, the theme remains... Theme provides this discovery, this understanding, this pleasure in recognizing 'Yes, that's the way it is!'" Since reading is a transaction between the reader and the text, a work of literature generally has several themes rather than one. Each reader constructs the themes that issue from the interaction of prior knowledge and the text itself. Underlying themes are valuable as a way of presenting conceptual, psycho-social, and moral challenges to students. Fully articulated stories permit the reader to learn and grow through the lives and dilemmas of others as the characters ask and pursue questions similar to the reader's.

Cautions. Many excellent pieces of children's literature are *not* narratives. While there are many fine books that have great utility in learning, only those which are actually stories will serve as narrative contexts. For example, *How Much Is a Million?* (Schwartz, 1985) is a delightful book that describes the value of a million in creative and humorous ways. Teachers and children may find it useful in studying number and scale. Yet, because it lacks a plot, we would not consider it as a context for curriculum. The essentials of *story* make narrative curriculum fundamentally different from curriculum arranged by topic or concept.

Teachers are sometimes encouraged to write their own pieces as ways to involve students in topic-specific inquiry. In addition, there are some published stories that are specifically designed for instructional purposes. You can imagine the nature of these creations: a simple, transparent story line, loaded with content details, a kind of elaborate word problem. These pieces are well-intentioned, but it is clear that these stories have only one purpose: to deliver information. One teacher, evaluating a presentation that encouraged teachers to write such lesson-stories, remarked, "If I thought I could write a decent piece of children's literature I would get out of teaching and become Beatrix Potter!" We certainly would not wish to discourage anyone from writing for children (or from writing)! But we are trying to discourage the preparation of pseudo-stories which have the primary purpose of transmitting information or hoodwinking children into studying something. These types of texts tend to be contrived and condescending. We believe that for the purposes of narrative curriculum, an authentic piece of literature is a requisite. Here the author does not have a hidden agenda of instruction. The story itself is the most important rationale for writing and only as much information is introduced as is needed to tell the story.

An Invitation.   How do you find literature for the narrative curriculum? Start by examining the ones we recommend to get the flavor of this type of literary work. Then, look. Spend a few hours in the picture book section of the local public library. Pull out a stack of children's books that might provide an opportunity for exploration in one or more disciplines. Read the book. Use the narrative filter. Is it a compelling story? Does it have a good setting, believable characters, tension in its plot, and a theme of transcendental value? We estimate that in a stack of a couple of dozen books you may find one or two that have possibilities. If you do find one that we have not listed in Appendix C, we would like to hear from you. As more practitioners try this form of curriculum and share their possibilities, we may yet assemble that comprehensive bibliography!

Historical Narratives

The word *history* often brings to mind a compendium of dates, places, facts, and figures. We have this association because most of us have learned history as macroevents. But there are incredibly rich narratives in history if we look more closely. History is constantly being made by the actions of real people in real places. It isn't something that happens to people; it is something that people live. It is the collective story of past and present humankind. The preface of an antique history reader reminds us of the intrigue of history:

It has become a commonplace remark that fact is often stranger than fiction. It may be said, as a variant of this, that history is often more romantic than romance. The pages of the record of man's doings are frequently illustrated by entertaining and striking incidents, relief points in the dull monotony of every-day events, stories fitted to rouse the reader from languid weariness and stir anew in his veins the pulse of interest in human life. There are many such... dramas on the stage of history, life scenes that are pictures in action, tales pathetic, stirring, enlivening, full of the element of the unusual, of the stuff the novel and the romance are made of, yet, with the advantage of being actual fact. (Morris, 1893)

The vignettes of microhistory are valuable sources for narrative curriculum because they contain the essential elements we have applauded in literary sources. Jean Fritz (1991, p. 610), a successful author of biographies for children, explains: "I think of history and biography as story and am convinced that the best stories are the true ones."

History becomes believable, interesting, and stimulating when it is presented as a story. If you have ever been enthralled with a historical talk, it is probably because the presentation was rich in the details of the people that made history. For example, consider what is presented in a history textbook about Alexander the Great and his empire. We find dates, maps, and sweeping generalizations about the rise of the Hellenistic world. In comparison, one small vignette in which Alexander risks all to conquer the city-state of Tyre reveals his personality and motivation, gives us insight to the events and times, and makes us beg for more. Told as a story, the siege of Tyre meets all of the requirements we presented in our discussion of literature. The characters are real people who interact with their world in believable ways. Alexander acted out of a sense of pride and possible delusion. His actions and decisions were limited by the possibilities of that particular time and place. Because this vignette is detailed and understandable in terms of the human condition, the characters perform the same function as they do in authored stories. In the examples shown in figure 7.3, notice that the historical vignettes contain the same essential elements as literary stories.

A historical vignette must evoke the tension of good literature. In "The Pine Tree Shillings," what will the mint master do with the coins on the scale with Betsy? Will Bell be able to save President Garfield's life? How will George Washington Carver ever be able to conduct his investigations if he has no laboratory or equipment? A historical context must allow the learner to participate and to speculate about the ending, just as we wonder "who dun it" in a mystery.

We recognize that it may be a challenge to find historical vignettes that are written with these parameters. Most accounts of history are written in an expository style. Expository text tends to wash characters into stick figures that make decisions without displaying human motivation. This kind

FIGURE 7.3 Historical examples of narrative contexts

Historical Source	Setting	Characters	Plot/Challenge	Theme
"The Siege of Tyre"	322 B.C. Palestine	Alexander the Great Tyrians	Alexander must decide how to take the fortress of Tyre	Technology, war, and social conditions are interactive
"The Pine Tree Shillings"	1670s Massachusetts colony	Sam Sewell, mint master, daughter	Coin maker gives dowry for daughter equal to her weight	Historical events at the national level have a parallel at the personal level
The Assassination of President Garfield	1881 U.S.	Alexander Graham Bell, James A. Garfield	A dying president precipitates the need to develop a device to detect hidden bullets	Humankind is uniquely capable of invention
The Life of George Washington Carver	Early 1900s U.S.	Carver, Booker T. Washington	Carver is hired as Tuskegee University's first professor of agriculture; He begins his work in an empty warehouse	Good science is not measured in the elaborateness of the laboratory, but rather in the habits of mind of the scientist

of historical approach often fails to excite students. Thus, stories from history may have to be presented as reenactments or recreations. Although we cautioned about creating a literary story from scratch, retelling history as story is a bit different. The teacher may need to develop skills as a storyteller, but the material is already available. With practice, success comes in finding a remarkable person or event and then retelling a small episode as a story—the siege of Tyre rather than the whole of Alexander's conquests, Betsy's dowry of pine tree shillings rather than the whole of colonial commerce. Because most available historical accounts are poor sources of narrative curriculum if left unaltered, we do need to consider ways of recreating them. For example, in textbooks we have found rather stiff, dry explanations of Archimedes and what he did. But we became fascinated with the story of Archimedes when we learned about all the aspects of his life. He was a man who claimed, "Give me a place to stand and a fulcrum and I will move the world." He ran naked in the streets when he discovered the principle of displacement. And he was killed by an invading soldier whom he scolded for stepping onto his beach "blackboard." A story of Archimedes' life incorporating these elements makes us want to know more. Appendix E contains a story about Thomas Edison told in the lively style we advocate. Other ideas for historical vignettes can be found in books such as *Strange Stories, Amazing Facts of America's Past* (*Reader's Digest*, 1989) and *Eccentrics* (Billings & Billings, 1987).

We choose our historical vignettes to consider not just the obvious historical, cultural, political, or geographical adjuncts but also to explore a multifaceted world. As Alexander makes a military decision about the logistics of siege it is against a backdrop that would interest a biologist (Is the lack of the snail species in the Mediterranean explained by over consumption over 2,000 years ago?), an engineer (How might these great engines of war have been constructed?), and an author (Who wrote the accounts of this siege and under what circumstances? What clues are there to suggest influences of other ancient literature?). We are intrigued by Ruth Law, a gutsy lady who acted beyond the narrow expectations and restrictions of women in her era when she attempted to set a record in 1916 by flying from Chicago to New York in a single day. Upon hearing this story, we can think like a historian (Could we get copies of the newspaper accounts? How does this flight compare to other "firsts" in aviation? Who are other significant female pilots?), a geographer (What is the route of Law's flight on a map?), a mathematician (How far did she fly and how fast did she go?), and a sociologist (Are women still pioneers in aviation? How did Ruth's choice of careers conflict with society's expectations?).

Once again, we invite you to participate in the process. Read some history. Find a person or event that interests you and pursue it. Remember to select a vignette, a small piece that can be retold as narrative and that has all the parts of a fully articulated story. The Civil War, for example, would be far too sweeping a time period and far too complex. Rather, a personal story that portrays human beings in the midst of events is more likely to captivate the heart and the mind. A good way to discover this for yourself is to read the Civil War chapter out of any elementary school social studies textbook and compare it to a human story such as *Pink and Say* (Polacco, 1994). People's lives often yield stories, but birth-to-death biographies rarely embody the qualities of story. Look for stories with surprise endings, elements of mystery, or incredible happenings. History abounds with these sorts of possibilities—for real life is very often stranger than fiction!

Collaborative Narratives/Simulations

Of all the forms of narrative contexts, collaborative story making is one of the most attractive because the stories are generated by teachers and students within a compelling context. It shares characteristics of both the literary and issue/problem narrative (fig 7.4). It differs from literature in that the story is lived rather than written, and from issue-centered narratives in that the problem is simulated rather than real. We have observed this form in action and have experimented with it in our own classes. The most well-known form of collaborative story making is called Scottish Storyline, a type of curriculum that has enjoyed a long and successful history in Scotland and has recently found many enthusiastic implementers in the United States.

Collaborative stories usually begin with an opening scenario or setting. The possibilities encompass past, present, and future, from far away to right at home. In our example of "The Town That Moved," we set the era and place and developed an opening setting that invited students to join in the simulation. Teachers usually pick a story line that has potential for exploration in a variety of areas. Voyages and the building of new communities are common milieus for units. Some teachers create cooperative storylines with other teachers so that a whole grade level becomes a new planet of pioneers or community members. Accompanying the opening scenario, a teacher creates a backdrop for the story. A large diorama, play

FIGURE 7.4 Collaborative/simulation examples of narrative contexts

Source	Setting	Characters	Plot/Challenge	Theme
"The Town That Moved"	Late 1800s Hibbing, Minnesota	Frank Hibbing, Olaf, Inga townspeople	A mining town is planned and populated only to discover the richest ore lies under the town	The pioneer spirit often meant a willingness to work hard
Seashore Community	Modern-day Oregon coast	townspeople	A stretch of beach is developed by a group interested in tourism. An oil spill changes their plans	With life's joys and accomplishments come challenges
Voyage to a Strange Planet	Future Space	travelers aliens	Travelers must determine what they will need on a new planet and discover that they are not alone	Every community requires individuals with special talents and interests

stage, or mural is crafted as the place where the story will be acted out. To start our town of Hibbing, we decided to create a $3' \times 8'$ model of the landscape where we could develop our community. Although a focal point is important as a place to continue the storytelling, teachers extend the setting to other places in and outside the classroom. In one example of children voyaging to another planet, a plastic bubble spaceship was assembled in the classroom and students donned space suits (painting coveralls) as they started their journey. Some teachers involve students in the creation of the setting itself. In a local school, the students decided to create an African village in their classroom. They made the murals, trees, huts, and clothing of the village members with the teacher providing resources and facilitating the process.

Once the setting is well established, students develop a plausible character for themselves. For example, as children planned to go on a voyage to another planet, each considered what role to play. Some became pilots or engineers. Others became merchants, teachers, tradespeople, or civil servants. Accuracy and completeness are encouraged by having students interview for the role that they have chosen. Once a role is determined, the students continue to build their character through daily development. During a visit to one school involved in this kind of simulation, a third grader came up to us beaming and pulled out his ID card—his assumed role ID card. He had donned this new persona and was proud of the knowledge and accomplishments of his character. Students may continue to develop their characters by their homes, businesses, modes of transportation, and professional or personal relationships. Model houses and vehicles can be added to the diorama or mural. In a seashore community simulation, students had each developed a business on the Oregon coast. When they had completed their work the display portrayed a miniature city.

Once the setting and characters are well developed, the teacher or other collaborator inserts an unexpected event into the story that causes students to grapple with a problem. In "The Town That Moved" we asked a colleague to play the role of a mine owner. He informed the proud members of the newly planned community of pioneers that their town would be destroyed because the best ore was located directly under it. The students who created the seashore community were greeted one morning with an oil spill on the beach. The planetary colonists discovered that there were inhabitants on the planet where their spaceship had landed. Each of the stories takes an unexpected twist that forces the students-as-characters to solve problems.

Resolution comes when the community develops strategies for dealing with the problem. The planetary colonists decided how they will live in harmony with another life form. The people of Hibbing contrived ways of moving their homes to a new site so they would not have to rebuild. The story is concluded as resolutions are reached and as the community returns to equilibrium. A story line can include several challenges (the people of Hibbing suffered a snowstorm, fire, and polluting smelted ore in the middle of their town). The degree of complexity is related to the ability of the story line to continue to motivate and interest students. Just as we would probably not have younger children read long, complex chapter books, we may limit the length and complexity of collaborative narrative according to the developmental level of our students.

What are the possibilities for collaborative stories that you might bring to a classroom? Where can students travel or build or explore? Take some time to examine the possibilities and sketch out the details. Then ask yourself:

- Will the setting lend itself to creating a classroom model?
- Will students have an opportunity to take on a real role?
- Is there potential for inserting a real problem or challenge into the story line?
- Can students bring about a resolution to the dilemma posed?
- What are the disciplinary perspectives that can be addressed?

Issue-/ Problem-Centered Narratives

A group of elementary school children met with city officials and school board members with an agenda for action. Armed with essays, data tables, photographs and arguments to support their cause, these children convinced the community to save a coastal stream from the ravages of pollution. After earning support from elected officials and public agencies, the elementary school children slowly restored the fragile stream into a healthy creek. With the help of local fishery experts, they raised salmon from eggs to smolt and released them in the stream. Watching the first salmon return from the sea after two years of waiting, the children knew they had made a difference in their world.

This true story, retold in *Come Back, Salmon* (Cone, 1992) helps us grasp the significance of what children can do when they are faced with a real-world problem or issue. The children in this story were compelled to ask: "What good is this polluted stream?" "How can anything live here?" From these questions they began to explore and to take action to resolve their questions. *Come Back, Salmon* is an issue-based narrative that exemplifies all of the criteria of an effective story.

Issues, or problems, become stories when learners participate in an authentic quest to seek resolution. The children and community members are the characters, the stream and surrounding land is the setting, the tension is the unknown results of their actions, and the underlying theme is that everyone can make a difference. When using an issue as a context, the story takes place in real time and the students are the characters. The problem, or issue, and the action the students take to resolution provide the conflict and plot of the story!

An issue can operate as a narrative context when several conditions are met:

1. The issue must be authentic.
2. Students must play authentic roles in the contribution toward resolution of the issue.
3. The issue must have opportunity for real solutions to be generated from student action.

Let us consider each of these further.

Come Back, Salmon is an example of an authentic issue. A natural opportunity for learning was provided by the polluted stream that ran past the school. In another example, a rural elementary school burned its trash in an incinerator each day, creating black sooty smoke and a noxious odor. Students developed a rationale for recycling and an enforcement plan in order to eliminate the need for the incinerator. In a southwestern city, students discovered an area where children played around a toxic waste dump. They took action which ultimately resulted in the dump being cleaned up. It is absolutely vital that the issue be authentic. To us, authenticity creates a context for learning that children can believe in and trust because it is a real situation in the world. In addition, the issue must make a personal connection with the child. For example, although we might study the desertification of central Africa and learn much about that endangered ecosystem, unless we allow students to take personal action and to have a role in change, the issue may be too remote and abstract to promote meaningful learning.

The students must have significant roles that impact the outcome of the process. In the examples listed in figure 7.5, every action taken by the students contributed to the resolution of the problem. For the children who cleaned the stream and raised and released the fish, the returning salmon were *their* salmon. The students who created a recycling system looked on the incinerator as a foe conquered. The children who got a hazardous waste cleanup law passed in their state legislature experienced the glow of democracy at work. All who contribute to the real world in a positive way own the outcome. They, personally, have made a difference.

Sources that discuss the use of issues in the classroom include *The Astonishing Curriculum* (Tchudi, 1993) and *The Kid's Guide to Social Action* (Lewis, 1991). These sources suggest many problems that students around the world have tackled. Although the resources are important guides, the actual selection of the problem or issue must be linked to what

FIGURE 7.5 Issue/problem examples of narrative contexts

Issue Source	Setting	Characters	Plot/Challenge	Actions Taken	Theme
Recycling	Local school	teachers students custodians school board	Trash is burned in furnace leaving a terrible stench: What can be done?	Students create recycling program at school	Humankind must be a good steward of natural resources
Homeless people	Any community	community members	People live without shelter: What can be done to help?	Students raise community's consciousness about problem	All persons should have an opportunity to live a quality life
Come Back, Salmon (Cone, 1992)	Coastal stream	school community	A stream that once supported salmon is now a trash dump: What can be done?	With the help of the local community, students repair ecosystem and facilitate return of salmon	Humankind must be a good steward of natural resources

students are interested in and the things which directly affect them. A local newspaper or a sharing circle in the classroom can generate many ideas that students will embrace. Younger children often contribute interests that are more personal or related to the classroom environment. Problem solving related to classroom rules, policies, environment, or activities can be real issues to children. Schoolwide issues such as violence in and around school, drug use, recycling, energy conservation, school lunches, school appearance, or playground procedures and equipment can provide compelling contexts. Older elementary school children can explore the relationship of school and community and delve into the legal, political, and social ramifications.

You may want to refer to some of the sources we have cited for examples of an issue-based curriculum before you plan this type of unit. The stories of other teachers and students involved in authentic problem solving are compelling narratives in themselves and are worth reading. Then consider: what issues could your students identify to tackle?

Additional Criteria for Selecting Narratives

We will leap to the conclusion that you have latched onto one of the possibilities we have outlined. We hope that you have found a piece of literature, a historical vignette, an issue, or an idea for a collaborative story. What other criteria are important in evaluating the potential of a context in a narrative curriculum? There are a few other important variables that should be considered before we take the plunge:

- Does the narrative allow teachers and students to inquire? Is it "writerly"?
- Does the narrative allow for disciplinary perspectives rather than just covering specific content?
- Does the narrative permit us to ask questions that lead to plausible explorations?
- Does the narrative have potential in helping students make progress toward the stated goals of schooling?

Writerly Versus Readerly Narrative

The first question we have posed relates to the style of the telling of the narrative. Consider two narrative selections and see if you can determine the difference between presentations. See figures 7.6, text from Jules Verne's *20,000 Leagues Under the Sea* and figure 7.7, text from Heide and Gilliland's *The Day of Ahmed's Secret*. Are we able to approach them as

---

FIGURE 7.6 Text from *20,000 Leagues Under the Sea* (Verne, 1968)

That day the *Nautilus* crossed a singular part of the Atlantic Ocean. No one can be ignorant of the existence of a current of warm water, known by the name of the Gulf Stream. After leaving the Gulf of Florida, we went in the direction of Spitzbergen. But before entering the Gulf of Mexico, about the forty-fifth degree of north latitude, this current divides into two arms, the principal one going towards the coast of Ireland and Norway, whilst the second bends to the south about the region of the Azores; then, touching the African shore, and describing a lengthened oval, returns to the Antilles. This second arm—it is rather a collar than an arm—surrounds with its circles of warm water that portion of the cold, quiet, immovable ocean called the Sargasso Sea, a perfect lake in the open Atlantic: it takes less than three years for the great current to pass round it. Such was the region the *Nautilus* was now visiting, a perfect meadow, a close carpet of seaweed, fucus, and tropical berries, so thick and so compact, that the stem of a vessel could hardly tear its way through it. And Captain Nemo, not wishing to entangle his screws in this herbaceous mass, kept some yards beneath the surface of the waves. The name Sargasso comes from the Spanish word "sartgazzo," which signifies kelp. This kelp or varech, or berry-plant, is the principal formation of this immense bank. And this is the reason, according to the learned Maury, the author of "The Physical Geography of the Globe," why these hydrophytes unite in the peaceful basin of the Atlantic. The only explanation which can be given, he says, seems to me to result from the experience known to all the world. Place in a vase some fragments of cork or other floating body, and give to the water in the vase a circular movement, the scattered fragments will unite in a group in the center of the liquid surface, that is to say, in the part least agitated. In the phenomena we are considering, the Atlantic is the vase, the Gulf Stream the circular current, and the Sargasso Sea the central point at which the float bodies unite.

FIGURE 7.7 Text from *The Day of Ahmed's Secret* (Heide & Gilliland, 1990)

My special colors are part of the city, too. Woven into the harness of my donkey are my own good luck ones, blue, green, and gold.

Hassan hands me a dish of beans and noodles and says, "And how goes the day my friend the butagaz boy?"

As I eat, Hassan and I laugh together at his jokes and stories. Always when I come home at sundown I tell his stories to my family, but tonight will be different. I will have my secret to tell them. I have been saving it until tonight.

Now someone else comes to Hassan's cart and I wave goodbye. I must hurry now if I am to get all my work finished today.

---

sources of inquiry in the same way? Which selection offers more opportunity for the reader to wonder and seek to learn more? Jules Verne provides us with a storehouse of information. His expository text embedded within the lines of the story tells us everything, and more, than what we might ever want to know! Called readerly texts (Obbink, 1992), this sort of narrative supplies the reader with the answers to all possible inquiries within the text itself. There are few if any opportunities to ask questions because they have all been answered with detail. One edition of Verne's book included diagrams such as the one in figure 7.8, which add to the readerly nature of the text. If we used *20,000 Leagues...* as a narrative framework, where and what would students be compelled to find out? We predict that by the time they had waded through all of the detail they would have found little left to inquire about! Please understand, we are not being critical of Jules Verne. This book is a valuable piece of literature, but it probably does not work very well as a narrative source for curriculum.

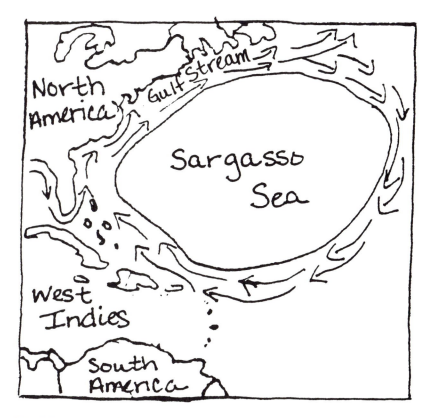

FIGURE 7.8 Illustration from *20,000 Leagues Under the Sea* (Verne, 1968), drawn by Anne Billing.

In contrast, *The Day of Ahmed's Secret* shows us the story instead of telling us all the detail. Readers of this story are invited to fill in the gaps and to invent possibilities for unanswered questions. In the passage quoted in figure 7.7 we are left with many puzzles: What is a butagaz boy? What does he deliver? Why the detail of colors? What were the stories that Ahmed took home? Even the artwork (fig. 7.9) from the stories helps us ask new questions about the setting, characters, and action of the story. *The Day of Ahmed's Secret* works well as a writerly text. Writerly texts (Obbink, 1992) invite participants to develop inquiries and to examine alternatives. Narratives that work best as curricular framework are writerly. As learners explore the story *they* create a readerly text by adding new information and meaning. The story works as a basis for curriculum because we can make the text readerly through research, added experience, or creative action.

Many narratives that otherwise have potential as context fail this criterion. Books by Jean Craighead George, such as *Minn of the Mississippi* (Holling, 1951), books by David Macaulay such as *Castle* (1977),

FIGURE 7.9 Illustration from *The Day of Ahmed's Secret* (Heide & Gilliland, 1990)

Scholastic's Time Quest books, and Windmill Press's Native American Legends are examples. In the case of the last two sets of books, they could be adapted so that only the story part of the text is used while the factual information is saved as resource material. It is important to examine a narrative source as a gateway for possibilities and not as a treasure of information in itself. It is easy to be persuaded to use one of the fine books mentioned above as a source of curriculum because they are so informative and interesting. Yet, if we want our students to engage in their own inquiries, to become explorers, and to construct their own meaning, then a self-contained source of narrative cannot serve our purpose.

Disciplinary Heuristic

The narrative context must be chosen to allow for disciplinary perspectives but not necessarily to cover specific subject content. The purpose of the narrative is not to transmit content but rather to encourage us to employ the tools of a historian, the strategies of a scientist, the eye of an artist, or the pen of an author. We honor the disciplines as ways of knowing and follow the inquiries that come from thinking like a practitioner of a discipline. You might examine some of the examples given in this chapter to determine if they allow for a disciplinary focus.

Potential for Explorations

Our third question about the narrative is interactive with the writerly nature of the context and the disciplinary heuristic. If there are opportunities to ask questions of the narrative, then what are those questions and do they lead to explorations that help students learn? Students must be able to follow their inquiries with explorations that lead to resolutions.

As we examine any context, we consider its potential to engage learners as active participants. If we are going to think and act like a scientist as we ask questions and explore possibilities, then we need to do science. If we ask the questions from an historian's vantage point, then we need to think like a historian and use primary sources. If we interpret the human experience from an artist's perspective, then we should create and interpret as an artist would. The narrative must allow us to perform these disciplines instead of simply reading about science or history or art. In the examples we have cited in all four genres of narratives we have employed a rigorous criterion: Unless children can be actively engaged in their own learning, then we must reconsider the viability of the context. We ask ourselves, "What will the students be able to do as they try to resolve this question?" "What experiments, constructions, dramas, writings, conversations, or mental inventions might students carry out?" The narrative curriculum must consist of much more

than posing questions whose answers can be looked up in an encyclopedia
Explorations must be just that—a voyage, a journey of knowing.

Goals

Finally we must ask, "Will the narrative help students make progress
toward the stated goals of schooling?" We are reiterating this crucial question. Will the narrative, inquiries, and possible explorations lead to the
fostering of skills, to the acquisition of knowledge, and to the development of an educated mind? In our zeal to create a wonderful piece of curriculum, we must focus on what we really want for children. What are the
things we want children to be able to do? In what areas do we want them
to grow? These questions must be considered as we select our narrative.

As we delineated in chapter 4, acknowledging goals is an interactive
process that requires conscious attention as curriculum is being planned. As
we examine the narrative we hear questions echoing in the background: "Will
this help students be better communicators? Will students be able to practice
cooperation and collaboration? Will science and mathematics relationships
be expounded? Will there be opportunity to use technology?" These internal
goal mechanisms need to interact with planning at every step of the process
as well. As explorations are conceived, the orientation is directed by our
selected goals. For example, in our *Galimoto* narrative, we focused on understanding science-technology-society relationships and the use of technology
as important goals for our learners. As we brainstormed possibilities from the
text it became clear that students could progress toward these goals if we oriented the exploration toward recycling and invention. Clear articulation of
goals helps us be aware of how to encourage our learners.

Summary: Story As Curriculum Framework

An appropriate narrative context meets all of the following criteria:

- Does the context have the essentials of story?
- Is it characterized by one of the narrative forms (literary, historical,
  issue, or collaborative)?
- Is it a writerly text that invites inquiry?
- Do the inquiries lead to active explorations that students can
  accomplish?
- Does it help forward the stated goals of schools?

And this, more personal, question:

- Is this a context that teachers and students will embrace and enjoy?

In the final analysis, the narrative you select must be one that has some pizzazz and some excitement. If we are going to work hard to create an environment of exploration in our classrooms, then we ought to be immersed in the quest as zealous learners ourselves. We must be sure to select a context that we believe our students will enjoy and that we are personally interested in. Examine the narrative context you have been considering as a possibility for a unit. Does it meet the criteria we have outlined?

We become redundant, but emphatic, when we celebrate story as the optimum context for curriculum:

- The narrative is the "container" of the curriculum. We start, learn, grow, and end within our story. The content of our study is based on what the narrative has to offer.
- The narrative is a fully articulated story that contains the essential elements of literary works. We look for stories that have rich settings, believable characters, and a well-conceived plot that offers a resolution to a conflict.
- The narrative is writerly, or open, providing the opportunity for inquiries which encourage the learner to interact and to make meaning with the story.
- The narrative has puzzles, questions, dilemmas, or challenges that can be resolved through inquiry. The story needs to stimulate a desire to know more.
- The narrative embodies an overarching theme or concept. The story must have a deep meaning and must convey a truth about what it means to be human in the real world.

Lingering Questions

How do teachers develop that intuitive sense for stories that are "just right" for the narrative curriculum?

Most of us learned subject content rather than the disciplines' methodologies. How can we model the heuristic of disciplines for students?

Companion Readings

Being alive in the world is the best way to find stories. Read everything! Watch documentaries. Attend lectures. Travel.

Current reviews of literature can also reveal possibilities. *School Library Journal, The Horn Book,* and *Booklist* as well as other periodicals include numerous reviews of young adult and children's books in each issue.

CHAPTER 8

Students As Co-Creators of Curriculum

Activating Prior Knowledge

What do you know about the development of children? How do they change in learning, reasoning, and social interaction as they grow physically?

Should this knowledge of development affect the practices of teachers?

Is curriculum responsive to the developmental needs of the learner? Can you think of examples?

Chapter Highlights

Curriculum planning is informed by an understanding of child development.

Modifications are discussed for planning the narrative curriculum with children as they grow from informants to negotiators to planners of curriculum.

In previous chapters, you have observed the narrative curriculum in action, dissected its parts, and begun to plan your own possibilities. Now consider how students participate in and interact with curriculum design. So far, in our examples, we have most often shown how the curriculum model works with a mixed-age group of elementary children. We recognize that there may be questions about how very young and more mature learners would be accommodated.

The purpose of this chapter is to examine the narrative curriculum with respect to what we know about the development of children. Since moral, social, perceptual, and conceptual differences are widely recognized as rationale for developmentally appropriate curriculum and teaching practices, we consider how these variables affect the narrative curriculum at various levels of schooling. The developmental levels and variables that we describe are general in nature. We fully realize that classrooms will have individual children that will extend beyond these descriptions of developmental stages. We have acknowledged from the outset of our work in curriculum that learning should emanate from, and center around, the child. We recognize the importance of individual differences, not only in development, but also in learning style, intelligence, personality, and culture. Although the discussion of these issues is beyond the scope of the book, we maintain that the narrative curriculum can embrace these differences. Because we honor students' unique interests, encourage personal construction of meaning, and provide opportunity for individual expression of learning, there are greater opportunities within the narrative curriculum to meet individual students' needs.

We begin this discussion by describing learners at the primary level. At this developmental level students can be *informants* in planning. The curriculum is created by the teacher as informed by the learner. As children mature, we shift into a *negotiated* curriculum. Planning with these students is a shared process where students and teachers together create learning opportunities. Ultimately, with self-directed learners, we view curriculum planning as the primary responsibility of the student. In this most advanced form of co-created curriculum, we view students as *planners* of curriculum. Figure 8.1 graphically displays the differentiated levels of development and the relative role of the teacher and student in the planning process.

❀ Students As Curriculum Informants

In this section we present a curriculum-planning process for primary grades that honors students while giving teachers most of the responsibility for planning the curriculum. Let's look at an example in detail to see how a primary teacher plans curriculum using students as informants.

FIGURE 8.1 A continuum of curriculum co-creation

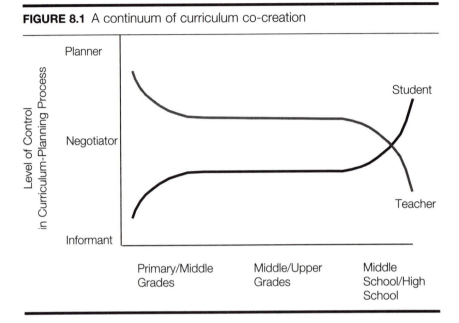

Carol Still, a kindergarten teacher, finds that springtime is an excellent setting for learning about growing things. (Please note that in this chapter "Carol" always refers to Carol Still.) She decided to read *The Tiny Seed* by Eric Carle (1990) to her kindergarten students to discover their response. According to Carol, these 5-year-olds

> loved it. They absolutely loved it. But the questions they had were not quite what I expected. First of all, they got into a discussion: Was the book real or was it not real? (It's really both but in the end the tiny seed grows into a flower bigger than the house.) Then we talked about what happened to all the seeds along the way. They got into an argument about whether seeds could come out of a flower and blow away. At this point we collected dandelions so they would go to seed and we experimented with them. We continued to explore real/make-believe because some of the children were still unclear about which aspects of the story were real. Even after the dandelion experiments, some of them weren't really convinced that seeds really blow away either. And I didn't want to just tell them.
>
> One of my goals was for the children to work cooperatively. It is my belief that a group of kindergarten children consists of two. They chose a partner and they decided what part of the story they would illustrate and dictated it to me. We put it all together and I read it back to them and they loved it. This fulfilled another goal of retelling a story. They thought their version was even better than Eric Carle's. Watching the cooperative groups was interesting. In some pictures there were two suns (fig. 8.2). In

The falr is Sow big and the PePl are a fad IT is big but the pepl are stl a fad.

FIGURE 8.2 Cooperative drawing

others, the sky appeared one way until the middle of the paper and then it changed. Listening to them work was fun and and informative to me.

As you can tell from this partial recounting of the interactions between the children and *The Tiny Seed*, Carol had definite goals in mind as she created this curriculum. It is also obvious that she is listening carefully to the children and using them as informants for inquiries that are compelling to them. The children had many questions:

Was the book real or was it not real?
Can seeds could come out of a flower and blow away?
What do seeds really need to grow?
Will a seed grow without dirt?
Can seeds grow in light that is not direct sunshine?
Are all seeds the same? Different?
How do they travel? Or do they move?

In her role as facilitator of the children's learning, Carol didn't just provide them with the answers to their questions. Instead, she listened to the children and allowed them to inform her of their interests and their need to know. From this information, Carol designed developmentally appropriate explorations that assisted students in their inquiries. To find out what seeds really need to grow, Carol gave all students an opportunity to plant seeds and play in the dirt. They also planted some seeds on paper towels. Some children were convinced the seeds on the paper towel would grow and others felt sure that they would not. The observations of the seeds provided the children with an opportunity to discover this for themselves. Through her careful listening, Carol realized that the children already knew that plants need sunshine. She found out that some children were convinced there is a difference between sunshine and light. So she had the children put some plants in the window where they got lots of light but no direct sunshine. Again, the children were encouraged to observe the seeds to satisfy their own need to know. These explorations also created new inquiries. For example, some children started thinking about what happens when a seed falls into the water. Some thought the seeds would drown. Carol facilitated a new exploration to help the children find out about what happened to seeds in water.

Carol found that the children read both the original story and their retelling over and over to one another. The arguments about the properties of seeds continued. Carol remarked, "That's okay. It's not important to have the answer. The children will satisfy themselves. I've provided them with the means for answering their own questions."

If we look at Carol's planning process we see that all of the planning was her responsibility. She chose the context, she identified the active goals, she created logical and developmentally appropriate explorations, and she assessed the learners. Carol was the curriculum planner and the students were informants. Because Carol is a good kid-watcher and listener, she synthesized what she knew about her learners and created appropriate learning

experiences. For students to be curriculum informants teachers must truly honor their ideas and interests by being keenly tuned to them. Figure 8.3 graphically portrays students as informants in curriculum planning.

In the primary grades the teacher has the critical responsibility to consider the interests and abilities of students. The teacher also creates the opportunities for student explorations and carefully orchestrates how students will engage in learning. To illustrate the careful planning required, let us examine another scenario of narrative curriculum in a primary-grade setting.

Pat, Karen, and Nancy spent hours creating a piece of curriculum with the goal of understanding aspects of the ecosystem. They chose a context that for them seemed appropriate for K–2 children, a field trip to a mountain-lake area within an hour's distance from the school. They anticipated what students might see, what questions they might have, and then planned for specific explorations that were appropriate for their students. The planning process was an informed one. Previous years' experience had acquainted them with the kinds of interests and abilities characteristic of this age student. Field trips in former years had provided insight into what children might do and say. And, experiences during the first few weeks of school helped inform teachers specifically about individual children.

This information required that they arrange logistical support to help students examine the forest, water, and riparian zones of the area. Parents

FIGURE 8.3 Students as informants

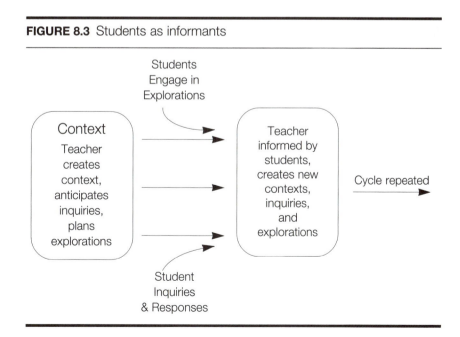

were trained to provide each small group of children with guidance so that they might make careful observations within each zone of the ecosystem. Nets, lenses, buckets, picture keys, and cameras equipped each small group with tools that helped students focus their attention. Parents served as note takers recording student questions and ideas. The teachers planned several follow-up explorations that provided students with opportunities to extend the field interests into the classroom. They wanted students to examine the materials they had collected and to use picture and print resources to create a display of their findings.

You may notice in this example that these teachers made almost all of the decisions about what children would be doing. They chose context and the manner in which children were invited into the context. They anticipated the kinds of questions that would be generated. They organized the exploration that would enable children to address their questions, and, finally, they set the expectations for how the products of inquiry would be displayed. The teachers worked within the narrative-curriculum model by anticipating students' interests and abilities. Nonetheless, the students were free to voice their personal inquiries, investigate what they were interested in, and share what they learned with others. Here teachers provide the kind of structure and options that gave students the greatest opportunities for success and the most appropriate challenges for achieving learning goals. While Carol Still created a curriculum-in-process by being informed by her students, these teachers, informed by their previous and current students, created the curriculum prior to implementation.

Chapter 10 gives two additional examples of the narrative curriculum in primary classrooms. In Gene Dunn's classroom, all children make pasta and have the opportunity to engage in other explorations. In Belinda Roberson's classroom, students decide how they will contribute to the construction of a model rain forest and are given wide latitude in the modality of that expression. The common elements in all of these primary examples are teachers who plan curriculum with careful and considerate knowledge of their children.

❖ Students As Curriculum Negotiators

In the previous section we have described the kind of curriculum planning that takes place at the beginning of the K–12 school experience. As learners become more sophisticated and able to assert new cognitive, social, and moral responsibilities, the planning process can be opened up to accommodate these learner attributes.

The curriculum described in chapter 1, *Very Last First Time,* is an example of a curriculum negotiation. In curriculum negotiation students are engaged by a context and they offer the inquiries they find interesting. Teachers may call attention to certain aspects of the context that the students have overlooked. Teachers can expand the students' horizons by offering their own questions. In *Very Last First Time*, for example, we inserted our own questions to serve as models of inquiry, to expose students to other disciplinary views, and to initiate explorations where students failed to see a potential. The inquiries from both students and teachers were then arranged into groupings of similar items. Teachers must model and scaffold this arrangement to help students learn to move from a specific question to a more abstract generalization. We find that reposing or summarizing the questions with a more global question is an effective way of simultaneously honoring student interests and focusing effort on the core issues embedded in students' specific questions. (You may wish to refer to figure 1.4 in chapter 1.)

As we hypothesize about explorations, teachers can help students articulate possibilities and can also add substantially to the possibilities. Less sophisticated learners are not apt to think of elegant possibilities for exploration or to know of available resources. For example, children were interested in the ice formations in *Very Last First Time*. They wanted to know how ice might form in the ocean considering the crashing surf. Their first thoughts of how to find out were to write to the author or go to the library to look it up. We knew that neither prospect had a high probability of success, so we suggested that they might undertake an experiment to find out. This was something that they hadn't considered, yet when offered the possibility, they found it logical and appealing. This kind of negotiation of possible explorations is important as teachers begin to help learners expand their own ways of knowing.

As the explorations are negotiated, teachers can direct the whole class toward efforts that seem critical to the understanding of the context, or provide essential skills for further work. Some lines of inquiry may seem unattractive to students on the surface; yet when converted to action in class, they become viable. Again, we call on our experience with *Very Last First Time*. As we investigated inquiries and explorations with the children, they selected several aspects that they thought sounded interesting. However, some aspects that we found vital to the understanding of the story—the geography of the arctic and the nature of the mussel—went unloved. Since we believed that these two areas provided excellent opportunities to practice map skills and observation techniques, we invited the children to their exploration. We asked children to use an array of maps to find the place names in the story. We showed them how to use the index of an atlas, flat maps, and globes to find latitudes and longitudes, to find similar locations on other continents, and to think about the effect of angled sunlight on this part of the world. We provided live mussels to observe. Students probed their anatomy, plopped them into steaming water, and finally tasted the cooked meat. Through these endeavors, children learned new skills and gained knowledge while having an enjoyable time.

We believe that teachers are responsible for bringing to the curriculum-negotiation process many of the explorations. The proportion will depend on how the inquiries and explorations are carried out, the extent of the children's prior knowledge, and the degree to which students have previously been involved in curriculum planning. Teachers at any level will generally be more knowledgeable learners than their students and will be able to offer ideas for inquiries and explorations that will expand their students' horizons.

As we complete the negotiated planning process with students we look at the results of learning. It is here that students think critically about the products and processes of their learning. "How will you (and others) know what you have learned?" is one entreaty that we use to focus students' attention on culminations. Again, we believe that for most elementary grades this is a negotiated process. Children will often suggest limited, routine products. Written and oral reports and tests are typical. Teachers can suggest and model other alternatives, especially those that foster multiple ways of knowing (Gardner, 1983): drama, art, electronic media, mathematics, music, and dance and movement. This is the time to help students see the relationship between the inquiry and the possible results of exploration. For example, students were keenly interested in the culture of the Inuits. How would they report their findings? Oral or written reports? Their brainstorming stalled. Reports were the only form they could think of at the moment. We suggested that they might recreate some of the cultural artifacts of the people and demonstrate their use. Could they recreate or dramatize a family setting? Could they prepare a script or dialogue that would communicate how these people lived? Would it be possible to make a video? Our interests here are to help students think about possibilities they might not have considered and that may be a best match for the resolution of an inquiry.

What is the role of teachers in negotiated curriculum? At this stage in a child's education, the teacher holds the vision for the learning and the goals of schooling. The teacher can select the contexts that will forward goals and introduce students to new ways of knowing. This is not meant to demean children's prior knowledge, but is a statement of fact. Children are often unfamiliar with the world of possibilities and often will not think of primary resources such as firsthand experimentation, interviewing, or use of archives. The teacher must help them recognize areas of inquiry, facilitate their question-generating abilities, and teach them the skills and information they need to make progress in their learning. In order to do this, the teacher must be a good listener and observer and be able to assess students' prior knowledge and level of understanding in order to promote each child's learning.

How can teachers bring children at this level into the planning process? Marilyn DeRoy, a fourth grade teacher, found an opportunity during recess.

> Mark, a student, brought me a pinecone and told me he knew how to get the seeds out. I didn't so he showed me and it started to dawn on me that this might be the way to approach science. We collected some pinecones for the class and also some rose hips from a bush on the playground. Over a weekend, when I was in the park, I found winged seeds from a Norway maple in the lawn. I noticed that those that had been positioned so as to have contact with the ground were already sprouting. I also collected pods of locust seeds. In class, the students and I read the book, *Miss Rumphius* (Cooney, 1982) together and discussed it. The students offered a number of comments on the author and illustrations. I moved the discussion to the idea of the flowers reseeding on their own. The students shared experiences they'd had with observing that same thing. We created a story map and then generated inquiries: What plants where we live disperse their own seeds? Where are the seeds located in the plant? What would we find if we cracked open these seeds? What would it take to make these seeds germinate? We then pursued scientific explorations of these questions.

Marilyn moved from a child's interest, related it to goals she had already outlined, offered a context, tapped into the students' prior knowledge, and then extended it through inquiries and explorations.

Roberta Gilmore and her third and fourth grade classes offer another example of negotiating curriculum.

> I read *The Green Book* and couldn't put it down. In my mind, I had many questions about happenings in the book and I knew the students in my classroom would have them also. Since I had only one copy of the book, I read it orally to the students at story time.
>
> As I read the book, I stopped at intervals to ask the students if they had any thoughts or questions about what they were hearing and processing in their minds. The students always had questions and thoughts. They were hooked on this wonderful book! As a class we listed questions the students had on a sheet of butcher paper hanging on the wall. After the questions were written, we arranged them into categories, for many were related to the same topics. It turned out that the questions concerned three areas. These were the "moth people" of Shine, the glasslike characteristics of the grass and wheat on Shine, and the death of Earth. The children had no idea how to approach the middle topic and I wasn't sure either so we didn't research it. I let the children decide which of the other questions they wanted to research. This procedure helped form their groups. They discussed how they would approach their research by asking themselves what information they needed to answer their question and deciding where they could look to find it. They were to turn in a conclusion or theory in answer to their question along with notes or something to show

where their thinking came from (fig. 8.4). Along with the written work, they created some type of visual aid (fig 8.5). I gave handouts to the group researching the question about evacuating Earth. These handouts contained information I had rewritten from other sources to make it understandable at the children's level. In the meantime, we were observing and studying mealworms. We would talk about the similarities between them and the "moth people." The children came to the conclusions I had hoped for and gained some knowledge I had not expected. They were enthusiastic and excited with the story and the research. They were eager to share their findings with their classmates as well as with me.

Roberta negotiated the curriculum with her students. She selected the context but solicited and listened carefully to the ideas of her students.

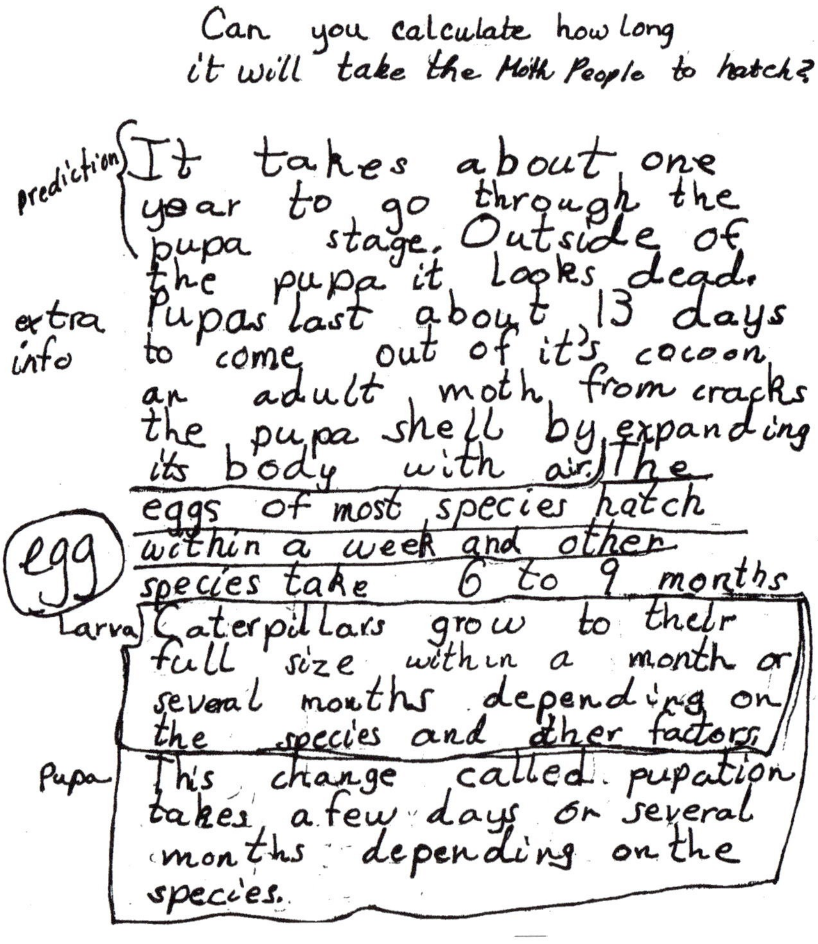

Can you calculate how long it will take the Moth People to hatch?

prediction) It takes about one year to go through the pupa stage. Outside of the pupa it looks dead.

extra info Pupas last about 13 days to come out of it's cocoon an adult moth from cracks the pupa shell by expanding its body with air. The

egg eggs of most species hatch within a week and other species take 6 to 9 months

Larva Caterpillars grow to their full size within a month or several months depending on the species and other factors,

Pupa This change called pupation takes a few days or several months depending on the species.

FIGURE 8.4 Student research conclusions

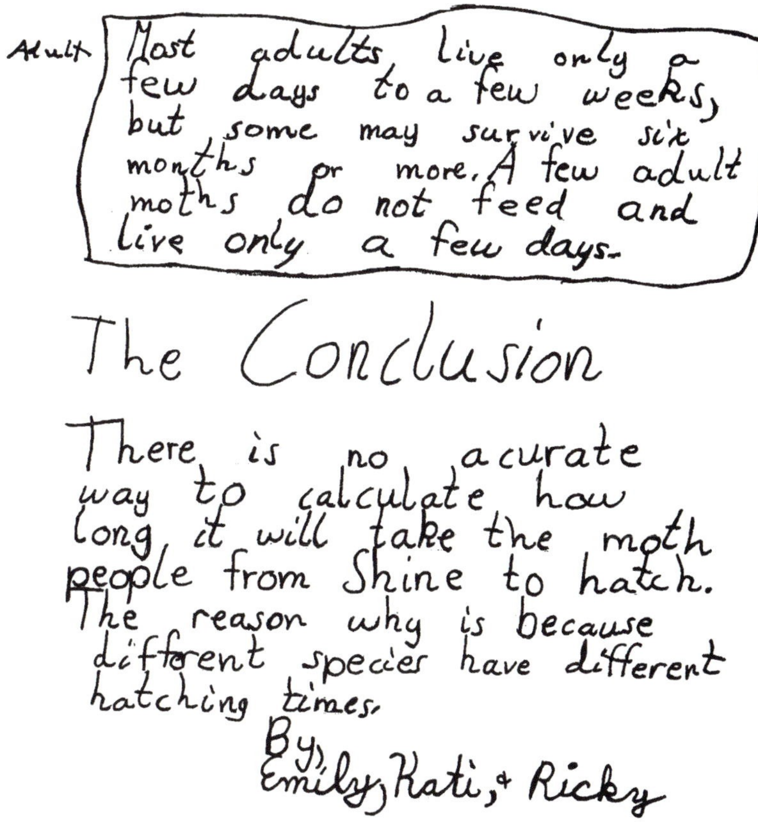

Adult | Most adults, live only a few days to a few weeks, but some may survive six months or more. A few adult moths do not feed and live only a few days.

The Conclusion

There is no acurate way to calculate how long it will take the moth people from Shine to hatch. The reason why is because different species have different hatching times.

By, Emily, Kati, & Ricky

FIGURE 8.4 Student research conclusions (continued)

They provided the questions but she helped to group them together. The students selected the question they wanted to research and formed their groups. Roberta provided information in a form the students could use and provided mealworms to be observed. She guided the students through a process of prediction, information gathering, and drawing conclusions. Because one of the active goals was communication, she asked for written work and a visual aid. She allowed for considerable student choice, but she also provided the scaffolding that allowed the students to be successful in their research.

In the negotiated narrative curriculum, students and teachers share in the planning. Teachers bring to the process a knowledge of goals to be reached, a grasp of the potential the context may offer, and the knowledge of a more advanced learner. Students bring ideas, possibilities, and interests. This type of co-created curriculum provides ownership and empowerment to all the members of the class.

Similarities of moths of shine, and

	Life Cycle ←
The life Cycle of a moth begins with the eggs then the larve (grub) next comes the pupa and last but not least the adult which lays more eggs and in a short amount of time the moth would die.	
	activities ↗
Moths live from high cold Mountain tops to hot deserts. In other words they live EVERYWHERE!	food →
	habitat ←

Moth of Earth about half this size

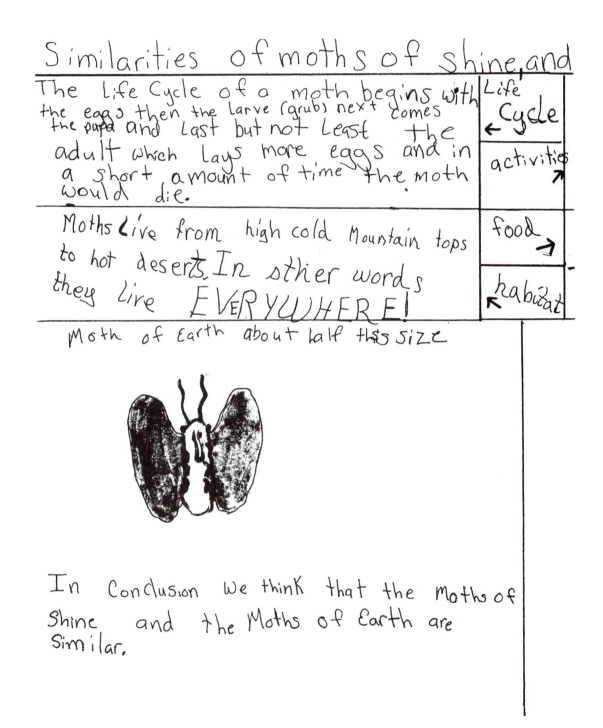

In Conclusion We think that the moths of Shine and the Moths of Earth are Similar.

FIGURE 8.5 Student-created visual aid

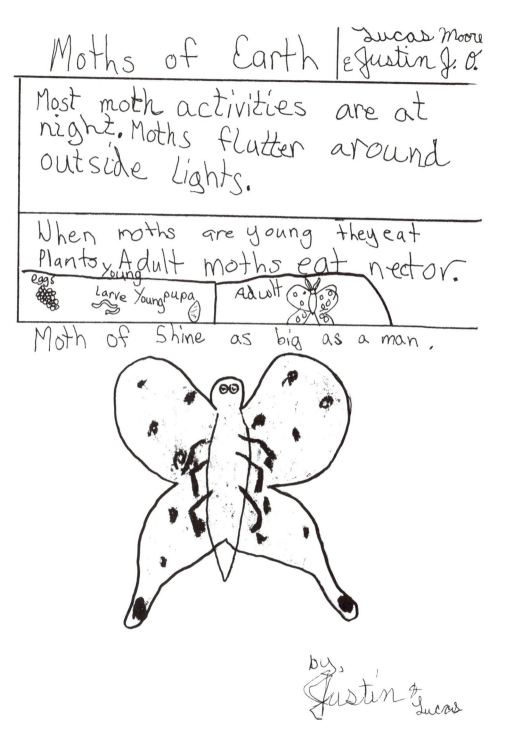

Moths of Earth | Lucas Moore & Justin J. O.

Most moth activities are at night. Moths flutter around outside Lights.

When moths are young they eat Plants. Adult moths eat nector.

eggs | Larve Young pupa | Adult

Moth of Shine as big as a man.

by, Justin & Lucas

FIGURE 8.5 Student-created visual aid

◈ Students As Curriculum Planners

What is our vision of students' achievements as they complete their high school years? They should be able to articulate a problem, pursue possible avenues of resolution using appropriate resources, feel confident in communicating solutions, and do all of these things without a manager or external control. The image of a local high school sophomore comes to our minds. Jerod had an opportunity to work at a local electronic instrument company during an open period in his school's schedule. He was assigned a mentor at the company who showed him the operation of the equipment, allowed him to explore, and answered his questions. For several weeks Jerod observed the operation of the business and developed an understanding of the basic concepts of spectrophotometers. By shining a light through various materials, he soon learned that each material had a particular fingerprint, displayed as absorption characteristics on the spectrophotometer. He applied quantitative knowledge and skills as he wrestled with numerical settings and measurements of machines, wavelengths, percents, and graphical displays of spectral absorption. In this instance, applied mathematical knowledge was essential in communicating how light was absorbed. Using the company's equipment and benefiting from the coaching of his mentor, Jerod became proficient at testing various materials and determining the proportions of their contents. Applying his learning to a new situation, Jerod flashed the light through a bottle of aspirin and recorded its signature. He found that he could determine the purity of the aspirin without disturbing the packaging. After several tests and collaboration with lab technicians, the process was verified. Company managers were so impressed that they encouraged Jerod to publish the results. Several journals accepted the student publication and he is often asked to present his findings in a public forum. Pharmaceutical companies are keenly interested in this technique to maintain quality control of products on store shelves.

Another image comes into view. The senior class of a small, rural high school planned their capstone project. A small grant from an electric power company prompted the students to use solar energy technology to solve a problem of their choice. With the help of a local engineer, they arranged for a three-week-long intensive course in solar power to learn all they could about how electricity is made from the sun and about the technology of solar energy. Although their science teacher made some arrangements for the students, most of the decisions about what they would do and how they would proceed came from the collective knowledge and work of the students involved in the project. Students debated the possibilities for applications of solar cells and batteries. They reached consensus to create a portable, solar-powered water pump, a machine that could be towed to a remote site where it would pump water out of a protected stream bed and into a stock tank. (Cattle are increasingly being denied access to small streams in this area because of their negative effect on the riparian zones.) During the next few months, the students engaged in a process of learning and in the practical application of knowledge: purchasing solar panels, contacting local pump suppliers, securing a donated trailer, and drawing initial designs. Students formed work teams and agreed to meet on alternate Saturdays to complete the project. In order to modify the trailer, one group learned to use an arc welder to install a platform for the solar apparatus. Another group assembled the solar panels and figured out how to connect the panels inside a watertight box. A final group worked out the details of the water pump, valves, and connections. As the subgroups finished their work, the entire project began to take form. A 4'-square rotating solar panel was mounted on the trailer, which was fitted with a large equipment box containing all of the materials necessary to connect a remote water pump. Initial tests were positive except that the stability of the panels was in question. Students solved the problem by adding stabilizing cables to the trailer. To complete the project, a set of instructions and explanations about the apparatus were needed. Students described the apparatus, wrote detailed sets of instructions, and developed a brochure that accompanied the equipment. For their culminating activity, they displayed their solar-powered water pump at the county fair and demonstrated its operation to thousands of fair-goers, many of whom were ranchers immediately interested in using it.

We hold these images up as exemplars. This is what we aim for in learning: self-directed, informed problem solving. Yet, these exemplars are rarities. For most students, their school experiences form a totally different picture: Problem solving is limited to the problems that can be completed in 50 minutes, within the confines of the classroom and with the materials at hand. They could be characterized as elaborate fill-in-the-blanks procedures. Self-directedness is prevented by a list of acceptable problems and processes. The curriculum is specific and contained. Our traditions have limited our ability to think beyond the scope of the textbook. Education becomes a chapter-by-chapter transmission of information. Traditional curriculum makes an assumption that students need to learn a compendium of information. Then, someday, when all of that information is accumulated, an individual may earn the right to solve a real problem. Rarely do students engage in real-world issues and rarely do they get to select what they truly want to learn.

We believe that the vision of students as informed problem solvers, as self-directed learners, as collaborators, and as effective communicators is much more attainable without the hegemony of traditional subject matter. Students can solve a problem without knowing everything; they can direct their own learning before they have an advanced degree; they can use language to learn across the disciplines; and they can collaborate with others without the managed system imposed by most schools. All these things are possible—but not if we retain a curriculum model based on the industrial model of the 19th century.

The concept is simple. If we want students to be informed problem solvers, we must engage them in the problem of determining their own curriculum. If we want students to be able to direct their own learning then we should allow them to do so. Learners preparing for the 21st-century world need a curriculum that provides these opportunities. New state mandates seem to agree. Therefore, educators are called upon to find a curriculum model that is congruous with these aims. The narrative curriculum has this potential. Experience in curriculum planning has enabled students like Jerod and the solar-power team to be able to select their own contexts from the world. With teacher scaffolding and facilitation, they have developed and maintained their intellectual curiosity and are able to find "strings to pull." They are able to gather their ideas together to form important questions and to apply what they know. They have the process skills to solve novel problems.

It may seem as though this shift in curriculum would require that we demolish school buildings and revamp the entire fabric of school schedule and culture. We believe, however, that this vision is attainable within the current structure of school. A flexible schedule and elaborate resources are desired and helpful, yet we find that given limited space, time, and money, we can still practice this curriculum. In our own meager situation, we teach within a busy school schedule, in a tiny basement room with erratic temperature control, where we are often interrupted with loud noises of machinery, and with almost no budget. Creating opportunities for learners can be at our fingertips. We must simply rethink the resources we already have and redirect their use.

The development of this type of learners needs to begin in the primary grades and continue onward into middle and high school. The role of the students as curriculum creators changes as they grow to maturity. They become curriculum planners by first being curriculum informants and curriculum negotiators. The narrative curriculum provides a structure for students to move through this continuum of responsibility for their own learning.

Co-Created Curriculum

Initially, the teacher selects contexts that have the potential to engage learners. Later, students may seek out and propose contexts. After students have been immersed in the context, they are encouraged to be reflective about the experience through means such as journal writing and dialoguing. The interests and questions the reflections produce are collected on a chart (fig. 8.6). The teacher acts as a facilitator of the group by urging participation, encouraging observations in overlooked arenas of interest, and promoting various disciplinary views. The teacher may act as a peer in the group by adding questions that are of personal interest. The compendium of ideas, including all student and teacher inquiries, are then reviewed by a process that is acceptable to the group. For example, if the list of interests is eclectic and ranges from narrow questions to more global ones, the teacher may suggest that the class employ a filtering, or classification, strategy to collect similar or repetitive questions. It is important that the students cooperatively create this scheme and that the true nature of their questions be honored.

As questions are clustered into natural groups, the teacher begins to ask students how one might explore these inquiries. The entire class provides a resource of prior knowledge to supply possibilities. A second column, a "how-to-find-out" section, is added to the chart. The teacher can add ideas but always after students have exhausted their own stock of possibilities. As in the collection of inquiries, the teacher's ideas should be offered as those of a more knowledgeable peer and *not* as a correction of the students' offerings or a prescription. Students come to class with a wide array of prior knowledge. This activity helps the teacher determine what is known and what learning might be needed.

When the possibilities for exploration have been listed, the teacher can then direct students to consider potential culminations—the demonstrations of learning. In other words, after the questions are researched and the inquiries are explored, what will the resolutions look like? What form will the communication of results likely take? For example, one advanced learning group was engaged in the context of the book *The Bamboo Flute* (Disher, 1993). They were interested in the bamboo flute in the story. How does the boy make a flute? The suggestions for exploration

---

FIGURE 8.6 Group planning chart

Inquiries	**Explorations**	**Potential Culminations**
Questions	Experiments	Written/oral communications
Mysteries	People to ask	Dramatic presentations
Ideas	Places to visit	Artifacts and constructions
Hypotheses	Reading	Demonstrations
etc.	etc.	etc.

included following printed directions, finding someone who knows how to make a flute, and using trial and error to make a flute. The possible culminations followed from the proposed inquiries and the explorations: bring a flute and show how it works, play some flute music, create a poster of flutelike instruments (fig 8.7). Students benefit from all of this work because the suggestions recorded on the chart give them ample flexibility to explore the questions of their interest, yet provide some general boundaries and expectations.

Even at this advanced level, teachers serve an important role in developing contexts that lead to authentic problem solving. If we are serious about students co-creating curriculum they need the support and framework that a writerly context provides. Without a context, students who are required to do research often pursue vacuous questions for which they have little interest or internal motivation. If we assign

FIGURE 8.7 *The Bamboo Flute* planning chart

Inquiries	Explorations	Potential Culminations
Flutes: How does a flute work? How did the boy make one? What is the history of the flute?	Use books; ask music and physics teachers Try to make one from description Contact local musicians	A diagram of a flute Simple instructions for playing Materials so others can make a flute Flow chart of the history of the flute Recording of flute music played
Australian geography and culture: What did the land around Tarlee look like? Was there a gold rush? Was the Australian depression like that of the U.S.? What are the people like?	Use library, CD-ROM, INFO Trak Personal contacts of known Australians Travel agencies Internet news groups	Maps of the region with Tarlee identified Pictures of the region Posters depicting region and people A skit depicting culture Oral presentation
Effects of war on veterans: Why did the father in the story seem so cold? What was the role of the letter opener? Did other Australian soldiers in WWI also make these things?	Movies—documentaries Personal contacts of vets Written histories of other wars VA Hospital Psychologists	Guest speaker Chart depicting effects Docudrama Read-aloud Skit
Swagmen: Who were the swagmen? Were they analogous to American hoboes? Do wars create these kind of men? Was "Waltzing Matilda" a stimulus for the book?	Literature of the time Australian histories Collaborate with other groups Lyrics of "Waltzing Matilda"	Interpretation of song Guide to special vocabulary Comparison chart of hoboes and swagmen Pictures or artistic rendition of swagmen

inane topics or default to letting students pinball about in the encyclopedia, they will rarely engage in real-world explorations. Thinking up good, important questions out of the blue is an extremely difficult task. Learning to frame inquiries that are researchable and doable requires the experience and support of teachers. The point we are reiterating here is that appropriate contexts impart the benefit of creating possibilities for authentic inquiries and problem solving. In addition, the well-chosen context can motivate students to move beyond their current areas of interest by offering the intrigue of new areas of study previously unknown to the student. If the only beginning point for curriculum is the students' interest, how will they ever discover new territory? Contexts can lead students to arenas they may never have found for themselves. If our students had not interacted with *The Bamboo Flute* context, it is unlikely they would have met Diep, who spoke poignantly of her flight from Cambodia, or Mary, who taught them to make flutes from cow-parsley stalks, or Eleanor, who shared treasures of her early life in Australia. Yet, the students became so highly involved in these experiences that they acquired new communication skills and enriched their personal lives.

Finally, having an entire class of students working within a context allows the teacher a better opportunity to meet the students' needs. We recall a teacher who had numerous small groups of students working on a variety of projects. All the groups had chosen interesting, worthwhile research. The teacher's frustration was not with the students' choices or their industriousness but with his own inability to facilitate the level of excellence he desired. One group was writing a grant for watershed management. A second group was learning bicycle repair. A third group was trying to build solar-powered model cars. And one student was building a wooden gun cabinet. There were just too many unrelated projects going on simultaneously for the teacher to deal with all of them adequately. All the students needed scaffolding to achieve at their highest potential, but the teacher did not have either the time or the resources to support the diversity of activity within the class. A context would have provided some boundaries within which the teacher could have worked more effectively with all the students.

Across the continuum of co-created curriculum, students need teachers. Teachers help students refine their ability to recognize areas of inquiry. They facilitate students' growth in generating and focusing questions. They listen carefully to help students determine if they have an internal motivation for the inquiry. Teachers help extend students' factual, process, and discipline knowledge. They guide students' choices regarding the means of exploring the inquiries. They foster explorations in the spirit of the way productive people solve problems that emerge from their real-world experiences with work, family, recreation, and social concerns. They serve as models of master learners and they apprentice their students into this type of learning.

💠 A Rationale of Reality

The rationale for co-creating curriculum with children is both developmental and realistic. It is realistic in that children create much of the curriculum of any classroom, whether it is recognized or not. Our classroom observations have revealed many examples of student-initiated curriculum that is disallowed or forced underground. Charlie is reprimanded by his fourth grade teacher for reading *Mort d'Arthur* instead of the assigned basal reader story. Doug, a first grader, makes Ninja swords from his Unifix cubes. A class watches its daily dose of current events on television and in great excitement wants to discuss the riots they have been viewing and the nature of race relations. Instead the teacher directs their attention to the chapter on Uruguay in their social studies textbook. Rachelle plans a family trip to Mexico while the teacher lectures on the history of that country.

Hubbard (1989) documents examples of underground literacy. Shelley creates a database of bathroom use while in the hall, supposedly occupied by peer writing conferences. Joe learns about statistics by tallying popular phrases on Star Trek. Three sixth grade girls pass 35 notes during a three-week period (a substantial amount of writing). Many children, either alone or with friends, create rich, out-of-school learning experiences involving elaborate games or pretend situations. *Roxaboxen* (McLerran, 1991), the recounting of a special place created in childhood, demonstrates how these child-created learning experiences are powerful memories. Perhaps you, too, had your own "Roxaboxen" or medieval castle or palace along the Nile. All these are examples of students engaging in a self-initiated curriculum. We recognize that students will always engage in their private curricula. We would not deny them this, but we highlight these examples as proof that kids are capable of curriculum planning. The energy and intellectual power apparent in students' underground curricula can be honored and channeled into the regular curriculum of the classroom through the process of co-creation. There would be less reason for students to create negative types of subversive curriculum if their voices were heard in the classroom.

💠 Developmental Considerations

The three levels of co-creating curriculum demonstrate different degrees of child involvement. Younger children participate in the planning process although the actual curriculum-planning responsibility resides with the teacher. Intermediate grade students have more involvement in planning their learning. This negotiated process shares the freedom and responsibility between teacher and student. Finally, more mature students develop into self-directed curriculum planners. From our perspective, these differences are intuitively and developmentally appropriate. That is, we believe that as children mature, they should take on more responsibility and more freedom in learning. However, there are additional compelling reasons for adopting a transitional co-creative approach to the narrative curriculum. The stages we have described in planning are directly related to what we know about how students develop cognitively, psychosocially, and morally.

We realize that within one chapter we cannot present a detailed picture of the characteristics of children at different developmental levels. That information is available in a variety of other sources. The list of companion readings at the end of the chapter provides references to Piaget, Kohlberg, and Erickson. In the previous sections we began with a discussion of younger learners and then progressed toward more mature learners. In this section we characterize the differences between young and more mature learners and build some rationale for the developmental appropriateness of the narrative curriculum and its planning process. We outline the major reasons why the narrative curriculum and the transitional planning process are developmentally appropriate. Much of the practical classroom view presented here was developed with a group of elementary and middle level teachers who joined us in our study of developmentally appropriate curriculum integration.

Primary Grade Learners

Much is known about how primary grade children reason, make decisions, and interact with others. The work of Piaget describes preoperational learners as children who tend to think concretely, who contain their belief systems in tangible explanations of events, and who tend to arrange their world in unidimensional packages. Erickson describes these young children as experiencing tension between feeling good about accomplishments and feeling inferior about failure. Kohlberg places these young students at a preconventional level of reasoning. Their moral decisions arise from pressure to act from fear of getting into trouble or for reward of being "good."

Teachers who work with primary grade students on a daily basis agree with these classifications, but tend to be more specific about other traits:

■ Children at this age learn by doing.
■ They encounter the world with all senses.
■ They engage in trial and error and learn from mistakes.
■ They learn concrete concepts best.
■ They need to "own" experiences.
■ They love play.

- They have egocentric interests.
- Personal needs are more important than the group's.
- They will cooperate but have trouble collaborating.
- They have a lot of psychomotor energy.
- These students ask questions, argue, and talk a lot.
- They often need direction to complete tasks or to display a certain behavior.

Primary grade children think, act, and learn in a special way, according to their level of development. The characteristics of this age group have several logical consequences for the construction of an appropriate curriculum and learning environment. For example, since primary grade learners tend to explain and interact with their world in tangible ways, then opportunities for learning should be highly tactile and real. Movement is critical as students practice the use of senses and newly acquired language to describe their world. Since these learners tend to think in simple, one-variable logical structures, the opportunities for inquiry should be arranged so that clear relationships between inquiries and explorations are evident. Because children make decisions based on perceived right and wrong and the consequences of those behaviors, curricular contexts should lead to clear and unambiguous resolution.

Because it is hazardous to engage in a process of prescribing do's and don'ts, we offer some strong suggestions. Teachers should take an active role in shaping the context for learning. They should arrange conditions that take advantage of the characteristics of primary grade learners. They should pick contexts, for example, that embody bold concepts such as change and cause and effect. Contexts should lend themselves to active and tangible explorations. Carol Still's decision to present a context that led to exploration of seeds was appropriate because it allowed students to be actively and sensorily involved in their explorations. An abstract organizer would be much less likely to match primary grade students either cognitively or morally. Because personal needs are so important to learners of this age, explorations should be shaped so that learners are allowed to make some personal choices. In the kindergarten classroom, all the children planted seeds and created pictures for a class book, yet they were all allowed to do it in their own ways. Students cooperated by sharing materials and space, yet they acted as individuals in creating their own designs.

The narrative curriculum addresses these developmental concerns. We believe that the process of child-informed planning, the development of inquires from the interests of students, and the crafting of developmentally appropriate exploration opportunities all present a good match to the developmental characteristics of primary grade students.

Mature Learners

As we move along the developmental spectrum to discuss middle school students, we encounter learners who exhibit more sophisticated traits. Psychosocially, students in this developmental category typically struggle with their identity in relation to the adult role they envision for themselves. Teachers characterize this group:

- They question authority often.
- Their behaviors range from sulking to enthusiasm.
- They like team sports.
- They develop cliques.
- They can be irrational and horrible.
- Peers are important.

Since these students are testing and forming adult roles and since they question authority, curriculum should not be solely teacher-directed. There should be opportunity for student-initiated curriculum planning. The choices they have and the empowerment they are given in this process match the learners' needs to test their wings and try something on their own.

Morally, students in this developmental category present what Kohlberg would call conventional reasoning. Typical kinds of thought processes that characterize this kind of thinking include:

- What is in it for me?
- What are the limits in this situation?
- Is what we are doing right?
- What are the consequences of these actions?

Again, if we develop appropriate practices that match this sort of reasoning, we create opportunities for students to engage in collaborative work, from which leaders and specific roles could emerge. Open-ended inquiry allows students an opportunity to answer their own questions about what is worth knowing and what is right. Narrative curriculum is ideally suited to this age range as it affords students room to explore their own definitions of truth while being challenged by different viewpoints.

Cognitively, students who have reached age 12 or so are starting to think abstractly. Piaget has described this formal operational stage exhaustively. What we would emphasize here is that learners who are starting to think abstractly need many opportunities to question, explore possibilities, manipulate ideas with materials, and depend upon concrete backgrounds, yet press on to communicate broader meaning. Because these learners need to meet challenges, have freedom to explore, and make meaning from experience, their curriculum should offer these opportunities.

The narrative curriculum that is planned primarily by students seems a perfect fit to the developmental needs of middle level students. These learners need to test their wings and this kind of curriculum model recognizes and validates that need. As students begin to realize that their real questions will be honored and that they are expected to create plans for investigating their questions, they find more interest in posing other inquiries and explorations. Their roles and identities can be transformed in this curriculum. One teacher using a co-created curriculum with a group of at-risk students reported that at first, students entering the class made little eye contact and rarely spoke unless spoken to. After weeks of working together in a simulated business, students willingly sought the roles of an accountant, a carpenter, an advertiser, and a salesperson. At the end of the enterprise, the teacher reported that the self-esteem of nearly all the students soared as they presented their work.

The student-planned narrative curriculum is an effective way of addressing the age-old problem of authority and compliance. When curriculum is a top-down, follow-the-rules, fill-in-the-worksheet design, it is no wonder that we see preadolescents and adolescents challenge the limits. If students generate much of the curriculum, we short circuit at least part of the conflict of "who's in charge." Society wants and expects marvels of our students, yet, ironically, by creating a dogmatic, transmissional curriculum, schools have only succeeded in exacerbating a developmental problem. A student-planned curriculum seems to ease many of these effects. In addition, it has advantages in providing learners a wide array of possibilities. Middle and high school learners bring to school an enormous amount of prior knowledge that is often ignored. If we employ a curriculum that respects what students already know and builds from that knowledge and skill base, then we have an opportunity to help learners make substantial individual progress. Engaging the students in the planning process allows us to identify those areas that are already a part of their backgrounds and to focus on those regions that are unknown. Working with the students to choose appropriate and meaningful contexts and inquiries honors their prior knowledge and experiences and addresses issues that challenge students to think abstractly and creatively.

Intermediate Grade Learners

Because learners in the intermediate grades (3–5) are in transition developmentally, they often display characteristics of both younger and older children. There are a few characteristics that may be helpful, however, in describing students at this level. Cognitively, students demonstrate remarkable growth. Becoming concrete learners, students are able to tackle more complex issues, wrestle with multivariate problems, and develop a sense of how various systems work. Morally, we also see an important change. Learners begin to interpret rules as important, unalterable givens. The formation of and allegiance to identified procedures and practices becomes their natural method of making decisions about the world. Psychosocially, students begin to identify gender roles and start to build personal relationships with others.

Teachers describe the needs of these students:

▌ Students in middle grades need opportunity to encounter open-ended inquiries.

▌ They need opportunities to explore both practical and creative aspects of their environment.

▌ They need to be involved in shaping the direction of their learning.

▌ They need to learn to take responsibilities for their actions.

▌ They need opportunity to share the products of their learning with peers and adults.

▌ They need to be offered a range of cognitive opportunity so that all can have success.

The negotiated narrative curriculum can provide a solution to the students' needs at this nexus of developmental stages. When we negotiate the curriculum with students we cede them certain powers and responsibilities. However, teachers must retain some control because they are more knowledgeable about contexts, potential explorations, and desired goals.

Teachers who employ a negotiated process in the middle grades notice that students find niches that are individually suited. For example, in our first chapter we chronicled the negotiated curriculum of *Very Last First Time*. The students in this group represented a range of abilities and developmental levels. There were great disparities in the level of questions that were posed and in the level of the children's sophistication for exploration. This eclectic group was well served because we honored all levels of understanding. From Karl and Vanessa, who made theoretical leaps about ice floes and electrical currents, to Jake who focused on using a glue gun to make a sugar cube igloo, each individual had the opportunity to work at his or her own level.

Balance is key in the negotiated process. Clearly, as teachers try to determine the proportion of student-created curriculum, they must consider their learners' developmental abilities. A third grade classroom may negotiate less responsibility than a fifth grade one, although individual students may have needs that differ from the group as a whole. The balance of how much to preplan and require versus how much to allow as personal choice is a matter of professional judgment. The important feature of an open, negotiated, co-created process is that the teacher can adjust the level of responsibility as learners grow accustomed to the pattern of learning, and as they develop cognitively, psychosocially, and morally.

Summary: A Continuum of Curriculum Planning

The transfer of curriculum-planning responsibility from teacher to student can be conceptualized as a continuum. Figure 8.1 delineates the changing roles of students and teachers as students mature as learners. As learners move along the continuum, they gain more and more responsibility for determining the curriculum. By the same token, teachers grant more and more responsibility for the curriculum to students, as they become more self-directed in their learning.

Allowing ourselves flexibility in planning the narrative curriculum also allows us to accommodate the wide skill ranges and developmental abilities of our learners. In the informed, negotiated, and student-planned curriculum there are opportunities for learners to act at their levels of cognitive ability. Our work with *Very Last First Time*, for example, has informed us about how different developmental levels and learner abilities interact with the planning and learning. Mature learners ask questions about earth-moon systems, about rites of passage, about technological dualities in the arctic, and about the effects of Euro-American cultures on Native American society. Mature learners delve into complex problems, use sophisticated language, explore nuances of problems, and interact with the material at their own level. Our younger learners found just as much to interest them in this context, yet their questions were less sophisticated, much less abstract, and demonstrated less prior knowledge of facts and ways of learning. Their questions related to more tangible topics of ice, sea, mussels, and the natural environment. Still, they worked from their level and grew in knowledge and skills as they developed meaning with the narrative. Narrative curriculum that is co-created with students makes it possible to address many of the developmental and individual differences that we find in our classrooms.

Lingering Questions

How do teachers learn to involve children in developmentally appropriate roles in curriculum planning?

How do our ideas about "control" influence how we plan curriculum?

Companion Readings

For general discussions of development, most educational psychology textbooks present adequate coverage. *Educational Psychology: Classroom Connections* (Eggen & Kauchak, 1992), and *Psychology Applied to Teaching* (Biehler & Snowman, 1986) both have chapters that describe Piaget's, Erikson's, and Kohlberg's theories. Both books also have chapters that explore appropriate classroom practices that emerge from these theories. Other reading that would help supplement your understanding of the ideas in this chapter focuses on developmentally appropriate practices. Bredekamp's (1987) *Developmentally Appropriate Practices in Early Childhood Programs: Serving Children from Birth through Age 8* is a standard reference for primary grades. *The Integrated Elementary Classroom: A Developmental Model of Education for the 21st Century* (Charbonneau & Reider, 1995) extends into the elementary grades. Middle-level needs are addressed by Manning (1993) in *Developmentally Appropriate Middle Level Schools.*

CHAPTER 9

Moving from Plans to Actions

Activating Prior Knowledge

What strategies or teaching techniques do you know that would help you implement the narrative curriculum?

What questions do you still have about planning or implementation?

Chapter Highlights

In this chapter we move from theory into practice to present some classroom-tested strategies and techniques that contribute to the success of the narrative curriculum. These pragmatic hints are organized within the structure of the planning template used in chapter 6.

*"We could hardly wait for morning to come
to get at something that interested us.
That's happiness."*

(Orville Wright as quoted by Freedman, 1991)

In previous chapters we have discussed the narrative curriculum in
more or less theoretical terms. The purpose of this chapter is to describe the
nuts and bolts of the model—how we offer the narrative context, how we
stimulate and collect inquiries, and how we manage day-to-day instruction.
The practical nature of this chapter will provide a resource as you begin to
implement curriculum. If you wish, for example, to investigate a particular
aspect of the planning process or seek an answer for a specific question, figure 9.1 provides a visual index to the information in this chapter.

Inviting Children into the Context

Once we have selected an appropriate context, with the potential to support further learning, the next task must be to help students become
involved and curious. Just reading a book, hearing a speaker, walking
along a creek, or watching a movie may not do the trick. As teachers we
must orchestrate the invitation. Our purpose is to provide students with as
many opportunities as possible to interact with the context, make observations, and come away with puzzles, questions, and unquenched curiosity. We have found several successful strategies that achieve these aims.

Books

Interactive Reading.   As described in the first chapter, the context of
Very Last First Time was presented to the students as an interactive read-
aloud. Carol wanted to share this well-crafted picture book in an intimate
reading circle so that the children could interact not only with the book's
text and illustrations but also with each other. Before the reading, Carol
had identified some points of tension and suspense in the story where she
could pause to invite the students to respond and make observations and
predictions. A transcript of this read-aloud is provided in Appendix D. The
dialogue is coded to show the kind of teacher talk that stimulates thinking,
questioning, and the sharing of ideas.

The interactive read-aloud provides a way to invite students into the narrative context and to conduct an initial pass at collecting inquiries from the
group. This experience can also provide a wealth of assessment information

FIGURE 9.1 Organization of chapter 9

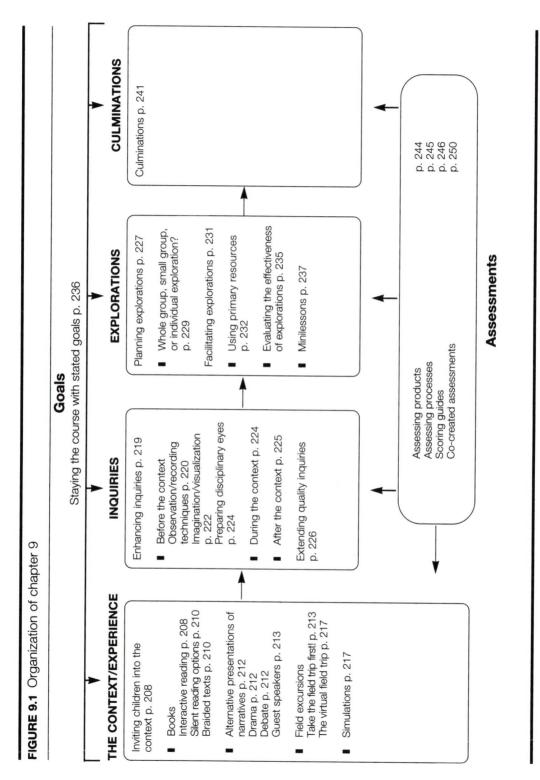

Goals

Staying the course with stated goals p. 236

THE CONTEXT/EXPERIENCE

Inviting children into the context p. 208

- Books
  Interactive reading p. 208
  Silent reading options p. 210
  Braided texts p. 210

- Alternative presentations of narratives p. 212
  Drama p. 212
  Debate p. 212
  Guest speakers p. 213

- Field excursions
  Take the field trip first! p. 213
  The virtual field trip p. 217

- Simulations p. 217

INQUIRIES

Enhancing inquiries p. 219

- Before the context
  Observation/recording techniques p. 220
  Imagination/visualization p. 222
  Preparing disciplinary eyes p. 224

- During the context p. 224

- After the context p. 225

Extending quality inquiries p. 226

EXPLORATIONS

Planning explorations p. 227

- Whole group, small group, or individual exploration? p. 229

Facilitating explorations p. 231

- Using primary resources p. 232

- Evaluating the effectiveness of explorations p. 235

- Minilessons p. 237

CULMINATIONS

Culminations p. 241

Assessments

Assessing products
Assessing processes
Scoring guides
Co-created assessments

p. 244
p. 245
p. 246
p. 250

to the teacher. In the *Very Last First Time* read-aloud, for example, it was clear from the questions about the ice and tides that some students could not conceptualize how this natural system worked. The students' questions and speculations provided information about their prior knowledge, concepts, and skills.

A variation of the interactive read-aloud is to read the book initially as a performance to which the students listen. After the reading, students and teacher respond to the story. Then during the second reading the students are invited to actively interact with the pictures, text, and other students. This is particularly effective with a short powerful text since it allows listeners to appreciate its full emotional impact. In addition, there is evidence that students develop greater insight and understanding through repeated experiences with the same text (Yaden, 1988).

Silent Reading Options for Interacting with Book Contexts. Sometimes the book or the circumstances of the classroom require a means other than the interactive read-aloud to create the context. An interactive read-aloud of a long chapter book, for instance, may be too cumbersome and slow. We may take so long reading and interacting that the inquiries and explorations would be stale by the time we have finished the story. Or we may weaken the impact of the text by fragmenting it. In addition, the plot may be too complex for students to remember their questions until the completion of the book. It may be easy to forget something that intrigued us at the beginning of the book because later in the book other considerations push it aside. If multiple copies of the text are available, students can read silently and write responses in a journal. This individual work can be followed by group discussion as is done in literature circles (Short & Pierce, 1990; Gilles, Dickenson, McBride, & Vandover, 1994). Some books such as *The Green Book* and *The Bamboo Flute* may be read in their entirety in a short time (one or two days). Longer, more complex books make be divided into sections and inquiries gathered for each section. Then, explorations can be initiated while the remaining portions of the book are read. Whatever the choice, the important consideration is to structure the reading so that the level of interactivity between students and text is similar to that of the read-aloud.

Braided Texts. A variation of creating context with one compelling piece of literature is to create a context with several interrelated texts. Selecting three books with similar themes, our colleague Ruth Davenport used *The Rag Coat* (Mills, 1991), *Only Opal* (Boulton, 1994), and *When I Was Young in the Mountains* (Rylant, 1992) as the context for her narrative curriculum (Davenport, Jaeger, & Lauritzen, 1995). Inquiries were created around each book as it was read and then discussions that examined the connections between the texts yielded even richer inquiries.

Two different procedures may be used. In the first option, all the texts are read in sequence and then the inquiries are generated. In the second option, inquiry and exploration of the first book could occur while a second book is introduced. The second and subsequent books are then interactive with the first and students use the cumulative experiences in each to shape more reflective questions.

The braided texts provide the learners with a more elaborate matrix from which to work and an opportunity to examine broad concepts and transcendental themes. In *The Rag Coat, Only Opal,* and *When I Was Young in the Mountains,* students could explore commonalities of the theme and the experiences of the characters. The students also learn to construct compare/contrast charts and Venn diagrams (fig. 9.2) as ways of organizing their ideas.

FIGURE 9.2 Venn diagram of braided stories

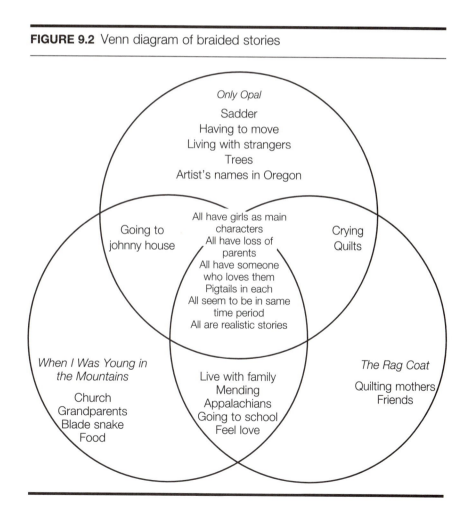

Alternative Presentations of Narratives

We need not always depend on children's literature to provide a context. In offering the stories of inventors, for example, we have sought alternatives to a written story. This repertoire adds interest and variety and allows the delivery of the context to be more closely matched to its content.

Drama. Role play is an effective means of engaging learners. The teacher can adopt the role of a historical person such as many professional actors have done (Hal Holbrook as Mark Twain, for instance). However, teachers need not feel they have to provide a polished performance. They must only be willing to take the risk of adopting a role and basing it on enough research to build a realistic character. Alternatively, students, faculty volunteers, and community members can be drafted into roles that the teacher has loosely scripted. For the "Thinking Like the Great Inventors" project (Jaeger, Munck, & Lauritzen, 1995), videotapes of the role play were created so that teachers unwilling to act in roles themselves could take advantage of the drama.

Role plays are varied. Rather than try to recreate a famous character, one might tell the story in the role of a minor character. For example, we created a story from the perspective of a scientist who knew Thomas Edison and presented the inventor through this idiosyncratic point of view. A written version of this oral story is in Appendix E. While the narrator was fictionalized, the information about Edison was accurate. This personal accounting requires a degree of sophistication in knowing the content thoroughly and adapting the character who delivers the information.

Question-and-answer sessions after dramatic presentations can entice learners to ask critical and detailed questions about the setting and characters in the role play. The storyteller stays in character and responds to the audience with improvisation. This can be particularly effective if the presenter then serves as a resource for students as they engage in their explorations. Michael has successfully employed this technique with students by playing two roles in the classroom during the exploration phase: one, as the teacher-facilitator, and the other as the "guest" persona. When he was himself, the teacher, he always stood. When he was responding as the "guest," he sat. In this way, he could indicate by his stance which of the roles he was serving.

Debate. Debate is another way we have introduced story. Two sides of an issue, concept, or historical event can be played by characters who have adequately learned about the situation and who have some improvisational skills. Again, interactivity can be an important feature using this kind of invitation. Students should be invited to interact with the debaters just as one would do in any public forum. The questions and interests generated from these exchanges can often bring about more possibilities for exploration.

Interviews. Interviews are also feasible for the classroom teacher. There are many people in the community who have a story to tell, and often the best way to hear the tale is through an interview. Even though interviewing can be difficult to do well and requires thoughtful, prepared questions as well as improvised follow-up questions, a successful interview can be a compelling context. Witness the success of talk shows in this media-rich world. Their popularity offers ample evidence of the appeal of the stories of regular people.

While most people are not very good solitary storytellers and/or do not realize their story is of interest or worth, they can tell their story if given opportunity and the right prompts. If teachers and students can learn to be good interviewers, then these stories are available to all learners.

Guest speakers. Inviting a guest speaker into the classroom is a common practice. Yet, in terms of the narrative curriculum, the guest presenter can be risky. In the other modes of presenting context, the teacher can control the variables of the story. However, we rarely have control over how a guest speaker will present a context or over the extent of the content they will present. Some are marvelous. Some are not! Good presenters for the narrative context show instead of tell. Good presenters encourage questions and provide appropriate responses. Good presenters involve children by listening to their interests. Good presenters limit the length of the presentation and focus on the most compelling aspects of their story. Good presenters leave students wanting to know more and wanting to find it out for themselves. The opposite of these results describes presentations that fail in providing a compelling context.

We have tried conferencing prior to the presentation, written guidelines, and coaching to help shape how our guests interact with children, but we have found no clear method of assuring the quality or the "writerly" nature of presentation. A trial run may be the best method of determining whether the guest presenter's style will create a suitable context.

Field Excursions

Take the Field Trip First! Most teachers view field trips as a supportive activity for instruction or as a closure for a unit. For example, classes visit tide pools to support a unit on oceans or go to the zoo as a fun trip and to provide closure to a study of animals. The field trip is like a reward for having studied the topic. In the narrative curriculum, the purpose of the field trip is quite different. In the traditional role of the field trip, the students have already studied the topic, written the reports, and taken the tests. They go on the field trip to confirm what they know. In the narrative curriculum, the students go on the field trip to discover the possibilities, to find areas of interest, and to whet their appetites for learning. From the field trip experience, the students and teacher generate inquiries. The field trip forms the context and therefore must come first.

Let us describe a field trip as a context. Near our school is an area of natural thermal springs. One place, called Hot Lake, is particularly interesting because of its long history as a hotel, resort, and hospital. Rumors circulated that the abandoned buildings were haunted and that mysterious creatures lurked in the hot water ponds. We believed Hot Lake would generate a lot of inquiry because of the eclectic nature of the area and because of the history and mystery surrounding humans' use of it.

The class toured the area on the first day of the unit. Readied by instructions to take down observations and questions, the students walked around hot water ponds, through overgrown wild areas, into eerie buildings filled with odd-looking medical equipment, through dilapidated barns and a dairy shed, through power generation facilities and bathhouses—all broken, vandalized, and mysterious. Questions abounded in the experience: "What did this place used to be? Who worked here? How old is it? What lives in the pond? What is the gray lacy stuff coming out of the hot water vent? What are these odd instruments in the hospital building?" and dozens more.

We spent several hours poking through the weeds, peering into dark rooms, skipping stones in the steamy pools. Michael, the science person, wondered out loud with students about the origins of the hot water, the ecosystem of the ponds, and the chemical and physical nature of the water.

Carol was curious about the people who worked, played, and were healed here. What were they like? What did they do here? Tom, the artist, thought metaphysically about the feeling of the site. "Can you feel the energy here?" he asked. He speculated about the healing, peaceful nature of the thermal springs and wondered about the Native Americans and early pioneers as they came upon these springs to rest and repair their physical and spiritual bodies.

We left Hot Lake with dozens of unanswered questions. There was plenty to wonder about. Students had jotted observations and questions in their notebooks. Our later examination revealed that they had addressed a multitude of disciplines: history, sociology, literature, biology, geography, geology, aesthetics, and technology. There were no shortage of interests to explore the next day when we started class. These interests led to hours of research, study, discussion, and sharing of results.

We had a strategic plan for this field trip. We did many things to try to ensure that the field trip would provide a compelling context for the days of exploration to come. First, we carefully planned the field trip beforehand. Scouting the area, we created a planning template anticipating student questions and interests and possible explorations. Keeping in mind the potential of the historic, medical, architectural, biologic, geologic, and aesthetic aspects of the site, we planned a tour that would help direct students' attention to these areas.

We had to design the experience to help students focus on experiences without providing a stream of information. The caretaker was informed that we wanted to see the buildings, the natural surroundings, and the artifacts, but that we were not interested in a narrated tour filled with facts about Hot Lake. If the students asked a question he was welcome to share what he knew, but we did not want a readerly field trip. (A readerly field trip is like a readerly text. One sits in a tour bus and the guide tells you everything you would ever want to know about the experience before anyone has asked a question!) Without this caution, tour leaders are inclined to tell students compendiums of information that often serve to negate the possibility of inquiry.

The purpose of a field trip, then, is not to gather a lot of facts or absorb a lot of information, although that may happen. Instead, it is to stimulate interest and provide a basis for inquiry. Requiring reflective writing in a journal helped shape student expectations about the purpose of the field trip. We asked them to record ideas, reflections, puzzles, and questions from each part of the trip. This requirement reminded students to remain in a state of mind that facilitated inquiry and helped direct their thinking away from a solely recreational stance.

The subtle encouragement of and modeling by the teacher is critical throughout this process. In our field trip we intentionally gathered students around certain items and encouraged oral questions and speculations in much the same way that we conduct an interactive read-aloud. In one area, for example, the students peered into a rock-lined opening and watched the water bubble up to the surface. "I wonder what the temperature of the water is?" Michael offered. One student speculated that it must be boiling because there were bubbles. Another student disputed the theory because the water did not seem that hot. Michael then asked how they might explore this question. Students started to speculate on how one might go about proving or disproving the theory. Later, inside the building, our artist friend Tom looked at peeling paint and commented, "I wish I had a roll of film for this wall." With this minimal prompting and modeling, students looked at the paint in a new way. These overt actions of teachers challenge students to observe and think in specific ways and are critical to generating worthwhile questions.

With our younger learners the case is even clearer. We doubt that students without guidance would generate as many detailed interests if we had not scaffolded them to observe carefully. Near a pond we asked students to dip in a bucket and retrieve a sample of water. Water lilies, bottom muck, and a host of critters emerged. Because of this, students wanted to know what kind of creatures lived in the weeds and why the black oozing mud smelled so bad. Later, we asked students to climb a hillside and collect as many different kinds of vegetation as they could. Because of these observations students wanted to know what these plants were and whether they were edible. Sitting down with the class on the cool grass, we

asked them to be quiet for a moment and think back to hundreds of years ago and imagine themselves as Native Americans. From this experience students recorded dozens of questions about the resources available to the Native Americans and the nature of the environment in the past versus the present. In each of these cases we expected students either to extend their observation skills or to focus their thinking in a certain way. These two features enhance the productivity of the field trip experience.

We encourage you to think creatively about field trip possibilities. They do not need to be elaborate, expensive affairs. We often try to plan field trips that our students can walk to. Consider the playground, the neighborhood, a historical building, a nearby business, a forest or stream, a craftsperson's workroom, a display or demonstration of someone's hobby, a cemetery, the school cafeteria, or the furnace room. There are opportunities right where you are—you just need to find them.

The Virtual Field Trip. Field trips are wonderful, but practitioners often report that either logistics or finances prevent their accessibility. Virtual field trips can fill the void in some cases. A virtual field trip can be a video-tape, slide show, or multimedia presentation of the experiences that one might have had on an actual trip. Although poor in sensory opportunities, a virtual field trip can bring auditory and visual stimuli to the learner.

A local teacher likes to use the virtual field trip to acquaint learners with experiences that they would otherwise be unable to have. A tour through a high-tech and high-danger lumber mill may be an important and appropriate context for upper-grade children, but, because of the legal and logistical ramifications, it is impossible. With supervision, Doug was allowed to record a tour with a video camera. The camera captured what he saw and the questions he asked. This personal trip became the context for students as they began their inquiries about the natural resources and economy of the region.

If a video is created it should be relatively short, detailed with close-up views of important aspects of the trip, and peopled with the conversations of knowledgeable individuals on site. The video should be lightly narrated and should avoid transmission of facts and information. The goal is not to produce a polished National Geographic-like video. Rather, it should be a personal account of a context so that the students can live through the experience and generate their own questions.

Simulations

Remember how we introduced the chapter on goals with "The Town That Moved?" This was a combination of role play and interactive drama. Olaf and Inge began the simulation with a conversation at the dinner table and then invited the audience to join their story. The story became a simulation as students took on the roles of characters interacting with Olaf and Inge. Olaf and Inge, not Michael and Carol, invited the learners into the context and created the opportunities for interaction. Each time we met with students we were in character and invited our learners into the drama.

In a similar example, groups of teachers have experimented with simulations in which students are invited into the context by assuming the role of an actual historical person, rather than a fictional character. In a simulation of Ellis Island, students were told in their classroom that they were going to immigrate to America. They then marched to another classroom, prepared to provide an Ellis Island atmosphere, where they were given name tags and the identities of actual Ellis Island immigrants. The teachers were in character as Ellis Island personnel and they treated the students as though they were immigrants. Throughout a week of intense activity the teachers and students stayed in role. Students learned about their home countries, the reasons for immigration, the procedures of Ellis Island, and the role of the immigrants in making a new nation as though the students were actual participants in that history. Moving through the simulation, students had to reconcile their characters according to the tensions and promises of a new land. This curriculum unit is presented in more detail in chapter 10.

Simulations require a time each day when students take on the role of someone else. Students need to spend significant time developing their own characters to fit into a larger story. Resumes, ID cards, personal histories, occupations, hobbies, and possessions are all synthesized as the children become Dust Bowl migrants, space travelers, cruise ship passengers, or business people creating a shoreline community. The teacher's role in a simulation is to encourage the students to develop full and accurate roles and to ensure that the simulation occurs for a designated portion of the day on a regular basis.

Story-making through simulation depends on the willingness of the teacher and learner to step into other characters. This is often easier for students than for teachers. The current popularity of role playing games demonstrates the appeal this approach has for students. Teachers may choose to remain outside the role playing as guides and facilitators. A group of teachers who arranged a simulation of migration along Route 66 during the Dust Bowl had initially intended to be part of the simulation. Each student was assigned an identity as a member of an actual migrant family. The teachers were going to be family members as well. However, as their planning proceeded, they realized it would be extremely difficult for them to stay in role and still meet the goals they had identified for the experience. They decided to remain outside the simulation as teachers/guides for the Dust Bowl travelers.

It is also important to realize that students need to remain somewhat aloof from their characters, always retaining the separation of themselves from the roles they are playing. However, as a precaution, it may be a good idea to set ground rules about the nature of events that will be allowed. For instance, it might be advisable to restrict the use of violence and to ban the death of characters during the role play. Finally, be reassured that we are not suggesting a reenactment such as those performed at Colonial Williamsburg or Plymouth Plantation. The simulation creates a story which will foster inquiry. Simulations that are lacking in details have a writerly quality that is beneficial to learners.

Enhancing Inquiries

As we plan to read the book, take the field trip, bring in the speaker, conduct the drama, or create the simulation, we think of possible questions and anticipate our students' responses. But how can we ensure that students will see what we know is there and be invited to bring their own interests to the context? Even the most compelling context can be passively accepted. We recall many family trips to wondrous vistas and natural phenomena in the western United States when our children were more interested in sleeping or in quarreling than in looking out the window at the glories of nature! What might be at work here? Is it the passivity that comes from 30-minute packaged television encounters or is it the jaded feeling that comes from living in a world of superlatives? While we are not certain of the reasons why students may opt out of responding to a context, we do know that it is critical that we do all we can to help learners experience the context to the fullest.

What can we as teachers do to heighten students' awareness and to encourage them to observe and value what they see, feel, hear, and touch? We recommend strategies such as prereading procedures, observation techniques, recording techniques, imagination/visualization, and preparing disciplinary eyes. During the unfolding of the context, these strategies can be extended through interaction. After the context has been experienced, it can be revisited through retelling and revisioning. Finally, the context is enhanced if students bring multiple modalities into play.

Planning for Inquiries Before the Context

Prereading strategies.   Reading techniques that attract and focus learners' attention before the context are often helpful in making the learner more apt to interact in a constructive way. In our opening example of *Very Last First Time*, Carol asked the students to speculate about the cover of the book and the title. Students looked at the cover picture and some saw ice while others saw a desert. Prior knowledge was activated and children contributed what they thought or knew about the pictures and the probable setting. Before Carol opened the book, students were engaged in wondering about it. The cover and title offered some critical clues, yet several schema were possible.

This strategy is not intended to supply students with the prerequisites for tackling the book, but rather to activate their prior knowledge and identify prior schema. In this sense, we use prereading strategies not to build up background, but to heighten anticipation and honor prior knowledge. By activating all of the possible schema before the reading, students are then able to decide as they read or interact which schema is in play. The prereading strategy helps each learner become expectant about whether their predictions will be confirmed. This heightened internal motivation helps students be more attentive to the experience itself.

Prereading strategies can be adapted for field trips, simulations, or guest speakers. In these situations we can create sufficient anticipation with titles of events, names and vita of speakers, maps or brochures of destination sites, or written excerpts of simulations. If we ask our students what they expect, what they already know, and what they speculate about what will happen, then we raise the consciousness of all learners.

We should be careful not to confuse a prereading strategy with an anticipatory set. An anticipatory set is a technique aimed at getting the student's attention. Our strategy is not an artificial stimulus to interest them in something they probably will find uninteresting. We intend prereading strategies to be honest attempts to draw out of learners what they already know and what they think will happen. Descriptions of prereading techniques such as KWL, anticipation guides, and structured previews are available in many sources (Cooper, 1993; Tierney, Readence, & Dishner, 1990).

Observation/recording techniques. Prior to immersion in the context, it is very helpful to have learners decide how they will keep track of observations, information, and questions. If we prepare learners ahead of time with the idea that they will be hearing, seeing, and touching, then we should negotiate ways for them to keep track of these observations. Journals, observation guides, and media devices are some tools we have used to help students record their responses to the context.

Most learners can learn to keep a simple journal. Prior to entering the context, we ask them to make field notes and model for them, if necessary, how to record observations, list questions, sketch things of interest, and write extemporaneously. After students have learned to keep notes of their experiences, more complex forms such as a dual column journal (fig. 9.3) can be introduced. One column is for observations and notes, the other for

FIGURE 9.3 Two-column response journal

Observations and Notes	Reflections and Questions
Title/Cover:	
Chapter 1:	
Chapter 2:	

reflections and questions about those notes. This type of journal allows the student to move beyond observation to thinking about the significance of those observations. Many resources describe the forms and functions of journal writing (Fulwiler, 1987; Calkins, 1990; Bromley, 1993).

There are many devices that can be used to respond to a text. For the interactive read-aloud we have used a group chart, as described in chapter 1. A public-domain text can be printed so that there is a wide margin for taking notes as the student reads. See Appendix A for the "The Pine Tree Shillings" example. Middle grade and older students can keep response

journals. We initially scaffold students by asking them to make at least one or two comments about each chapter and to record their questions and interests or the things that they would like to know more about. In a long chapter book, we may choose to collect responses after a few chapters. This may be especially true if the book contains a number of diverse areas of interest, as does *The Bone Wars* (Lasky, 1988), which deals with paleontology, historical figures of the West, Native Americans, natural environments, and interpersonal struggles. In books of this sort, the students read a designated number of chapters, write journal reflections, and engage in discussion to elicit questions evoked by the designated chapters. Explorations are determined and initiated even while the rest of the book is being read. These explorations interact with the text and enhance the students' understanding of their reading. We want the interaction with the literature to be an experience of grand conversation (Edelsky, 1988; Peterson & Eeds, 1990) and intellectual curiosity. We need to maintain careful timing so that the study culminates on a still-rising sense of enjoyment. The students should still view the book as a treasure to be kept, not as a limp dirty rag to be discarded.

Observation guides are more directed and can help some learners focus their attention. We have used prompting questions such as "What did you see? What did you hear? What did you feel?" to help each learner utilize all the senses. Humans don't usually observe all the details unless they take the time and focus their attention carefully. If, before the experience, we ask our students to sit in a quiet spot and close their eyes and listen, or look carefully for certain details, or feel the textures, we are helping them focus their attention.

For field trips, media devices such as video cameras, CCDs, and tape recorders are effective ways of encouraging students to interact with the experience. We may also employ instruments or tools to enhance observational skills. If you give students a magnifying glass, a paper cone for their ears, or a plastic container for collecting, the tool becomes a way of focusing students' attention. Before our explorations of Hot Lake, students were given a thermometer. Because of this device they predicted that there must be something thermal to observe—their attention was alerted to look where they might not have looked before. Other students had insect nets or fish nets. Again, these tools indicate a specific way to focus on the experience.

Imagination/visualization.   Sometimes it is impossible to physically participate in the experience. In these cases children become spectators. To supplement the spectator role, we can ask our students to create a way of interacting in their minds. Learners can imagine or visualize the experience as though they were there—as though they were participants. One teacher team decided to make designing and building an airplane the

context for explorations. They asked a local model airplane pilot to fly his remote control airplanes on the school grounds. The context did not allow the students any direct participation—they could only watch while another person worked the controls to launch, fly, and land the plane. We suggested to the teachers that they have students imagine that they were in the plane, shrunk to the size of a miniature pilot. What would they see? Feel? Hear? Most elementary school students have little difficulty imagining being small. They have seen movies or read stories that have taken the viewpoint of tiny characters. Encouraging learners to become virtual participants can lead to many more intimate questions about the context. If we read with the notion that we become the character in the story, if we watch while also imagining ourselves in the shoes of the demonstrator, if we listen and visualize ourselves in the action, then new possibilities for interacting with the context emerge.

Preparing disciplinary eyes. Suppose the compelling experience you choose for your students is the zoo. You plan possibilities for students to elicit their questions about the biology of animals, the aesthetics and beauty of animal form, the ecological settings observed, and the technology of zoos. To encourage students to think in novel ways, you broaden their ability to create inquiries with the following prompts:

- Suppose you are a materials engineer on this trip today. What would you see? What would interest you? What questions might you have?
- You are an artist and have an entire hour just to roam around the zoo. What do you want to do?
- The zoo has just hired you as their waste manager. What will you want to look at? What will you be interested in?

If we prepare ourselves in a certain way, we are apt to see different things and to think differently about what we see. As we mentioned in an earlier chapter, disciplinary eyes are important in crafting explorations and in honoring the way in which each discipline organizes the natural world. By asking learners to train their eyes in specific ways, we encourage them to develop another perception. It may be an imperfect perception, but it does provide the function of broadening the way in which a learner interacts with the experience. With our explorations at Hot Lake, for example, we asked students to think like scientists, artists, writers, architects, and historians: "If you were a professional in this area, what would you find interesting? What would you spend your time looking at? What questions would you ask?" Asking questions from someone else's viewpoint certainly enhanced and broadened the inquiries that were generated. It is necessary to model the thinking, the questions, and the tools of the disciplines for students who do not have an understanding of them. The teacher can act as this model or can invite a professional in the discipline to do so.

Enhancing Inquiries During the Context

Each of the strategies that we employ before the initial immersion in context has an extension during the context, as we continue to encourage students to interact with their environment. As learners write, sketch, record, imagine, and think, we continuously return to the prompts we used to set the learners' anticipation of the event. If a journal has been established to record inquiries, then we call attention to their writing. If we want students to think as a particular professional would then questions and reminders during the experience should direct their efforts. If we want students to imagine or visualize, we ask them to share the images they are creating.

Another strategy that works well during the immersion experience is to immediately record student questions as they ask them. We have used clipboards, videotapes, tape recorders, overhead projectors, and blackboards to collect the questions and insights. We do not mean that teachers should bounce about posing strategic questions at every circumstance, but teachers can help students remember their ideas and record their insights while the students encounter the context. This strategy is especially important for younger students whose minds generate questions and observations much faster than their hands can write them. At the same time, these recordings suggest to students that their ideas are important and this further encourages them to respond.

Enhancing Inquiries After the Context

Once we have read the book, enjoyed the trip, engaged in the simulation, or seen the event, what can we do to encourage learners to inquire further? Even if we engage all of our strategies before and during the experience, there is a need to revisit the context afterward to provide the classroom community with a sense of shared inquiry. There are several possibilities for eliciting responses after the experience.

One effective way to get learners to generate ideas and to ask questions about the context is to have them retell the experience. By recasting the story, reliving the experience, or summarizing the event, the whole class has an opportunity to revisit the context. Prompts from the teacher and students can facilitate this retelling, so that comments lead to responses by other students which in turn lead to comments, and so forth. A chain reaction of observation, assertion, and counter-assertion is established and generates a host of inquiries about the context.

As we retell a story and brainstorm possibilities, we observe rules for student contributions. We encourage any and all responses and observations no matter how spurious, inappropriate, illogical, or impossible they may seem initially. When students speculated about Ungava Bay from *Very Last First Time*, for example, and suggested we go there to find out what it looked like, we recorded that idea along with all the others. After writing everything out we went through the process of selecting which inquiries and possible exploration fit within our probable capacities. As students see the suggestions displayed, they are likely to dismiss undoable or impractical suggestions. On the other hand, ideas that seemed "far-out" may, upon examination, be very fruitful pursuits. By delaying feedback, we respect all learners—both those who offer impractical, yet sincere, ideas and those who make humorous or interfering commentary. To do so honors the former student and avoids confrontation with the latter. In addition, it sets a tone that allows students to offer what they consider "wild" ideas. For example, in one classroom where this type of brainstorming took place, a student timidly suggested making a video with the disclaimer, "but you'd [the teacher] never let us do it." However, she would and they did and it was a valuable learning experience.

Collecting ideas about the context is certainly dependent on a high degree of interactivity between students and between students and the teacher. We have practiced this strategy with many age groups and note that prompts, active listening, and other communication skills are essential in helping learners articulate their inquiries and ideas. With one group of learners, for example, we read a story, asked them to record questions they had about the story, and collected their responses afterward. We first prompted their questions with a very general inquiry: "What questions did you have about the story you just read?" Because the piece we had given them was full of the unfamiliar vocabulary of a different era, students asked many questions about word meaning. They contributed very few other ideas or inquiries until we restated the question and asked, "What would you like to know more about?" After this prompt, we had a chorus of suggestions. We recognized that to give students alternative wordings of the invitation was critical. Consequently, we invite inquiries through prompts such as: "What does this make you want to know more about?" "What does this make you curious about?" "What feelings did you have during this experience?" "What things did you do that you'd like to do more of?"

◈ Extending Quality Inquiries

In seeking to stimulate inquiries, we are trying to encourage quality rather than quantity. After all, in order to solve problems, deal with issues, and think critically, we need a critical question to act on. Initially, most learners who are offered the opportunity to ask questions about a context are likely to ask information-like questions. When fifth graders responded to "The Pine Tree Shillings," for example, we found that, at first, they asked basic questions such as: "What does this word mean?" or "What is a _____?" This first layer of questions tends to be superficial and unsuited to the kind of exploration that we desire for students.

We have found several effective strategies to help students ask questions that explore conceptual relationships and disciplinary perspectives. First, as we solicit inquiries from students, we can be aware of our own wording and the nature of our own questions. A prompt such as "What questions do you have?" tends to get literal responses, while questions such as "What do you find puzzling here?" or "What did you wonder about?" tend to elicit more thoughtful inquiries. Sometimes the students' responses are nebulous or just hint at what they are thinking. In these cases we must have the patience and skill to help them find the wording to express their ideas. We can add to the student's repertoire of inquiry creation by modeling our own critical thinking questions.

Second, when students think and question from different disciplinary viewpoints, they generate a greater diversity of responses. If students suggest possible disciplines that might be appropriate to the context and then ask questions from the those perspectives, we could expect different responses to the same stimuli. We find it important to model these kinds of questions for students, especially when we know they have limited experience with a disciplinary perspective. With "The Pine Tree Shillings" story, Carol prompted many more questions during brainstorming when she modeled these inquiries: "What do you think a newspaper account of this event would look like? What if it were on the social page? What if it were on the editorial page? What would the writer want to know about the event?" Students could relate to this perspective and immediately contributed many more possibilities for inquiries.

Finally, we can, with the students, develop classification schemes of lower-level questions that yield more conceptual questions. The teacher and students can group all of the questions about the coins, for example, in one column and then think about all the questions together. "What is common about all these questions? or "What is one question we could ask that would help us answer all the rest?" Students had low-level questions such as: What is a doubloon? What is a shilling? What is a mint master? What is barter? Although each of these questions alone called for simple dictionary exercises, grouping these questions together encourages more global thinking. The larger questions about the origin of coins, the need for an economic system of exchange, and technology of minting emerged. Again, modeling of this process is essential. Teachers must set the pace to help students see the possibilities. With practice, students feel they have permission to ask challenging and therefore compelling questions.

Planning Explorations

We have thus far delineated how we discover much about what students already know through interaction with the context. In the same fashion, we also see their ideas about how they think their questions can be resolved. Students offer possible resolutions of inquiries before the teacher establishes explorations. Recording these early ideas allows us to engage in cooperative planning. We choose to have the entire class speculate about all inquiries and to list possibilities about experiments, readings, interviews, media, and other research possibilities. This way we enjoy the broadest thinking for all the questions posed. Some teachers invite students to complete their own planning charts as they try to determine how they might explore their inquiries and what products might result. This would be most appropriate after students have had the benefit of the group planning process and as they move toward independent learning. However, we favor cooperative planning at least some of the time because in most situations today, whether in employment, community projects, or family, people do need the collaborative planning skills that can be fostered through a group inquiry process.

When our possibility chart is completed, we help students think about what these explorations might look like and what the products and culminations might be for each. In our *Very Last First Time* example, we helped students envision their work ahead of time so that they could choose the inquiry which sounded the most appropriate:

> If you are interested in the question of Inuit culture, you will be looking at videos, reading printed resources, calling resource people, and perhaps creating facsimiles. If you are interested in how the ice caves are made you may be creating an experiment to simulate waves and tides. If you are interested in how long Eva had under the ice you may be doing experiments with candles and learning about tide tables.

When students, limited by their prior experience, think of how they might explore, they often see the finding out as tedious and unappealing. On the other hand, some questions sound too esoteric to students and they reject them as unobtainable. Offering students a glimpse of the exploration ahead of time counteracts both these possibilities by accurately setting the expectations and clearly matching learner interests to actual activities.

The next step requires good classroom logistics. Once we have established the areas of inquiry, the kinds of exploration, and the probable products, how will students move to the area of most interest? There are some positive things to consider and some pitfalls to avoid. We do suggest that groups be formed based on interests, rather than on popularity contests or social cliques. We can use a secret ballot to have students commit to an inquiry before checking on what their friends are doing, but it is preferable to build a classroom community where students will trust themselves and their peers enough to make good choices. It is also important to be careful to explain each kind of exploration so that they each have parallel appeal. If students are given a choice, for example, between an inquiry in which the exploration involves batteries, wires, and glue guns and an inquiry where students read encyclopedias, we can predict what children will choose! Therefore we might have one workshop time that is devoted to quiet types of exploration and another that is more active. If one exploration is incredibly compelling, then perhaps all students should have the opportunity to participate. If materials are scarce, allow enough time for the explorations so that students can rotate through the desired exploration. If there is only one facility or set of materials and many students are interested, then it may be important to find more materials. It is unsatisfying for learners to default to what is to them a less interesting question because there are not enough books, microscopes, computers, or maps.

Whole-Group, Small-Group, or Individual Exploration?

So far we have entertained only one kind of possibility for exploration—that small groups of learners will explore separate inquiries. There are several other possibilities. As we considered *Very Last First Time* we knew that most of the exploration would be done in small groups. We knew that the diversity of interests would likely generate at least four or five different groups. As we examined some of the explorations, we decided that it was critical for all students to participate and practice certain skills. We decide to invite all students to explore one of the inquiries, "Where was Ungava Bay and what was it like?" The whole class pored over maps, globes, atlases, and books to determine the answer. Similarly, we also chose a whole group exploration at the end of the unit when we invited students to explore the nature of the mussels. In the first case of exploring geography we made the decision based on the students' academic needs. In the second we made the decision for logistical and aesthetic reasons. We could get our supply of mussels only once during the week due to the delivery schedule at the local supermarket. We also wanted to have a common experience to conclude our context.

Some may question the validity of small group experiences rather than whole group ones. Why would a teacher allow one group to do something different from another? Isn't that unfair or, at the very least, unequal preparation? Won't the children know different things after they are finished with their explorations? We recognize the importance of all learners engaging in enjoyable experiences that foster the achievement of the identified goals. In some cases we would say, yes, every child should have the opportunity to do this one thing. Still, there are many times when students may not need to do everything. Some of our students made igloos, others made fishing spears, some conducted ice experiments, others made candle explorations. These explorations were valuable, but not critical in themselves to learning content or a skill. Igloo building, spear construction, and candle burning are not core knowledge. These explorations simply proved that all students experimented, used their hands and tools, created something, and communicated their findings. In this way the explorations were parallel and equal because each enabled students to pursue the intended goals.

Although we form groups to promote the goal of cooperation and collaboration and to facilitate the social nature of learning, there are often wonderful opportunities for individuals to engage in explorations as single inquirers as well. Students should be free to pursue inquiries that hold interest only for them and in which they will direct their own learning. Learning centers, individual choice times, mentoring, and out-of-class study are options that allow students to take personal inquiry beyond the mainstream of curriculum. When we elicit inquiries from students about the context, we honor *all* as valid. Because we are interested in forwarding certain goals and because we are limited in what we can facilitate as teachers, we can marshal resources for only a small number of the possible explorations that emerge from the context. It is at this point that students with compelling personal questions have the opportunity to go beyond the classroom fare. Parents and community mentors can become involved with individual students and their explorations.

The braided text unit discussed earlier offers a good example. The teacher planned certain logical adjuncts relating to the study of logging, quilts, and the history and sociology of the era. Some children became interested in trees and asked questions about the age of trees. An inquiry about growth rings arose and a group experimented with cross sections. One exploration led to several others and before the end of the week one student brought in a fossilized limb cast of a tree, another a leaf collection, another a taxonomic key about trees. The teacher encouraged her students to tackle these explorations during their individual study time in class and

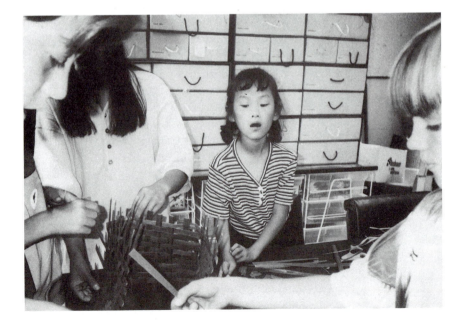

checked in with them as they made discoveries or ran into difficulties. Meanwhile, the teacher continued to foster the main adjuncts of the text in whole and small group activities.

Facilitating Explorations

We have been using the word *explorations* to designate how students in this curriculum resolve inquiries that they formulate. How do we help students create an exploration? As we have so often stated, acknowledging and serving the goals of instruction is foremost in our minds as we start to plan explorations. We desire much more for our students than a simple acquisition of information. Although we are confident that learning of meaningful and connected information (content) emerges from this kind of curriculum experience, we stress other goals. We care that students learn how to formulate questions, access and process information, experiment, draw conclusions, and communicate effectively.

A second critical aspect of planning explorations is the employment of a constructivist learning theory. We want explorations to be open-ended and contain a degree of uncertainty. Because we want children to explore, the answers are not as critical as the seeking. Therefore, we are not really focused on helping students discover a particular concept or relationship, but rather on their formulating their own concepts and generalizations about the questions they ask. We may want students to learn specific skills and processes while resolving their questions, but that is a different kind of learning that we will discuss in the section on minilessons.

Consider, as an example, the exploration of finding out about Ungava Bay. There are many ways of describing where this place is in the world. We could cite latitude and longitude, draw a map, point to it on a globe, relate its position to other cities, or describe how to get there. Knowing the range of possibilities, we simply allowed students to decide for themselves how to describe where Ungava Bay was. We left the exploration open-ended. There were no work sheets to fill in or right answers to get. Students came to know the place in their own ways.

What makes this kind of teacher facilitation possible is the collection of appropriate tools and resources that fosters student success. As teachers we scramble to find as many possibilities for students as we can. This is not easy, but then, teaching is no easy proposition! For the candle explorations, for example, we collected a number of different types of candles, matches, pie plates, a scale, rulers, and a ring stand. Because we knew the students would be interested in the dripping wax, we set up a station where they could experiment safely. After they had a chance to play around with the materials, we helped them think about how they might collect and interpret data related to their questions. The presence of a ruler suggested to them that they measure a candle before and after burning it. After working with the scale they decided they could also use this tool as a before-and-after measure. Students generated their own ways of finding out by using some of the materials we had carefully selected. If we had handed the students step-by-step instructions on how to measure, weigh, burn, and interpret candle data the experience would have been ours, not theirs.

We are not trying to cleverly get students to do what we want them to do. Rather, we provide what we think they will logically need to conduct the inquiry. It is our best guess of what we think they will ask for and what we think they will need to do their work. Often we find that students will not use some materials that we provide them and other times they openly reject what is available and ask for other things. We are always gratified when students supply their own materials for the inquiry because it indicates a high level of involvement. We want students to engage in meaningful explorations—we do not want the curriculum to distill to students following our recipes. This is a subtle difference but a crucial one, in that it separates a constructive versus a discovery approach.

A third important consideration for facilitating explorations is the role of talk. "Learning awakens a variety of internal processes that operate only when the child is interacting with others in his environment and in cooperation with his peers" (Peterson, 1992, p. 3). We benefit from the insights and experiences of others that are shared with us through talk.

> Learning benefits when partners co-produce meaning. Ideas get a better workout. No one truly learns in a vacuum. Students need informed feedback on how they are doing and an audience that will appreciate their efforts as well as their results. (Peterson, p. 79)

Watson (1993) asserts that talk is fundamental in meaning making. Barnes (1993) found that students working together can provoke each other to formulate explicit explanations in science and to interpret literature in a thoughtful way. "Since the most significant learning is likely to take place when young people are talking about something that matters to someone who wants to hear, it makes sense for students' talk to play a central part in all schooling." (Barnes, p. 33)

Using Primary Sources

Our examples in this text feature students interacting with primary sources: experimentation, people, community resources, documents, phone contacts, newspapers, Internet news groups. These types of sources are the mainstay of explorations. The experiences of our students who explored

The Bamboo Flute are a good example. Their first stop was at the library where they checked the usual resources: encyclopedia, card catalog, *Reader's Guide to Periodical Literature.* They came back saying, essentially, "We can't find anything!" We directed the students to primary sources, a reservoir they had never before tapped. We suggested several routes:

> Talk to the local geography professor. Maybe he can give you some leads. Call a woman we know who lives in a little town west of here. I think she knows something about Australia. Check with a woman in town who makes flutes out of plant stalks. She might be able to help. Post a note on the Internet news group dedicated to the culture of Australia. Do a CD-ROM search using keywords for post-traumatic stress disorder on the interlibrary database. Check the Internet for Australian resources using Netscape or some other search. Try to find a telephone number for someone in Tarlee.

All of these suggestions were like revelations to students. They thought that the only place one did research was in the library. If they bottomed out there, then there must be no solution.

The students tried everything we suggested and were amazed with what they found. Their telephone call to a local woman who used to teach in Australia yielded personal recollections, memorabilia, and printed resources about Australia. An Internet gopher source led them to the postal code for Tarlee so that its existence as a real place was confirmed. The geography professor helped them locate the tiny town on a more detailed map. He gave them several leads for contacts in Adelaide. A series of phone calls later they were speaking to a helpful woman in a town near Tarlee whose promises to send information were peppered with a phrase that became the catchword of the group: "no worries." The Internet news group provided a conversation about "Waltzing Matilda" and the history of swagmen as well as leads to other current sources of the history and culture of Australia. A local craftsperson showed one group how to make flutes from simple materials and gave them the tools and materials to make their own. Other local musicians provided insight into the therapeutic effects of music. Finally, through a psychologist, students met a college student who had lived in Cambodia during the purge of the Khymer Rouge and she provided a moving firsthand account of her escape and how post-traumatic stress disorder has affected her life.

Primary sources are key in this curriculum. Students need to see that to generate solutions to questions, we must go beyond the confines of textbook and school sources. Real resources are people who have their own stories to tell. There is a wonderful bonus in connecting with others in the search for solutions. We meet people that we would not have known otherwise. The students studying Australia interacted with the geography professor on a one-to-one basis. They made friends with a local musician and the Australian woman from a nearby town. The conversations and relationships that developed were powerful in shaping the students' ideas about their projects and affecting their ownership of the exploration.

The use of primary sources is not restricted to older students. We find elementary school students are also capable and gain a great deal from their use. Often the greatest benefits for these younger students are the relationships they establish with adults. For example, one of our 11- and 12-year-old groups worked on city issues. They wanted to see if they could design some alternative community recreation sites and built three-dimensional models to demonstrate their ideas. Even though students were motivated and interested in their projects, they were transformed when they began to interact with a city council member, the local theater owner, and other community members. The personal conversations and the authentic nature of their interests were confirmed by these adults; and that made all the difference to these students. The benefits work the other way as well, illustrating that these young people are assets to their community.

Personal contacts also help students sort out possibilities and leads that would otherwise take long periods of tedious study. Students who were interested in geothermal hot springs found that they had too little background to do the necessary research to understand how hot springs originate. So they enlisted the help of a local geologist. In two hours they learned the core elements of what they needed to know.

We live in a small community and we often hear laments that there are few local resources for learners. Yet, when we look at the people in the community we are constantly impressed with the wonderful collected talent and information base we have. The problem is often in making connections with the right people! We have used informal networks, bulletin boards, and newspaper advertisements to find people who have information, skills, and the willingness to work with students. We have found that the older people in our community offer a marvelous wealth of skills and information and often have the time and desire to work with young people. If college or university help is needed, the college relations office will usually supply a list of faculty and areas of expertise. Our geologist friend who is a college professor has been answering questions from a third grade class thousands of miles away via e-mail. The telephone directory is another place to start looking for contacts and it can be a challenge for students to learn to use telephone technologies, practice proper etiquette, and employ effective interview techniques.

Parents and other caregivers are the first place to turn. Each time a piece of narrative curriculum is planned, parents should be informed of the inquiries and invited to offer their talents in helping children explore them. Parents want to know what their children are studying and they want to know how they can be an integral part of their child's schooling. The narrative curriculum offers many opportunities for parents to be models, mentors, and co-learners with their children.

Evaluating the Effectiveness of Explorations

How do we know if the students' explorations are effective? What makes one set of actions preferable to another? The way we have informed ourselves is to watch and listen to students carefully. If students' language and actions demonstrate volitional behaviors, we know immediately that an exploration is well designed. Volitional learners are motivated to pursue their explorations and look forward to digging deeper into the areas of interest on their own time. They "can hardly wait for morning to come."

We often hear or read that it is important in a curriculum plan to make activities varied for students because their attention will wander. In this MTV society, we are, after all, used to microsecond flashes and sound bites. Management pundits say, "We shouldn't expect students to concentrate on any one task for more than fifteen minutes in the classroom." This is probably true if the curriculum originates from the teacher or textbook. We expect, however, that children will sustain their attention to a single task for a very long time if they are volitional learners. Even very young children are capable of long periods of focused attention if what they are doing is of their own design and interest. Michael vividly remembers his 4-year-old son Aaron spending almost five uninterrupted hours on Christmas Day playing with a Sesame Street™ Playhouse and characters— he was incredibly focused and volitional. Carol can recall her son Nathan and his group of friends occupied for hours with a feudal system they had invented, based on a castle community built out of Legos™. It is this kind of behavior and interest from students that we look for as we monitor our curriculum. We know it is possible because we have seen it happen. A student identified with attention deficit disorder spent nearly an hour collecting copper fragments and hammering out "coins." He learned that the Colonial mint master got paid by keeping one of every twenty coins he minted. Our student came to the conclusion that working on a commission is a hard way to make a living. Another student who was easily distracted from most classroom activities explored the signatures left on Register Rock along the Oregon Trail and spent many contented minutes carving on his own register rock. He came to an understanding of the determination people feel to leave their mark in the world. Later in the year, his teacher wrote about him in her journal:

> Today we explored food preparation. [Student] spent the entire time grinding corn and he really liked it. He said, "I found something I'm good at." He said it would probably take a year to grind enough for meals for everyone. He is very proud of his work.

Students involved in a community action unit made many efforts to talk to parents, faculty, and community leaders outside their classroom time. They used recess time, lunch time, and before- and after-school time to pursue their interests. Students who used a computer program to design gliders used all their workshop time and voluntarily used their recesses to build and test their gliders. We could easily continue this list, but these few examples prove that this type of student engagement is possible.

If sustained attention to exploration is not evident, it is important that the teacher conference with the individual or group to help rethink or redirect the learning. Children approaching a problem sometimes try one route and get frustrated if that route yields no fruitful outcome. For example, Elizabeth had lost her sustained interest in igloo building. A conference with Carol about other materials and possibilities restored her interest. For the children who were making wave machines, a similar teacher intervention helped students redirect and sustain interest. After one group had constructed a wave machine, they were unsatisfied with the speed of their motor and the size of the waves it produced. Michael conferenced with the group and suggested that they might use a speed control. Employing the rheostat Michael had provided, the group renewed their interest and experimented with wiring variable control into their circuit.

As we help students direct their interests and explore their questions, it is critical that the prompts, the encouragements, and the stimuli help students reflect on their learning and make comments about the context from which the inquiry emanates. We engage our learners in reflection by asking questions such as: "Has this exploration helped you understand the story any better? Does this exploration give you any insight about the issue? Will doing this experiment help you answer your question?" As teachers we want to help students direct their questions and explorations so that they can assess whether their work will contribute to an understanding of the context and a resolution of their inquiry. It is very easy for learners to leap from an authentic inquiry to a more spurious one. Although this isn't necessarily wrong and may be quite natural as one thing leads to another, it is nonetheless critical that we use the time our learners have in school to the best advantage. Teacher guidance during explorations is essential in keeping students on track.

Staying the Course with Stated Goals

Just as it is important for the community of learners to keep each other focused on the context, it is important to be persistent with the goals that have been selected. In each scenario that we have described, goals were an active moderator in the selection of the narrative and in the exploration phase of the curriculum. In the *Very Last First Time* unit we urged students to communicate each day by listening, writing, and oral reporting in order to assess our progress toward the goals. As we conferenced with students about their work, we encouraged effective writing, asked questions that required reflective thinking and oral responses, and asked students to listen critically as information was shared by class members. In the *Galimoto* unit, we wanted students to use technology and be creative—two goals that we continued to address during explorations. We asked questions about where they got their ideas, how they were thinking, and what they were creating. We encouraged the application of new materials and tools as they did their work. With "The Town That Moved" we wanted students to apply quantitative relationships, so as they mapped and built scale models we continued to encourage them to think about measurement and proportions.

Persisting with our goals as we engage in learning is a critical tenet of the narrative curriculum, and it is in the exploration phase where these goals are most active. The teacher's function in making these goals come alive is one of constant vigil, assessing activities to determine if they provide opportunities for reaching toward goals. Teachers must ask this critical question during explorations: "Considering my goals, is this the most appropriate thing these students could be doing right now?"

Maintaining our perspective about the disciplines is also important at this stage. If we have stated early on that we want to think like artists as we engage in the exploration, then we should honor that discipline as we learn. If we want our students to think like artists, how can we help explore that way of thinking? Modeling by the teacher or by a professional in a discipline can be a powerful way of supporting learners. In a direct way, teachers can share with students what they know about how disciplines operate. As an artist we can help students think about form, function, aesthetics, and craftsmanship, for example. If we do not understand a discipline, then it would be appropriate to get help. When teachers began a narrative curriculum unit concerning aeronautical engineering they were unschooled about how engineers think and act, so they asked a local pilot and airplane builder to help them understand the discipline's perspective and to model to the class how he worked and thought.

Minilessons

The issue of content and skills usually arises much earlier in our conversations about curriculum because it is an important issue for teachers, students, and parents. Teachers ask us pointed questions such as, "Where do students learn the stuff we are expected to teach them—the traditional content of the scope and sequence mandates and the core skills that are tested by the state?"

Content and skills are alive in the narrative curriculum. They do not take an organizing role, but they are needed as students develop their explorations. Several examples will demonstrate this idea:

▌ As students built wave machines, Michael had to help them understand how a circuit works so they could hook up the motor and add the parallel cells.

▌ As Debra and Holly melted candles and experimented with measurement, they needed direction to use a triple-beam balance to weigh the candle.

▌ As the children looked through an atlas, Carol helped them review how to read latitude and longitude so that they could locate the position on the globe.

▌ As the class examined the live mussel, Michael explained about the biology and ecology of the mollusca.

Students in the process of an exploration take a small side journey to learn a skill, concept, or essential piece of knowledge. Sometimes these journeys are entire class lessons that are focused and preplanned; other times they are personal and spontaneous. Their purpose is supportive in nature. Learners need these pieces of information and skills

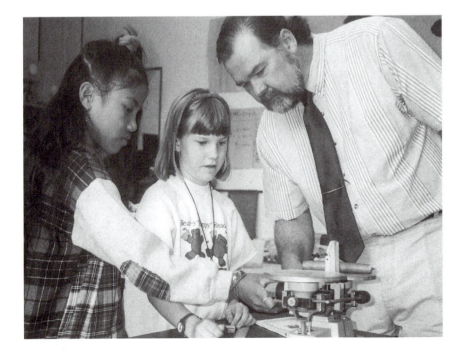

to continue their explorations successfully. We know that students gain information and skills through these informal means. Students learned about mussels from firsthand observations and from others' observations. Exposed to a new vocabulary, many used words like bivalve, byssal fiber, and muscular foot as they wrote about their experiences in their journals. We had not set out to teach these bits of information directly, but because we were in the neighborhood, students picked up the vocabulary.

Minilessons are ideal ways to provide specific skills and information to learners when they need it. This is not a front-loaded process. We do not hammer students with skills practice and compendiums of information before they engage in inquiry. Rather, we carefully set the minilessons in strategic places in the learning cycle to help students hurdle difficulties they are having, or are about to have, with their projects. Students began their search for Ungava Bay first. We gave them time to engage in free exploration. After a time we brought them into a group, took ten minutes and explained how to use an atlas and latitude references to find a place on a map. Some students knew how to do this already so we used their skills to help guide the discussion. After the minilesson we supported individuals' use of the skill and as soon as they demonstrated an understanding, they continued their explorations using the new or refreshed skill in their work. The timing of the minilessons in the workshop cycle is determined by assessing what learners know and need to know to continue their work (fig. 9.4). Many useful skills, such as how to use a video recorder and camera, how to make an effective telephone call, how to conduct an interview, how to use information technologies, and how to use hand tools, may not appear on a typical curriculum guide. Yet they are critical to helping learners make progress in finding, processing, and communicating. New skills, processes, and information are acquired in the minilesson and applied immediately in the explorations. Minilessons are explained in other sources (Atwell, 1987; Calkins, 1994; Cooper, 1993; Graves, 1994). We encourage teachers to master the use of minilessons during explorations to provide learners with skills and information they need to be successful.

Minilessons are powerful in helping students progress in areas where they have special interest or in acquainting learners with new areas in which they may develop expertise. A local fifth grade student we know had a reputation as a reluctant learner. The child had not demonstrated any active engagement in the classroom until he and his class began to explore a local aquatic habitat. In one minilesson the teacher brought in small, individual microscopes and a more powerful microscope that projected its images on a screen for group viewing. The student learned how to make slides and manipulate the instruments and

FIGURE 9.4 Workshop cycle with minilessons (Developed with
M. Ruth Davenport)

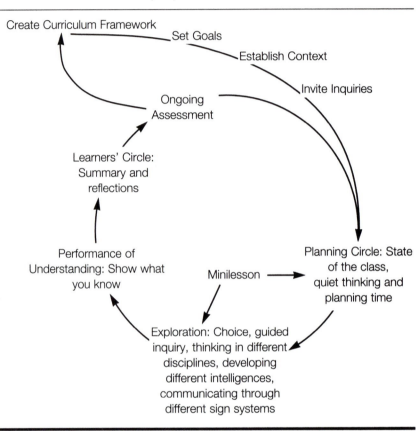

soon found himself tutoring every other student in the class and all of
the second graders who were collaborating in the study. When Carol visited the class to watch the unit, she noticed the boy and thought that he
was a high school student assistant for the class. His professional
demeanor and his skillful communications led Carol to believe that he
was a top student! In this case the minilesson had empowered the learner with special talents and had invited the student into the context and
community of learners in an important way.

The teacher is certainly not the only person who can facilitate a minilesson. Our colleague Ruth maintains a standing operational policy in her
intermediate level elementary classroom to develop expertise in her students. It is common in her room, for example, to find students helping one
another with such things as technology, special skills, and areas of personal

interest or expertise. Rather than personally filling requests for help, Ruth directs the children to find a peer who can teach them. She maintains lists of "experts" for various skills that the children need. Because the narrative curriculum depends on a community of learners to construct meaning from experience, an individual in the community who can provide special talents and resources is a valued and important member.

🏵 Culminations

As we have related earlier, providing learners with authentic opportunities to share their learning is a rewarding aspect of school. The joy in celebration of learning is one that begs our attention and diligence.

Culminations are planned events during which students and teachers can share what they have learned. There are many possibilities depending on the nature of the inquiry, the level of the students, the environment, and the cultural setting. Determining what sort of culminating event is most appropriate should occur early in the co-created curriculum-planning process, although the decision may be modified later. As students think about their questions and develop plans for learning, they can also think about what form their findings will take and in what setting or circumstances they will present them. A teacher can post or provide a list of possibilities so that students can consider what would be most appropriate.

Audience is a critical aspect of culminations. Fellow students as well as other members of the community can serve this role. Parents, grandparents, neighbors, friends, interested school patrons, school board members, administrators, teachers, high school students, reporters, and other interested members of the community add significance to the event. The concomitant bonus of inviting the community to celebrate with children in culminations of learning is that it communicates children's achievements resoundingly. Parents are amazed at and proud of what children have learned, school principals are reassured that the noise and seeming confusion had a real point after all, and community members are shown that schooling is a worthwhile endeavor. Although public relations are not the reason for creating the culminating event, we recognize the value of sharing what we are doing outside the small circle of the classroom. It is on these occasions that we communicate best what we value and how we work. It is also on these occasions that we can make new alliances with those in the community who see the power in giving children permission to own their learning. These liaisons may also provide resources for future explorations.

Culminations, because they are much like celebrations, should be recorded. Videotape, still photography, and newspaper reports are powerful

reminders to learners that wonderful journeys were taken and new territories were studied. Once archived, these data also create anticipation in new groups of learners that something wonderful will happen in their future years of schooling. Students' work can also provide a trail of evidence that helps unseasoned learners envision possibilities. We save examples of student work and presentations that will help others think about their own work without providing a pattern for cloning.

Assessments

As we have emphasized throughout this book, the reason we teach is to facilitate and monitor learners' progress toward goals. We have crafted the narrative curriculum to honor this basic rationale. Assessment is important because it informs the school community, including students, teachers, and parents, about the progress each child is making toward the goals. Assessment also helps us plan future instruction.

Identifying our expectations of learners in terms of observed processes and demonstrated products helps ensure progress toward stated goals. If we state a goal such as, "each student will work as a member of a cooperative team," then the description of the learning might be something like:

Each learner will demonstrate the following collaborative skills:

▌ Engages in brainstorming without criticizing suggestions
▌ Acts as an individual to generate ideas and possibilities in a group setting

- Listens patiently and politely to others' ideas
- Refrains from personal "put-downs"
- Takes a role in the group and contributes to the process and product of the work

If we state a goal such as, "each student will communicate through effective writing," then the demonstrated product might be:

Each learner will produce a sample of writing which shows the following characteristics:

- The writing is clear, focused, and interesting.
- Words convey the intended message in an interesting, precise, and natural way.
- The order, structure, or presentation is compelling and moves the reader through the text.
- The writer demonstrates a good grasp of standard writing conventions.
- Sentences are well built, with consistently strong and varied structure that makes expressive oral reading easy and enjoyable.
- The writer speaks directly to the reader in a way that is individualistic, expressive, and engaging.

Products and processes are described specifically enough that we know what it looks like when we have arrived. As we planned *Very Last First Time* we decided in advance what we expected from the children's work. Because we had said that communication, technology, and self-directed learning were the active goals in this instructional opportunity, we crafted a picture of what students might produce and how they might act in the process. The goal of communication led us to create opportunities for listening, reading, writing, and speaking. We decided that learners will demonstrate their ability to communicate by:

- writing observations in a field note journal
- orally sharing resolutions of their findings
- asking interactive questions, generated by listening to the story and others' ideas.
- reading and interpreting resource information that contributes to their inquiry

These kinds of descriptors gave us a clear idea of what students needed to do and demonstrate before we started instruction.

The process of planning for assessment opportunities is interactive with all other features of the curriculum. In the example above, we wanted students to engage in self-directed learning and to explore some technologies. It seemed logical to us that as they made observations and discovered things, they should keep record of that information. A field note journal was an ideal way to record the process of this activity. Because we knew they would want to share what they had learned with us and the other students, an oral presentation would be an appropriate summative activity. Because we wanted students to research their own questions, they would need to read for information. It was logical to expect that they cite the resources that they used to find that information.

The planning of products, although seemingly restrictive, still allows flexibility. Each child enjoyed a wide berth in what and how their personal field note journals were created, how the oral presentations were made, and what information resources were used. Children demonstrated progress toward stated goals through a variety of means—showing their ability to communicate while retaining their individuality.

In planning for processes and products, we describe the kinds of things we expect, but they are not always specific. Self-directed explorations lead children on many different paths. Specific pieces of information or the content of the product differ from group to group. What is consistent is the structure we require of all students. Even though in the *Very Last First Time* unit we had wave machines, igloos and spears, candle experiments, and mollusk research, all students communicated in both written and oral forms. As teachers we could monitor these demonstrations as students engaged in the process and as they presented their products.

Assessing Products

Products come at the end of an instructional opportunity. Products are the neat, packaged summations of our learning and take forms such as oral presentations of projects, models, drawings, data sets and summaries, essays, dramatic events, or skill demonstrations. Lately, we have heard the term *portfolio* used in this sense. But portfolio may suffer from the same catch-all definition to which other buzz words in education have succumbed. In one definition, a portfolio is the container in which artists place examples of all their best work. This material is presented to potential employers or buyers and the artists say through its display: "This is what I can do. This is what I am capable of. This is what I know." However, other portfolio definitions may include work in progress or multiple drafts of writing. If we define a portfolio as a way to provide possibilities for engaging students in self-assessment of growth over time, then the term serves the purpose of describing how both products and processes may be assessed.

Products, or summative expressions of learning, can represent progress toward the stated goals. If we say that we want learners to be excellent communicators of written and spoken language, then a summative portfolio of that work can be a way of showing that proficiency. If a student creates a technologically rendered product, then we can draw conclusions about the skills that were required to accomplish that task. If a student shows the results of an experiment and summarizes the findings, then we can surmise that the requisite science skills were operational as the student conducted the work. Products are ways of demonstrating what we know, and often they celebrate our accomplishments. Kristin and her spear, Mike and his wave machine, Holly and her candle data, Jake and his igloo—each product is a tangible demonstration of learning.

Still, using products alone as a way to discern student progress can limit the teacher's vision. When we ask our preservice teachers to plan opportunities for assessment they usually suggest that students can write a report, make a model, or give a presentation. These are appropriate suggestions, but we ask them, "What if the report is poorly rendered, or worse, lost? What if the model that they made is unattractive and disheveled? What if the oral presentation is unsatisfactory? Will that mean the student has learned nothing?" Thus, products can be only part of our assessment.

Assessing Processes

Process is the other part. Processes are the behaviors, skills, and knowledge that students demonstrate as they are conducting an inquiry. For example, Holly and her partners conducted several experiments about candles. They wrote cursory notes in their journals and gave brief oral reports at the end of their work. If we only had looked at the products of their work, we might have thought that they had not accomplished much. We saw little in their presentation that assured us that they had applied technology, developed an experimental method, or really were self-directed in their work. The product alone was an imperfect window for viewing learning.

But we had interacted a great deal with Debra, Holly, and Anne as they explored candles, and we kept careful observations of their behaviors during the processes of finding out. The students had used rulers, balances, ring stands, glassware, and matches in appropriate and safe ways. They made observations, developed questions, posed hypotheses, experimented, and drew conclusions as they discovered how to find out. They worked on their own, used resources, asked questions, decided what to do, organized materials, and stayed on task. We observed all of this as they engaged in exploration. We would not have been able to infer this learning from the product alone.

It is critical, then, that we use the "during" time as a way of knowing about our learners. Our planning had to accommodate process assessments. We knew that children would be manipulating materials and using tools. We knew that we wanted them to learn how to use things like glue guns, wire strippers, and hacksaws; to employ problem-solving skills as they made models and did experiments; and to make plans for learning as they pursued their own interests. We chose these active tasks as places to observe and collect assessment information.

Both process and product observations are needed in assessment. Processes usually give us insights about skills, attitudes, manipulative abilities, critical thinking, creativity, and collaborative social attributes. Products show resolution of problem solving, presentation skills, and knowledge.

Scoring Guides

Scoring guides are documents that we use to help organize our observations of student work. They describe behaviors that we hope to see in processes and products and they provide an effective and efficient means to characterize the learner's abilities without an inordinate amount of anecdotal narrative. A process scoring guide we use with our students serves as an example (fig. 9.5).

Scoring guides may be created by agencies other than the classroom teacher. The state of Oregon (Oregon Department of Education, 1994), for example, has created several assessment guides, including one for open-ended problem solving (fig. 9.6). This scoring guide has three basic levels of achievement. The first level, or "proficient" rank, is a listing of the kinds of attributes or behaviors one might see in a student who has met this goal. If we looked at Jerod, the student described in chapter 8 who did the spectrographic research, we would check off every category under the proficient

---

FIGURE 9.5 Scoring guide for process assessment

Process Assessment: Check one box from each pair listed below that best describes the work of your team members.

☐ Collaborated with team members effectively
☐ Cooperated reluctantly at times

☐ Was enthusiastic
☐ Tasks perceived as hurdles to overcome

☐ Problem solver
☐ Followed lead of others in solving problems

☐ Directed own learning
☐ Required reminders and deadlines to complete work

☐ Communicated effectively and appropriately
☐ Communication skills adequate, yet uninspired

FIGURE 9.6 Problem-solving scoring guide

☐ Proficient (Learner demonstrates mastery of the stated outcome)
    ☐ Understands self as learner
        ☐ Identifies own interests (Personal area of research selected despite peer influence)
        ☐ Identifies own aptitudes and abilities
        ☐ Identifies personal educational and career aspirations
    ☐ Identifies and accesses the resources necessary to obtain needed skills or knowledge
        ☐ First finds ways of knowing without help from instructional leader
        ☐ Uses multiple resources such as primary sources in research
        ☐ Establishes clear goals and high standards for personal performance
    ☐ Timelines are established
        ☐ Is accountable to those standards
    ☐ Learner evaluates work and makes improvements according to own feedback
        ☐ Perseveres when faced with difficult situations (Repeats work on own volition after failure)
        ☐ Analyzes different learning environments and adapts strategies to improve learning

☐ Progress/Developing (Learner demonstrates progress toward the stated outcome)
    ☐ Understanding of self as learner is emerging yet mixed with the expectations of others
        ☐ Personal areas of research are influenced by others
        ☐ Aptitudes and abilities are imperfectly self-assessed
        ☐ Personal educational and career aspirations are not well articulated
    ☐ Identifies and accesses some resources in obtaining needed skills or knowledge
        ☐ Help from instructional leader is essential in forwarding research
        ☐ Resources selected usually center around traditional secondary references
        ☐ Goals and standards for personal performance negotiated with instructional leader
    ☐ Timelines are required and established through negotiation
    ☐ Accountability is in the hands of the instructional leader
    ☐ Learner makes improvements according to others' feedback
        ☐ Repeats work only through encouragement of others
        ☐ Takes advantage of different learning environments established by instructional leader and adopts new strategies from others' direction

☐ Not Understanding/Emergent
    ☐ Does not understand the idea of self as learner
        ☐ Interests almost always adopted from the interests of others
        ☐ Cannot identify own strengths and abilities
        ☐ No personal educational or career aspirations articulated

---

FIGURE 9.6 Problem-solving scoring guide (continued)

☐ Cannot identify or access resources necessary to obtain needed skills or
knowledge
   ☐ Depends solely on instructional leader for direction
   ☐ Cannot use resource material to find information
   ☐ Goals are externally created and maintained
☐ Learner cannot complete work within established timelines
☐ Student takes no responsibility for outcome of learning, behaviors generally
off task
☐ Learner makes no improvements in work after feedback
   ☐ When faced with difficult situations student is frustrated and quits work
   ☐ Faced with different learning environments learner expresses frustration
and fails to adapt

---

rank. Jerod demonstrated in both process and product the exemplar of self-directed learning. Many of our mixed-age-group students are marked as "making progress" toward the goal of becoming self-directed learners because they required some encouragement, a significant amount of help in accomplishing their study, and external guidance in establishing timelines and expectations. The behaviors of a few learners suggested that they were functioning at the lowest level because they were unable to stay focused on their own learning and little progress was demonstrated in the area of self-directed learning.

Many scoring guides show more than these three levels of attainment. Some five- and six-point scoring guides are extensions of this basic design and accommodate the middle ground between each level. We find that the basic three-level scoring guide is satisfactory as a starting place.

The purpose of these written instruments is not to grade students, but rather to inform instruction. In operation, we focus on sections of these guides as we give feedback to learners. For example, we may desire to help students grow in the area of identifying and accessing resources. We may wish to put all of our energy into examining this aspect and these guides help us give feedback on specific traits. Ideally, scoring guides are helpful to all participants in the learning process because they articulate expectations clearly and help students self-assess their work.

Creating Scoring Guides. When should these scoring guides be made and who creates them? Our preference is to establish assessment instruments as we plan the unit. Scoring guides are created as early as we begin to understand our goals for our learners. This is a departure from traditional practice. In a former paradigm we made tests to correspond to the content we had covered in class. The test was made as we looked back on instruction and made a decision about what information students should have obtained. This post-test paradigm uses the idea that whatever goes into the system should be what is assessed—whether it is integral to the stated goals or not!

Creating the assessment instruments ahead of time drives instruction in a purposeful manner. Because we know we are going to assess how students use technology, for example, the opportunities we provide students, the questions we ask, and the observations we make are directed to that aim. It may seem like a tyranny of control, but we think of it instead as a rudder that keeps us on course, because the assessment is securely tied to the goals. Creating the assessment instruments at the beginning of the instructional cycle identifies where we want students to grow and demystifies for students the expectations of learning.

The idea of "no surprises" is an appealing one to us. Students should have a clear idea of what is expected of them and they should have every resource they require to meet those expectations. It is absurd to think that assessment should be some kind of cosmic guessing game where the teacher creates the "test" and the learners try to figure out what is on it. Our purpose is to help learners be successful. Our evaluation system communicates to students: "This is the vision of what we want to see, this is an example of what we want you to be able to do, this is the way we will look at your work and evaluate it." This provides learners with every opportunity to meet the challenge.

Scoring guides (rubric) make the job of assessment easier. In many of the examples that have been used in this manuscript, student projects are varied. Students create written work, make models, give dramatic presentations, prepare speeches, and so forth. Without a scoring guide to direct student work and assess learning, the teacher has difficulty providing feedback. We are relegated to construct arbitrary measures to cover the territory: a number of points for quality of written essay, a number of points for neatness, a number of points for references, and so on. The evaluation becomes invalid and unreliable. Without a scoring guide we are likely to give products that look good higher scores than less attractive ones of better substance.

If we create a specific scoring guide with students before they begin to render their products, then we can expect students will have an opportunity to plan their work in accordance with expectations. As students proceed with their work, they and we are reminded of what they will be accountable for. By the time the project is completed, students already have an idea of how their work compares to expectations. Evaluation takes place openly with the student as an active participant.

Several important observations have resulted from use of scoring guides. First, students have poor initial performance because scoring guides represent a major shift from how they have formerly been assessed. For example, in the assessment of mathematics, students were able to produce correct answers to the problems, but failed miserably in expressing their thought processes for reaching solutions. Their school experience had trained students to do the computations and circle the correct answer. To them, "show your work" meant to put all the numerals in the correct places on a piece of paper. Students were not prepared to communicate their reasoning.

The second benefit derived from the use of scoring guides is that they alerted teachers to the need for and joy of helping learners think more globally about problems. No longer is the correct answer the sole item of importance. We are now interested in how children understand the problem, how they interpret the feasibility of the solution, and how they communicate the reasoning processes that they used. Scoring guides have influenced instruction for the better.

Our statements about assessment may seem to contradict our position on constructivism and child-centered curriculum. Let us explain their compatibility. It is important to remember the nature of the goals that are being assessed. These are not content-specific; instead they are broad descriptions of core skills and abilities, both coginitive and social. The child still has every opportunity to construct meaning from experience. The flexibility of narrative curriculum and the establishment of broad goals allow the child to remain at the center of the experience. In addition, children are actively involved in the assessment process.

Co-created Assessments

The rationale for involving learners in the identification of inquiries and exploration is based on the belief that students make insightful offerings to the content of the curriculum. The same belief holds true for assessments. Children have much to say about what can be expected as a result of their own learning.

In the process that we have outlined for identifying inquiries and planning explorations, we have shown how the teacher helps guide discussions about possible consequences of learning. Students are often insightful about the culminations of their learning and are equally insightful about the quality of their work. When we asked students what might be expected if they were to construct models, for example, students are quick to create a checklist of expectations. Often, their expectations will match or even exceed those suggested by the teacher.

Co-creating the scoring guides and negotiating expectations is one more way students share in the narrative curriculum. Consider this from a student's point of view:

If I find something that interests me, if I think clearly about what I might do to find out more about that question, if I set standards that will help me know that I have done everything possible to reach that solution, and if I share that process with others, then I make a strong commitment to the construction of my own knowledge. Learning becomes a central and vital aspect of who I am as a person.

After all, the fundamental rationale for all of schooling is to empower a new generation of lifelong learners.

Lingering Questions

A question we often get from teachers thinking about this style of learning and teaching is, "How will I ever start such a risky endeavor?" My students have never done anything like this. Won't they just get out of control if I let them do their own thing? How do we begin to engage in child-centered constructive learning, especially with older students who are used to teacher-controlled classrooms?

What teacher traits and what preparation is necessary to engage in this kind of risk taking?

Companion Readings

You may wish to consult some of the resources that explain specific strategies discussed in this chapter. Insights about literature circles can be found in Short and Pierce (1990) and Gilles, et al. (1994). Prereading techniques are addressed by Cooper (1993) and Tierney, et al. (1990). Fulwiler (1987), Calkins (1990), and Bromley (1993) present many ideas about journal writing. The concept of grand conversation is developed by Edelsky (1988) and Peterson and Eeds (1990). The chapters in *Cycles of Meaning* (Pierce & Gilles, 1993) discuss exploratory talk. Minilessons are explained by Calkins (1994), Cooper (1993), and Graves (1994).

CHAPTER 10

Curriculum Exemplars

Activating Prior Knowledge

What curriculum do you remember from your school days? What made it memorable?

Chapter Highlights

We describe narrative curriculum planned and implemented by teachers with whom we are personally acquainted. Then we present a rationale for the narrative curriculum in other settings. Finally we express our values which support the narrative curriculum.

Throughout this book we have primarily used our own teaching experiences as we described both the theoretical and practical aspects of the narrative curriculum. Now we would like to share with you how others have gone through the process of narrative curriculum development and what they have learned from their attempts to implement constructive learning in the classroom.

We have selected pieces of curriculum, the process or results of which we have personally observed over the past few years. The examples vary from primary to middle school, from rural to town settings, and from small to large classes. The students involved represent the whole spectrum of public school children—the gifted and talented as well as those addressed in federal law 94–142, the children of affluence as well as the children of poverty, and the children of white middle-class America as well as those for whom English is not a first language. Contexts range from picture books and chapter books to field trips, simulations, and issues. These stories are summarized in each of the accompanying templates. The teachers who participated are varied in personality, but share a few common traits:

- They were willing to take a risk and try something new.
- They expressed a belief that all children can succeed and that each child should be honored for whatever contributions they can make in the classroom.
- They have explored alternatives to traditional methodology and were searching for an optimum way to facilitate learning in the classroom.

For each contributor in this section we have prepared a short biographical sketch, a description of the setting where the curriculum was planned and implemented, a brief explanation of how the context was introduced, a planning template of the unit, sample explorations, and reflective comments.

While it may seem that our examples are limited by our geographical region, we believe the students who have been engaged by the narrative curriculum are representative of the diversity of the student population in American schools. In the second section of this chapter we relate some examples that lead us to believe that the narrative curriculum will be effective with children in other regions and environments.

In the final section of this chapter we bring the text to a close by presenting what we value for our children and how we believe the narrative curriculum sustains these values.

◈ Teachers and the Narrative Curriculum

Belinda Roberson
June 1993
Riveria School
La Grande, Oregon

At the time of this unit, Belinda taught in an elementary school which included a large population eligible for free lunches and compensatory services. Her class, consisting of 24 children in second and third grades, was a typical cross section of the community and the students showed a wide range of abilities.

After examining dozens of books, Belinda chose *The Great Kapok Tree* (Cherry, 1990) because of its presentation of the rain forest ecosystem and because it matched the goals she had for her learners. Belinda and her colleague, Sue Taylor, planned the unit together. They brainstormed first, predicting areas that students would find interesting, and then created opportunities for exploration. They also planned that at the end of the unit, each class would be an audience for the presentation of other's learning.

Belinda's students were accustomed to gathering together for story time. She had planned four guiding questions to help the students interact with the book as she read it aloud. However, she used only one, "What do you see?" The students generated the rest of the discussion as Belinda stopped after every second page to facilitate student talk. Most of the student talk had to do with plants and animals. After reading and responding to the entire book, Belinda and the children grouped the responses into three main questions. The second day Belinda told the class she had found information to answer their questions and from then they clamored: "Show us that," "Read this to us," and "What does that say?" As one of their explorations students created a rain forest environment in the classroom. Paper trees, plants, and animals that the children made surrounded the room. Each student posed a personal research question about an animal that they saw in the book. Class discussions, research, and oral reports helped students add to their understanding of the rain forest ecosystem.

Toward the end of the exploration, Belinda came to school early and "chopped down" the largest of the trees, the great kapok. When the children arrived at school that morning they were shocked to find their creation on the floor with their animals lying around it. The children knew who cut down the tree: "It was the man from the book!" Then they decided to reuse (recycle) the old paper to make new trees to "plant" in their forest!

Belinda reflected on her first attempt to facilitate a narrative-curriculum unit in her class:

> Once it started it wasn't a big deal—once you see them start to do their own thing, and make their own decisions about what they're going to do and how they are hoping to do it.
>
> I stood on a ladder for most of two days while the students were doing the creating. I moved the ladder around to put things up where they wanted. From the ladder I checked out the groups' progress and talked to them about what their part of the rain forest looked like and how they might build it.
>
> The animal research part of it was really interesting because we went down to the library and the librarian showed us the reference section and showed them a computer program that also had information they could use. I found that I needed a lot of help to read to them the information they found. Once we read it to them they were able to find it again and copy that part down on their paper.
>
> They definitely worked better on this project than any other they have worked on before. I think some of them learned how to be more sensitive to each others' questions and feelings and they learned the confidence of being able to help each other. They learned factual things. I bet that every one of those kids could tell about the four levels of the rain forest. They learned about some environmental issues as far as recycling and why we cut trees. They learned about where the rain forests are. It's incredible.
>
> The students had tremendous ownership. They brought anyone who would listen into our room to show and explain about their rain forest. Lessons were interrupted more than once with "Mrs. R., there goes_____. Can we show him/her our forest?"

What I have learned from this is don't be afraid to jump off the bridge. Don't be afraid to let the book do the teaching or afraid of the kids doing the learning. If we set it up for them and guide them along but let them learn what they want to learn they are going to end up learning what they need to know at that point.

See figures 10.1 and 10.2: planning template and exploration for *The Great Kapok Tree.*

Gene Dunn
June 1993
Humboldt School
John Day, Oregon

As a primary level teacher in a rural school, Gene is responsible for 20 active youngsters. He is a good listener. He knows what students are interested in, what they know, what they fear, and what they enjoy. Gene also has a good sense of what he wants for his learners. Foundational goals are embedded into the way he thinks about curriculum.

He began his planning process with a book and the goals he wanted his learners to address. Meeting with the students in an interactive read-aloud of *Gino Badino* (Engel, 1991), Gene listened carefully to student questions and ideas. He found his students relating to the character of Gino who wanted so badly to be included in the family's work. They were pleased when Gino's talents were finally recognized. They were also interested in many things related to the story: "What is pasta? How do you make it? Can we make it? Can we make animals? Can we sell it?"

Because he had thought through the planning process and predicted the inquiries, Gene could provide students with explorations that fit both the goals and the students' interests. To answer the question of what pasta was, Gene had some examples for children to see. To answer the question of how to make pasta, Gene gave students a recipe and directions for preparing dough. Students became pasta makers and soon discovered the joy of mixing flour and water. Gene helped them differentiate teaspoons and tablespoons as they developed an understanding of the reason for measuring and following the directions carefully. To answer the question of how to make shapes, students had both patterns to copy and open-ended opportunities to shape dough. Gene stopped short of fulfilling the final student question (Can we be like Gino and sell the pasta?) because he was careful not to violate USDA rules prohibiting that sort of activity. Following their explorations, the students had more empathy with Gino and his family and their understanding of the story was deepened.

FIGURE 10.1 Planning template for *The Great Kapok Tree*

Foundational Goals: Solve Problems - Think Critically, Creatively - Use Technology - Communicate - Quantify - Direct Own Learning - Collaborate/Cooperate
Applications: Ability to Deliberate on Public Issues, to Interpret Human Experience; to Understand Diversity, Health Habits, Science/Math Relationships, Humanities

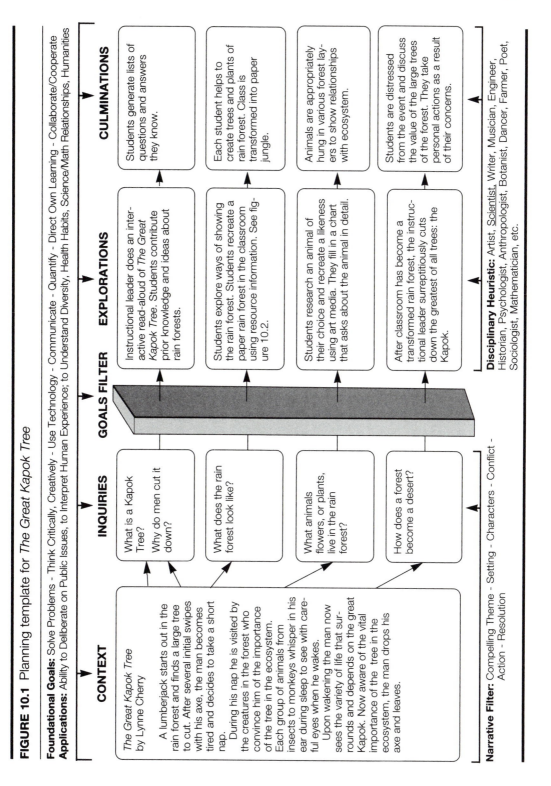

CONTEXT

The Great Kapok Tree by Lynne Cherry

A lumberjack starts out in the rain forest and finds a large tree to cut. After several initial swipes with his axe, the man becomes tired and decides to take a short nap.

During his nap he is visited by the creatures in the forest who convince him of the importance of the tree in the ecosystem. Each group of animals from insects to monkeys whisper in his ear during sleep to see with careful eyes when he wakes.

Upon wakening the man now sees the variety of life that surrounds and depends on the great Kapok. Now aware of the vital importance of the tree in the ecosystem, the man drops his axe and leaves.

INQUIRIES

What is a Kapok Tree?
Why do men cut it down?

What does the rain forest look like?

What animals flowers, or plants, live in the rain forest?

How does a forest become a desert?

GOALS FILTER

EXPLORATIONS

Instructional leader does an inter-active read-aloud of *The Great Kapok Tree*. Students contribute prior knowledge and ideas about rain forests.

Students explore ways of showing the rain forest. Students recreate a paper rain forest in the classroom using resource information. See figure 10.2.

Students research an animal of their choice and recreate a likeness using art media. They fill in a chart that asks about the animal in detail.

After classroom has become a transformed rain forest, the instructional leader surreptitiously cuts down the greatest of all trees: the Kapok.

CULMINATIONS

Students generate lists of questions and answers they know.

Each student helps to create trees and plants of rain forest. Class is transformed into paper jungle.

Animals are appropriately hung in various forest lay-ers to show relationships with ecosystem.

Students are distressed from the event and discuss the value of the large trees of the forest. They take personal actions as a result of their concerns.

Disciplinary Heuristic: Artist, Scientist, Writer, Musician, Engineer, Historian, Psychologist, Anthropologist, Botanist, Dancer, Farmer, Poet, Sociologist, Mathematician, etc.

Narrative Filter: Compelling Theme - Setting - Characters - Conflict - Action - Resolution

FIGURE 10.2 Exploration for *The Great Kapok Tree*

Inquiry: What does the rain forest look like?

Exploration Overview: Students explore ways of showing the rain forest. Students create a paper rain forest in the classroom using resource information.

Guided Inquiry: While reading *The Great Kapok Tree* interactively, students are urged to generate questions with a minimum of prompts:

"What do you see in the picture?"
"Where do you think this place is?"
"Who is this man and what does he do?"

The questions stimulate a host of other ideas that are collected on a chart. The teacher guides students through a few general explorations about the Kapok tree as a whole group first. Afterward, students relate to the size and general function of the trees in the forest. Given resource sheets on the canopy levels in the rain forest, the teacher guides group discussion about what the layers really look like.

In small groups, student discuss ways that they might show the layers of the forest by using colored paper. The teacher asks each group to decide what materials and what tools they will need to complete their task. "What will the class look like/sound like when we are doing this work together?"

For the next two days, student work in cooperative groups to make trees and plants out of paper. At the beginning and end of each work period, the class meets to discuss what they will be trying to accomplish and what they have completed.

Teacher Facilitation: In a primary-level setting it is important that the teacher is well prepared for students' needs and is able to supply information and materials when needed. Knowing the skill levels of the students, appropriate technologies are arranged: scissors, large pieces of colored paper, marking pens, tape, staplers.

In planning the exploration, behavior standards and agreements on how the class should look and sound during construction are established.

Although the teacher in this case provides the story, resource information, and raw materials, the product of the exploration is primarily driven by the students. As groups design and build pieces to the rain forest, the teacher asks, "Where do you suppose this part would fit best?" The students direct the development of their own classroom rain forest.

Culminations: What emerges from this work is a classroom transformed into a model rain forest. Large tree trunks made of brown paper climb up the wall. Green puffs of paper line the canopy and smaller plants line the forest floor. Two entire walls show the cooperative effort of all children in the class. Children show off their forest to all who pass by.

Assessment: The teacher records anecdotal information about the activities of students for a classwide assessment of the impact of this unit. (Several interesting concomitant products and processes demonstrated that students are immersed in the context of the rain forest:

- During the first exploration stage children saw resource information and said things like: "Show us that" or "read us that."
- During a thunderstorm one afternoon children said, "It was because of our rain forest!" (They had learned that in a rain forest it rains almost every afternoon.)
- One boy said that there was no way that anyone would ever cut down the tree that he made!)

This anecdotal information contributes to an overall sense that children are learning to appreciate the rain forest.

If we look closely, we see that all of the planning was really Gene's responsibility. He chose the context, identified the goals that were active, he brainstormed possible questions, created logical and developmentally appropriate explorations, and devised an assessment tool. Gene was the curriculum planner in this setting and the students were his informants.

Gene's Reflections

I had been examining some literature for second grade readers and found a few books that fit the narrative filter: a compelling theme, rich setting, characters, action, and resolution. The story I thought that I could use to get groups to collaborate and cooperate was *Gino Badino*.

As I thought about this book, it came to mind that the students would want to make pasta. This would be a wonderful project that would lend itself to group cooperation. The students would also learn to make measurements of volume. They could see how technology works by examining and using a pasta machine and writing about how it works. They could examine different kinds of pasta and see how commercial products compare to the ones they make. Students could probably be led to the inquiries on the planning template. If they had other ideas we could easily use the materials to explore what they are interested in. It is important that they are able to explore their own ideas. That is important!

After completing the planning template I assembled all of the materials: ingredients, mixing bowls and cups, commercial pastas, drawing paper and patterns, and a pasta machine. I set up three pasta-making stations and two additional stations to examine the pasta machine and to design shapes.

After reading the story, collecting questions, and having a discussion about pasta, everyone wanted to make pasta. We divided into three groups and went to the pasta-making stations. It's really fun to watch second graders follow a recipe and make pasta dough. To my amazement, every group was able to break an egg without spilling it or getting shells into the bowl. They were able to beat the egg and blend the ingredients to make dough. One table was too cooperative and all five group members put their hands into the bowl to mix the flour and other ingredients. When they removed their hands from the bowl, presto! No pasta in the bowl. That group made another batch and learned "Too many cooks spoil the pasta!"

One student asked, "How do you measure half and half?" I explained that half and half was one of the names of the ingredients!

When the students came in from music [class], they took turns looking at the pasta maker, put dough through it, and explained how it worked in their journals. They did this while others were examining other types of pastas by tracing around the shapes. Some designed their own patterns. They even colored some of their pasta shapes.

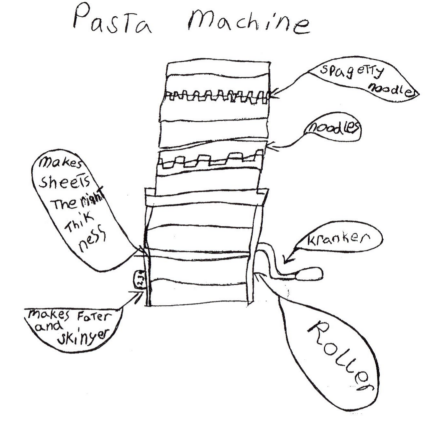

Next time I do this we could have parents buy the ingredients and help fix the pasta. Afterward we could have a pasta feed in the multi-purpose room!

See figures 10.3 and 10.4: planning template and exploration for *Gino Badino*.

Betsy Sadowski, Kathy O'Hara, and Jenni Fager
Winter 1993
Ackerman Laboratory School
La Grande, Oregon

Betsy, Jenni, and Kathy were student teachers at the time they collaboratively developed this unit. The trio of teachers wanted to design curriculum that would help a group of 16 mixed-age, upper-grade students appreciate

FIGURE 10.3 Planning template for *Gino Badino*

Foundational Goals: Solve Problems - Think Critically, Creatively - Use Technology - Communicate - Quantify - Direct Own Learning - Collaborate/Cooperate
Applications: Ability to Deliberate on Public Issues; to Interpret Human Experience; to Understand Diversity, Health Habits, Science/Math Relationships, Humanities

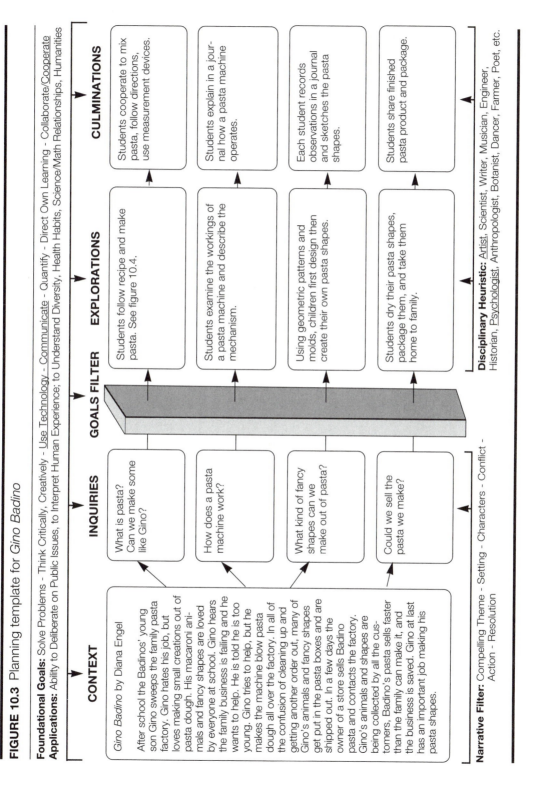

CONTEXT

Gino Badino by Diana Engel

After school the Badinos' young son Gino sweeps the family pasta factory. Gino hates his job, but loves making small creations out of pasta dough. His macaroni animals and fancy shapes are loved by everyone at school. Gino hears the family business is failing and he wants to help. He is told he is too young. Gino tries to help, but he makes the machine blow pasta dough all over the factory. In all of the confusion of cleaning up and getting another order out, many of Gino's animals and fancy shapes get put in the pasta boxes and are shipped out. In a few days the owner of a store sells Badino pasta and contacts the factory. Gino's animals and shapes are being collected by all the customers. Badino's pasta sells faster than the family can make it, and the business is saved. Gino at last has an important job making his pasta shapes.

INQUIRIES

What is pasta? Can we make some like Gino?

How does a pasta machine work?

What kind of fancy shapes can we make out of pasta?

Could we sell the pasta we make?

GOALS FILTER

EXPLORATIONS

Students follow recipe and make pasta. See figure 10.4.

Students examine the workings of a pasta machine and describe the mechanism.

Using geometric patterns and molds, children first design then create their own pasta shapes.

Students dry their pasta shapes, package them, and take them home to family.

CULMINATIONS

Students cooperate to mix pasta, follow directions, use measurement devices.

Students explain in a journal how a pasta machine operates.

Each student records observations in a journal and sketches the pasta shapes.

Students share finished pasta product and package.

Narrative Filter: Compelling Theme - Setting - Characters - Conflict - Action - Resolution

Disciplinary Heuristic: Artist, Scientist, Writer, Musician, Engineer, Historian, Psychologist, Anthropologist, Botanist, Dancer, Farmer, Poet, etc.

FIGURE 10.4 Exploration for *Gino Badino*

Inquiry:
What is pasta? Can we make some like Gino did?

Exploration Overview: Students work in cooperative groups, follow a recipe, and make pasta.

Guided Inquiry: Three pasta-making stations are set up for this exploration. After reading the story, students are immediately interested in making pasta and are divided into three groups. The following recipe is given to the children on cards at each station.

- Mix 1 teaspoon salt, 1 egg, ½ cup half and half (add enough flour to make a soft dough).

- Knead until smooth.

Also at each station are a variety of mixing bowls and measuring cups. Children follow the recipe and make pasta.
Parental help is suggested to assist students in cooperating and solving problems when they occur.

Teacher Facilitation: Students should be able to experiment and follow a recipe without much direct instruction from the teacher. The ability to discover ways to solve measuring problems, breaking eggs, blending, and making dough are part of the learning process.

Culminations: Students are excited by the prospect of sharing the pasta they have made with others. The products are cooked and eaten or given to parents. These authentic culminations of learning direct students to the possibility of marketing their ideas just like Gino Badino.

Assessment: If students cooperate to make edible pasta then they have been successful. Following directions and cooperation are the key elements in this exercise.

Students can assess themselves about their abilities in making pasta:

- Did they follow instructions?
- Did they measure carefully?
- Did they share materials?
- Did they clean up after themselves?

A Pasta Machine can Roll Pasta Dogh The right Langht. The nob can make iT FaTer and skinyer. The FaT noodles are chiken noodles. The skiney noodles are sagetey noodles.

diversity and have a better understanding of human experiences. They decided a simulation was the best means of fostering these goals. They created an immersion experience based on the historical events of Ellis Island at the turn of the 20th century. Arranging a multipurpose room, the teachers converted the space into testing areas, meeting rooms, media and resource tables, and quarantine zones.

To initiate the simulation, the teachers met the "immigrants" at the door of their regular classroom, gave them general instructions about what was to happen, gave them new identities, and then marched them "off the ship onto Ellis Island." Students were required to take various tests and fill out forms just as immigrants would have had to do coming to America. They experienced waiting in line, engaging in some menial tasks, trying to communicate in an unknown language, being anxious about not passing a screening, and dealing with a number of official-looking documents that were created by the teachers.

Throughout the unit, the teachers acted as Ellis Island officials and stayed within their characters to encourage the immigrants to role-play their own characters. They interacted with the students to invite improvisation and further research. The officials showed American indoctrination films (a documentary about Ellis Island), insisted that the immigrants document their potential earning power, and focused the immigrants on the task of meeting the citizen requirements.

At the end of the experience, when students had accrued appropriate passing marks on all tests for immigration, they were sworn in as citizens. A ceremony and celebration welcomed the new citizens into a nation of immigrants.

Jenni's Reflections

Doing the Ellis Island simulation was very enjoyable, both for the students and for us, the teachers. It was such a different mode of instruction. When we threw ourselves into the roles and let ourselves go and try it, it was very rewarding. When we could see the students enjoying themselves, it was even more enjoyable for us. We just fed off one another. All the kids reacted positively and each day the students got more into it. By the end, some of the students were doing things on their own. Several students dressed specially for their roles. Others adopted an accent. We tried to give them opportunities to be creative such as having them bring their most prized possession, and many students took advantage of the opportunity. They were engaged easily in the role. They were not on the outside looking in.

Our team felt the experience was so successful that Betsy adapted the unit for her student teaching experience. Now that she is a practicing teacher, the Ellis Island experience has become a tradition in her classroom that students look forward to.

See figures 10.5 and 10.6: planning template and exploration for Ellis Island.

Sarah Bennett and Kermit Kumle
Fall 1994
Union Elementary School
Union, Oregon

Sarah and Kermit worked together on this unit during a student teaching experience in a small, rural elementary school in eastern Oregon. Because they were both interested in the natural resources of the region and in the Hot Lake area in particular, they planned a collaborative unit for their fifth- and second-grade classes.

Sarah and Kermit arranged their classes in multiage teams for a field trip to Hot Lake, a thermal hot spring that had been a stop on the Oregon Trail and later developed into a hospital and resort. At the site, students observed their surroundings at several stations. Sarah and Kermit designated one to collect animal and plant life, one to collect the physical measurements of water temperature and pH, and one to collect other descriptive information about the site.

Each second grader had a fifth-grade buddy to work with as they gathered data using microscopes, plant presses, thermometers, field nets, reflective journals, and maps. Students became proficient at making slides,

FIGURE 10.5 Planning template for Ellis Island simulation

Foundational Goals: Solve Problems - Think Critically, Creatively - Use Technology - <u>Communicate</u> - Quantify - <u>Direct Own Learning</u> - Collaborate/Cooperate
Applications: Ability to Deliberate on Public Issues; <u>to Interpret Human Experience</u>; to Understand Diversity, Health Habits, Science/Math Relationships

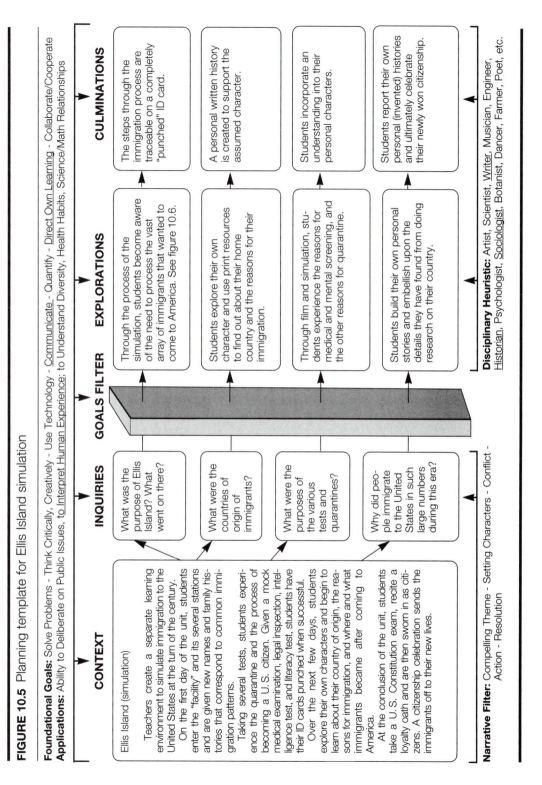

CULMINATIONS

The steps through the immigration process are traceable on a completely "punched" ID card.

A personal written history is created to support the assumed character.

Students incorporate an understanding into their personal characters.

Students report their own personal (invented) histories and ultimately celebrate their newly won citizenship.

EXPLORATIONS

Through the process of the simulation, students become aware of the need to process the vast array of immigrants that wanted to come to America. See figure 10.6.

Students explore their own character and use print resources to find out about their home country and the reasons for their immigration.

Through film and simulation, students experience the reasons for medical and mental screening, and the other reasons for quarantine.

Students build their own personal stories and embellish upon the details they have found from doing research on their country.

GOALS FILTER

INQUIRIES

What was the purpose of Ellis Island? What went on there?

What were the countries of origin of immigrants?

What were the purposes of the various tests and quarantines?

Why did people immigrate to the United States in such large numbers during this era?

CONTEXT

Ellis Island (simulation)

Teachers create a separate learning environment to simulate immigration to the United States at the turn of the century.

On the first day of the unit, students enter the "facility" and its several stations and are given new names and family histories that correspond to common immigration patterns.

Taking several tests, students experience the quarantine and the process of becoming a U.S. citizen. Given a mock medical examination, legal inspection, intelligence test, and literacy test, students have their ID cards punched when successful.

Over the next few days, students explore their own characters and begin to learn about their country of origin, the reasons for immigration, and where and what immigrants became after coming to America.

At the conclusion of the unit, students take a U.S. Constitution exam, recite a loyalty oath and are then sworn in as citizens. A citizenship celebration sends the immigrants off to their new lives.

Disciplinary Heuristic: Artist, Scientist, <u>Writer</u>, Musician, Engineer, <u>Historian</u>, Psychologist, <u>Sociologist</u>, Botanist, Dancer, Farmer, Poet, etc.

Narrative Filter: Compelling Theme - Setting Characters - Conflict - Action - Resolution

FIGURE 10.6 Exploration for Ellis Island simulation

Inquiry: What was Ellis Island? Why was it necessary? Initially, students understand that they are immigrants to America and that they are taken to a place called Ellis Island. The murmurings of "what is an 'Ellis Island'" are common as students depart for new surroundings.

Exploration Overview: Students are told that they will be going on a journey. In this case it will be to the multipurpose room (Ellis Island). To prepare for the journey they will all be given new identities. On the first day of their indoctrination at Ellis Island they engage in several mock tests and as they complete each task their ID card is punched as "passed." There are papers to fill out, simple tests to take, questions to answer.

Guided Inquiry: Since this is a simulation, teachers take the role of Ellis Island staff. They stay in role the entire time and give directions and respond to questions as though they were officials in 1901. On the first day, students are given their roles. A laminated manila card outlines a brief history of the individual, country of origin, and occupation. Around the edge of the card are markings and numbers that correspond to tests and processes that each immigrant will be required to pass. As they complete tasks, a hole is punched to indicate a "pass" for the immigrant.

The stations are simple, but require time and patience: A mock intelligence test consisting of simple oral tasks, a physical exam that checks hearing and eyesight, a legal inspection that requires immigrants to answer questions about their background, and a literacy test comprise the four stations.

Teacher Facilitation: The goals for this unit are to help students experience the human condition. It is important that students gain a personal feeling through experience. The teacher's role in the simulation is to create the experience and to stay as close to role as possible so that students are personally confronted with new experiences. Instead of disseminating information, the goal is to make students "feel" the information through experience. To help them experience quarantine, for example, teachers tie a yellow ribbon around students' arms who "failed" the medical exam and make them go to a separate area where there are resource materials on disease. In this way the student discovers the concept of quarantine.

Culminations: Students share their personae with others in round-table discussions. This dialogue encourages students to ask about each others' hopes, dreams, and plans for the future.

At the conclusion of the experience, students participate in a citizenship ceremony if they have all of their "punches." This ceremony has students say the Pledge of Allegiance, recite parts of the Constitution, and sing the National Anthem. After the students are sworn in, they are invited to a welcome reception.

Assessment: Students should leave the Ellis Island experience with an understanding of the human events of the time. Through their personal experience they should emerge with a broader understanding of what it might have been like to be an immigrant and the reasons for migration. Students should be able to discuss the major events that are happening to them, reflect on their own feelings and ideas, and play a role that is consistent with the character that they have been asked to assume.

In addition to completing the punched card activity, students are required to keep a journal of their experiences. As immigrants they are struggling to retain ties to their home countries and the journals will record these reflections as they interact in the new world. Journals are collected at the end of each day's experience and the teacher responds to them.

Students are also asked to debrief in the last few minutes of the session to ask questions or share discoveries. After the first day, students start to adopt their characters and show interest in developing their personal histories.

observing creatures under the projection microscope, and viewing the animals on an overhead screen.

At the end of the unit each group presented their findings to the fourth-grade class and interested parents. Students showed the maps they had drawn, the plants they had pressed, the pictures they had drawn, and the experiments they had conducted. The local newspaper featured the students on the front page.

Kermit's Reflections

We set the foundation with the field trip and that foundation allowed the students to say "I know where this water came from. I'm familiar with it and now I want to look at it." If we had given them a bottle of water and said "This is from Hot Lake," half of the kids would have said "What's Hot Lake?" The foundation of the field trip allowed these kids to take that ownership. They even referred to the samples by who had collected them, such as "This slide was made from Mike's sample" or "I got this leaf from Christi's sample." When they have that ownership they run with it—they want to know. I've got one kid that we consider an underachiever in school, who has samples that he's not going to give up until he knows what those things are: "What's that spider?" "What's that thing running around in that stream?"

One thing that I liked about the curriculum was that the kids were responsible for the most part. I wasn't there at the station always. I was getting materials that they asked for so they took responsibility. The kids were responsible for running the microscopes and talking about the stations.

They learned the different areas of sciences—maybe not to a T, maybe not in depth… In the traditional setting we're just going to give a child information that will be retained for a short time: This is what a biologist does, this is what a geologist does. I pretested them. I asked them, "What is a biologist?" They couldn't tell me. These kids didn't know. Now if I ask them what a biologist is, they know. These kids came away with not only what we showed them but they're also going to take the real live information that they've got inside their heads and be able to make sense of it. They can do things like using microscopes. Actual hands-on skills of technology use were clearly demonstrated. So now a kid can use those things and know their purpose.

Sarah's Reflections

One thing I really liked about this unit was the collaboration between the second and fifth graders. Kermit and I tried to match our students together in a way that would benefit both students. I have several nonwriters and we made sure that they would be paired with a fifth-grade buddy that would help them with their work and not do it for them. I also have a hearing-impaired student. She was wonderfully matched with a fifth-grade boy that made sure she was able to hear everything that was going on.

The pre/postassessment I gave the students was one sheet of paper with "Hot Lake" written at the top and the different science disciplines written along the left side. This sheet was used to measure their critical thinking and the cooperation/collaboration goal. Students were allowed to work with their partners. They were told to write everything they knew about Hot Lake. During the preassessment some students crossed off the discipline areas because they did not know what they meant. They included what they knew about the building and ghost stories they had heard. By the time they did the postassessment the students were able to put information in each of the discipline areas about what they knew about the science of Hot Lake.

See figures 10.7 and 10.8: planning template and exploration for Hot Lake.

Richard Meyer and Sharon Lester
Music Specialists
La Grande School District
La Grande, Oregon

Richard and Sharon are music specialists in the five elementary schools of La Grande, a community of approximately 10,000 people. Their responsibilities take them through the full gamut of music curriculum. They have both experimented with using context to make music meaningful, and they

FIGURE 10.7 Planning template for Hot Lake

Foundational Goals: Solve Problems - Think Critically, Creatively - Use Technology - Communicate - Quantify - Direct Own Learning - Collaborate/Cooperate
Applications: Ability to Deliberate on Public Issues; to Interpret Human Experience; to Understand Diversity, Health Habits, Science/Math Relationships, Humanities

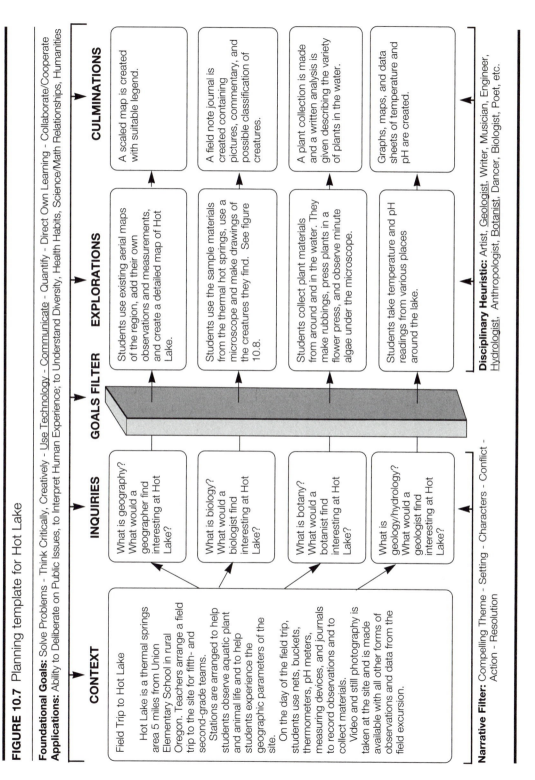

CONTEXT

Field Trip to Hot Lake

    Hot Lake is a thermal springs area 5 miles from Union Elementary School in rural Oregon. Teachers arrange a field trip to the site for fifth- and second-grade teams.

    Stations are arranged to help students observe aquatic plant and animal life and to help students experience the geographic parameters of the site.

    On the day of the field trip, students use nets, buckets, thermometers, pH meters, measuring devices, and journals to record observations and to collect materials.

    Video and still photography is taken at the site and is made available with all other forms of observations and data from the field excursion.

INQUIRIES

What is geography? What would a geographer find interesting at Hot Lake?

What is biology? What would a biologist find interesting at Hot Lake?

What is botany? What would a botanist find interesting at Hot Lake?

What is geology/hydrology? What would a geologist find interesting at Hot Lake?

GOALS FILTER

EXPLORATIONS

Students use existing aerial maps of the region, add their own observations and measurements, and create a detailed map of Hot Lake.

Students use the sample materials from the thermal hot springs, use a microscope and make drawings of the creatures they find. See figure 10.8.

Students collect plant materials from around and in the water. They make rubbings, press plants in a flower press, and observe minute algae under the microscope.

Students take temperature and pH readings from various places around the lake.

CULMINATIONS

A scaled map is created with suitable legend.

A field note journal is created containing pictures, commentary, and possible classification of creatures.

A plant collection is made and a written analysis is given describing the variety of plants in the water.

Graphs, maps, and data sheets of temperature and pH are created.

Disciplinary Heuristic: Artist, Geologist, Writer, Musician, Engineer, Hydrologist, Anthropologist, Botanist, Dancer, Biologist, Poet, etc.

Narrative Filter: Compelling Theme - Setting - Characters - Conflict - Action - Resolution

FIGURE 10.8 Exploration for Hot Lake

Inquiry: What is biology? What would a biologist find interesting at Hot Lake?

Exploration Overview: Students use the sample materials from the thermal hot springs, use a microscope, and make drawings of the creatures they find.

Guided Inquiry: Materials from the site are collected in plastic jars or other containers. The jars are labeled, as the same organisms may be resident in different environments.

Bringing materials back to class, students make simple wet mounts on glass slides. (The pairing of second and fifth graders worked well for this process. Simple compound microscopes and a projection microscope were borrowed from other classrooms. Minilessons on microscope technique helped older children learn techniques so that they in turn could assist younger children.)

Teacher Facilitation: Two things were the focus of this exploration: 1) allowing students to explore as a biologist might, and 2) giving students an opportunity to practice using the technology of science. Although children are always interested to name and classify, especially in second grade, the processes of observing, recording, sketching, and using the microscope are more important than the actual analysis of creatures in the pond water. Naming and classifying the creatures accurately is less important than the process. Accurate analysis requires a great deal of experience and sophistication.

Teachers should prompt with encouragement, ask questions about what they have seen and what characteristics the organisms have, and what role that they might have in the pond ecosystem.

Culminations: A field note journal is created containing pictures, commentary, and possible classification of creatures. The findings can be displayed or used in oral or media presentations. Parents and other classes are invited to view journals and samples on the projection microscope.

Assessment: A process checklist of behaviors is used at each station. A simple check next to each criterion indicates whether the student is using technology effectively, whether the student remains on task, and whether the student works collaboratively. A product checklist lists the criteria relating to the features of the field note form.

- Have students rendered observations in drawings?
- Have they made written comments?
- Have they made an attempt to relate their observations to resource materials about pond life?

eagerly attempted a narrative curriculum design as a way to weave music goals into the curriculum.

They selected the picture book *Chicken Sunday* (Polacco, 1992), a story of Russian and Ukrainian people at Easter time. The story contained puzzles about the two cultures and explored how some of the people reconciled their differences through personal relationships.

The story presented at least four leads to inquiry:

1. the origin and customs of the two cultures mentioned in the text
2. the tradition of making Pysanky Easter eggs
3. the nature of the music that is described in the book
4. the issues of diversity and bias

Richard and Sharon assembled the materials that they believed would be appropriate for student inquiry: maps, resource texts, various pieces of sacred music, eggs, wax, needles, and dyeing solutions.

The intrepid pair tested the story on a small group of upper elementary school students. They wanted to give the students a wide array of opportunities to study things that interested them.

Sharon's and Richard's reflections clearly demonstrate the recursive nature of the narrative curriculum—the children's explorative experiences helped them understand the story more deeply.

Sharon's and Richard's Reflections

The students' primary questions were how to decorate the Pysanky eggs and what kind of song would sound like "slow thunder and sweet rain." The egg process was lengthy and showed students the time and effort that must have taken place to create such beautiful eggs. It was definitely a project that made the students realize the children in the story were trying to make Mr. Kodinsy know that they did not egg his shop. This proved to him they were good kids that were willing to spend a great deal of time to verify it.

From a group of songs that we presented ("Christ the Lord Is Risen Today," "Jubilate De Rejoice in the Lord, Alleluia," "City Blues," and "Climbing Up the Mountain"), children selected the most appropriate song for Miss Eula to sing.

We felt as music teachers we probably would not be able to carry out the Pysanky egg exploration or writing activity in our regular music class because of our limited time. However, we would be able to use the story to integrate literature. We would use the ethnic discussion and dramatize the story. We would also have movement and unpitched instrumental improvisation.

See figures 10.9 and 10.10: planning template and exploration for *Chicken Sunday.*

Community Action Curriculum
Wendi Johnson, Cynthia Foy, Chandra Wilson
Ackerman Laboratory School
La Grande, Oregon

These three student teachers created an issues-based curriculum for 17 mixed-age, upper elementary school students. These teachers planned an experience (for a 90-minutes-per-day block) that would help students see possibilities and take some responsibilities for action.

To prepare for the unit, the teachers brainstormed the kind of problems that students could effectively identify, research, and act on in a short period of time. Scanning the community they found several possibilities that might interest students: a lack of playground equipment, few appropriate and low-priced motion pictures at the local theater, a dilapidated and nonfunctional community pool, a dangerous skate park, and so forth.

FIGURE 10.9 Planning template for *Chicken Sunday*

Foundational Goals: Solve Problems - Think Critically, Creatively - Use Technology - Communicate - Quantify - Direct Own Learning - Collaborate/Cooperate
Applications: Ability to Deliberate on Public Issues; to Interpret Human Experience; to Understand Diversity, Health Habits, Science/Math Relationships, Humanities

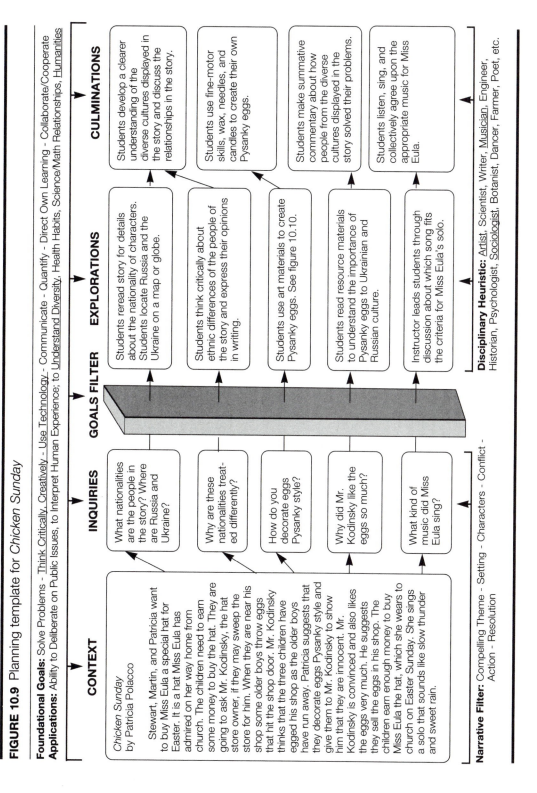

CULMINATIONS

Students develop a clearer understanding of the diverse cultures displayed in the story and discuss the relationships in the story.

Students use fine-motor skills, wax, needles, and candles to create their own Pysanky eggs.

Students make summative commentary about how people from the diverse cultures displayed in the story solved their problems.

Students listen, sing, and collectively agree upon the appropriate music for Miss Eula.

EXPLORATIONS

Students reread story for details about the nationality of characters. Students locate Russia and the Ukraine on a map or globe.

Students think critically about ethnic differences of the people of the story and express their opinions in writing.

Students use art materials to create Pysanky eggs. See figure 10.10.

Students read resource materials to understand the importance of Pysanky eggs to Ukrainian and Russian culture.

Instructor leads students through discussion about which song fits the criteria for Miss Eula's solo.

GOALS FILTER

INQUIRIES

What nationalities are the people in the story? Where are Russia and Ukraine?

Why are these nationalities treated differently?

How do you decorate eggs Pysanky style?

Why did Mr. Kodinsky like the eggs so much?

What kind of music did Miss Eula sing?

CONTEXT

Chicken Sunday
by Patricia Polacco

Stewart, Martin, and Patricia want to buy Miss Eula a special hat for Easter. It is a hat Miss Eula has admired on her way home from church. The children need to earn some money to buy the hat. They are going to ask Mr. Kodinsky, the hat store owner, if they may sweep the store for him. When they are near his shop some older boys throw eggs that hit the shop door. Mr. Kodinsky thinks that the three children have egged his shop as the older boys have run away. Patricia suggests that they decorate eggs Pysanky style and give them to Mr. Kodinsky to show him that they are innocent. Mr. Kodinsky is convinced and also likes the eggs very much. He suggests they sell the eggs in his shop. The children earn enough money to buy Miss Eula the hat, which she wears to church on Easter Sunday. She sings a solo that sounds like slow thunder and sweet rain.

Disciplinary Heuristic: <u>Artist</u>, Scientist, Writer, <u>Musician</u>, Engineer, Historian, Psychologist, <u>Sociologist</u>, Botanist, Dancer, Farmer, Poet, etc.

Narrative Filter: Compelling Theme - Setting - Characters - Conflict - Action - Resolution

FIGURE 10.10 *Exploration for* Chicken Sunday

Inquiry: How do you decorate eggs Pysanky style? Most students are familiar with some sort of egg dyeing but are unfamiliar with the term used in the story.

Exploration Overview: Pysanky eggs are made using a waxy coating and a sharp object to score away areas that are to be dyed. A simplified process is as follows:

1. Choose a simple design first.
2. Use a hard-boiled egg.
3. Cover areas that are designed as white with white crayon.
4. Use vinegar, water, and dye solution to dye the egg.
5. All the areas unprotected by the wax will be dyed.
6. Cover the dyed areas with another pattern of wax (this will protect any previously dyed area).
7. Redye the egg with a darker color; this will give a two-tone image on the egg.

A more complicated process requires that liquid wax be applied to the egg with a pin or stylus. This will make sharper and smaller patterns.

Guided Inquiry: For younger children the white crayon technique adequately illustrates the process. Use tape or rubber bands stretched around the egg to help children draw straight lines. Planning is important and sketching the design ahead of time helps students see how the patterns will need to be planned.

Teacher Facilitation: Proper modeling of techniques is required. A display of eggs at each stage of the process helps students visualize the purpose of each instruction.

Once eggs have been dyed the first time they can be redyed in a darker mix. Therefore, lightest dyes should occur first.

As students are engaged in the process of patterning and dyeing they soon realize the difficulty of the task. The "specialness" of the Pysanky egg to Mr. Kodinsky is revisited as is the value of hand skills in this process.

Culminations: Students use fine motor skills, wax, needles, and candles to create their own Pysanky egg. Students see the value in patience and planning and appreciate why the eggs are so valued in the Russian and Ukrainian culture. A display or other presentation of the eggs creates an appropriate setting for discussion of these values.

Assessment: Students produce a Pysanky egg, but the product is not critical in the assessment of hand skills.

- Did students follow directions?
- Did students use materials and tools properly and safely?
- Did students cooperate by sharing and cleaning up?

The teachers assembled a slide show of these features and role played the problems in front of the class.

Encouraging students to pick a problem that they found interesting, the trio of teachers worked hard to help students see past their pessimism about doing anything that would be important. To help show students that it was possible, they read stories from *The Kid's Guide to Social Action* (Lewis, 1991). Each story was selected to show what one person can do to change the world for the better.

After identifying a problem, students engaged in basic research about the issue. They read newspaper stories, talked to owners, community planners, and politicians to find out the facts about their problem. Once the students began to understand the problem, their teachers encouraged them to design alternative solutions to the problem by writing persuasive letters, making models, or communicating through dramatic presentations. Minilessons were offered to students to help them acquire skills necessary to carry out their projects. As the groups generated ideas, sketched plans, and crafted three-dimensional models of the features that they hoped to see in the community, they were engaged, eager learners.

Their work produced interesting child-oriented perspectives on what recreation opportunities ought to look like. City council members, the mayor, the owner of the local theater, and parents were invited to listen to presentations by the students. One council member was so impressed by the children's insights that she asked that the models and presentations be shown to a city planning committee. The following is an excerpt from an article in the the local newspaper:

> Sixteen Ackerman Laboratory School students have crafted what they hope is La Grande's future. The students made models or blueprints of facilities they believe the community needs. These include a swimming pool, a theme park, a roller skating rink, and a playground for older children.
>
> The students made presentations about these projects recently to a group made up of La Grande City Counselor Sue Hottois, several Eastern Oregon State College education professors, and a representative from the Granada Theater. Hottois was struck by the similarity between the students' ideas and those submitted by adults during a recent Town Hall meeting. She was so impressed that she asked the students to present their projects to the La Grande Parks Commission, a committee appointed by the City Council. Hottois, who served as a consultant for the students, wants them to see that they can be a part of the city government process.
>
> The students' work has been part of the Social Action Project. It involves children ages 10 to 12 in Ackerman's upper-level program. It was directed by student teachers Wendi Johnson, Cynthia Foy, and Chandra Wilson. Johnson will never forget the children's reaction when they made their pre-

sentations to Hottois and others. "It was a 'Wow!'" she said. "They finally understood that kids can make a difference that is real." She added that one student said, "Gosh, I didn't know it would go this far!" (Mason, 1995)

Cynthia's Reflections

It has been an experience full of ups and downs plus a lot of growth. I learned a lot about how students respond and I believe that the students in our room also learned a lot during this week.

We tried to have students research and learn all they could about the subject before they built models. Looking back at it, I think it might have worked better to build the models and then have them research the information about them. They could make any changes they needed before presenting their ideas to an appropriate audience. The students had a difficult time doing research on something that they were not very involved with at first. If they built the models first they would have more involvement from the start.

See figures 10.11 and 10.12: planning template and exploration for community action.

FIGURE 10.11 Planning template for community action

Foundational Goals: Solve Problems - Think Critically, Creatively - Use Technology - Communicate - Quantify - Direct Own Learning - Collaborate/Cooperate
Applications: Ability to Deliberate on Public Issues; to Interpret Human Experience; to Understand Diversity, Health Habits, Science/Math Relationships, Humanities

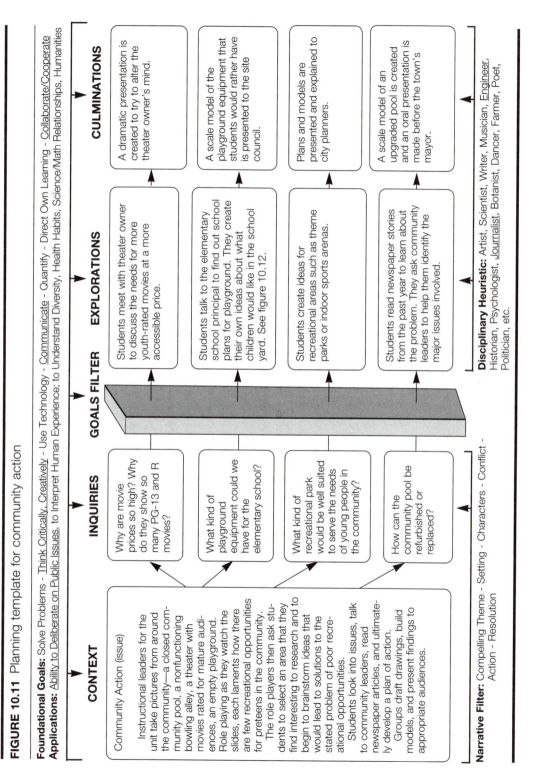

CONTEXT

Community Action (issue)

Instructional leaders for the unit take pictures from around the community—a closed community pool, a nonfunctioning bowling alley, a theater with movies rated for mature audiences, an empty playground. Role playing as they watch the slides, each laments how there are few recreational opportunities for preteens in the community.

The role players then ask students to select an area that they find interesting to research and to begin to brainstorm ideas that would lead to solutions to the stated problem of poor recreational opportunities.

Students look into issues, talk to community leaders, read newspaper articles, and ultimately develop a plan of action.

Groups draft drawings, build models, and present findings to appropriate audiences.

INQUIRIES

Why are movie prices so high? Why do they show so many PG-13 and R movies?

What kind of playground equipment could we have for the elementary school?

What kind of recreational park would be well suited to serve the needs of young people in the community?

How can the community pool be refurbished or replaced?

GOALS FILTER

EXPLORATIONS

Students meet with theater owner to discuss the needs for more youth-rated movies at a more accessible price.

Students talk to the elementary school principal to find out school plans for playground. They create their own ideas about what children would like in the school yard. See figure 10.12.

Students create ideas for recreational areas such as theme parks or indoor sports arenas.

Students read newspaper stories from the past year to learn about the problem. They ask community leaders to help them identify the major issues involved.

CULMINATIONS

A dramatic presentation is created to try to alter the theater owner's mind.

A scale model of the playground equipment that students would rather have is presented to the site council.

Plans and models are presented and explained to city planners.

A scale model of an upgraded pool is created and an oral presentation is made before the town's mayor.

Disciplinary Heuristic: Artist, Scientist, Writer, Musician, Engineer, Historian, Psychologist, Journalist, Botanist, Dancer, Farmer, Poet, Politician, etc.

Narrative Filter: Compelling Theme - Setting - Characters - Conflict - Action - Resolution

---

FIGURE 10.12 Exploration for community action

Inquiry: What kind of playground equipment could we have for the elementary school? (Former playground materials have been removed because they were either deemed too dangerous or because they were old and rusty. The school yard is now a bare playing field and there have been discussions and plans regarding the purchase of additional equipment.)

Exploration Overview: After students first identify their interest in the issue they brainstorm with the class possible avenues for exploration. Choosing strategies they begin to gather information. Students talk to the elementary school principal to find out what plans the school has to install playground equipment. As a result they formulate their own plans and design ideas that suit their interests.

Guided Inquiry: Since the goals for this lesson are problem solving and deliberating on public issues, the research requires the use of primary resources. Students are encouraged to talk to people they know and to formulate their own ideas based on the input from students and school personnel. After the problem is identified, a brainstorming session helps students identify the possible sources for inquiry. Interview skills, telephone etiquette, and data gathering techniques are minilessons provided for the group as they assemble ideas and information about the problem.

After students have gathered basic information they design their scale models of the playgrounds that they would like to see. Materials such as sticks of wood, foam blocks, cardboard, paper, plastic, and tools are made available so that students can go from plans to model.

Minilessons on scale and measurement as well as safe tool use accompany the planning of the model. At this point students engage in free exploration in creating their three-dimensional model.

When the students complete their model they organize a media presentation that combines oral and written portions with the three-dimensional model.

Teacher Facilitation: The instructional leader in this unit sets up the possible questions, provides basic strategies and procedures for collecting information, makes contacts with resource personnel ahead of time, procures necessary materials and tools, and encourages the students to find alternative solutions.

Arranging students in interest groups, the teacher facilitates the groups' exploration by providing access to telecommunications, primary resources, and other media. Suggesting alternative possibilities is the ongoing responsibility of the teacher if groups become frustrated with specific explorations.

Culminations: Students should have the opportunity to share their models and ideas with members of the community who have interests in their area of study. Specific feedback to the student in intimate, personal settings is especially powerful.

Assessment: Both process and products are evident in this work. How students collect information, how they relate to one another, how they solve problems, and how they use material and technology are all aspects of process. The product of their work, the actual model and presentation, is appropriately linked to goals such as communication, self-directed learning, and ability to use technology. A checklist is used for each of the stated goals:

Communication (process assessment)
Student uses reading, writing, listening, and speaking to:
_____ explain ideas clearly
_____ record information
_____ work effectively in a group, listening to others' ideas

Collaboration (process assessment)
Student does his or her "fair share" to:
_____ help the group
_____ do the job given each day (gopher, leader, recorder, encourager)
_____ encourage other group members to be involved

Presentation (product assessment)
_____ The presentation is a clear explanation of the problem
_____ The presentation is a clear explanation of the solution
_____ The presentation involves all members of the group

M. Ruth Davenport,
with Michael Jaeger and Carol Lauritzen
Winter 1994
Ackerman Laboratory School
La Grande, Oregon

Ruth Davenport is the instructional leader for a group of mixed-age students at the college's laboratory school. Her classroom centers around student-generated curriculum and a workshop cycle similar to that presented in chapter 9. Students are often self-directed in their studies and enjoy explorations in areas around the room. Ruth worked with Carol and Michael to test the narrative curriculum.

To begin, Ruth elucidated some of the broad goals that she has for all her learners: Learners must be actively involved in the process of learning. They demonstrate this by writing to know, writing to communicate, and thinking in a discipline. With these goals in mind, we examined the samples of curriculum possibilities that we wanted to try in the classroom. We found a classic fictionalized biography of Benjamin Franklin by Robert Lawson (1939) called *Ben and Me*. Carol first suggested the idea to use several chapters as contexts for inquiries about static electricity. Michael read the story and assembled some manipulatives that would match the ideas presented in the text. Since Ben was experimenting with different materials to create static charges, we assembled different types of plastic, glass rods, pieces of silk, and strips of fur so students could try these experiments if the appropriate inquiry arose. Other possibilities included making an electroscope and letting children explore different static-producing devices.

Highlighting Ruth's stated goals on a planning template helped us focus as we considered explorations for the students. After reading a portion of the book interactively with the students, Carol asked them to write their questions and ideas in a science lab log. Students were then gathered in a learner's circle and were asked to share their ideas. From these initial interests it was clear that the first exploration that we had conceived would respond to students' desires to understand how Ben made static electricity. The students, working in pairs, tried various combinations of materials to see which could pick up the most pieces of paper confetti. Exploratory talk was heard around the room as students suggested combinations to each other and shared their results. The logs were used to record data. The teachers modeled the type of questions students could ask to explore why the confetti stuck to the rods. Bringing together prior knowledge and the current experiences, the children talked about getting shocks from door knobs and pet dogs. They made analogies to what they knew by referring to the phenomenon as "magnetism."

Michael's Reflections

I was impressed with Ruth's notion about having students think in a discipline. This influence increased my dissonance with the lesson we were teaching because on one hand we were creating an open exploration for students to find interesting static phenomena and on the other hand I was anxious inside that students would come to the appropriate scientific explanation. This dissonance was borne out in how the lessons proceeded.

At first I was relaxed as students freely explored the materials combinations to find the most effective static generators. Making the electroscopes was a bit more constraining because if the devices are not made to specifications they may not operate correctly. Trained as a scientist, I wanted the equipment to be made to specific, predictable standards. Anything less gave me an uneasy feeling! Yet, I had to let the children build them for themselves.

As we demonstrated the static generator, I asked children to speculate about the sparks they saw and the sparks they heard or saw when they made static from their materials. By asking guiding questions about lightning and friction, I was hoping that students would integrate the experience and arrive at what Ben Franklin did some 200 years ago.

At times, my frantic inner voice wanted to try to talk these children out of their fresh and sometimes unsophisticated view of the world. I had to keep reminding myself that helping them to think like a scientist did not consist of forcing them to concur with my belief system.

See figures 10.13, 10.14, and 10.15: planning template and explorations for *Ben and Me.*

Dale Holland
Ione Junior/Senior High School
Ione, Oregon

Dale teaches science in a rural junior and senior high school. (If you want to understand how rural, find Ione on a map.) Responsible for a wide array of subjects and grade levels, Dale was interested in bringing projects into the classroom that would help students incorporate the skills of a scientist. Realizing that most of his students had seen the movie *Jurassic Park*, Dale reminded them of key concepts by reading excerpts from the book. Using this context and dinosaurs in general, Dale asked students to generate project ideas. Three general areas of study were initiated:

1. Dinosaur excavation. An area would be excavated that contained remains of recently buried animals. The same process a paleontologist would use would be followed.
2. Dinosaur tracking. Using prints from fossilized tracks, students made ratio comparisons of people to dinosaurs in order to relate similarities and predict dinosaur attributes.
3. Dinosaur reconstruction. Finding remains of an unknown animal, the project was designed to rearticulate the bones as a paleontologist would.

Other projects were planned, but because of time constraints, only these three were feasible. Students selected the research area that interested them the most; they all spent hours making observations, collecting data, and constructing models. At the conclusion of their work, students met to compare data. They commented in their conclusions about their explorations and reflected on their findings.

Bridget M. had researched how dinosaur tracks might be used to estimate the creature's size, using a human model for comparison. She wrote:

In this lab we found that our measurements of the Anatosaurus did not match those that the scientists found. For the Iguanadon we found it to be 19 cm., not 55.2 cm. We also found the mass to be 5.2 metric tons. We learned how to find the surface area and stride of people. We also graphed

FIGURE 10.13 Planning template for *Ben and Me*

Foundational Goals: Solve Problems - Think Critically, Creatively - Use Technology - Communicate - Quantify - Direct Own Learning - Collaborate/Cooperate
Applications: Ability to Deliberate on Public Issues; to Interpret Human Experience; to Understand Diversity, Health Habits, <u>Science/Math Relationships</u>, Humanities

CONTEXT

Ben and Me
by Robert Lawson

Chapters 3 and 6:
Benjamin Franklin and his faithful mouse friend Amos agree to be partners—Ben to give Amos food and shelter, and Amos to give Ben advice and assistance in all his scientific endeavors.

Ben and Amos explore how static electricity can be made by rubbing certain materials together. Amos receives more than one shock from Ben as they develop apparatus to make electricity and to study how it works.

Ben plans a grand exposition of his discoveries for the governor and his lady. Amos discovers that Ben has wired the apparatus incorrectly and takes it upon himself to set the apparatus straight. In the middle of the demonstration Ben announces that by pressing on a certain knob, the electrical forces displayed will be amazing. They are. Amos has wired the governor's chair to the static machine, giving him a profound jolt! Ben is pleased that he has discovered the effects of electricity on the human body!

INQUIRIES

What were the materials Ben used to make static electricity? What combinations of materials are most efficient?

What devices did Ben use to study the nature of static electricity? What did he show the Philosophical Society?

What is the nature of a circuit? What does it mean to have the wires connected correctly?

GOALS FILTER

EXPLORATIONS

Students explore the nature of generating static electricity by combining cloth and fur with glass and plastic. Used in a certain way, rubbing the combinations yields two distinct types of charge. Placing a charged rod or fork near a pile of shredded newspapers causes an excited leap of letters! See figure 10.14.

Using the directions for making a pop bottle electroscope, students make a device like the one Ben used to make several of his more profound discoveries of electricity. The electroscope is sensitive to the presence of charge and can be used to demonstrate that there are two distinct kinds of charges. See figure 10.15.

A Leyden jar (two plastic cups and foil) can be made to store electrical charge. By using silk thread or fine wire, charge can be transmitted from place to place. Students can experiment with the circuits necessary to try to "shock" the governor!

CULMINATIONS

Students manipulate variables and communicate findings.

Students construct an electroscope and communicate their findings orally and through field journals.

Students utilize electroscopes, Leyden jars, and wires to make static circuits.

Disciplinary Heuristic: Artist, <u>Scientist</u>, Writer, Musician, Engineer, Historian, Psychologist, Anthropologist, Botanist, Dancer, Farmer, Poet, etc.

Narrative Filter: Compelling Theme - Setting - Characters - Conflict - Action - Resolution

FIGURE 10.14 Exploration 1 for *Ben and Me*

Inquiry: What were the materials Ben used to make static electricity? What combinations of materials are most efficient?

Exploration Overview: Students explore static electricity by combining cloth and fur with glass and plastic. In certain combinations, rubbing the materials yields two distinct types of charges. Placing a charged rod or fork near a pile of shredded newspapers causes an excited leap of letters!

Guided Inquiry: Direct students' attention to materials at hand: newspaper, cloth, plastic forks, glass rods, and fur. Challenge students to use the combinations of plastic or glass and fur or flannel to determine effect on newsprint pieces. "What combinations will cause the most effect?

Try suggesting various ways of rubbing the materials together. "Do the number of strokes, direction, or rate of rubbing change the amount of static produced?"

Teacher Facilitation: As students explore combinations of the materials, ask questions such as:

"Do you notice any difference between the combinations of materials?"
"What seems to be the best combination?"
"Does it matter how you rub the fork or rod?"
"Do you notice any interesting behavior of the newsprint when you change from one combination to another combination?

Culminations: Students record findings in field notes that use both words and pictures. Oral contributions may also accompany the notes. Teacher questions that help focus students' attention back to the story may close this lesson. "What do you suppose Ben did to shock Amos? What might he have rubbed together to generate a charge?"

Assessment: This inquiry leads to the exploration of the causes and effects of static electric interactions. Assessment of student work follows both processes and concepts as students use materials. One process goal that may be applied here is critical thinking. We may assess this with a check sheet:

____ Does the student make observations of phenomena?
____ Does the student invent a possible explanation?
____ Does the student design any opportunity to validate the explanation?
____ Does the student reflect on the explanation in light of new observations?

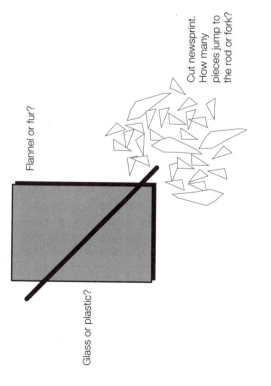

Flannel or fur?

Glass or plastic?

Cut newsprint. How many pieces jump to the rod or fork?

FIGURE 10.15 Exploration 2 for *Ben and Me*

Inquiry: What devices did Ben use to study the nature of static electricity? What did he show the Philosophical Society?

Exploration Overview: Using the directions for making a pop bottle electroscope, students make a device like the one that Ben used to make several of his more profound discoveries of electricity. The electroscope is sensitive to the presence of charge and can be used to demonstrate that there are two distinct kinds of charge.

Guided Inquiry: Using the instructions below, have students create their own electroscope. (This device was known at the time of Ben Franklin and he received instructions similar to this to make his own device.)

"What can this device tell us about static electricity? Students can then use the electroscope to explore more qualitative variables about electrical charge.

- Place an aluminum wire through the cap in a clean soda bottle.
- Make a ball of aluminum foil as round as possible and rest it firmly on the wire end as shown.
- Glue a portion of tinsel on the end of the wire so that two equal pieces hang limply from the end.
- Screw the cap on the bottle and orient the aluminum wire so that the tinsel hangs freely without touching the sides or bottom of the bottle.
- Use static electricity combinations to test the electroscope.

Tin foil ball

Clean pop bottle with hole in lid

Aluminum wire bent at end

Tinsel glued to wire

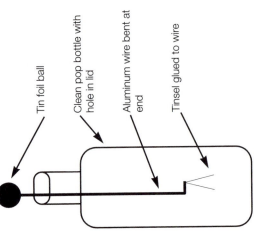

Teacher Facilitation: As students explore combinations with the materials, ask questions such as "What happens to the tinsel when the glass or fork is placed near the aluminum ball?" "Why do you suppose the tinsel spread apart?" "Do both combinations cause the same effect in the tinsel?"

The teacher may then suggest that one student place one combination of static materials near the aluminum ball and then have another student bring a combination near. "What happens to the tinsel?" (This is the essence of what Franklin did to prove that there were two types of charges. Because the leaves spread with both combinations, yet collapsed when placed on the ball at the same time, he deduced that the one combination made a negative charge and the other made a positive charge. When they were put together they collapsed and neutralized the charge. An elegant proof of electrons and protons! Note: This parenthetical explanation is provided not for transmission to students, but to give the teacher background information.)

Culminations: Students create an electroscope, demonstrate its actions, record field notes in their journal, and communicate their findings. "How were you like Ben, the scientist? What have you discovered about the nature of static electricity?"

Assessments: We are interested here in helping students test hypotheses and make generalizations about what they observe. These are process goals that we find within the science and mathematics area of the goals filter.

To check for progress in these processes, teachers should listen carefully to students' talk about what they are doing.

A check sheet that helps to identify the processes is given as follows:

— Has the student manipulated materials?
— Has the student made observations?
— Has the student suggested a possible reason for these observations? (A hypothesis?)
— Has the student made any further attempt to corroborate ideas with experimentation?
— Has the student recorded these data?

and created tables. If I were doing this again I would make sure that the things were a little more organized. I would also have compared the stride to something like a dog instead of a person.

Jerad A. added his ideas:

Next time if I were to do this I would get all supplies before we start. Sometimes during the project it wasn't so much the work but the hunting for rulers, markers, dinosaur information, etc. I would definitely be better equipped next time.

A third student wrote:

We had a precise purpose for the lab. Instead of following some instructions we had to do some research and to find the better way to do our purpose. That was what made it interesting. …This was maybe the most

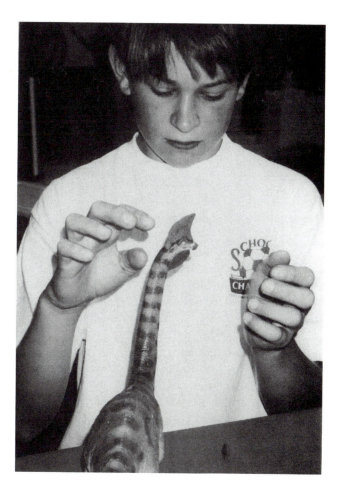

interesting lab we have done so far because we had to do our own research to create something that can have a utility in life.

Dale Holland's Reflections

I had students begin excavating in an area near the school where we had buried five cats from an advanced biology class the year before. Only three of the cats were recovered.

The third project, "Dinosaur Reconstruction," was derived from students that went out looking for an animal bone to compare. We had planned to reconstruct a cow. With the help of an anatomy book, we found just about all the bones for a cow. The class put the cow together in the back of the classroom (laid flat on the floor). We were planning on making a standing model with the help of rebar, nuts, bolts, and glue. Also, we wanted to label the skeleton with the proper names of all of the bones.

As the projects were being written up, students were very confused with the huge amount of data that they collected. When the data and calculations were compiled, students began to understand how it all fit together. The students came up with a lot more questions and ideas on how to make these projects better, but we ran out of time to test these ideas!

Now that I have jumped into these projects and have a better understanding of the time and inquiry involved, I could do a better job of organizing this task.

See figures 10.16 and 10.17: planning template and exploration for *Jurassic Park.*

◈ The Narrative Curriculum in Other Settings

In the following sections we present other examples that illustrate that the narrative curriculum is viable with multicultural populations, in urban settings, and with students with special needs. Teachers have incorporated the critical aspects of the narrative curriculum in a variety of ways. While the needs of mainstreamed students will still have to be carefully considered through individualized programs, the narrative curriculum offers many opportunities for such children to share the curriculum with other learners. Teachers have also found that the narrative curriculum benefits children with diverse learning needs, due to its multiple entry points and explorations that spring from a variety of learning styles. Teachers can spontaneously adapt the curriculum to foster these children's learning by taking advantage of the many teachable moments that the narrative curriculum provides.

FIGURE 10.16 Planning template for *Jurassic Park*

Foundational Goals: Solve Problems - <u>Think Critically</u>, Creatively - <u>Use Technology</u> - Communicate - Quantify - Direct Own Learning - Collaborate/Cooperate
Applications: Understand Diversity, Wellness, Human Condition, <u>Understand Science/Math Relationships</u>, Humanities

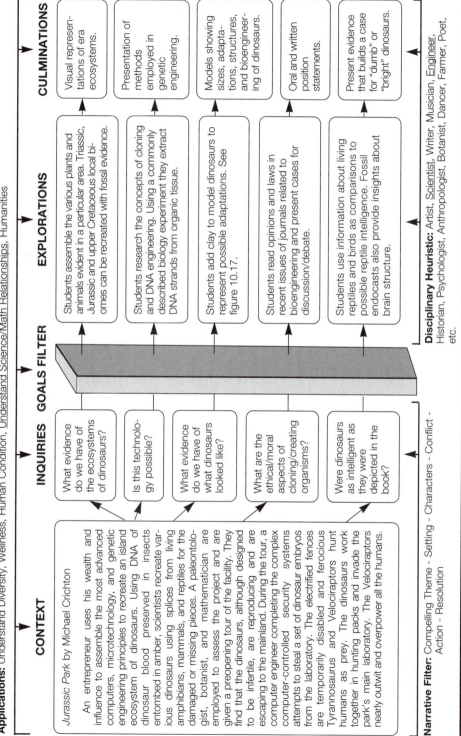

CONTEXT

Jurassic Park by Michael Crichton

An entrepreneur uses his wealth and influence to assemble the most advanced computers, microtechnology, and genetic engineering principles to recreate an island ecosystem of dinosaurs. Using DNA of dinosaur blood preserved in insects entombed in amber, scientists recreate various dinosaurs using splices from living amphibians, mammals, and reptiles for the damaged or missing pieces. A paleontologist, botanist, and mathematician are employed to assess the project and are given a preopening tour of the facility. They find that the dinosaurs, although designed to be infertile, are reproducing and are escaping to the mainland. During the tour, a computer engineer completing the complex computer-controlled security systems attempts to steal a set of dinosaur embryos from the laboratory. The electrified fences are temporarily disabled and ferocious Tyrannosaurus and Velociraptors hunt humans as prey. The dinosaurs work together in hunting packs and invade the park's main laboratory. The Velociraptors nearly outwit and overpower all the humans.

INQUIRIES

What evidence do we have of the ecosystems of dinosaurs?

Is this technology possible?

What evidence do we have of what dinosaurs looked like?

What are the ethical/moral aspects of cloning/creating organisms?

Were dinosaurs as intelligent as they were depicted in the book?

GOALS FILTER

EXPLORATIONS

Students assemble the various plants and animals evident in a particular area. Triassic, Jurassic and upper Cretaceous local biomes can be recreated with fossil evidence.

Students research the concepts of cloning and DNA engineering. Using a commonly described biology experiment they extract DNA strands from organic tissue.

Students add clay to model dinosaurs to represent possible adaptations. See figure 10.17.

Students read opinions and laws in recent issues of journals related to bioengineering and present cases for discussion/debate.

Students use information about living reptiles and birds as comparisons to possible reptile intelligence. Fossil endocasts also provide insights about brain structure.

CULMINATIONS

Visual representations of era ecosystems.

Presentation of methods employed in genetic engineering.

Models showing sizes, adaptations, structures, and bioengineering of dinosaurs.

Oral and written position statements.

Present evidence that builds a case for "dumb" or "bright" dinosaurs.

Disciplinary Heuristic: Artist, <u>Scientist</u>, Writer, Musician, <u>Engineer</u>, Historian, Psychologist, Anthropologist, Botanist, Dancer, Farmer, Poet, etc.

Narrative Filter: Compelling Theme - Setting - Characters - Conflict - Action - Resolution

FIGURE 10.17 Exploration for *Jurassic Park*

Inquiry: Students are interested in the depiction of dinosaurs in the book and the movie. Where do the writers, producers, and scientists get their ideas about what dinosaurs really looked like?

Students may be guided to challenge these views: "What evidence do we have of what dinosaurs looked like?"

Exploration Overview: Most of the evidence we have of dinosaurs is limited to that which comes from bones. These do provide many possibilities for bone structure, but do not show fleshy adaptations that may have been present. Using information about modern reptiles and mammals, students add to models made from pure skeletal derivation.

Guided Inquiry: The teacher helps students with their questions and guides them to be critical about the way in which Hollywood depicts the dinosaur. Humorous examples such as Godzilla are presented so that students can see the possibility for error.

Examples from nature are also important. Given a series of pictures of modern-day reptiles that exhibit fleshy appendages, students can speculate about their purpose and then decide whether dinosaurs might have also had similar appendages.

Soft clay added to a plastic model can simulate protective layers, defensive devices, cooling vanes, or sexual attractors. Students create these additions and defend the plausibility of such an adaptation based on modern function.

Teacher Facilitation: Several examples are helpful in giving students some background help as they form their own adaptations. American chameleons, for example, puff up their bodies and look ominous as they challenge each other's territories. To attract females, the male inflates the lower part of the throat and the color changes to bright pink. Fleshy adaptations can be controlled, colored, or deleted (as in the case of a removable tail).

Other mammalian adaptations such as trunks, fleshy ears, noses, fat layers, and hair may also be applicable.

Culminations: Students create a new vision of a dinosaur based upon the probable natural history of the animal and the possible adaptations that would assist the animal in being successful in its environment. One way to show their ideas is to present a modified model to the class, accompanied by a chart that shows the adaptation and rationale for adding it to dinosaurs.

Assessment: Assessment of this project is based upon creativity:

- the actual model created
- the plausibility of the adaptation based on the likely characteristics of the dinosaur's life history
- the evidence from modern animals that this adaptation is plausible

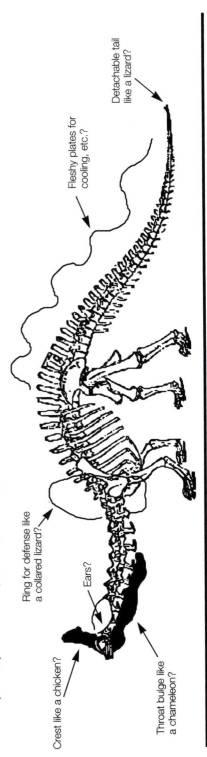

Crest like a chicken?

Ring for defense like a collared lizard?

Ears?

Throat bulge like a chameleon?

Fleshy plates for cooling, etc.?

Detachable tail like a lizard?

On a Reservation

As a group, children living on the reservation of the Confederated Tribes of the Umatilla tend to score poorly in mathematics and sciences. These test scores, among other indicators of academic difficulties, have alerted teachers to the need to find new ways to help Native American children be successful in school. A narrative curriculum has made an impact in this particular community of learners. For example, one unit used the context of *Rainbow Crow* (Van Laan, 1991), a Lenape legend which describes the crow as a bird with rainbow-colored feathers. Students generated questions about how the bird developed its black, shiny coloration and whether the rainbow seen in the black feathers is the same as a rainbow in the sky. Students explored color through experimentation with spectroscopes, prisms, and chromatography. In the culminations, they related their observations to their cultural heritage of story.

This powerful link between context and the child's background is important, first, because it verifies a community that seeks to perpetuate and honor cultural traditions and, second, because new meanings about the physical universe have a point of reference. The acknowledgment and advancement of their cultural point of view provided these children with access to the empiricism and special vocabulary of the discipline of science.

In the Inner City

The initial experience for a group of K–6 Chicano children in a summer educational program was to brainstorm everything in their community that needed fixing. These inner-city youths in San Diego found plenty of things to complain about. From the list of problems, students decided to study the issue of school lunches. Where did they come from and why were they so bad?

> Thus began a summer-long odyssey in which students wrote letters, made phone calls, traced their lunches from the catering truck through the school's contracts office, figured out taxpayers' cost per lunch, made records of actual services received from the subcontractors, counted sandwiches and tested milk temperatures, and finally, compared their findings with contract specifications and found that there was significant discrepancy... Both the local television stations and the major networks responded to the press releases sent out by the students, who held a press conference to present the facts and answer reporters' questions. (Nifto, 1994, p. 421)

The students learned how to push the system for information. Quizzed about their methods, one 9-year-old girl responded: "We found this stuff out. Nobody had to tell us anything. You know, you adults give yourselves too much credit" (Nifto, 1994, p. 421).

Dramatic stories from other inner-city schools demonstrate the power of the student-centered curricula. Fort Pitt Elementary School had established a reputation as the most dreaded of all Pittsburgh schools. Over a period of two years, however, that image has radically changed. The school has posted 29 to 47 percent gains in writing scores, discipline referrals have dropped 71 percent, and the general school climate has dramatically improved. What caused this turnaround? Teachers and administrators attest that the curriculum has made all the difference.

> One week each month for four months intermediate teachers dispense with normal routine and lead groups of 10 students each in an in-depth look at one topic. Like college students perusing a catalog, the children get to select their research team from a changing menu. (Hartman, et al., 1994, p. 46)

The students take field trips, engage in research, and share findings.

> In an Electricity Independent Research Project, students went to Pittsburgh's Science Center on Tuesday afternoon and the electric company on Wednesday afternoon, then helped teach third graders about electricity on Thursday... As their group project, children constructed a model city of cardboard, then lighted it up with battery-powered lightbulbs and some circuitry. On Friday, they gave culminating presentations on their work to peers, parents, and community members. (Hartman, et al., 1994, p. 46)

In these examples we see the power that personal story holds in curriculum. These children were allowed to direct their own curriculum and share their discoveries with significant audiences. Here we see vital elements of a narrative curriculum at work: the identification of a rich context for learning, the belief that all students are capable of learning at high levels, and the conviction that learners will succeed in finding personal meaning within their learning environment.

In a Resource Room

Eric and his brother Mark were identified as trainable mentally retarded very early in life. The parents, although not abusive, severely restricted the two boys and isolated them from the rest of the world until the state forced the parents to send them to school. They had developed their own language and way of coping with the world. School presented incredible challenges for them: acculturation, new language, little appropriate prior knowledge, and socialization. To accommodate for some unknowns, the resource room teacher decided to provide the boys with an initial experience in the school's garden. The boys would interact with tangible items like sunflowers, soil, and garden tools. Guided by their abilities and interests, their teacher would create new opportunities for them to grow seeds, learn new vocabulary and practice writing, use tools, and communicate in a "second" language.

The narrative curriculum serves special needs students well because it provides a tangible starting place from which to assess students' abilities and knowledge. It can then help develop new territories for exploration. Because the context is engaging, this preassessment can be a dynamic process. We can understand in a more holistic way the true abilities of special needs students. Further, if we can use these encounters as a way to determine which areas are of continued interest, we may be able to avoid the overly behavioral nature of much special education curriculum.

What We Value

In these examples we note commonalities in what teachers have valued in education. The idea of values leads us to a final consideration about the narrative curriculum. So far we have made a case for the narrative curriculum from theoretical and practical bases. We have asserted our learning theory and verified it through evidence and examples. We have supported the adoption of goals with both practical and political rationale. We have postulated story as the structure of the curriculum and justified how and why it is effective. And because of personal experience and the confirmation of others, we can support a model for implementation that is effective in the classroom. The essential rationale behind our belief in the narrative curriculum, however, can be explained by naming what we truly value:

- ▎ Children are important for who they are now, not just for who they might become.
- ▎ We teach who we are, not just what we know.
- ▎ We care about caring.

Children Are Important for Who They Are Now

It is a common misperception, held by many people, including educators, that children are a deficit model of adults. That is, children are looked upon as unable, immature, unproductive, and uninformed versions of the adult ideal. If we apply the deficit model of children, we are forever wishing, prodding, and pushing learners to be something they are not. We value a different perspective. Children are who they are. We recognize and celebrate their developmental differences as we provide opportunities for growth and maturation. Because this perspective allows us to respect our learners for who they are now, for what they know and are able to do now, they in turn develop for themselves a sense of self and self-worth. We believe in and trust children. They are immensely capable of a world of possibilities. Like Dewey and others (Winograd & Higgins, 1994/1995), we believe that children have a natural tendency to be curious and to ask questions. We believe that children exemplify "the having of wonderful ideas" (Duckworth, 1972) and that children's perspectives form a legitimate framework for generating ideas. They may not have the skills, tools, and knowledge of adults, but they can and do contribute to this world. We "celebrate the children" (Myers, 1990).

No curriculum can be of value if it is not centered in the lives of students. Honoring and respecting all children's stories (by helping them create the events that lead to a positive resolution of their personal needs) forms the core of a curriculum that believes in children. If we create learning environments that depend on this value, then we may expect generous returns for our efforts. Curriculum must allow students to work at their own level, to engage in exploration appropriate to their physical, cognitive, and emotional maturity, and to have ever-present opportunities for challenge and growth. We believe that the narrative curriculum honors this value. Because we expect students to generate their own questions, act on their own ideas, and culminate their findings in ways they believe are important, students are honored for who they are now.

We Teach Who We Are

Our friend made a lasting impression when he said: "I teach who I am, not what I know" (Hooshang Bagheri, personal communication, October 20, 1992). By these meaningful words, our eyes were opened to see teachers as influential human beings rather than simply holders of certificates, licenses, lettered degrees, or titles. Our impetus for teaching is the desire to share with other human beings that which we embrace as precious and meaningful. The knowledge, degrees, and awards that we have acquired are unimportant compared to who we are and the way we act as we live (and write) our lives as teachers.

In translating this value to our own practice, we must grapple with the key question: What kind of learning environment will best allow us to teach ourselves and best allow our learners to teach themselves? You anticipate the answer, of course. The environment the narrative curriculum creates, with its purposeful embracing of student interests, its open-ended explorations, and its opportunities for shared culminations of learning, enables us to teach who we are.

We Care About Caring

This value synthesizes our beliefs about curriculum and learning. Let us tell one last story, one that creates a vision dear to us. It is a true story that a friend shared about his father. His father came home each night, exhausted from a long day at the middle school. He complained rarely. Rather he would tell stories about what had happened that day. His recollections were most often positive and humorous. Many years after he had retired, when his son had a sense of the awesome challenge of teaching, the more remarkable aspect of the story became known. When asked by his son how he managed to survive those thirty-plus years in the middle school classroom, he looked at him and softly told him how he would start each day. Every day he would get to school an hour early before any of the other students or teachers would arrive. Every morning he would look out over the empty desks and wonder about what the day would bring. Then he would move through the room and place his hand on each desk and pray for the child who sat there. He tried to see all the children as the special people they were and he hoped for them a positive and successful day.

We relate this story because it communicates the foundation of teaching—caring. Without caring we have a world devoid of meaningful human interaction. "Caring is not a program or activity; rather, it is a *value* that is grounded in relationships—the kinds of relationships that good teachers have cultivated for years" (Chaskin & Rauner, 1995, p. 673). Caring is an

ethic that requires commitment, continuity, and community. As teachers we must care for our students. Caring requires that we listen, respect, advocate for, learn from, encourage, and celebrate with our students.

We can certainly care for students without a discussion of curriculum, but we cannot have a valid discussion of curriculum without caring. We advocate that if we truly care about our students, then we will care about everything with which they interact. Curriculum is certainly the most pervasive element in their environment of learning and it can set the tone and the starting place for relationships. Noddings (1995 b) says that caring must be woven into the curriculum so that its presence is felt by the learners. Lantieri (1995, p. 392) asserts, "To care about one's thinking and to think about what one cares about: these I submit, are goals worth aiming for." We must care about who we are, how we teach, and what we teach, before themes of caring can be realized.

We care about the curriculum and the learning environment because they are a significant and formative portion of our children's lives. As we face each day look out on a classroom of empty desks, what kind of curriculum do we choose that allows us to care the most? We choose a narrative one.

APPENDIX A

Aids for the Planning Process

Appendix A contains three items that may be used in conjunction with the planning process explained in chapter 6. The first item is the story "The Pine Tree Shillings." This story is a possible context for curriculum. The margins can be used by students to take notes, make drawings, ask questions, or record wonderments as they read. The second item is a story map outline that can be used to record the essential elements of any narrative context that is being considered for curriculum development. The third item is a blank planning template on which to read a one-page overview of the essential elements of the narrative curriculum design.

"The Pine Tree Shillings"

In the early colonial days Captain John Hull was the mint master of Massachusetts and coined all the money that was made there. This was a new line of business; for, in the earlier days of the colony, the current coinage consisted of gold and silver money of England, Portugal, and Spain. These coins being scarce, the people were often forced to barter their commodities instead of selling them. For instance, if a man wanted to buy a coat, he perhaps exchanged a bear's skin for it. Musket bullets were used instead of farthings. The Indians had a sort of money, called wampum, which was made of clamshells; and this strange sort of specie was taken in payment of debts by the English settlers. Bank bills had never been heard of.

As the people grew more numerous and their trade with one another increased, the want of current money was more sensibly felt. To supply the demand, the General Court established a coinage of shillings, sixpences, and threepences. Captain John Hull was appointed to manufacture this money and was to have about one shilling out of every twenty to pay him for the trouble of making them. Then all the old silver in the colony was handed over to Captain John Hull. The battered silver cans and tankards, and silver buckles, and broken spoons, and silver buttons, and hilts of swords were thrown into the melting pot together. But by far the greater part of the silver consisted of bullion from the mines of South America, which the English buccaneers had taken from the Spaniards and brought to Massachusetts.

All this old and new silver being melted down and coined, the result was an immense amount of shillings, sixpences, and threepences. Each had the date 1652 on the one side and a figure of a pine tree on the other. Hence they were called pine tree shillings.

When the mint master, Captain John Hull, had grown very rich, a young man by the name of Samuel Sewell came a-courting his only daughter. His daughter Betsy was a fine, hearty damsel; by no means as slender as some young ladies of our own days. On the contrary, having always fed heartily on pumpkin pies, doughnuts, Indian puddings, and other Puritan dainties, she was as round and plump as a pudding itself. With this round, rosy face did Samuel Sewell fall in love. As he was a young man of good character, the mint master very readily gave his consent. "Yes, you may take her," said he, in his rough way; "and you'll find her a heavy burden enough!"

On the wedding day, John Hull dressed himself in a plum-colored coat, all the buttons of which were made of pine tree shillings. The buttons of his waistcoat were sixpences, and the knees of his small-clothes were buttoned with silver threepences. Opposite to him between her bridesmaids sat Miss

Betsy. She was blushing with all her might and looked like a full-blown peony, or a great red apple. There, too, was the bridegroom, dressed with as much finery as the Puritan laws and customs would allow. His hair was cropped close to his ears, because Governor Endicott had forbidden any man to wear it below his ears.

The mint master was pleased with his son-in-law, especially as he had courted Miss Betsy out of pure love and had said nothing at all about her portion. So, when the marriage ceremony was over, Captain Hull whispered a word to two of his men, who immediately went out, and soon returned lugging a large pair of scales. "Daughter Betsy," said the mint master; "get into one side of these scales." Miss Betsy—or Mrs. Sewell, as we must now call her—did as she was bid, like a dutiful child, without any question of the why and wherefore. But what her father could mean, unless to make her husband pay for her by the pound, she had not the least idea.

"And now," said honest John Hull to the servants, "bring that box hither." The box to which the mint master pointed was a huge, square iron-bound, oaken chest. The servants tugged with might and main but could not lift this enormous receptacle and were obliged to drag it over the floor. Captain Hull then took a key from his girdle, unlocked the chest, and lifted its ponderous lid. Behold! it was full to the brim of bright pine tree shillings, fresh from the mint, and Samuel Sewell began to think that his father-in-law had got possession of all the money in the Massachusetts treasury.

Then the servants, at Captain Hull's command, heaped double handfuls of shillings into one side of the scales, while Betsy remained in the other. Jingle, jingle, went the shillings, as handful after handful was thrown in, till, plump and ponderous as she was, they fairly weighed down the young lady from the floor. "There, son Sewell!" cried the honest mint master, "take these shillings for my daughter's portion. Use her kindly, and thank Heaven for her. It is not every wife that's worth her weight in silver!"

(Story excerpted from *Stories of Our Country* by James Johonnot, 1887.
This particular entry was cited simply as — Hawthorne.)

Appendix A Blank story map

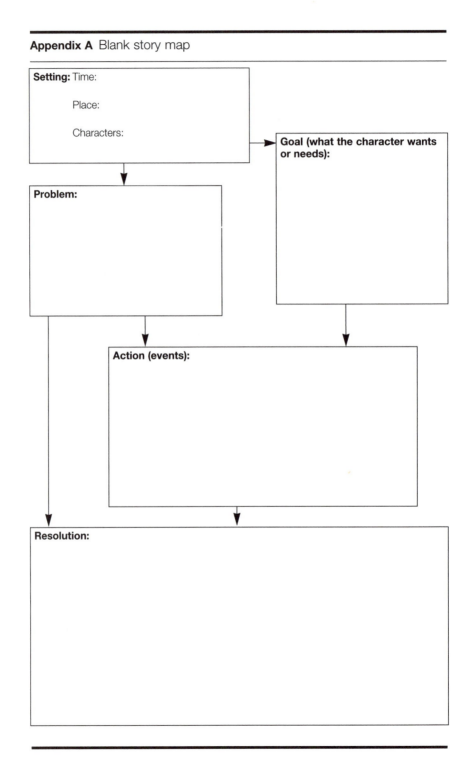

Appendix A The narrative curriculum planning template

Foundational Goals: Solve Problems - Think Critically, Creatively - Use Technology - Communicate - Quantify - Direct Own Learning - Collaborate/Cooperate
Applications: Ability to Deliberate on Public Issues; to Interpret Human Experience; to Understand Diversity, Health Habits, Science/Math Relationships, Humanities

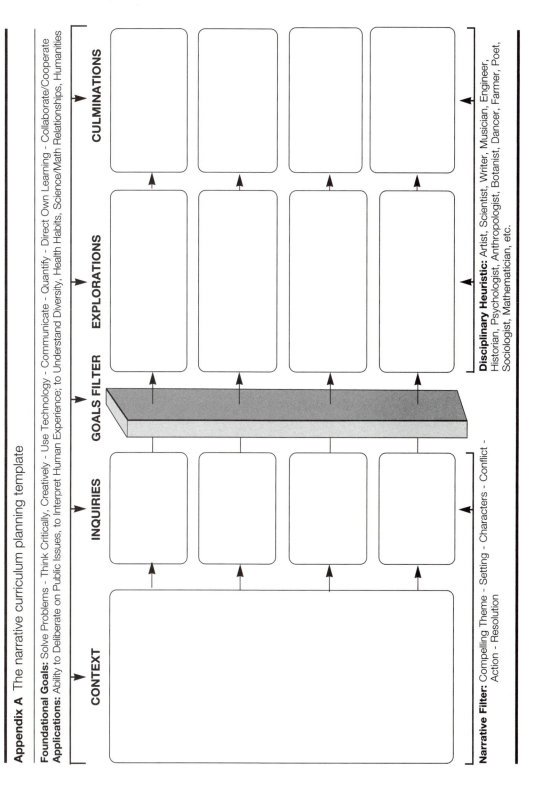

CONTEXT   INQUIRIES   GOALS FILTER   EXPLORATIONS   CULMINATIONS

Disciplinary Heuristic: Artist, Scientist, Writer, Musician, Engineer, Historian, Psychologist, Anthropologist, Botanist, Dancer, Farmer, Poet, Sociologist, Mathematician, etc.

Narrative Filter: Compelling Theme - Setting - Characters - Conflict - Action - Resolution

APPENDIX B

Sample Planning Templates

Appendix B contains sample planning templates for five of the contexts described in the book: *Very Last First Time* (Andrews, 1985), *The Green Book* (Paton Walsh, 1982), *Galimoto* (Williams, 1990), "The Town That Moved," and "The Siege of Tyre."

Appendix B *Very Last First Time* planning template

Foundational Goals: Solve Problems - Think Critically, Creatively - Use Technology - Communicate - Quantify - Direct Own Learning - Collaborate/Cooperate
Applications: Ability to Deliberate on Public Issues; to Interpret Human Experience; to Understand Diversity, Health Habits, Science/Math Relationships, Humanities

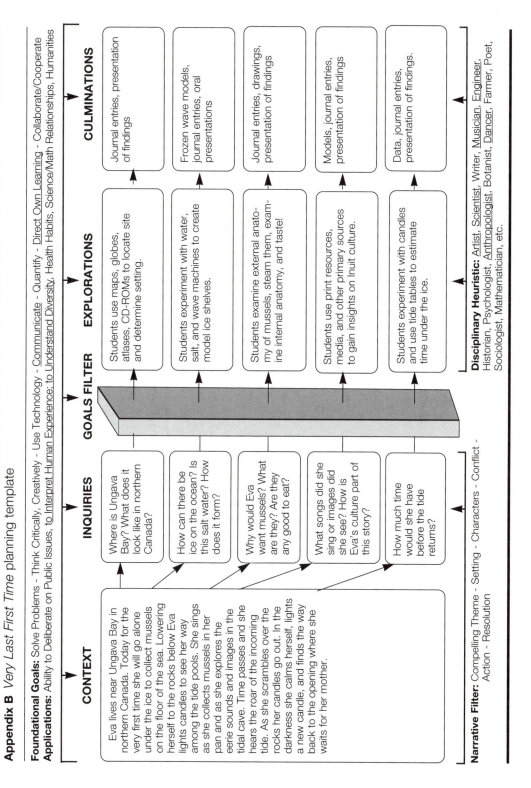

CONTEXT

Eva lives near Ungava Bay in northern Canada. Today for the very first time she will go alone under the ice to collect mussels on the floor of the sea. Lowering herself to the rocks below Eva lights candles to see her way among the tide pools. She sings as she collects mussels in her pan and as she explores the eerie sounds and images in the tidal cave. Time passes and she hears the roar of the incoming tide. As she scrambles over the rocks her candles go out. In the darkness she calms herself, lights a new candle, and finds the way back to the opening where she waits for her mother.

INQUIRIES

Where is Ungava Bay? What does it look like in northern Canada?

How can there be ice on the ocean? Is this salt water? How does it form?

Why would Eva want mussels? What are they? Are they any good to eat?

What songs did she sing or images did she see? How is Eva's culture part of this story?

How much time would she have before the tide returns?

GOALS FILTER

EXPLORATIONS

Students use maps, globes, atlases, CD-ROMs to locate site and determine setting.

Students experiment with water, salt, and wave machines to create model ice shelves.

Students examine external anatomy of mussels, steam them, examine internal anatomy, and taste!

Students use print resources, media, and other primary sources to gain insights on Inuit culture.

Students experiment with candles and use tide tables to estimate time under the ice.

CULMINATIONS

Journal entries, presentation of findings

Frozen wave models, journal entries, oral presentations

Journal entries, drawings, presentation of findings

Models, journal entries, presentation of findings

Data, journal entries, presentation of findings.

Disciplinary Heuristic: Artist, Scientist, Writer, Musician, Engineer, Historian, Psychologist, Anthropologist, Botanist, Dancer, Farmer, Poet, Sociologist, Mathematician, etc.

Narrative Filter: Compelling Theme - Setting - Characters - Conflict - Action - Resolution

Appendix B *The Green Book* planning template

Foundational Goals: Solve Problems - Think Critically, Creatively - Use Technology - Communicate - Quantify - Direct Own Learning - Collaborate/Cooperate
Applications: Ability to Deliberate on Public Issues, to Interpret Human Experience; to Understand Diversity; Health Habits, Science/Math Relationships, Humanities

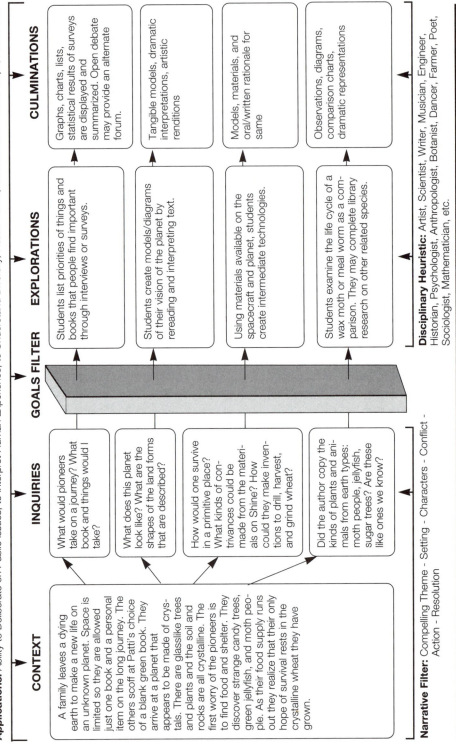

CONTEXT

A family leaves a dying earth to make a new life on an unknown planet. Space is limited so they are allowed just one book and a personal item on the long journey. The others scoff at Patti's choice of a blank green book. They arrive at a planet that appears to be made of crystals. There are glasslike trees and plants and the soil and rocks are all crystalline. The first worry of the pioneers is to find food and shelter. They discover strange candy trees, green jellyfish, and moth people. As their food supply runs out they realize that their only hope of survival rests in the crystalline wheat they have grown.

INQUIRIES

What would pioneers take on a journey? What book and things would I take?

What does this planet look like? What are the shapes of the land forms that are described?

How would one survive in a primitive place? What kinds of contrivances could be made from the materials on Shine? How could they make inventions to drill, harvest, and grind wheat?

Did the author copy the kinds of plants and animals from earth types: moth people, jellyfish, sugar trees? Are these like ones we know?

GOALS FILTER

EXPLORATIONS

Students list priorities of things and books that people find important through interviews or surveys.

Students create models/diagrams of their vision of the planet by rereading and interpreting text.

Using materials available on the spacecraft and planet, students create intermediate technologies.

Students examine the life cycle of a wax moth or meal worm as a comparison. They may complete library research on other related species.

CULMINATIONS

Graphs, charts, lists, statistical results of surveys are displayed and summarized. Open debate may provide an alternate forum.

Tangible models, dramatic interpretations, artistic renditions

Models, materials, and oral/written rationale for same

Observations, diagrams, comparison charts, dramatic representations

Narrative Filter: Compelling Theme - Setting - Characters - Conflict - Action - Resolution

Disciplinary Heuristic: Artist, Scientist, Writer, Musician, Engineer, Historian, Psychologist, Anthropologist, Botanist, Dancer, Farmer, Poet, Sociologist, Mathematician, etc.

Appendix B *Galimoto* planning template

Foundational Goals: Solve Problems - Think Critically, Creatively - Use Technology - Communicate - Quantify - Direct Own Learning - Collaborate/Cooperate
Applications: Ability to Deliberate on Public Issues; to Interpret Human Experience; to Understand Diversity, Health Habits, Science/Math Relationships, Humanities

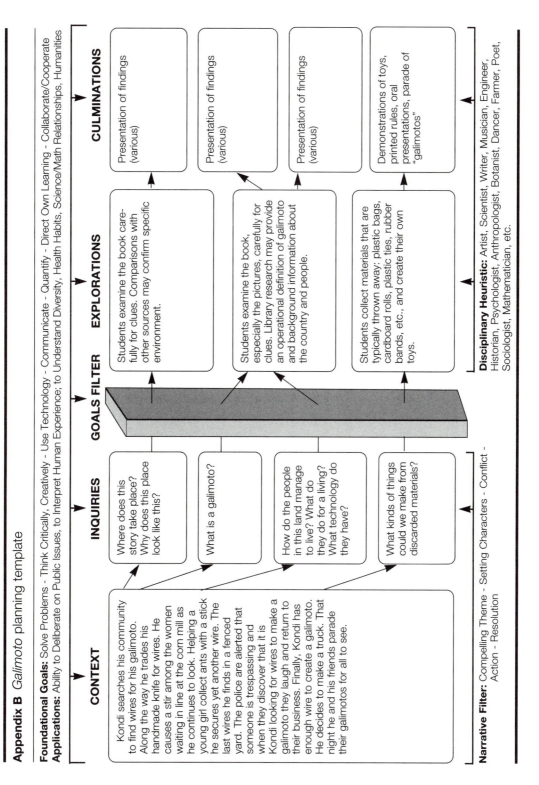

CONTEXT

Kondi searches his community to find wires for his galimoto. Along the way he trades his handmade knife for wires. He causes a stir among the women waiting in line at the corn mill as he continues to look. Helping a young girl collect ants with a stick he secures yet another wire. The last wires he finds in a fenced yard. The police are alerted that someone is trespassing and when they discover that it is Kondi looking for wires to make a galimoto they laugh and return to their business. Finally, Kondi has enough wire to create a galimoto. He decides to make a truck. That night he and his friends parade their galimotos for all to see.

INQUIRIES

Where does this story take place? Why does this place look like this?

What is a galimoto?

How do the people in this land manage to live? What do they do for a living? What technology do they have?

What kinds of things could we make from discarded materials?

GOALS FILTER

EXPLORATIONS

Students examine the book carefully for clues. Comparisons with other sources may confirm specific environment.

Students examine the book, especially the pictures, carefully for clues. Library research may provide an operational definition of galimoto and background information about the country and people.

Students collect materials that are typically thrown away: plastic bags, cardboard rolls, plastic ties, rubber bands, etc., and create their own toys.

CULMINATIONS

Presentation of findings (various)

Presentation of findings (various)

Presentation of findings (various)

Demonstrations of toys, printed rules, oral presentations, parade of "galimotos"

Disciplinary Heuristic: Artist, Scientist, Writer, Musician, Engineer, Historian, Psychologist, Anthropologist, Botanist, Dancer, Farmer, Poet, Sociologist, Mathematician, etc.

Narrative Filter: Compelling Theme - Setting Characters - Conflict - Action - Resolution

Appendix B "The Town That Moved" planning template

Foundational Goals: Solve Problems - Think Critically, Creatively - Use Technology - Communicate - Quantify - Direct Own Learning - Collaborate/Cooperate
Applications: Ability to Deliberate on Public Issues, to Understand Diversity, Health Habits, Science/Math Relationships, Humanities

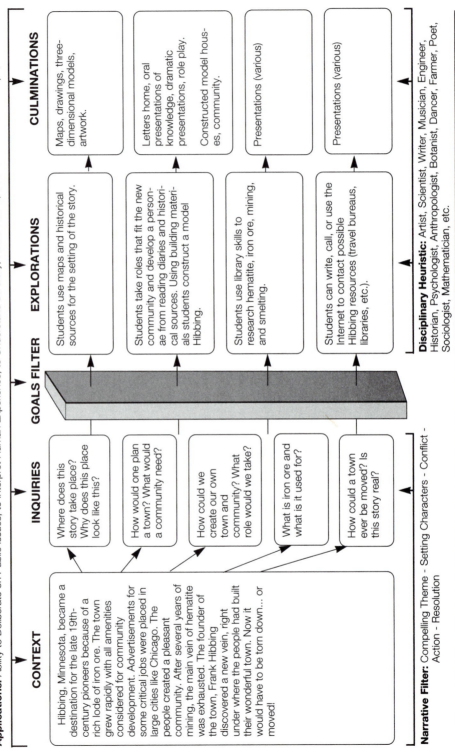

CONTEXT	INQUIRIES	GOALS FILTER	EXPLORATIONS	CULMINATIONS
Hibbing, Minnesota, became a destination for the late 19th-century pioneers because of a rich lode of iron ore. The town grew rapidly with all amenities considered for community development. Advertisements for some critical jobs were placed in large cities like Chicago. The people created a pleasant community. After several years of mining, the main vein of hematite was exhausted. The founder of the town, Frank Hibbing, discovered a new vein, right under where the people had built their wonderful town. Now it would have to be torn down... or moved!	Where does this story take place? Why does this place look like this?		Students use maps and historical sources for the setting of the story.	Maps, drawings, three-dimensional models, artwork.
	How would one plan a town? What would a community need?		Students take roles that fit the new community and develop a persona from reading diaries and historical sources. Using building materials students construct a model Hibbing.	Letters home, oral presentations of knowledge, dramatic presentations, role play. Constructed model houses, community.
	How could we create our own town and community? What role would we take?		Students use library skills to research hematite, iron ore, mining, and smelting.	Presentations (various)
	What is iron ore and what is it used for?		Students can write, call, or use the Internet to contact possible Hibbing resources (travel bureaus, libraries, etc.).	Presentations (various)
	How could a town ever be moved? Is this story real?			

Narrative Filter: Compelling Theme - Setting Characters - Conflict - Action - Resolution

Disciplinary Heuristic: Artist, Scientist, Writer, Musician, Engineer, Historian, Psychologist, Anthropologist, Botanist, Dancer, Farmer, Poet, Sociologist, Mathematician, etc.

Appendix B "Siege of Tyre" planning template

Foundational Goals: Solve Problems - Think Critically, Creatively - Use Technology - Communicate - Quantify - Direct Own Learning - Collaborate/Cooperate
Applications: Ability to Deliberate on Public Issues, to Interpret Human Experience; to Understand Diversity, Health Habits, Science/Math Relationships, Humanities

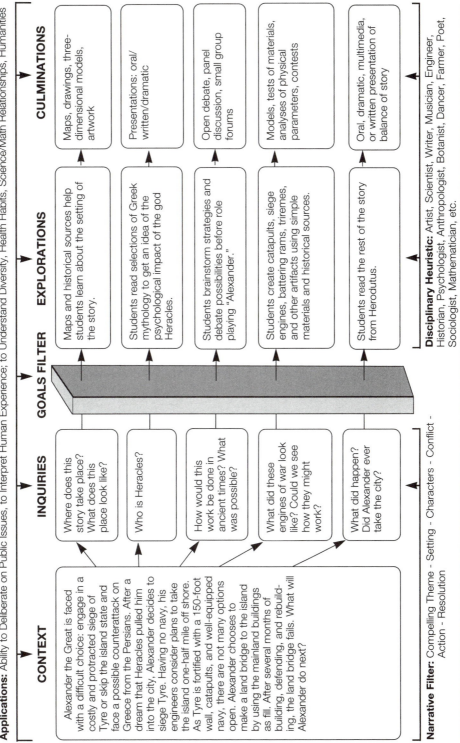

CONTEXT

Alexander the Great is faced with a difficult choice: engage in a costly and protracted siege of Tyre or skip the island state and face a possible counterattack on Greece from the Persians. After a dream that Heracles pulled him into the city, Alexander decides to siege Tyre. Having no navy, his engineers consider plans to take the island one-half mile off shore. As Tyre is fortified with a 150-foot wall, catapults, and well-equipped navy, there are not many options open. Alexander chooses to make a land bridge to the island by using the mainland buildings as fill. After several months of building, defending, and rebuilding, the land bridge fails. What will Alexander do next?

INQUIRIES

Where does this story take place? What does this place look like?

Who is Heracles?

How would this work be done in ancient times? What was possible?

What did these engines of war look like? Could we see how they might work?

What did happen? Did Alexander ever take the city?

GOALS FILTER

EXPLORATIONS

Maps and historical sources help students learn about the setting of the story.

Students read selections of Greek mythology to get an idea of the psychological impact of the god Heracles.

Students brainstorm strategies and debate possibilities before role playing "Alexander."

Students create catapults, siege engines, battering rams, triremes, and other artifacts using simple materials and historical sources.

Students read the rest of the story from Herodutus.

CULMINATIONS

Maps, drawings, three-dimensional models, artwork

Presentations: oral/written/dramatic

Open debate, panel discussion, small group forums

Models, tests of materials, analyses of physical parameters, contests

Oral, dramatic, multimedia, or written presentation of balance of story

Narrative Filter: Compelling Theme - Setting - Characters - Conflict - Action - Resolution

Disciplinary Heuristic: Artist, Scientist, Writer, Musician, Engineer, Historian, Psychologist, Anthropologist, Botanist, Dancer, Farmer, Poet, Sociologist, Mathematician, etc.

A Selected Bibliography of Children's Literature

The works of literature listed in this bibliography have been selected from among the many possibilities from the world of children's literature. They have been included because they meet the following criteria:

- Each book has strong literary qualities.
- Each tells a compelling story with conflict and resolution.
- Each exhibits a writerly style. The author has left open many possibilities for inquiry.
- Each encourages inquiry from varied disciplinary perspectives.
- Each book is one with which we have had personal experience. Thus, we feel confident that it will provide a successful context for curriculum.

The books represent a wide spectrum of geographical locations from Africa to the Arctic and Australia to the Americas. Females and males are equally represented among main characters who are ethnically diverse. Inquiries generated by these works of literature range across the disciplines from the arts to math and science. The books are varied in terms of length and difficulty. Some are simply told stories in picture books while others are complex chapter books. We have not, however, put a level on the books since we have found that all of them can be used successfully with students at a variety of levels.

You may find some books absent from the list that you feel belong there. Try them with a group of students and if you find one that meets our criteria, let us know. We are eager to see the bibliography grow.

■ Andrews, Jan. (1985). *Very last first time*. New York: Atheneum.
Genre: Picture book
About the book: It is the first time for Eva, a young Inuit girl, to gather mussels alone under the ice while the tide is out.
Possible inquiries:
Where does this story take place and what is it like there?
What are the social and cultural customs of this community?
What is it like under the ice in the tidal zone?
How do the tides work?
How long is Eva under the ice?

■ Brown, Don. (1993). *Ruth Law thrills a nation*. New York: Ticknor & Fields.
Genre: Picture book
About the book: Based on newspaper articles, this book chronicles the events of the attempt by Ruth Law to set a record in 1916 by flying from Chicago to New York in a single day.
Possible inquiries:
How can an airplane fly?
How is temperature related to elevation?
Are women still pioneers in aviation? What are other kinds of records set by women? Who are other significant female pilots?
What is the route of Law's flight on a map?
Could we get copies of the newspaper accounts?
How does this flight compare to other "firsts" in aviation? Books which describe some of these include: *The Glorious Fight: Across the Channel with Louis Blériot July 25, 1909* (Provensen & Provensen, 1983), *Flight: The Journey of Charles Lindbergh* (Burleigh, 1991), *The Wright Brothers: How They Invented the Airplane* (Freedman, 1991).

■ Buss, Fran L. (1991). *Journey of the sparrows.* New York: Dutton.
Genre: Modern realistic fiction
About the book: Along with her sister, brother, and a boy named Tomás, María is smuggled into the United States in a fruit crate. Despite the ordeals of illegal status, María's story demonstrates hope, courage, and caring.
Possible inquiries:
> How many illegal aliens are in the United States? Why and how do they come? Where do they go? What is their life like? Other books which tell related stories are *Lupita Mañana* (Beatty, 1981) and *Grab Hands and Run* (Temple, 1993).
> How far did María travel? What was her route?

■ Calhoun, Mary. (1981). *Hot-air Henry.* New York: Morrow.
Genre: Picture book
About the book: Henry, an adventurous cat who stows away on a hot air balloon, demonstrates the principles and perils of balloon flight.
Possible inquiries:
> How do things look from the air?
> Where might this story take place—its geographic location and features?
> What are the principles of balloon flight?
> What are the sensory experiences of a balloon ride?
> Could a cat either intentionally or coincidentally do the things suggested in the book?
> How does this fictional flight compare to a real one? See, for example, *Fire and Silk: Flying in a Hot Air Balloon* (Johnson, 1991).

■ Campbell, Eric. (1994). *The shark callers.* San Diego: Harcourt.
Genre: Modern realistic fiction
About the book: Alternating chapters tell how the eruption of a volcano in Papua New Guinea brings together the lives of two teenage boys, one a native, being initiated as a shark caller, and one a white American on a sailboat.
Possible inquiries:
> What is the culture of the natives of Papua New Guinea?
> What would be the effects of an underwater volcanic eruption and the ensuing tidal wave? Is the book scientifically accurate?
> What actually happened to the sailboat? Why didn't the same thing happen to the canoe?
> Are there any historical eruptions on which to base this account?
> Could we make the sound of the *larung*? How far does this sound travel underwater?
> How is shark behavior understood and used by the shark callers?

▌ Cherry, Lynne. (1990). *The great kapok tree: A tale of the Amazon rain forest*. San Diego: Harcourt.

Genre: Picture book

About the book: While the woodcutter sleeps, the animals that depend on the great kapok tree convince him not to chop it down.

Possible inquiries:

Where are the world's rain forests?

Who are the native people of the rain forest and what is their culture?

What is the ecosystem of the rain forest?

▌ Coerr, Eleanor. (1993). *Sadako*. New York: Putnam's.

▌ Coerr, Eleanor. (1977). *Sadako and the thousand paper cranes*. New York: Putnam's.

Genre: Picture book (biography)

About the book: Sadako is an energetic schoolgirl in the late 1940s in Japan. Leukemia from exposure to radiation from the Hiroshima bomb causes her early death. She keeps her hope by folding paper cranes.

Possible inquiries:

How is a paper crane made?

Why, what, and when was the Hiroshima bomb?

How many others were affected by radiation?

Was leukemia the major aftereffect of the bomb or were there other problems?

What is the current situation in Hiroshima?

What are the characteristics of Japanese culture—its holidays, beliefs, language, etc.?

▌ Crichton, Michael. (1990). *Jurassic park*. New York: Knopf.

Genre: Science fiction

About the book: An entrepreneur uses his wealth and influence to assemble the most advanced technologies to recreate an island ecosystem of dinosaurs. A paleontologist, botanist, and mathematician are given a preopening tour to assess the project. Sabotage which frees the dinosaurs to go hunting, combined with human relationships and emotions, makes for lots of action.

Possible inquiries:

What evidence do we have of ecosystems of dinosaurs?

Is the technology used in this book currently available?

What evidence do we have of what dinosaurs looked like?

Were dinosaurs intelligent as they were depicted in this book?

What are the ethical/moral aspects of cloning/creating organisms?

▎ De Angeli, Marguerite. (1949). *The door in the wall.* New York: Doubleday.

Genre: Historical fiction

About the book: Robin, the son of a 14th-century English nobleman, is crippled by an unknown illness. Nursed and educated by the brothers of St. Mark's, he overcomes his handicap to perform an act of heroism.

Possible inquiries:

What does being educated mean in the fourteenth century?

What are the crafts that Robin learns? Could we do them too?

Why does building a harp and learning to play it have an important place in the story?

What illness did Robin have? What were the diseases that caused mass deaths in medieval times?

Were the health practices of the brothers sound?

Where are the places mentioned in the book? Are they still in existence? What did they look like then? What do they look like today?

▎ Disher, Gary. (1992). *The bamboo flute.* New York: Ticknor & Fields.

Genre: Historical fiction

About the book: People in the rural town of Tarlee, Australia, are feeling the effects of the aftermath of World War I and the Depression. Twelve-year-old Paul risks contact with a swagman to bring music and hope back into his life.

Possible inquiries:

How does the trauma of war affect people?

What are the psychological effects of music?

How is a flute made? Can I make a flute from natural materials?

What was Australia like in the 1930s? How did it compare to the American Depression and Dust Bowl experience?

▎ Engel, Diana. (1991). *Gino Badino.* New York: Morrow.

Genre: Picture book

About the book: Gino's artistic talents go unappreciated by his family in the pasta business. When hard times come, Gino's sculpted dough mice save the family from failure.

Possible inquiries:

How is pasta made? Can we make some?

How does a pasta machine work?

What is the role of the artist in a community?

▎ Finsland, Mary Jane. (1983). *The town that moved.* Minneapolis: Carolrhoda.

Genre: Easy-to-read illustrated book

About the book: The town of Hibbing, Minnesota, had to be moved when iron ore was discovered under it.

Possible inquiries:

What are the weather and climate of northern Minnesota?

What makes a good town? How is a community planned? How does a place become a town?

Where did the people come from to make this community? Were they immigrants? Where did the people come from who make up our own community?

How would you move buildings without modern equipment?

How did the people feel about moving?

Are there other towns or towns in our region that have been moved? Why were they moved?

▮ Harrah, Madge. (1990). *Honey girl.* New York: Avon.

Genre: Historical fiction (based on a true story)

About the book: In 1908, Dorothy and her family journey down the Mississippi River from Wisconsin to Arkansas on a houseboat, along with a barge loaded with beehives.

Possible inquiries:

What was the Mississippi River like in 1908? What were its dangers? How was it navigated? How many boats were on the river?

What were the places like that they traveled by?

What were the customs in 1908?

How do clams make pearls? Why were they valuable?

What are the habits of honeybees? How do beekeepers "keep" bees?

Why did so many people die of diseases such as influenza and measles?

▮ Heide, Florence, & Gilliland, Judith. (1990). *The day of Ahmed's secret.* New York: Lothrop.

Genre: Picture book

About the book: All during the day, Ahmed works delivering butagaz to the people of Cairo until he is able to share his secret with his family—he has learned to write his own name.

Possible inquiries:

What are the social, cultural, and religious customs of modern Cairo? Is there a mixture of the traditional and the modern?

What is Ahmed's job like? How is he paid? How hard is the work?

Why is knowing how to write one's name a secret? Does he go to school? Is literacy uncommon?

How does Ahmed find his way around Cairo? How big a city is it? Is it located within sight of the pyramids as the pictures show?

What is the desert like?

■ Isadora, Rachel. (1991). *At the crossroads.* New York: Greenwillow.
Genre: Picture book
About the book: Children anticipate the return of their fathers from the
  mines. As they wait through the night they make instruments and
  sing.
Possible inquiries:
  Where does this story take place and what is it like there?
  What are the social and cultural customs of this community?
  What is it like to have your loved one away for long periods of time
    working in a dangerous occupation?
  What kind of materials did the children use to make instruments?
    Could we make instruments and play them?
  What is the music like for these people and what is the role of music in
    their lives? How does it compare to the role of music in our lives?

■ Lasky, Kathryn. (1988). *The bone wars.* New York: Morrow.
Genre: Historical fiction
About the book: The lives of Thaddeus Longworth, orphan and tracker,
  and Julian Demott, pampered son of a world-famous English paleon-
  tologist, intertwine in the rugged badlands of Montana where they
  are working for competing fossil-hunting teams.
Possible inquiries:
  What was the Native American perspective? How have things
    changed from then to now?
  How are dinosaurs excavated and reconstructed in museums?
  What biographical information can be gleaned about the famous peo-
    ple mentioned in the book, such as Custer, Buffalo Bill, Calamity
    Jane, Black Elk, Red Cloud, and Sitting Bull? Is the book histori-
    cally accurate?
  What was the region like that is depicted by the book? What are its
    geology and geography? Were the travels of Thad geographically
    and physically possible?
  What was the elitism note in the book? What were the sources of
    elitism?
  Were the bone wars real?
  What was the motivation for the actions taken by pioneers, explor-
    ers, and industrialists?

■ Lawson, Robert. (1939). *Ben and me.* Boston, MA: Little, Brown.
Genre: Historical fiction/fantasy
About the book: Amos, Ben Franklin's faithful mouse, narrates the "true"
  story of Ben's accomplishments, including those in electricity, states-
  manship, inventing, and printing.

Possible inquiries:

> What are the facts about Benjamin Franklin's life?
>
> How does a printing press work?
>
> How did Ben's experiments in electricity work? Could we make static electricity and circuits?

❚ Markun, Patricia. (1993). *The little painter of Sabana Grande.* New York: Bradbury.

Genre: Picture book

About the book: Fernando, a young Panamanian boy, knows how to make paint but lacks paper. He gains acceptance after painting the available surface—the walls of his adobe house.

Possible inquiries:

> Where is Sabana Grande and what is it like there?
>
> What is the culture like?
>
> How long will the paint stay on the walls of the house?
>
> Can we make paint from natural products?
>
> How does it feel to want to paint the way Fernando does?
>
> What is the significance of the designs? How would an artist view what Fernando has done?
>
> Is this story true? Are there places in the world where people do paint designs on their houses?

❚ Meyer, Carolyn. (1994). *Rio Grande stories.* San Diego: Harcourt.

Genre: Modern realistic fiction (a collection of connected stories)

About the book: A group of seventh graders engages in the Heritage Project, a celebration of the diverse community and culture in which they live. They discover interesting things about themselves, their families, and their city.

Possible inquiries:

> Can we make the recipes in this book?
>
> Can we make clay pots and luminarias?
>
> Can we build something from adobe?
>
> What are the social and religious values of the Hispanics of the Rio Grande region? Of our region? Of the Native Americans of the Rio Grande region? Of our region?
>
> Where is the Rio Grande region? What is it like there? What are the different cultures and ethnic groups of this region?
>
> What art forms are found in this region?
>
> Are there stories like these about our own region that we can write?

❚ Mikaelsen, Ben. (1993). *Sparrow Hawk Red.* New York: Hyperion.

Genre: Modern realistic fiction

About the book: Since his mother's death, 13-year-old Ricky has been learning to fly from his father, a former DEA agent. His father has attempted
to give him pride in his Mexican-American heritage. Ricky learns the
realities of the homeless children in Mexico when he tries to steal a
high-tech airplane from drug runners to avenge his mother's death.

Possible inquiries:

What are the realities of drug cartels, street children, and DEA
agents? Has the author used stereotypes or accurate portraits of
these people?

Why is crossing the border into Mexico so much easier than crossing
from Mexico into the United States?

What are the social and political conditions in Mexico?

What are the medicinal properties of the desert plants?

What are the technicalities of trick flying such as loops and rolls?

How do children of Mexican descent view their heritage?

▮ Olson, Arielle. (1987). *The lighthouse keeper's daughter.* Boston: Little,
Brown. (A similar story is told by Roop & Roop (1985) in an easy-to-read
book, *Keep the Lights Burning, Abbie.*)

Genre: Picture book

About the book: During her father's absence, Miranda tends the light in
the lighthouse during a violent storm even though she becomes ill.
She is rewarded for her heroism by the seamen who bring soil to the
island for her springtime garden.

Possible inquiries:

How does the light work?

What causes the storms?

Where are lighthouses located? Why are they needed?

What would a girl in a lighthouse write in a journal? (An example can
be found in *Celia's Island Journal*, Krupinski, 1992.)

Would plants grow on the rocks of a barren ocean island?

▮ Parenteau, Shirley. (1978). *Blue hands, blue cloth.* Chicago: Children's
Press.

Genre: Easy-to-read illustrated book

About the book: Iman, a west African girl, longs to be recognized as an
expert indigo dyer in the tradition of her mother and grandmother.

Possible inquiries:

Is indigo dyeing still taking place in Africa today? Where? What is it
like there? Is this where the idea of tie-dyeing came from?

How is indigo dye made and how does a yellow dye make blue cloth?

How are patterns made on the cloth?

Where do ideas for patterns come from?

▮ Paton Walsh, Jill. (1982). *The green book.* New York: Farrar.

Genre: Fantasy

About the book: Due to a disaster on Earth, a colony is formed on the new planet Shine. Patty keeps a diary of their struggle to survive.

Possible inquiries:

What causes a planet to "die"?

What does the new planet look like and what are its physical properties?

What were the crystals like? Can plants really have crystalline structures? What happens when crystals are eaten?

What is a contriver and what could be contrived from the materials on Shine?

What are the moth people like? How does their life compare to life on Earth?

What could we record in our own green book?

What stories are precious to us?

▮ Polacco, Patricia. (1992). *Chicken Sunday.* New York: Philomel.

Genre: Picture book

About the book: Three cultures come together in this story of caring, as three children make Pysanky eggs to convince an old shopkeeper that they didn't vandalize this shop.

Possible inquiries:

Is this a true story? When and where did it take place?

What music sounds like "slow thunder and sweet rain?"

Can we make Pysanky eggs? What is their significance?

What story would Mr. Kodinsky tell of his life? What is the blue mark on Mr. Kodinsky's arm?

What are each of the cultures represented in this book?

▮ Polacco, Patricia. (1994). *Pink and Say.* New York: Philomel.

Genre: Picture book

About the book: The story of Pinkus Aylee and Say Curtis was handed down from generation to generation as a reminder of the shared humanity in the world.

Possible inquiries:

Is this a true story?

How accessible was President Lincoln to ordinary people as compared to current presidents?

Why is literacy important to slaves and other oppressed people?

Did boys have a big role in fighting the Civil War? Were there many black soldiers?

What was Andersonville and what happened there?

▌ Ringgold, Faith. (1991). *Tar beach.* New York: Crown.

Genre: Picture book (based on a quilt made by the author)

About the book: In Cassie's imagination, she flies from the mattress on the tarred roof of her apartment building over the city of New York, remembering its people and places.

Possible inquiries:

How is a picture story quilt designed?

How were African-Americans and Hispanics excluded from the unions?

How was the George Washington Bridge built and how does its form relate to its function?

How is the flying in this book related to the flying in books such as *The People Could Fly* (Hamilton, 1985) or *Abuela* (Dorros, 1991)?

▌ Temple, Frances. (1994). *The Ramsay scallop.* New York: Orchard.

Genre: Historical fiction

About the book: Elenor and Thomas, betrothed through family and financial arrangement, are assigned a pilgrimage to Santiago de Compostela as penance for their entire community. The pilgrimage through France and Spain is filled with the romance and adventure of 1300.

Possible inquiries:

How and why were cathedrals made?

How was writing done at this time? What did the manuscripts look like? *Catherine, Called Birdy* (Cushman, 1994), is a book set in this time period that focuses on writing and illustrating.

What is the process of glassmaking and how were the stained glass windows made? Can we make glass or design windows?

What was the route of the pilgrimage and what did it look like along the way?

What was 14th-century culture like—arranged marriages, feudal society, medical care, role of religion, treatment of pilgrims?

What is the truth about the Crusades and fighting the Moors?

What stories were told during this time and why were they told?

What are the facts and fictions of St. James's body in Spain?

▌ Williams, Jay. (1965). *The question box.* New York: Norton.

Genre: Picture book

About the book: Maria foils the invasion of her village because her curiosity has led her to discover the mystery of the town clock.

Possible inquiries:

What were the social and cultural customs during the time period described in this book?

How do gears in a clock work?

Where are there clocks like the one described in the book?

What kinds of information are in the library that we don't know about?

▌ Williams, Karen. (1990). *Galimoto*. New York: Lothrop.

Genre: Picture book

About the book: Kondi begs, borrows, and gathers enough wire from members of his community to make a galimoto.

Possible inquiries:

Where does this story take place and what is it like there in terms of climate and land forms?

What are the social and cultural customs of this community—the juxtaposition of traditional and modern technologies; the roles of females, males, children; the monetary system?

How could we use our trash to make something precious?

▌ Williams, Karen. (1994). *Tap-tap*. New York: Clarion.

Genre: Picture book

About the book: Sasifi and her mother earn enough money at the market in Haiti to ride home in the tap-tap, a truck that lets off passengers when they bang on its side.

Possible inquiries:

Where does this story take place?

What is the culture like?

What products support local commerce and the economy?

Do the designs on the tap-tap have any significance?

How can this peaceful event take place in a country that in news reports is characterized by conflict and violence?

▌ Yep, Laurence. (1975). *Dragonwings*. Boston: New York: Harper & Row.

Genre: Historical fiction

About the book: The Chinese community in San Francisco in the early 20th century is portrayed through the eyes of Moon Shadow, a recently arrived Chinese boy. Events include the San Francisco earthquake and the making of an airplane by the boy's father.

Possible inquiries:

What was life like among the Chinese in America and what were their ties to China? Who were the Tang?

What were the historical events of the 1903 San Francisco earthquake? *Earthquake at Dawn* (Gregory, 1992) may serve as a resource book.

How was it possible for the man to build an airplane and why are his achievements so little known?

▌ Yolen, Jane. (1992). *Letting Swift River go.* Boston: Little, Brown.

Genre: Picture book

About the book: Sally Jane remembers the drowning of Swift River towns to create the Quabbin reservoir.

Possible inquiries:

How do different people feel about losing their homes and familiar places?

How and why are decisions made about creating dams?

How is a dam built?

Are there local dam-building stories which could be compared to this story?

Are there examples in which "letting Swift River go" means that the river was not dammed?

Interactive Storybook Reading and Analysis of Teacher Behavior

Interactive storybook reading is an approach to reading aloud that invites students to respond to the text as it is being read. During this type of read-aloud, children's prior knowledge becomes apparent, their interpretation of the text is immediately shared, and their interests and questions about the text are conveyed. Morrow (1993) researched and synthesized categories of adult behavior that elicited student responses.

Managing (M) includes introducing the story, providing background information, and redirecting irrelevant discussion back to the story. *Prompting* (P) refers to those behaviors that invite children to ask questions or make comments, scaffold responses for children to model, and relate responses to real-life experiences. *Supporting and Informing* (S) behaviors are those in which the teacher answers questions, reacts to comments, and invites comparison to real-life experiences. (S) behaviors also include responses which provide positive reinforcement.

As you examine the following transcript of an interactive storybook reading, note several characteristics:

- Few managing behaviors are needed. The children are comfortable with this procedure and take advantage of the setting to share their ideas. When the teacher pauses in the reading, they spontaneously offer their thoughts and questions.
- The teacher's comments fall mainly into the categories of Prompting (48%) and Supporting (37%).
- Prompts are worded to encourage the children to share their ideas; they are not specific questions about content generated by the teacher. They can be a rephrasing of the children's ideas to ask them to expand on an idea that has been mentioned.
- The Supporting comments are mostly responses to the content of the students' comments and rarely take the form of verbal praise.
- There are many student comments in a row without teacher questioning or interference.
- The students often prompt and support one another.
- The teacher does not always answer students' questions or correct their interpretation of the text. The teacher, instead, tries to foster participation and the sharing of the students' ideas.

Very Last First Time Interactive Storybook Reading

Student:	It's a story.
Student:	It's named *Very Last First Time.*
Teacher (M):	What do you notice about the cover of the book?
Student:	He's digging a hole.
Student:	Eskimos!
Student:	He's in the north.
Teacher (P):	Where do you think it is?
Student:	It looks like a desert with some snow there.
Teacher (S):	That's an interesting description. You're close to the truth.
Student:	It looks like he's ice fishing.
Teacher (P):	Have some of you gone ice fishing?
Students:	No. Yeah.

Teacher (P): What's it like to go ice fishing?

Student: Well, it's kind of cold. You just sit around.

Student: You try to catch fish.

Teacher (M): This story is written by Jan Andrews. She lives in Ottawa, Canada. The illustrations are by Ian Wallace. I hope you'll talk about the book and share what you are thinking.

Student: There's cats.

Student: Those aren't cats. They're dogs.

Student: It looks like that's the same Eskimo that was on the [note]books.

Student: It gives a symbol [sic] that you're going to be talking about Eskimos.

Teacher (M): Here's the beginning page. "Eva Padlyat lived... walk on the bottom of the sea alone." So what do you think? What did you notice?

Student: She's like not going to like it maybe.

Student: And it's gonna be cold.

Student: It's a very strange custom. People don't need to walk on the bottom of sea, especially in the winter.

Student: It'd be frozen.

Student: She doesn't want to do it.

Teacher (P): Why do you think she wouldn't want to do it?

Student: Because it's the first time and she might not know where to go.

Student: And I don't think she should go. She might drown. Because if you go to the bottom, it's really dark down there.

Student: Then it will be the last time she does it.

Student: Her first and last time.

Teacher (P): Anything else? Some of you noticed the dogs?

Student: The different furs.

Student: There's like fur being stretched.

Student: They're like wool.

Student: And there's snowshoes that you walk on top of the snow.

Student: And then there's a little town in the background.

Student: And there's a little sled.

Teacher (S): Up close Kristen sees a little sled right here.

Student: Almost like a box. I thought it was something like a box.

Teacher (S): You are very observant. (M) Let's see what happened next. "Eva got ready... and disappeared into the distance."

Student: They both have the same sled. It looks the same. They're exactly alike, identical.

Student: I think there are no trees because they can't live there because it's too cold. I think it's above the tree line or something.

Teacher (S):   Chris is having some ideas about where this place is.

Student: There are more people stretching furs.

Student: There's a burning barrel.

Student: The village is very isolated from any of the. . .

Student: There's a burning barrel at the side of the. . .

Student: It seems like it's really sort of old, but it's not. I mean it's not an old time, it's modern.

Teacher (S):   So you see some old things, like some old traditions and you see some modern things too. What are some of the modern things?

Student: Corn flakes.

Student: Electricity.

Student: Snowmobiles.

Student: An airplane in the background

Teacher (P):   Where do you suppose the electricity comes from?

Student: The electric company.

Student: A generator.

Student: They might have phone lines on the electrical wires too.

Student: Probably a lot of people are stretching more fur because it's really cold and they need new coats maybe.

Teacher (S):   You're making a prediction about why they are doing what they do.

Student: In the other picture they had like a sink with running water and all that stuff.

Teacher (P):   What are some of the old traditions you noticed? We noticed the stretching of the furs as a kind of an old thing.

Student: The sleds.

Student: Little boxes with little skis on them.

Teacher (P):   They're not going with snowmobiles, are they?

Student: I'd go out with a sled.

Teacher (M):   Let's go ahead. "Down by the shore... and wander about on the sea floor."

Student: Now that would be scary.

Student: And there's a kite.

Student: There's an airplane in every picture.

Teacher (M):   I heard you say that would be really scary.

Student: Oh, I get it now.

Teacher (P):   What do you get, Mike?

Student:	How they do it. There's like a sheet of ice over it and when the tide goes out, the ice stays there and there's like air space when the water is farther down.
Teacher (P):	Anybody else?
Student:	What if the tide comes back in and drowns them?
Student:	What if they can't find the hole?
Student:	Then you're in big trouble.
Teacher (S):	So Steve and Vanessa are thinking about what-ifs. Right? "Eva and her mother walked carefully… made a hole."
Student:	The ice is yellow.
Teacher (P):	Oh, you want to talk about that?
Student:	Well, the reflection of the sun, well, it shined on the ice and it's yellow. It doesn't really look like ice.
Student:	When it was high tide the ice probably wouldn't be yellow because there's a pool of water under it and when it's low tide there's no water under it and the sunlight goes straight through.
Teacher (S):	For you that might be a way of checking whether the tide's in or out?
Student:	It is also probably the color of the sand.
Teacher (P):	For a second you thought it was sand, but do you still think so?
Student:	Sand could have gotten, like it could have like floated to the surface as the ice was forming and gotten stuck.
Teacher (P):	So do you have some ideas about what this ice was like?
Student:	It would be hard.
Teacher (P):	Hard?
Student:	Rough.
Teacher (P):	Rough?
Student:	Abrasive.
Teacher (S):	Abrasive, I like that word, that's a neat word. We'll see what happens. "Eva peered down into the hole… let go of the ice above."
Student:	So there's no water?
Teacher (P):	Is there?
Student:	It sounds like there's no water.
Student:	Why don't they have like a flashlight?
Student:	Maybe it wasn't invented.
Teacher (P):	Maybe it wasn't invented yet? What do you think?
Student:	They have a lamp.
Teacher (S):	A lamp? Well, you said they had electricity.
Student:	Yes.

Student: And they have airplanes.

Student: I see a snowman back there.

Teacher (S): Wow, you noticed that? I saw one of those earlier.

Student: It looks like rocks.

Student: Yeah, yeah, it looks like rocks.

Teacher (S): Aren't those curious? Maybe we can find out what they are.

Student: Rocks... totem pole.

Teacher (S): A rock totem pole, that's a good guess. You might want to find out what those are. (M) Well, we need to find out why she doesn't have a lamp going down in there.

Student: Well, maybe it's part of their customs.

Student: Yeah.

Teacher (P): Do you want to talk about that?

Student: Well, it sounds like it's their custom to go down under the ice. Well, maybe they are not to use any light.

Student: She might not need a light because the sun's out and it's shining in and she might not go very far.

Teacher (S): So you think maybe the sun's bright enough to go through the ice? Those are all interesting speculations.

Student: It doesn't look like water.

Student: It's a cave.

Teacher (S): It looks like a cave? "In a minute she was standing on the seabed... 'I'd better get to work,' she said."

Student: So people had gone down there before and carved into the ice?

Teacher (P): What do you guys think? Have people been down there carving?

Student: It was probably just her imagination.

Student: The ice would probably like disappear in summer. So once you carved in it, it wouldn't do any good.

Student: Somebody could have gone down before her maybe, but...

Student: Maybe they were frozen animals.

Teacher (S): You said you thought maybe it was just her imagination?

Student: Yeah, probably.

Student: Because the water when it came up it would wash away the ice a little bit.

Student: I think it would be frozen animals.

Teacher (S): Real animals frozen? Shadows, Debra says.

Student: It says it is shadows in the book.

Teacher (P): So are they real or are they shadows or are they imagination?

Student:	Maybe rocks.
Student:	Probably the water just kind of wore out some spots and then she probably imagined what she saw.
Teacher (P):	Oh, do you ever do that?
Student:	Yeah.
Teacher:	And see things that aren't really there? Jacob, what was that?
Student:	I don't see how she could get to the bottom of the ocean. It's pretty deep.
Student:	How can she get to the bottom?
Student:	But, that's not very deep down there because the tide's out and the tide doesn't go out in the middle of the ocean.
Teacher (P):	So how deep is it under there? (S) That's a good question. (M) We have to go back and take a look at what the book says with some of our other ideas. Well, let's see what happens now that she's got her candle lit. "Lighting three more candles… into her pail."
Student:	She's collecting mussels.
Teacher (S):	Somebody sees a crab.
Student:	I saw a starfish. By the candle. Shaped like a spider. That's not a spider, that's a crab. It looks like a spider.
Teacher (P):	Where would you see those kind of animals?
Student:	Tide pools.
Student:	In the tide pools.
Teacher (P):	Anybody ever seen mussels?
Group:	Yeah.
Student:	I collected them once.
Teacher (S):	You did? What did you do with them, Steve?
Student:	I don't know.
Teacher:	You just collected them?
Student:	I don't know. I threw them away.
Teacher (P):	Anybody have an idea what they think is going to happen now?
Student:	An avalanche.
Student:	They stick to rocks.
Teacher (P):	The mussels do?
Student:	They also stick to whales and stuff.
Student:	I think a crab will eat them.
Teacher (S):	You won't have a funny ending.
Student:	I also think the mussel is like a clam with the mouth gone and the nose off.
Teacher (M):	Do you think that is going to happen in this story?

Student: I doubt it.

Student: I see two starfish.

Student: I see three starfish.

Student: How can you light a candle under water?

Teacher (P): How can you light a candle under water?

Student: She's not under water.

Student: On matchboxes there's a little thing that you scrape the match against and it lights the candle.

Student: On rocks too.

Teacher (M): So where is she now —is there water here?

Group: No.

Teacher (P): Where's the water?

Student: The water's out—it's a tide. It won't be back in.

Student: What if the tide comes in and washes it away?

Teacher (M): One of the things you might like to do in your journals is to see if you can draw a little diagram of what's happening here—where she is and where the water is and where the ice is. "Soon her mussel pan was full... tickled her wrist."

Student: She should collect crabs too, and shrimp.

Teacher (S): Are those edible too?

Student: Yes.

Teacher: "Beyond the rock pools... heaps and masses."

Student: It might be her reflection.

Student: Might be her shadow.

Teacher (S): Good for you for noticing that. "Eva scrambled out of the seaweed... when the tide comes in."

Student: Maybe those are rocks instead of ice and maybe like you can carve them permanently so that the water doesn't wash them away.

Teacher (S): Because you think that if it was ice, the water would melt it and wash it away, but on rocks it would be permanent?

Student: I see another person right there.

Student: Well, it might not melt since it's so cold up there.

Student: Maybe that isn't her reflection.

Teacher (P): What would it be then?

Student: A person who stayed down there too long.

Teacher (P): Do you think it's for real?

Student: I doubt it.

Student: Maybe people had been down there and they carved it.

Teacher (S): On the rock? You think maybe like Chris that during some other time of year instead of winter they were down there?

Student:	Maybe some other people...
Teacher:	"Eva listened... and whoosh again."
Student:	She'll get washed away.
Teacher:	"Eva jumped off the... dark all around." (P) Was anybody there to come?
Student:	Dead people.
Student:	No.
Teacher:	"Help me she called... help me quickly." (P) Was anybody there to come?
Student:	When she gets back her mom probably won't let her go collect mussels again on her own.
Teacher:	Do you think she'll tell her mom?
Student:	Yeah.
Teacher:	"Eva closed her eyes... the moon in the sky."
Student:	There's a little picture.
Student:	There are dead people.
Student:	No neck.
Teacher:	"The moon was high... "my very last first time," Eva said."
Student:	You mean she's not going to do it again?
Teacher (P):	Is that what that means? What do you think? What does that mean when she says that was "my last very first— my very last first time"?
Student:	Well, you can't have the first time for the same thing twice.
Student:	It was her first time to go down.
Student:	She's not ever going to do it again.
Student:	Not go off by herself.
Student:	Maybe it was her first time to get lost down there.
Teacher (S):	Okay.
Student:	No, it was the first time she went down there by herself.
Teacher (S):	So when she goes again she won't be by herself?
Student:	Maybe that's the last time she'll ever go down or the first time she's ever been down there.
Student:	It's the first time she's ever been down there.
Teacher (S):	So you think this is her first time to go and her last time to go.
Student:	By herself.
Teacher (P):	By herself? What do you think, Karl?
Student:	I think that she's going to go again but probably with somebody like her mom.
Student:	Like she did before.
Teacher (S):	Like she did before?

Student: She said that this was her first time for going alone.

Teacher (P): Does anybody think that she'll ever go alone again?

Student: No.

Student: Maybe, yeah.

Student: I doubt it.

Teacher (P): Why?

Student: Actually because she said that this was like my very first last time.

Teacher (M): Let's look at the very last picture. What do you see her doing?

Student: Eating.

Student: Eating.

Student: Eating.

Student: Eating mussels.

Student: Eating mussels. She's going to get more muscles like Arnold Schwartzenegger.

Teacher (P): Brian, would you eat some mussels?

Student: No.

Teacher (P): Would you do what Eva did?

Student: Yeah.

Teacher (P): Would you try that?

Student: I would.

Teacher (P): Would you?

Student: I would. I think I wouldn't get lost.

Teacher (S): You wouldn't get lost? Because you wouldn't go exploring?

Student: I would just stay there.

Teacher (P): Have any of you had first times like Eva where you did something for yourself for the first time. Some things for yourself?

Student: I... one time I watched my two brothers by myself and one time I went to Bi-Mart by myself.

Teacher (S): So those were first times to do those things by yourself. Anybody else done some things for the first time by themselves?

Student: I do a lot of things by myself.

Teacher (P): Can you remember your first time to do it?

Student: No.

Student: Um, like the first time I went to my grandma's house about 10 blocks away.

Teacher (S): And so it was the first time to try something like that by yourself?

Teacher (M): What I'd like you to do is to go back to where your journals are and write one more time—draw a line where you were last time—and write what you think a very last first time is. And what we'd like to do is to hear your ideas—you can either read to us what you wrote in your journal or if you have other things you'd like to say that you didn't write down, you can.

Retelling of a Historical Event: "Thomas Edison Invents the Lightbulb"

Michael retells the events of the invention of the lightbulb using an invented narrator—a college professor friend of Edison's giving an after-dinner speech to a scientific society in the early 1900s. This character is a fictional composite created from biographical references.[1] Note the familiar voice of the storytelling.

Groups like this always ask me to speak to them, especially on these auspicious occasions—this auspicious occasion being, again, another anniversary of Edison's invention of the lightbulb. And groups always ask the same question, "How did he do it? What was Edison really like?" Well, I was a friend of Edison before he became well-known and since this is polite company I won't tell you what many would say of him.

When I met Edison for the first time, I was a professor in New York. Thomas had developed a wonderful device—the phonograph—and I was enamored of that device and we spent many long hours in conversation. Tom and I would wax philosophic about everything in the world. He rarely would pay heed to my ideas, though, because after all I was an academic type and Thomas always said he wouldn't do anything unless he could get a buck out of it. You can see that might lead to a rocky relationship. I really respected his mind and his eager desire to think of things but he was an entrepreneur at heart.

Well, anyway, let me just tell you one story that will help you understand a little bit about Tom and maybe about how he thought about the lightbulb. It's an interesting story to me and I'll never forget it. And I bet you won't either.

Tom and I were talking with some other groups of scientists and inventors. We had a little society to ourselves and we would meet periodically and have some brandy, and he would smoke cigars and we'd have a grand old time talking about inventions that were probably going to be made in the new century. Because so many things had been found already, we had grand ideas for all the tasks that electricity might be able to do. One of the devices that had just been invented was a new thermometer. Tom was eager to go try it out to see whether he could measure very small temperature differences. He got the idea to go out west to Wyoming where there was supposed to be a full eclipse. He got us so excited we all trooped onto a train and went out to Wyoming. We had a grand time out there testing this instrument to determine if there were temperature differences that could be measured as the sun was occluded by the moon.

On the way to Wyoming, all Tom did was talk about possibilities and ideas and inventions and all we academics did was say, "Well, Tom, how do you think that works?" Tom would say, "All you guys think about is how things work. I think about how things will work, make them, and then improve the way people live." He was always like that, practical and pragmatic. He had been burned, you know, by the first thing he made. He invented this thing that he thought was really keen, an automatic vote-counting gizmo. He made one of those and went up to Congress and he tried to sell it to them and they said, "Wait a minute. We don't need that thing because part of our political process is being slow about how we vote

---

1. Heyn, E. V. (1976). *The fire of genius.* New York: Anchor Press/Doubleday, pp. 107–157.

and that's part of the business." After that, Tom swore he would never make anything unless there was profit in it.

Well, anyway, back to the story. We were in Wyoming and Tom got this wild hair to keep on going to Sacramento. You know what I think it was? This is just speculation, mind you. Since he's long gone I guess I can speculate all I like. I told him about the work that had been going on in Europe with arc lamps and about the different kinds of things that had been invented with those arc lamps and how light from electricity was just waiting to be created. Tom got to chewing on that idea and wouldn't let it go. He convinced the engineer of the train to let him set a pillow on the cow-catcher and he proceeded to sit on that pillow from Wyoming to Sacramento. He was perched on the front of that train the whole way thinking about that incandescent lightbulb idea. Now, can you imagine that? He would come out to take his meals and, of course, he went back to the Pullman to take a few hours' nap, but everyone knows that when Tom got an idea he could make do with just a catnap. He would sleep on his desk, he would drool all over his notes, he would never even see his family as soon as he engaged his brain on one of his projects.

I didn't hear much from Tom after that. But the next fall, I heard that he had gone up to see a friend of mine up at the dynamo factory. They'd been building dynamos up at Albany for a while. Tom was up there asking my friend's partner, a fellow who was involved in arc lamps, how the business was going and how the inventions were coming and as he watched them work apparently Tom said, "You're on the wrong track, I can beat you." The press got hold of it and started to print Tom's wild tale that he'd have a solution in six months for how to make an incandescent bulb. Well, as you know, the rest is history. He spent the next year and a half going after the lightbulb and one of his best traits was perseverance. I know you've probably heard the axiom, "99% perspiration, 1% inspiration." Tom really didn't say that. What he said was, "to be able to do a job, to be able to invent something, it was 99% knowing what didn't work and 1% keen observation and perseverance to keep looking." So the press kind of changed what he'd said on that. Tom has had a lot of bad press, let me give him that. He had a wife and child that people say he abused. But I think if you looked at his notes… I remember looking over his shoulder one time at his notes. He had little anecdotes in his notes. He was thinking so hard and he'd written 40,000 pages about the lightbulb and the possibilities— 40,000 pages, handwritten. Over in the right-hand column, he'd written, "My wife, poopsy-woopsy, can't invent." From that, you get an insight into the humanity that the man had. I knew right then that even though he spent all those days and hours in the lab, he still loved his family.

In any case, we all know the rest. Tom was the kind of guy that once he got hold of an idea, he wouldn't let it go until he succeeded. For the lightbulb, at first he tried platinum. He thought he'd have it within a month. Well, it wasn't platinum. He had his workers go all over the world to try every known substance, all kinds of things, things in the Orient, things in the tropics, every known element. He tried every wire and substance known to mankind in his incandescent bulb. And absolutely nothing seemed to work right. Well, we know it did work out and we know that Tom was successful.

He was an odd character, Tom. But he certainly knew a lot of the stuff that had happened before. I'll have to give him credit—he was the guy who invented the lightbulb. But, I really think it was my doing. After all, I gave him the idea that got him started. I suppose in a few years I'll be asked to give another commemorative speech. I know a lot more about good ol' Tom Edison. Maybe if you want to stay on afterward, I'll be glad to discuss some other fine details of that poor fellow's life.

Kaempffert, W. (Ed.) (1924). *A popular history of American invention.* New York: Scribner's, pp. 566–572.

Josephson, M. (1959). *Edison: A biography.* New York: McGraw-Hill.

Oliver, J. W. (1956). *History of American technology.* New York: Ronald Press.

Thomas Alva Edison Foundation. (1960). *Edison experiments you can do.* New York: Harper & Row.

Thomas Alva Edison Foundation. (1988). *The Thomas Edison book of easy and incredible experiments.* New York: Wiley.

334

 ## Professional Works Cited

American Association for the Advancement of Science. (1990). *Science for all Americans.* New York: Oxford University Press: Author.

Anderson, R. C., Reynolds, R. E., Schallert, D. E., & Goetz, E. T. (1977). Frameworks for comprehending discourse. *American Educational Research Journal,* 14 (4), 367–381.

Applebee, A. (1978). *The child's concept of story.* Chicago: University of Chicago Press.

Atwell, N. *In the middle. Writing, reading, and learning with adolescents.* Portsmouth, NH: Heinemann, 1987.

Ausubel, D. (1968). *Educational psychology: A cognitive view.* New York: Holt, Rinehart & Winston.

Avi. (1992, January/February). The true confessions of Charlotte Doyle. *The Horn Book Magazine,* 24–27.

Baker, L., & Stein, N. (1981). The development of prose comprehension skills. In C. M. Santa, & B. L. Hayes (Eds.), *Children's prose comprehension: Research and practice* (pp. 7–43). Newark, DE: International Reading Association.

Barnes, D. (1993). Supporting exploratory talk for learning. In K. M. Pierce & C. J. Gilles (Eds.), *Cycles of meaning: Exploring the potential of talk in learning communities* (pp. 17–34). Portsmouth, NH: Heinemann.

Barone, T., Eeds, M., & Mason, K. (1995). Literature, the disciplines, and the lives of elementary school children. *Language Arts,* 72, 30–38.

Barthes, R. (1977). Introduction to the structural analysis of narratives. In R. Barthes (Ed.), *Music, Image, Text.* (S. Heath, Trans.). London: Fontana/Collins.

Barton, B., & Booth, D. (1990). *Stories in the classroom: Storytelling, reading aloud and roleplaying with children.* Portsmouth, NH: Heinemann.

Beane, J. (1991). The middle school: The natural home of integrated curriculum. *Education Leadership,* 12, 9–13.

Beane, J. (Ed.). (1995). *Toward a coherent curriculum: 1995 yearbook of the Association for Supervision and Curriculum Development.* Alexandria, VA: Association for Supervision and Curriculum Development.

Biehler, R. F., & Snowman, J. (1990). *Psychology applied to teaching* (6th ed.). Boston: Houghton Mifflin.

Blais, D. M. (1988). Constructivism: A theoretical revolution in teaching. *Journal of Developmental Education, 11* (3), 2–7.

Bloome, D., & Green, J. (1985). Looking at reading instruction: Sociolinguistic and ethnographic approaches. In C. N. Hedley, & A. N. Baratta (Eds.), *Contexts of reading* (pp. 167–184). Norwood, NJ: Ablex.

Boomer, G., Lester, N., Onore, C., & Cook, J. (Eds.). (1992). *Negotiating the curriculum: Educating for the 21st century.* London: The Falmer Press.

Bredekamp, S. (1987). *Developmentally appropriate practices in early childhood programs: Serving children from birth through age 8.* Washington, DC: National Association for the Education of Young Children.

Bromley, K. (1993). *Journaling.* New York: Scholastic.

Brooks, J. (1990). Teachers and students: Constructivists forging new connections. *Educational Leadership,* 47 (5), 68–71.

Brooks, J. G., & Brooks, M. G. (1993). *The search of understanding: The case for constructivist classrooms.* Alexandria, VA: Association for Supervision and Curriculum Development.

Brown, R. (1991). *Schools of thought: How the politics of literacy shape thinking in the classroom.* San Francisco: Jossey-Bass.

Brown, R. T. (1872). *Elements of physiology and hygiene.* Cincinnati, OH: Wilson, Hinkle.

Bruner, J. (1990). *Acts of meaning.* Cambridge, MA: Harvard University Press.

Caine, R. N., & Caine, G. (1991). Making connections: Teaching and the human brain. Alexandria, VA: Association for Supervision and Curriculum Development.

Calkins, L. M. (1991). *Living between the lines.* Portsmouth, NH: Heinemann.

Calkins, L. M. (1994). *The art of teaching writing.* (Rev. ed.). Portsmouth, NH: Heinemann.

Callison, P. (1991, June). *Naive conception in science.* Paper presented at PIMCES summer institute at California State University at Long Beach.

Chaille, 1991 (p.82a)

Chaille, C., & Britain, L. (1991). *The young child as scientist: A constructivist approach to early childhood science education.* New York: HarperCollins.

Charbonneau, M. P., & Reider, B. E. (1995). *The integrated elementary classroom: A developmental model of education for the 21st century.* Boston: Allyn & Bacon.

Chaskin, R. J., & Rauner, D. M. (1995). Youth and caring: An introduction. *Phi Delta Kappan,* 76 (9), 667–674.

Coles, R. (1989). *The call of stories: Teaching and the moral imagination.* Houghton Mifflin.

Connelly, E. M., & Clandinin, D. J. (1988). *Teachers as curriculum planners: Narratives of experience.* New York: Teachers College Press.

Cooper, J. D. (1993). *Literacy: Helping children construct meaning.* (2nd ed.). Boston: Houghton Mifflin.

Darling-Hammond, L. (1994). National standards and assessments: Will they improve education? *American Journal of Education,* 102, 478–510.

Davenport, M. R., Jaeger, M., & Lauritzen, C. (1995). Negotiating curriculum. *The Reading Teacher,* 49 (1) 60–62.

Davies, P. (Ed.). (1975). *The American Heritage Dictionary of the English Language.* New York: Dell.

Denman, G. A. (1991). *Sit tight, and I'll swing you a tail: Using and writing stories with young people.* Portsmouth, NH: Heinemann.

DeVries, R., & Kohlberg, L. (1989). *Constructivist early education: Overview and comparison with other programs.* Washington, DC: NAEYC.

Dewey, J. (1938). *Experience and education.* New York: Macmillan.

Didion, J. (1979). *The white album.* New York: Simon & Schuster.

Drake, S. M. (1991). How our team dissolved the boundaries. *Educational Leadership, 49* (2), 20–22.

Driver, R., & Bell, B. (1986). Students' thinking and the learning of science: a constructivist view. *Studies in Science Education, 13,* 443–455.

Driver, R., & Easley, J. (1978). Pupils and paradigms: A review of literature related to concept development in adolescent science students. *Studies in Science Education, 5,* 61–84.

Duckworth, E. (1972). The having of wonderful ideas. *Harvard Educational Review, 42* (2), 217–231.

Eastern Oregon State College. (1990). Ackerman Laboratory School broad goals. La Grande, OR: Author.

Edelsky, C. (1988). Living in the author's world: Analyzing the author's craft. *The California Reader, 21,* 14–17.

Edelsky, C., Altwerger, B., & Flores, B. (1991). *Whole language: What's the difference?* Portsmouth, NH: Heinemann.

Eeds, M., & Peterson, R. (1991). Teacher as curator: Learning to talk about literature. *The Reading Teacher, 45* (2), 118–126.

Egan, K. (1979). *Educational development.* New York: Oxford University Press.

Egan, K. (1990). *Romantic understanding: The development of rationality and imagination, ages 8–15.* New York: Routledge.

Egawa, K. (1990). Harnessing the power of language: First graders' literature engagement with *Owl Moon. Language Arts, 67,* 582–588.

Eggen, P. D., & Kauchak, D. (1992). *Educational psychology: Classroom connections.* New York: Merrill.

Erasmus, C. C. (1989). Ways with stories: Listening to the stories aboriginal people tell. *Language Arts, 66,* 267–271.

Feher, E., & Rice, K. (1988). Shadows and anti-images: Children's conceptions of light, and vision. II. *Science Education, 72* (5), 637–649.

Finley, F. (1985). Variations in prior knowledge. *Science Education, 69* (5), 697–705.

Fitzgerald, J., & Spiegel, D. (1983). Enhancing children's reading comprehension through instruction in narrative structure. *Journal of Reading Behavior, 15,* 1–17.

Fosnot, C. T. (1989). *Enquiring teachers, enquiring learners: a constructivist approach for teaching.* New York: Teachers College Press.

Freire, P. (1973). *Education for critical consciousness.* New York: Seabury.

Fritz, J. (1991). Through the eyes of an author: On writing biography. In Norton, D. *Through the eyes of a child: An introduction to children's literature.* (3rd ed.). (p. 610). New York: Merrill.

Frye, S. M. (1989, May) The NCTM standards—Challenges for all classrooms. *Arithmetic Teacher, 36,* 4–7.

Fulwiler, T. (Ed.). (1987). *The journal book.* Portsmouth, NH: Heinemann.

Gardner, H. (1983). *Frames of mind: The theory of multiple intelligences.* New York: Basic Books.

Gardner, H. (1991). *The unschooled mind: How children think and how schools should teach.* New York: Basic Books.

Gergen, J. (1982). *Toward a transformation in social knowledge.* New York: Springer-Verlag.

Gilles, C. (1990). Collaborative literacy strategies: "We don't need a circle to have a group." In K. G. Short & K. M. Pierce (Eds.), *Talking about books: Creating literate communities* (pp. 55–70). Portsmouth, NH: Heinemann.

Gilles, C., Dickinson, J., McBride, C., & Vandover, M. (1994). Discussing our questions and questioning our discussion: Growing into literature study. *Language Arts, 71,* 499–508.

Godolphin, F. (Ed.). (1942). *The Greek historians, Vol. II, Arrian.* New York: Random House.

Godolphin, F. R. B (Ed.). (1942). *The Greek historians: The complete and unabridged historical works of Herodotus, Thucydides, Xenophon, [and] Arrian.* (Vol. 2). New York: Random House.

Goodlad, J. I. (1979). *What schools are for.* Bloomington, IN: Phi Delta Kappa Educational Foundation.

Goodlad, J. I. (1984). *A place called school: Prospects for the future.* New York: McGraw-Hill.

Graves, D. H. (1994). *A fresh look at writing.* Portsmouth, NH: Heinemann.

Guthrie, J. T. (1995). *A vision of the engaged reader.* Paper presented at the Annual Convention of the International Reading Association, Anaheim, CA. (ERIC Document Reproduction Service No. ED 263 136).

Guthrie, J. T., Bennett, L., & McGough, K. (1994). *Concept–oriented reading instruction: An integrated curriculum to develop motivations and strategies for reading.* Reading Research Report #10, National Reading Research Center, Athens, GA. (ERIC Document Reproduction Service No. ED 366 927).

Hahn, J. (1994). *Framework for aesthetic literacy: Montana arts and English curriculum.* Helena, MT: Montana Office of Public Instruction.

Harris, T. L., & Hodges, R. E. (1981). *A dictionary of reading and related terms.* Newark, DE: International Reading Association.

Harste, J. C. (1994, February 26). *Multiple ways of knowing: Curriculum in a new key.* [video presentation] Whole Language Videoconference.

Hartman, J. A., DeCicco, E. K., & Griffin, G. (1994). Urban students thrive as independent researchers. *Educational Leadership, 52* (3), 46–47.

Hartsfield Elementary School. (1995). *Belief statements* [On-line]. Available: http://144.174.177.33/vision1.html—goals.

Hewson, M. (1986). The acquisition of scientific knowledge: Analysis and representation of student conceptions concerning density. *Science Education, 70* (2), 159–170.

Hickman, J. (1992). What comes naturally: Growth and change in children's free response to literature. In C. Temple & P. Collins (Eds.), *Stories and readers: New perspectives on literature in the elementary classroom* (pp. 185–194). Norwood, MA: Christopher-Gordon.

Hillman, J. (1979). A note on story. *Parabola, 4,* 43–45.

Hirsch, E. D., Jr. (1987). *Cultural literacy: What every American needs to know.* Boston: Houghton Mifflin.

Hubbard, Ruth. (1989). Notes from the underground: Unofficial literacy in one sixth grade. *Anthropology and Education Quarterly, 20,* 291–307.

Iran-Nejad, A., McKeachie, W. J., & Berliner, D. C. (1990). The multisource nature of learning: An introduction. *Review of Educational Research, 60,* 509–517.

Jaeger, M. (1991). The siege of Tyre: Technology of ancient war. In D. W. Cheek (Ed.), *Broadening Participation in Science Technology and Medicine:*

Proceedings of the Sixth Annual Technological Literacy Conference. Bloomington, IN: ERIC for Social Studies/Social Science Education. (ERIC Document Reproduction Services, No. ED3JO #248)

Jaeger, M., & Lauritzen, C. (1992). *Curriculum integration: A constructivist approach.* Paper presented at the fifth Conference of the North America Construct Network, Seattle, WA.

Jaeger, M., Munck, M., & Lauritzen, C. (1995). *Thinking like the great inventors.* Unpublished manuscript, Eastern Oregon State College at La Grande.

Jensen, J. (Ed.). (1989). *Stories to grow on: Demonstrations of language learning in K–8 classrooms.* Portsmouth, NH: Heinemann.

Kamii, C. (1985). *Young children reinvent arithmetic.* New York: Teachers College Press.

Kamii, C. (1989). *Young children continue to reinvent arithmetic.* New York: Teachers College Press.

Kamii, C., Lewis, B. A., & Jones, S. (1991, Fall). "Reform in primary mathematics education: A constructivist view." *Educational Horizons, 70,* 19–26.

Kauffman, G., & Yoder, K. (1990). Celebrating authorship: A process of collaborating and creating meaning. In K. Short & K. M. Pierce (Eds.), *Talking about books: Creating literate communities* (pp. 135–154). Portsmouth, NH: Heinemann.

Kent School District. (1995). *Language arts district-wide goals* [On-line]. Available: http://www.kent.wednet.edu/KSD/IS/SLO/00-kindergarten.html#objectives.

Kohlberg, L., & Meyer, R. (1972). Development as the aim of education. *Harvard Educational Review, 42,* 449–496.

Kyle, W., & Shymansky, J. (1989, April). Enhancing learning through conceptual change. *NARST, 21.*

Lantieri, L. (1995). Waging peace in our schools: Beginning with the children. *Phi Delta Kappan, 76* (5), 386–392.

Lauritzen, C. (1991, Fall). Stories in the curriculum. *Oregon English, 13,* 24–25.

Lauritzen, C. (1992). When children write math stories. *Northwest Reading Journal, 1* (1), 42–46.

Lauritzen, C., & Jaeger, M. (1994). Language arts teacher education within a transdisciplinary curriculum. *Language Arts, 71,* 15–21.

Leal, D. J. (1993). The power of literary peer group discussions: How children collaboratively negotiate meaning. *The Reading Teacher, 47* (2), 114–120.

Levstik, L. S. (1989). Historical narrative and the young reader. *Theory into Practice, 28,* 114–119.

Lipson, M. Y. (1982). Learning new information from text: The role of prior knowledge and reading ability. *Journal of Reading Behavior, 14* (3), 243–261.

Lipson, M. Y. (1983). The influence of religious affiliation on children's memory for text information. *Reading Research Quarterly, 18* (4), 448–457.

Lipson, M. Y., Valencia, S. W., Wixson, K. K., & Peters, C. W. (1993). Integration and thematic teaching: Integration to improve teaching and learning. *Language Arts, 70,* 252–263.

Lukens, P. (1990). *A critical handbook of children's literature* (4th ed.). New York: HarperCollins.

Mandler, J. (1984). *Stories, scripts, and scenes: Aspects of schema theory.* Hillsdale, NJ: Erlbaum.

Mandler, J. M., & Johnson, N. S. (1977). Remembrance of things parsed: Story structure and recall. *Cognitive Psychology, 9,* 111–151.

Manning, M. L. (1993). *Developmentally appropriate middle level schools.* Wheaton, MD: Association for Childhood Education International.

Manning, M., Manning, G., & Long, R. (1994). *Theme immersion: Inquiry-based curriculum in elementary and middle schools.* Portsmouth, NH: Heinemann.

Martin, K., & Miller, E. (1988). Storytelling and science. *Language Arts, 65* (3), 255–259.

Mason, D. (1995, February 20). Students give dreams touch of reality. *The Observer,* p. 2.

Michigan Department of Education. (1994, August). *Mathematics content standards and benchmarks* [On-line]. Available: gopher://mdenet.mde.state.mi.us:70/00/serv/curric/corecur/Mathematics.

Mish, F. C. (Ed.). (1989). *Webster's ninth new collegiate dictionary.* Springfield, MA: Merriam-Webster.

Morris, C. (1893). *Historical tales: The romance of reality.* Los Angeles: The Angelus University.

Morrow, L. M. (1993). *Literacy development in the early years* (2nd ed.). Boston: Allyn & Bacon.

Myers, W. D. (1990, January/February). Let us celebrate the children. *The Horn Book Magazine, 66,* 46–47.

National Center for History in the Schools. (1995). *National Standards for History Grades K-4: Expanding Children's World in Time and Space* [On-line]. Available: http://www.iac.net/~pfilio/.

National Committee on Science Education Standards and Assessment. (1994). *National science education standards* (draft document). Washington, DC: National Academy of Sciences Press.

National Council of Teachers of English & International Reading Association. (1995). *Standards for the English language arts.* Urbana, IL: National Council of Teachers of English.

National Council of Teachers of Mathematics. (1989). *Curriculum and evaluation standards for school mathematics.* Reston, VA: Author.

National Council for the Social Studies. (1994). *Curriculum standards for the social studies* (Bulletin 89). [On-line]. Available: http://www.iac.net:80/~pfilio/geo.txt.

National Education Goals Panel. (1992). *The national education goals report: Building a nation of learners.* Washington DC: U.S. Government Printing Office. [Also available on-line: http://www.ed.gov/legislation/GOALS2000/index.html].

National Research Council. (1994). *National science education standards.* Washington, DC: National Academy Press.

National Science Teachers Association. (1993). *The content core: A guide for curriculum designers* (vol. 1). Washington, DC: Author.

Nifto, S. (1994). Lessons from students on creating a chance to dream. *Harvard Educational Review, 64* (4), 392–426.

Noddings, N. (1995a). A morally defensible mission for schools in the 21st century. *Phi Delta Kappan, 76* (5), 365–368.

Noddings, N. (1995b). Teaching themes of care. *Phi Delta Kappan, 76* (9), 675–679.

Nussbaum, J. (1979). Children's conception of earth as a cosmic body: A cross age study. *Science Education, 63* (1), 83–93.

Obbink, L. A. (1992). The book needs you: Gary Paulsen's *The Winter Room* as a writerly text. *The New Advocate, 5* (3), 175–186.

Ogle, D. (1986). K-W-L: A teaching model that develops active reading or expository text. *The Reading Teacher, 39,* 564–570.

Ohio State Board of Education. (1995, February). *Guide to proposed pre-kindergarten through grade 12 standards* [On-line]. Available: gopher.ode.ohio.gov/000gopher_root1%3a5b_ode_standard%5d_FebP.

O'Neil, J. (1992). Wanted: Deep understanding: "Constructivism" posits new conception of learning. *ASCD Update, 34* (3), 1, 4, 5, 8.

Oregon Department of Education. (1988). *Science education common curriculum goals.* Salem, OR: Author.

Oregon Department of Education (1993). *Report on the certificate of initial mastery.* Salem, OR: Author.

Oregon Department of Education. (1994). [Scoring rubrics] (draft document). Salem, OR: Author.

Pappas, C. C., Kiefer, B. Z., & Levstik, L. S. (1995). *An integrated language perspective in the elementary school: Theory into action* (2nd ed.). White Plains, NY: Longman.

Perrine, K. (1983). *Literature: Structure, sound, and sense* (4th ed.). San Diego: Harcourt.

Peterson, R. (1992). *Life in a crowded place: Making a learning community.* Portsmouth, NH: Heinemann.

Peterson, R., & Eeds, M. (1990). *Grand conversations: Literature groups in action.* New York: Scholastic.

Pierce, K. M., & Gilles, C. J. (1993). *Cycles of meaning: Exploring the potential of talk in learning communities.* Portsmouth, NH: Heinemann.

Pines, A., & West, L. (1986). Conceptual understanding: An interpretation of research within a sources-of-knowledge framework. *Science Education, 70* (5), 583–604.

Posner, G., Strilke, K., Hewson, P., & Gertzog, W. (1982). Accommodation of a scientific conception: Toward a theory of conceptual change. *Science Education, 66* (2), 211–227.

Resnick, L. (1985). *Cognitive science and instruction.* Paper presented at the annual meeting of the American Association for the Advancement of Science, Washington, DC. (ERIC Document Reproduction Service No. ED 263 136).

Reynolds, R. E., Taylor, M. A., Steffensen, M. S., Shirey, L. L., & Anderson, R. C. (1982). Cultural schemata and reading comprehension. *Reading Research Quarterly, 17,* 353–366.

Riley, M. K., Morocco, C. C., Gordon, S. M., & Howard, C. (1993, Summer). Walking the talk: Putting constructivist thinking into practice in classrooms. *Educational Horizons, 71,* pp. 187–196.

Rosen, H. (1986). The importance of story. *Language Arts, 63,* 226–237.

Rosenblatt, L. M. (1938/1976). *Literature as exploration.* (4th ed.). New York: Modern Language Association of America.

Routman, R. (1991). *Invitations: Changing as teachers and learners K–12.* Portsmouth, NH: Heinemann.

Short, K. G., & Pierce, K. M. (Eds.). (1990). *Talking about books: Creating literate communities.* Portsmouth, NH: Heinemann.

Shymansky, J. A., & Kyle, W. C., Jr. (1988). Learning and the learner. *Science Education, 72* (3), 293–304.

Smith, L. C., Readence, J. E., & Alverman, D. C. (1984). Effects of activating prior knowledge on retention of expository text. In J. A. Niles & L. A. Harris (Eds.), *Thirty-third yearbook of the National Reading Conference* (pp. 188–192). Rochester, NY: National Reading Conference.

Steele, J. D. (1891). *Popular physics.* New York: American Book Company.

Steffensen, M. S., Joag-Dev, C., & Anderson, R. C. (1979). A cross-cultural perspective on reading comprehension. *Reading Research Quarterly, 15* (1), 10–29.

Stein, N. L., & Glenn, C. J. (1979). An analysis of story comprehension in elementary school children. In Freedle, R. O. (Ed.), *New directions in discourse processing*. Norwood, NJ: Ablex.

Stevens, A. D. (1993, May). *Learning for life through universal themes*. Portland, OR: Northwest Regional Educational Laboratory.

Stowell, C. H. (1893). *A healthy body: A textbook on anatomy, physiology, hygiene, alcohol, and narcotics*. New York: Silver, Burdett.

Tchudi, S. (Ed.). (1993). *The astonishing curriculum: Integrating science and humanities through language*. Urbana, IL: National Council of Teachers of English.

Temple, C., & Gillet, J. W. (1989). *Language arts: Learning processes and teaching practices* (2nd ed.). Glenview, IL: Scott, Foresman.

Temple, C., Nathan, R., Temple, F., & Burris, N. A. (1993). *The beginnings of writing* (3rd ed.). Boston: Allyn & Bacon.

Templeton, S. (1995). *Children's literacy: Contexts for meaningful learning*. Geneva, IL: Houghton Mifflin.

Tierney, R. J., Readence, J. E., & Dishner, E. K. (1990). *Reading strategies and practices: A compendium*. (3rd ed.). Boston: Allyn & Bacon.

U. S. Department of Labor, The Secretary's Commission on Achieving Necessary Skills. (1991). *What work requires of schools: A SCANS report for America 2000*. Washington, DC: U. S. Department of Labor.

Watson, D. J. (1993). Community meaning: Personal knowing within a social place. In K. M. Pierce & C. J. Gilles (Eds.), *Cycles of meaning: Exploring the potential of talk in learning communities* (pp. 3–16). Portsmouth, NH: Heinemann.

Wells, C. G. (1986). *The meaning makers: Children learning language and using language to learn*. Portsmouth, NH: Heinemann.

Wells, G., & Chang-Wells, G. L. (1992). *Constructing knowledge together: Classrooms as centers of inquiry and literacy*. Portsmouth, NH: Heinemann.

Wheatley, G. (1991). Constructivist perspectives on science and mathematics learning. *Science Education, 75* (1), 9–21.

Wiggins, G. (1995). Curricular coherence and assessment: Making sure that the effect matches the intent. In J. Beane (Ed.), *Toward a coherent curriculum: 1995 yearbook of the Association for Supervision and Curriculum Development* (pp. 101–119). Alexandria, VA: Association for Supervision and Curriculum Development.

Williams, H. (1907). *The historians history of the world*. London: Hooper & Jackson.

Winograd, K., & Higgins, K. M. (1994/1995). Writing, reading, and talking mathematics: One interdisciplinary possibility. *The Reading Teacher, 48* (4), 310–319.

Wyatt, M., & Pickle, M. (1993). "Good teaching is good teaching": Basic beliefs of college reading instructors. *Journal of Reading, 36* (5), 340–423.

Yaden, D. (1988). Understanding stories through repeated read-alouds: How many does it take? *The Reading Teacher, 41*, 556–560.

Yager, R. E. (1991). The constructionist learning model. *The Science Teacher, 58* (6), 52–57.

Trade Books Cited

Andrews, J. (1985). *Very last first time*. New York: Atheneum.

Beattie, O., & Geiger, J. (1992). *Buried in ice: The mystery of a lost arctic expedition*. Toronto, Canada: The Madison Press Limited [Time Quest Books].

Beatty, P. (1981). *Lupita mañana*. New York: Morrow.

Billings, H., & Billings, M. (1987). *Eccentrics*. Providence, RI: Jamestown.

Bisel, S. C. (1990). *The secrets of Vesuvius*. Toronto, Canada: The Madison Press Limited [Time Quest Books].

Bonsall, C. (1973). *Mine's the best*. New York: Harper & Row.

Boulton, J. (1994). *Only Opal: The diary of a young girl*. New York: Philomel.

Brown, D. (1993). *Ruth Law thrills a nation*. New York: Ticknor & Fields.

Burleigh, R. (1991). *Flight: The journey of Charles Lindbergh*. New York: Philomel.

Buss, F. L. (1991). *Journey of the sparrows*. New York: Dutton.

Calhoun, M. (1981). *Hot-air Henry*. New York: Morrow.

Campbell, E. (1994). *The shark callers*. San Diego: Harcourt.

Carle, E. (1970). *The tiny seed*. New York: Crowell.

Carroll, L. (1866/1963). *Alice's adventures in Wonderland*. New York: Macmillan.

Cherry, L. (1990). *The great kapok tree: A tale of the Amazon rain forest*. San Diego: Harcourt.

Coerr, E. (1977). *Sadako and the thousand paper cranes*. New York: Putnam's.

Coerr, E. (1993). *Sadako*. New York: Putnam's.

Cohlene, T. (1990). *Ka-ha-si: An Eskimo legend*. Mahwah, NJ: Watermill.

Cohlene, T. (1990). *Turquoise boy: A Navajo legend*. Mahwah, NJ: Watermill.

Cone, M. (1992). *Come back, salmon*. San Francisco: Sierra Club Books.

Cooney, B. (1982). *Miss Rumphius*. New York: Puffin.

Cowcher, H. (1988). *Rain forest*. New York: Farrar, Straus & Giroux.

Crichton, M. (1990). *Jurassic park*. New York: Knopf.

Cushman, K. (1994). *Catherine, called Birdy*. New York: Clarion.

De Angeli, M. (1949). *The door in the wall*. New York: Doubleday.

Disher, G. (1993). *The bamboo flute*. New York: Ticknor & Fields.

Dorros, A. (1990). *Rain forest secrets*. New York: Scholastic.

Dorros, A. (1991). *Abuela*. New York: Dutton.

Dwyer, J. (Ed.). (1989). *Strange stories, amazing facts of America's past*. Pleasantville, NY: Reader's Digest.

Engel, D. (1991). *Gino Badino.* New York: Morrow.

Finsland, M. J. (1983). *The town that moved.* Minneapolis: Carolrhoda.

Freedman, R. (1991). *The Wright brothers: How they invented the airplane.* New York: Holiday.

George, J. C. (1990). *One day in the tropical rain forest.* New York: HarperCollins.

Gregory, K. (1992). *Earthquake at dawn.* San Diego, CA: Harcourt.

Hamilton, V. (1985). *The people could fly.* New York: Knopf.

Harrah, M. (1990). *Honey girl.* New York: Avon.

Heide, F. P., & Gilliland, J. (1990). *The day of Ahmed's secret.* New York: Lothrop.

Holling, H. C. (1951). *Minn of the Mississippi.* Boston: Houghton Mifflin.

Isadora, Rachel. (1991). *At the crossroads.* New York: Greenwillow.

Johnson, N. (1991). *Fire and silk: Flying in a hot air balloon.* Boston: Little, Brown.

Johonnet, J. (1887). *Stories of our country.* New York: D. Appleton and Company.

Krupinski, L. (1992). *Celia's island journal.* Boston: Little, Brown.

Lasky, K. (1988). *The bone wars.* New York: Morrow.

Lawson, R. (1939). *Ben and me.* Boston, MA: Little, Brown.

Lewis, B. (1991). *The kid's guide to social action.* Minneapolis, MN: Free Spirit.

Macaulay, D. (1977). *Castle.* Boston: Houghton Mifflin.

Markun, P. (1993). *The little painter of Sabana Grande.* New York: Bradbury.

McCloskey, R. (1948). *Blueberries for Sal.* New York: Macmillan.

McLerran, A. (1991). *Roxaboxen.* New York: Morrow.

Meyer, C. (1994). *Rio Grande stories.* San Diego: Harcourt.

Mikaelsen, B. (1993). *Sparrow Hawk Red.* New York: Hyperion.

Mills, L. (1991). *The rag coat.* Boston: Little, Brown.

Olson, A. (1987). *The lighthouse keeper's daughter.* Boston: Little, Brown.

Parenteau, S. (1978). *Blue hands, blue cloth.* Chicago: Children's Press.

Paton Walsh, J. (1982). *The green book.* New York: Farrar, Straus & Giroux.

Polacco, P. (1992). *Chicken Sunday.* New York: Philomel.

Polacco, P. (1994). *Pink and Say.* New York: Philomel.

Provensen, A., & Provensen, M. (1983). *The glorious flight: Across the channel with Louis Blériot July 25, 1909.* New York: Puffin.

Reeves, N. (1992). *Into the mummy's tomb: The real-life discovery of Tutankhamun's treasures.* Toronto, Canada: The Madison Press Limited [Time Quest Books].

Ringgold, F. (1991). *Tar beach.* New York: Crown.

Roop, P., & Roop, C. (1985). *Keep the lights burning, Abbie.* Minneapolis: Carolrhoda.

Rylant, C. (1992). *When I was young in the mountains.* New York: Dutton.

Schwartz, D. (1985). *How much is a million?* New York: Lothrop.

Temple, F. (1993). *Grab hands and run.* New York: Orchard.

Temple, F. (1994). *The Ramsay scallop.* New York: Orchard.

Van Laan, N. (1991). *Rainbow crow.* New York: Knopf.

Verne, J. (1968). *20,000 leagues under the sea.* Chicago: Children's Press.

Viorst, J. (1974). *Rosie and Michael.* New York: Atheneum.

White, E. B. (1952). *Charlotte's web.* New York: Harper

Williams, J. (1965). *The question box.* New York: Norton.

Williams, K. (1990). *Galimoto.* New York: Lothrop.

Williams, K. (1994). *Tap-tap.* New York: Clarion.

Yep. L. (1975). *Dragonwings.* New York: Harper & Row.

Yolen, J. (1987). *Owl Moon.* New York: Philomel.

Yolen, J. (1992). *Letting Swift River go.* Boston: Little, Brown.

Author and Title Index

Subject Index

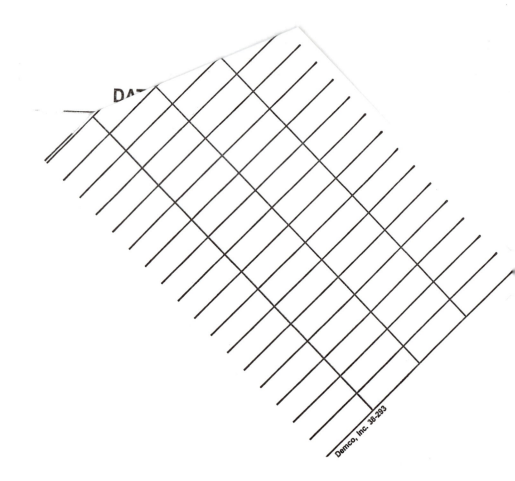

DAT

Demco, Inc. 38-293